MANUAL OF COLOUR PHOTOGRAPHY

Manual of
Colour Photography

by

EDWARD S. BOMBACK

SOUTH BRUNSWICK AND NEW YORK:
A. S. BARNES AND COMPANY

First Published 1964

© reserved

Fountain Press Limited, 46-47 Chancery Lane,
London WC2

First American edition 1966

A. S. Barnes and Co., Inc.
Cranbury, New Jersey

Printed in Great Britain by
Headley Brothers Ltd., 109 Kingsway, London WC2
and Ashford, Kent

Contents

List of Colour Illustrations

(Page numbers given in brackets)

Author's Preface

IT WAS NOT until the beginning of the present century that colour photography emerged from a jungle of strange and unpredictable processes, for it was only in 1907 that the first satisfactory colour material, Lumière Autochrome Plates, appeared on the market. These offered a workable and satisfactory method of producing colour transparencies, based on the additive mixture of light passing through a three-colour reseau: they were still in production nearly thirty years later. However, this process offered no solution to the making of colour prints, and for this purpose a succession of processes involving the making of colour separation negatives appeared over the next forty years, culminating in the Trichrome Carbro process, which was also a product of Lumière Autochrome. Until very recently, the Carbro process was considered the best available for making colour prints of first class quality.

Today such processes are of little more than historical interest, and colour photography has undergone a complete revolution in the form of multi-layer or tri-pack materials based on a subtractive colour system. The first commercially-successful multi-layer colour film appeared in 1935 under the name Kodachrome, as an 8 mm. film for making colour movies. A year later it was made available to users of 35 mm. cameras for making colour slides.

The second step in the colour revolution occurred in 1942 with the introduction of Kodacolor Film and its associated colour paper which provided the amateur photographer with a true negative-positive process for making colour prints. At about the same time, the production of a reversal-type white-base material made it possible for users of reversal colour film to obtain Kodachrome Prints.

But for a further decade the photographer in search of high grade colour prints still made use of such processes as Carbro or Kodak Dye Transfer, and it is only within the last ten years that colour negative processes have become the most common method of making colour prints. It can be safely said that Ektacolor and Kodacolor films plus their companion printing material, Ektacolor Paper, now offer a standard equal to the best obtained with the Carbro process plus the many advantages that go with a negative-positive printing process.

13

The serious photographer interested in producing photographs rather than accumulating experience in the many brands of colour film now available must, of necessity, restrict his use of materials to those he has found to be accurate, easy to handle, and consistent. For various reasons the author adopted those produced by Kodak Ltd., and it is on very nearly thirty years' experience with Kodak colour films that the present book has been based. The wide variety of colour materials manufactured by Kodak has made it possible to cover all practical aspects of modern colour photography, while at the same time avoiding the unwieldiness of providing full and up-to-date information on materials of other manufacture.

In a century notable for its spectacular inventions, that of colour photography must rank among the most enjoyable and useful. As well as providing a valuable recording medium for commerce and science, it has become the hobby of millions, for it is not necessary to be a technical expert to enjoy taking colour photographs. The famous Kodak slogan 'You press the button, and we do the rest' applies as much to colour photography as it did to black-and-white. Why then, might the reader ask, does it need a 400-page manual? The answer is simple; much of the success of colour photography depends on knowing when and under what conditions the camera button should be pressed. It is in answer to this that the first 250 pages of the book have been written. There remains the hard core of photographers who want to do the 'rest' themselves, and it has needed a further 80 pages to deal adequately with the processing and printing of Kodak colour films. In view of the wide-spread use of miniature colour slides, further chapters have been devoted to advice on their presentation. The last two chapters before the data section deal with the making of colour separation negatives and the Kodak Dye Transfer process, and have been added by way of a postscript. Materials for the Dye Transfer process are still available and offer a useful method for making both straight colour prints and colour derivatives.

The author finally wishes to express his gratitude to that great pioneer of colour photography, Ralph M. Evans, whose books have contributed so much to the proper understanding of the principles of colour photography.

Alghero, Sardinia
June 1st 1964   EDWARD S. BOMBACK

The author wishes to acknowledge the help given by Messrs. Kodak Ltd. in checking the information relating to Kodak products and processes, and in supplying many of the illustrations

The Nature and Perception of Colour

PHOTOGRAPHY has been described as 'painting with light', and this description, originally coined in the 'black-and-white' era, is perhaps even more apt today now that colour photography has become the accepted standard. But while the term painting is somewhat fanciful, it is very much to the point to say that photography is the product of light and is concerned with the action of light both on sensitized materials used in a camera and darkroom, and on the retina of the eye. It is the action of light through the lens of a camera which records an image on the film, and the action of light through the lens of the eye which stimulates the retina thereby causing impulses to be sent to the brain. It is tempting to draw a comparison between the retina and a colour film, and from this to conclude that, if the reaction to light of a colour film were identical to that of the retina, we could then produce a photograph which was identical in appearance to the original scene. Such a likeness between the photograph and the original subject has always been the principal goal of the photographic inventor, but its realization has proved to be extremely complex. Indeed more than a hundred years after the theoretical basis of modern colour photography was described there still remains a gap, albeit a small one.

However, while verisimilitude is a major requirement of modern photo-graphy, particularly in its many technical applications, it must be noted that a photograph may also be considered as an object in its own right. In other words a photograph may be viewed as a record of some object and therefore be compared either directly, as in the case of a copy of a painting (or even another photograph), or indirectly in terms of our visual memory of the original scene, or it may be viewed as an object itself without reference to, or knowledge of, an original object. This dual nature of a photograph is an important one to keep in mind, since the aim of a photographer may be as much to create a new object as to present a faithful copy of some existing object. Indeed the popular conception of photography as a means of recording some attractive scene, a personal likeness or some other object of interest is very far from being adequate for anyone who intends to make intelligent and creative use of colour photography. One of the principal aims of the present book is to discuss the basic difference between objects as seen by the eye, and objects seen via the lens of a camera as recorded and reproduced by modern colour processes. And it is logical and necessary to begin this discussion with some knowledge of the nature of light, the vital ingredient both to our sense of sight and to photography.

Light

We can define light as that form of radiant energy to which the retina of the eye is sensitive. It is a small region of the electromagnetic spectrum – radiant energy which travels in wave motions – embracing at one end the extremely short gamma rays emitted by certain radioactive materials, and at the other end the radio waves which extend to a mile in length (fig. 1.1). These forms of energy all travel at 186,000 miles per second, a speed commonly known as the 'speed of light'. The wavelength or the distance between one crest and the next is usually measured in metres or fractions of a metre. Thus short-wave radio transmissions are in the 20 to 50 metre band, medium waves in the 200 to 500 metre band and long waves 1,000 or more metres in length. Towards the middle of the electro-magnetic spectrum it is necessary to resort to millimicrons – millionths of a millimetre – and we find light in the wave band of from 400 to 700 millimicrons. These are not exact limits since the eye is relatively insensitive to the extremes of the light spectrum. Immediately beyond 400 millimicrons are the ultra-violet rays and beyond 700 millimicrons are the infra-red rays. Although invisible to the human eye they are similar to light and may be utilized in photography.

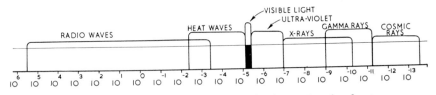

Fig. 1.1. Spectrum of electromagnetic radiation in wavelengths of metres.

Light as radiant energy exists independently of the human observer and in this sense is purely physical; but in its reaction on the retina, which gives rise to the sensation of vision and hence visual perception, we are dealing with mental or psychological expressions. Thus the definition of light as radiant energy which gives rise to visual perception is a physico-psychological one. But like all human responses to physical stimuli, that of the eye to light and of the mind to the sensations aroused by the electrical impulses conveyed by the optic nerve to the brain are not rigidly exact ones such as those which can be made with measuring instruments. Human beings vary both in their physical and psychological reactions and it is therefore necessary to discuss visual processes in terms of a person having an average or normal response. Thus on the physical side we have various degrees of colour blindness and on the psychological side the effects of conditioning and habit formation. Lacking full telepathic communication there is no way of determining whether two people respond in exactly the same way to the same stimulus.

White light

When light of all wavelengths from 400 to 700 millimicrons reaches the eye in very nearly equal quantities we have the sensation of colourless or white light. However there is no absolute standard for white light since we are able to adapt ourselves both physically and mentally to certain variations in the composition of light. Thus we tend to accept all but extreme variations in the qualities of daylight as white light – only at sunrise and sunset do we become conscious that it is noticeably yellow – and in the absence of daylight we accept considerable variations in artificial light, though we are usually conscious that it is somewhat yellower than daylight. In the presence of daylight we can, however, perceive that the light of an ordinary tungsten lamp is considerably yellower than daylight. On the other hand, should daylight and tungsten light be compared at roughly equal intensities in a darkened room then daylight will appear distinctly blue. This effect also becomes noticeable towards dusk when looking out of a window of a room lit with tungsten lighting, see plate 10.

The colour spectrum

The eye – or that part of the retina which is fully colour-sensitive – responds to the total effect of groups of wavelengths falling on any given point and is not able to analyse the light fully. Until Newton demonstrated the composition of white light by means of a glass prism, it was commonly held that 'white' was as separate and distinct a colour as blue, green or red. The existence of the rainbow in nature did not in fact provide a simple answer since its colours are not spectrally pure. However, we now accept the colour spectrum, along with the rainbow and the jewelled colours of dewdrops, as the result of refraction and dispersion of white light. In the spectrum of white light we can broadly identify violet, blue, blue-green, green, yellow, orange and red, but a critical inspection of the band of colours formed with a glass prism shows a continuous change and in fact the normal observer can distinguish several hundred different hues. The separation of white light into different colours by means of a glass prism is explained by the fact that the speed of light is reduced in glass by different amounts for different wavelengths and when entering a flat glass surface at an angle, differing wavelengths are therefore bent or 'refracted' by different amounts, the shorter wavelengths being refracted to a greater degree than the longer wavelengths. It is worth noting that the colours of the spectrum are the purest possible since each is seen in isolation, whereas generally speaking the colours in nature are mixtures of all wavelengths.

The colours of the spectrum can be related to their wavelengths by a diagram of the kind shown in fig. 1.2. The spectral composition of any light-source or colour is conveniently shown by a curve of the kind shown in fig. 1.3 known as a spectral energy curve. Thus fig. 1.4 shows the curves for three different light-sources, skylight, sunlight, and a tungsten lamp.

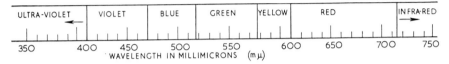

Fig. *1.2.* Principal colours of the visible spectrum related to wavelength.

Selective absorption

A surface which appears white when illuminated with a white light-source does so because it reflects all colours of the spectrum in equal amounts and also reflects a very high percentage of the total incident light. Such a surface may be called non-selective, but when it absorbs in equal amounts a considerable part of the incident light it will appear grey, the degree of greyness depending on the amount of absorption.

With almost total absorption of all regions of the spectrum the surface appears black. Thus on the one hand a surface coated with magnesium oxide presents a very white surface, while one coated with soot or lamp-black gives a very black surface. White, grey and black are said to be hueless or to have zero colour saturation.

If the surface absorbs certain regions of the spectrum to a greater extent than others, then it takes on a coloured appearance when viewed in white light. We call these absorbing elements pigments and dyes, and it is their presence on the surface of an object which gives it its characteristic colouring. For an example an unripe tomato appears green because it absorbs a great deal more blue and red light than it does green, but when it becomes fully ripe the

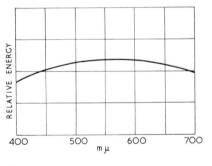

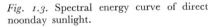

Fig. *1.3.* Spectral energy curve of direct noonday sunlight.

Fig. 1.4. Spectral energy curves for (1) Light from blue sky, (2) Noonday sunlight, and (3) Tungsten filament lamp. The curves are plotted so that the relative energy in the visually brightest part of the spectrum, 550 mμ., is the same.

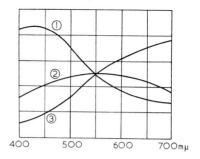

absorption becomes greater in the blue and green and very much less in the red regions. This is known as selective absorption and is by far the most common cause of the coloured appearance of objects which surround us. It is also the basis of colour vision and modern colour photography.

Colour filters

White light will also take a coloured appearance if it is made to pass through a transparent or translucent material which absorbs certain wavelengths while freely transmitting others. Such materials applied to photography are known as colour filters and are used extensively in both black-and-white and colour photography. Thus material which absorbs all the greenish parts of the spectrum while freely transmitting bluish and reddish parts will give the transmitted light a strongly reddish-blue (or magenta) appearance. White light, which has been modified by such a filter, will give a white surface a coloured appearance much as it would appear as if the surface itself contained a pigment of similar absorption characteristics, but viewed with white light.

This distinction between the colour of the incident light or source of illumination, and the colour of the surface itself when viewed in white light, is an important one in colour photography and colour evaluation generally, and will be dealt with in various aspects in later chapters.

Structural colours

In addition to colours caused by selective absorption, there commonly exist in nature colours which arise from the structure of the reflecting surface. These can be due to one of four phenomena, (a) interference, (b) diffraction, (c) dispersion and (d) scattering of light. The first two give rise to iridescent colours, that is, colours which change according to the angle from which the surface is seen.

Colours due to interference are typified by the soap bubble and film of oil on water. Light is reflected from both outer and inner surfaces of the film, but that reflected from the inner surface travels further. If the extra distance is an odd number of $\frac{1}{2}$ wavelengths, part of the spectrum is reduced or cancelled out, and we see the sum of the remainder. As the thickness of the film varies – particularly in the case of a soap bubble which is changing all the time – there is a play of colours. The colours may also vary with the angle from which the surface is viewed, since a change of angle alters the path-difference between interfering rays of light.

Iridescent colours can be produced by a diffraction grating, a structure often embedded on the surface of insects giving rise to intense blues and greens. An artificial diffraction grating can be made by scratching a series of fine lines very close together on a polished metal surface. On either side of a beam of light that falls across these lines and is reflected, there appear spectra which give an iridescent appearance to the surface. This effect is often to be seen in the reflections from the surface of a long-playing gramophone record. The effect of dispersion is to be seen in the rainbow.

The most common example of colour produced by scattering is that of the blue sky. The phenomenon was first explained by Tyndall and is sometimes named after him. It is due to the fact that water molecules in the upper atmosphere, and dust particles lower down in the air, scatter and send back a high proportion of the shorter wave radiation of sunlight, namely, the violet and blue light.

Fluorescent colours

Certain compounds when irradiated by ultra-violet radiation emit visible light. This phenomenon is often made use of in stage spectacles, various parts of the performers' costumes being treated with different compounds, so that when the normal stage lights are extinguished and the stage flooded with ultra-violet radiation, brightly coloured phantoms appear to be floating in the darkness. Modern detergents also make use of fluorescence to give brighter 'whites' and fluorescing compounds have been used in the base of photographic printing papers for the same purpose. The term fluorescent is applied to colours which disappear when the source of excitation is discontinued. A second term, phosphorescence, is used when the visible light continues for some time after the excitation ceases.

Colour mixtures

We have seen how white light can be broken down into its various colours either by the absorption characteristics or by the structure of a surface, and it remains to see what happens when we reverse the process. This was also demonstrated by Newton by using a second prism to collect the colour spectrum formed by the first prism so as to form a single beam of white light again. However the experiment can be simplified by mixing the beams from three projectors, one fitted with a filter which transmits only reddish light, one that transmits only greenish light and one only bluish light – in other words each of the filters transmitting about one third of the spectrum. Assuming the intensity of each of the beams of light is approximately adjusted, then where they overlap a white surface such as a projection screen will appear white. If the beams are displaced

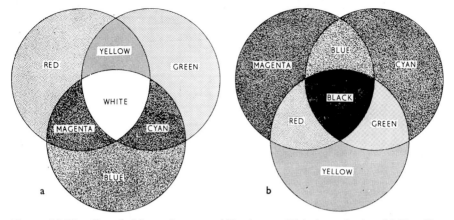

Fig. 1.5. (a) The effect of adding red, green and blue beams of light by projection. (b) The effect of superimposing magenta, cyan and yellow filters over a single light-source. The central area will be grey or black when the filters are equally desaturated.

in the manner shown in fig. 1.5(a), then we get a condition where the outer zones appear red, green and blue, the intermediate zones, where only two beams overlap, appear yellow (red+green), magenta (red+blue) and cyan (blue+green), while only the centre zone appears white. The outer colours are known as the primary colours or more specifically the additive primaries because various mixtures of light of these three colours can be made to match almost all other colours. This method of reproducing colours photographically was first put forward by Maxwell and, independently, du Hauron, a little more than a hundred years ago, and Maxwell in fact attempted a practical demonstration before the Royal Institution in 1861 of what can be considered the first colour photograph based on the use of three projectors.

Additive colour mixtures were the basis of the more successful colour photographic processes invented in the earlier part of the present century, but the theory of reproducing colour by using the subtractive primaries – yellow, magenta and cyan – had been put forward by du Hauron as early as 1862. The subtractive primaries are so-called because each represents white light *minus* one of the three additive primaries. For example yellow can be considered as white light minus blue, magenta as white light minus green, and cyan as white light minus red.

Such a colour method offers considerable advantage over an additive mixture. Filters designed to transmit the subtractive primaries each, in fact, transmit two-thirds of the spectrum, the total absorption of any two filters transmitting only one of the additive primaries. Thus we can superimpose them over a single light-source to produce other colours as shown in fig. 1.5(b) and fig. 1.6. In the case of the additive primaries the superimposition of any two filters merely results in total absorption.

The first successful colour process to make use of subtractive colour mixtures was, in fact, Kodachrome film first introduced in 1935 for narrow-gauge cine cameras and in 1936 for 35 mm. still cameras. But we shall be dealing with colour processes more fully in Chapter 3 and having briefly discussed the nature of light and the formation of colours it is opportune to learn something about the nature of colour vision.

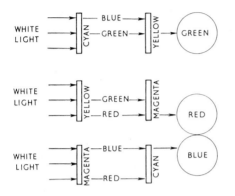

Fig. 1.6. The diagram shows how the primary colours, green, red and blue are produced by combinations of two of the subtractive primaries, cyan, yellow and magenta.

How we see colour

Although there have doubtless been theories of colour vision since the dawn of reasoning, it was not until Newton demonstrated the nature of white light and the effects of mixing various coloured lights that the ground was prepared for the recently-established chemical basis of three-colour vision. Newton himself, although not principally interested in the nature of vision, made very penetrating observations in his famous *Opticks* as can be seen from the following extract from Query 13 at the end of the book.

'Do not several sorts of rays make vibrations of several bignesses which according to their bignesses excite Sensations of several Colours, much after the manner that the Vibrations of the Air according to their several bignesses excite Sensations of several Sounds? And Particularly do not the most refrangible Rays excite the shortest Vibrations for making a Sensation of deep violet, and the least refrangible the largest for making a sensation of deep red, and the several intermediate sorts of Rays, Vibrations of several intermediate bignesses to make the Sensation of the several intermediate colours?'

But Newton, of course, had in mind the analytical capacity of the prism in suggesting such a capacity for the eye. Much later Young proposed his simplified theory of three-colour vision, suggesting that three receptors only would be needed for the eye to transmit colours to the brain. It remained for Maxwell to demonstrate that all colours can be almost perfectly matched by a mixture of the three primaries. He chose blue, green and red for his primaries, but it does not matter what colours are chosen so long as their mixture in some proportion can form white. The effects of colour matching were shown strictly to obey Newton's centre-of-gravity rule, and the relations of colour matching were shown by the geometric properties of Maxwell's colour triangle, fig. 1.7.

Extensive study over the last few decades on the nature of the retina as a light-receptor revealed the existence of photo-sensitive pigments in the rods and cones of the eye. The first to be isolated was rhodopsin or visual purple which was found to fill the outer segments of the rods. These exist in something like 100 million in number in all but the foveal area of the retina, and are particularly abundant in nocturnal animals. The rods are of extremely high sensitivity and provide the means for twilight vision. This, as we know, is virtually colourless, and it is on the cones, which occupy exclusively the small area of acute vision, the fovea, that we rely for perception of colour. Working on the basis that only three primary colours are needed to produce all other colours, Rushton in 1957 demonstrated in a most convincing manner the existence of two of the three pigments in the cones. He named the pigments 'erytholabe' (red-sensitive), 'chlorolabe' (green-sensitive) and 'cyanolabe' (blue-sensitive).

The existence of three photo-sensitive receptors does not explain more than the physiological basis of vision. The rods and cones are connected to the optical centres of the brain by means of a complex nerve system. Just how complex this system is can be judged by the fact that the optic nerve carries over a million separate nerve fibres, each carrying to the brain impulses which are interpreted into all the aspects of visual perception – colour, shape, lightness, detail, movement and so on.

Fig. 1.7. Maxwell's colour triangle showing geometric relations of colour matching.

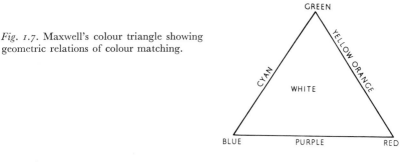

Adaptation

Were the retina of the eye a light-receptor having a fixed sensitivity range, it might be possible to produce a colour film of like sensitivity with the technical knowledge now available to the photographic industry. But the eye is an extremely complex receptor which serves our needs in a multitude of different conditions. A study of the eye structure of other living organisms shows an interesting variety which ranges from the most rudimentary 'light-detectors', raised patches designed to detect shadows passing over a sensitive area, to the complex eyes of man and the higher vertebrates. But the eye is merely the outer receptor of the actual seat of visual perception in the brain, and it is man's peculiarly complex brain which directs, interprets and gives meaning to the things seen.

As a physical receptor of light the eye is capable of adapting itself to the general brightness level over a range of intensities considerably in excess of 1 to 1,000,000,000. This range extends from complete dark adaptation to brightness levels almost too painful to observe. Part of this brightness adaptation is obtained through the two kinds of visual receptors, the rods and the cones. At low brightness levels vision is effected exclusively through the large area of the rods and is known as twilight or scotopic vision. At somewhat higher levels there is a change-over to the cones, which not only give colour vision but a much higher degree of visual acuity. Cone vision is known as photopic vision. At intermediate brightness levels both rods and cones are effective. The photo-sensitive pigments in both rods and cones are themselves capable of building up or reducing their sensitivity. This fact becomes evident when entering a cinema during daylight, the first sensation being that of total darkness (save for the screen). However after ten minutes or so the internal lighting seems almost sufficient to read a newspaper. The reverse happens on leaving the cinema and going out into a sunlit street, but in this case the eyes more rapidly adapt themselves to the dazzle.

Part of this brightness adaptation is achieved by the variable iris diaphragm of the eye, and in the case of a very bright scene to the rather cruder method of screwing up the eyes or nearly closing the eyelids.

But while this brightness adaptation is extremely valuable to the normal function of vision, it makes the eye a very unreliable guide to the actual intensity of light, and hence the exposure requirements for a photographic material of fixed sensitivity range.

Unlike the camera lens, which takes in a wide angle of view at one time, the eye observes objects by a process of scanning, since the angle of acute vision is a very narrow one. During this process the eye tends to adapt itself to local brightness levels or, in other words, to equalize the overall lighting contrast of a scene. This form of adaptation is yet another pitfall to the unwary photographer in attempting to achieve a suitable lighting contrast for his subject. The existence of local adaptation becomes very apparent after looking for a few moments at a very bright light, when we become aware of an after-image due to the time lag in the recovery of the local sensitivity of the retina. The image of a lamp, for example, is apparent as a dark or coloured image when viewing a white surface.

Yet another effect of brightness adaptation is that the decrease in sensitivity of the retina caused by a light area may extend to an adjacent region of the retina so that a dark image appears darker than it really is. Thus a grey patch viewed with a white surround appears considerably darker than when viewed with a black surround. Such changes in appearance of adjacent objects are known as simultaneous contrast effects. An example of this is to be found in plates 67 and 68 where the same subject is photographed against different backgrounds.

26

Colour adaptation

As well as adapting its overall sensitivity, the eye adapts its colour sensitivity so that the illumination tends to appear colourless. This allows us to view an object or scene rather more as it would appear under normal conditions of daylight. Thus tungsten light, although much yellower than daylight, appears almost colourless so long as it cannot be compared with daylight. However, even when the scene is lit by two light-sources which differ in colour quality, the eye tends to minimize the difference by adapting to an intermediate level of colour quality.

Local colour adaptation also occurs and after the eye has observed a particularly strong colour for a short time, a change to a lighter surface reveals the existence of a coloured after-image. Thus although we may not always be aware of it, various colours in a brightly coloured scene or painting tend to modify each other as the eye moves from one part to another. A closely related effect is that known as simultaneous colour contrast where the effect of two adjacent colours is an enhancement of the colour contrast. Artists are aware of these effects and frequently make striking use of them.

Psychological effects

The act of seeing is not a simple and spontaneous action such as that of breathing. With a gentle slap on the back a newborn baby starts breathing with as much efficiency as an adult with many years of practice. But this is not so with the use of his eyes: not only must he learn to control them – to direct and focus them on what he wants to see, but he must learn to interpret the meaning of the various patterns presented to the visual centre of the brain. Owing to the fact that our memory does not extend to this period, we are tempted to believe that we have always seen objects just as we see them now from earliest infancy. During its first few months the child is chiefly aware of light and shade, and of movement. In the process of learning to see, forms, shapes, patterns, colours, textures are associated and imprinted in the visual memory, and become part of the process by which we see. These visual habits tend to impose themselves on the actual light-rays reaching our eyes both by influencing the sensitivity characteristics of the eye, and in the interpretation of the impulses reaching the brain.

Needless to say the psychological aspects of vision are extremely complex and in some respects are probably beyond our capacity for investigation. Nevertheless certain aspects are worth noting in the present chapter, and others will be mentioned later in the book as the need arises.

Constancy effects

Among the many mental adjustments we are continually making, for the most part unconsciously, to what we see, are the various 'constancy' phenomena. Important among these is 'size' constancy whereby the size of an object at a distance does not look smaller than when close at hand, although in fact the image on the retina is much smaller. This difference in the size of the image merely tells us that the object is farther away. Another effect is that of 'shape' constancy where we see, for example, a round plate as round although, when viewed obliquely, its outline is oval. Yet another is 'brightness' constancy, whereby we tend to see objects in terms of their reflecting power rather than the actual amount of light they reflect under given lighting conditions. For example, a sheet of white paper is seen as white even when in deep shadow and when it may be reflecting much less light than a sheet of grey paper in full illumination. It is unfortunate for the photographer that brightness constancy effects are much stronger in an original scene than in a photograph of the scene. This fact explains why photographs of interiors, where the lighting is often far from uniform, appear excessively contrasty unless specially illuminated for photography.

From the point of view of colour photography the effect known as approximate colour constancy is probably the most important. As we have already shown, the colour of an object is determined as much by the spectral quality of the light falling on it as by the selective absorption characteristics of the surface. Thus if we illuminate a blue object with strongly red light, it will appear dark grey or black since most of the light will be absorbed. This is an extreme example and in every-day life we are far more concerned with relatively small, though none the less significant, changes in the colour quality of illumination. Thus an object illuminated with tungsten illumination receives a higher proportion of red and a lower proportion of blue light than when it is illuminated with sunlight. Assuming it reflects some part of all the colour spectrum, then it must clearly reflect more red and less blue than it would in sunlight. Owing to colour constancy the difference is much less than might be expected and is in fact often unnoticed. Being predominantly creatures of daylight, we tend to see colours as they appear in daylight and our mind therefore presents these colours as it expects them to be.

However this effect is far weaker with objects which have highly selective absorptions or show sharp peaks or depressions in their spectral-reflectance curves, and similarly when the source of illumination itself has this characteristic. This applies to certain types of gas discharge lamps which emit very strong radiation in certain wavelengths and relatively little in others. Mercury and sodium street lighting are common examples, the latter being almost totally devoid of red (in spite of its orange appearance) giving red objects, such as pillar boxes and pink complexions, a dirty grey appearance.

Colour memory

From infancy we build up a memory of colours usually in association with familiar objects such as food, toys, flowers, foliage, the sky and common objects such as letter boxes, and public transport. With objects of almost daily occurrence this memory can be quite accurate since it is constantly being refreshed, and it is usually on this basis that we judge the accuracy of a colour photograph. However with colours less frequently seen, or indeed seen on a solitary occasion only, our memory of them may be very approximate. To some extent also we tend to memorize colours in terms of verbal classification or by the names of objects which commonly possess the colour. Thus we have the basic term yellow, itself evolved from the old English word for gall, which can be qualified with such terms as canary, buttercup, lemon and so forth. The pigments used by artists are themselves rich in associations – rose madder, crimson lake, red ochre and the like. But while an artist or person trained in colour recognition may be able to apply these verbal labels with considerable accuracy, the average person uses them far more loosely.

The strength and persistence of the memory of a particular colour may depend also on the intensity of any emotion which is experienced at the time. It is likely that a woman would retain a very clear memory of the colour of her bridal dress, or a man the colour of his school blazer. The naturalist, the gardener, the philatelist and others interested in growing or collecting things all gain a considerable repertoire of colours. But these are individual and personal memories, and at best form only a rough and ready means of classifying or matching colours. It may be noted here that, in viewing a new colour on a single occasion, our memory of it will be based on the colour quality of the illumination. Thus the colour of a dress seen in artificial lighting may not be recognized later when seen in daylight or in a colour photograph which has been taken with a colour film balanced for artificial light. It is upon the memory of colours associated with strong emotional experiences that we gain certain likes and dislikes of colours. The sight of a severe accident in childhood involving a good deal of spilt blood may create a lifetime's aversion to the colour of blood. Or, on a pleasanter note, a girl may have received some of her most flattering attentions at a time when she was wearing a green dress, and unconsciously adopt this colour ever after as the one which suits her best. Psychiatrists often read surprising meanings into their patient's choice of a favourite colour.

It is also reasonable to suppose that our reactions to colours are to some extent conditioned by our surroundings. These undoubtedly influence our conception of harmony and discord in colour mixtures. Tradition, religious beliefs, fashion and more recently the influence of colour charts and other propaganda devised by paint and wall-paper manufacturers are all factors in our use of colour.

Colorimetry

From what has already been said it may be appreciated that the measurement or matching of colours (other than by direct comparison) presents a problem since no two observers react in entirely the same way to the same spectral stimulus. We have to rely therefore on the reactions of an average or standard observer. However, the need for an accurate method of specifying colours when conditions do not permit of direct comparison is clearly of great importance in many branches of science and industry.

When the eye views a colour it can distinguish three main properties, *lightness*, *hue*, and *saturation*. The *lightness* of a colour refers to the amount of grey which it appears to contain. The second property, *hue*, relates to the shade or variety of colour. Thirdly a *saturated* colour contains a large proportion of a spectral colour with very little white, the colour becoming desaturated – or washed-out – as the amount of white light increases. Spectral colours thus have 100 per cent saturation, while white, grey and black may be said to have zero saturation.

One of the most important and widely used systems of colour specification is the Munsell system. It is based on the three-dimensional arrangement of all colours which can be represented by samples prepared from stable pigments (see fig. 1.8). It takes the form of a cylinder in which the vertical axis corresponds to the achromatic grey colours with black at the bottom and white at the top. Hue varies with the angle round the cylinder and the five major hues, red, yellow, green, blue and purple are spaced in planes at equal angles. Chroma (saturation), which starts at zero from the achromatic axis, is proportional to the radial distance from the axis. The Munsell Handbook contains 400 charts of colours arranged page by page with variations in intensity and hue. Needless to say it takes time and considerable experience to achieve satisfactory results in colour specification.

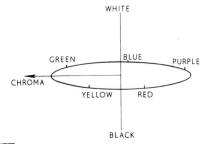

Fig. 1.8. Munsell colour system based on a cylindrical solid. The vertical axis corresponds to achromatic colours, hue varies with the angle round the cylinder and chroma is proportional to the radial distance from the axis. Hue is divided into five principal colours, red, yellow, green, blue and purple.

CIE system

We have already seen that mixtures of three primary colours can be made to match almost all other colours and it is upon this fact that the Commission Internationale de l'Eclairage introduced in 1931 a reference system for the precise definition of a colour, based on three numerals indicating the quantities of each primary necessary to produce a visual match of a given colour. Measurement is made by means of a colorimeter, an instrument which is essentially a photometer enabling a coloured beam of light to be compared with a beam made up by the addition of various amounts of three primaries. The three colours chosen for reference are in fact hypothetically supersaturated colours, designated X (red), Y (green) and Z (blue).

It is of course not possible to plot three variables on a flat sheet of graph paper but in fact this is not necessary, for the *total* amount of light present in any colour must be $X + Y + Z$ and the *fraction* of X light in this is $\dfrac{X}{X + Y + Z}$ (for convenience referred to as 'x', or 'little x'), and the fraction of Y light present is

$\dfrac{Y}{X + Y + Z}$ ('y'). Similarly the amount of Z light present is $\dfrac{Z}{X + Y + Z}$ ('z').

From the above it will be seen that

$$x + y + z = \dfrac{X}{X + Y + Z} + \dfrac{Y}{X + Y + Z} + \dfrac{Z}{X + Y + Z} = 1,$$

and so $z = 1 - (x + y)$.

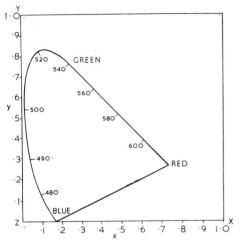

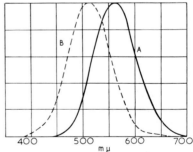

Fig. 1.9. CIE chromaticity diagram where the real primaries, red, green and blue, are shown in relation to the hypothetical CIE primaries X, Y and Z. The boundary line shows the position of the pure spectrum colours, some of which are indicated by values in mμ units.

Fig. 1.10. Luminosity curves of (A) photopic vision and (B) scotopic or twilight vision.

This now leaves the way clear to plot all colours on the graph, given their x and y values. This is shown on fig. 1.9. The curved line running from blue through green to red shows the position of pure spectral colours, representing the maximum saturation possible. The straight line joining blue to red direct covers the purples and magentas, colours which do not occur in the spectrum. All colours of less saturation must lie inside this 'triangle' and there is one point which is colourless. The position of this point is governed by the colour of the illumination used when making the measurements and it is therefore important to specify which illuminant was used. There are three standard illuminants, A, B and C. A is a tungsten lamp operating at a colour temperature of 2,854°K., while B and C are the same lamp filtered through liquid filters to give colour temperatures of approximately 4,800°K. and 6,500°K.

For more detailed information on the complex subject of colour specification the reader is referred to 'Colour as Seen and Photographed' (Kodak Limited) or 'The Reproduction of Colour' by R. W. G. Hunt (Fountain Press).

One of the features of the CIE system of specifying colours is the ease with which the X, Y, and Z coordinates of any coloured light can be calculated from the spectral absorption curves and tables without lengthy and sometimes unreliable visual measurements. The basis of these calculations are the CIE tables which give values of mixture curves.

In the colorimetric measurement of colour it is of course necessary to take into account the brightness sensitivity of the eye to the various wavelengths of light. For an average person this is shown by the curve, fig. 1.10, where relative luminosity is plotted against wavelength. This curve is for normal levels of illumination (photopic vision) and a second curve in broken lines shows the response to low levels (twilight or scotopic vision). However it is necessary to bear in mind that many individuals show marked departures from the average.

Some observers suffer from some form of colour blindness. Such a defect could seriously handicap a photographer attempting to achieve accurate colour matches.

Terminology of colour

While the reader may be familiar with all the terms already used in the present chapter and of those in subsequent chapters, there exists a certain confusion in the usage of words relating to light and colour. For this reason it is useful to conclude this chapter with a few definitions so as to avoid possible ambiguity. *Light* has already been defined as visible radiation and the term *radiation* is therefore reserved for radiant energy in the ultra-violet and infra-red regions of the spectrum. The term *hue* refers specifically to the type of colour such as red, yellow and green. However it is convenient to use the term *colour* when speaking of hue in the more general sense. *Lightness*, often referred to as brightness, is the characteristic of a surface or transparent medium by which it is said to reflect or transmit a greater or lesser amount of the light falling on it. Thus the steps on a grey scale from near-white to near-black differ in their lightness. *Luminosity* is the characteristic by which the eye judges the relative brightness or luminousness of the various parts of a subject. It is subjective in the sense that a candle will appear very luminous in a dark cellar, and little more than a feeble glimmer in the presence of sunlight; but the *luminance* – the actual amount of light emitted as measured by an illumination meter – remains the same. *Dominant wavelength* is the wavelength of that spectral colour which, with an appropriate amount of white light, it can be made to match the colour. *Saturation* or chroma denotes the purity of a colour; the greater the saturation the smaller the amount of white or grey mixed with it. Pale or pastel colours have a low saturation, vivid colours a high saturation.

2

The Nature of the Photographic Image

WHILE it is not essential to the practice of photography to know anything about the theory of lenses, some knowledge of the way a lens behaves and the nature of the image formed by it, may be considered indispensible to anyone wishing to make full and intelligent use of a camera. It is proposed therefore to confine the present chapter to practical aspects which have a bearing on colour photography, and to refer the reader desiring some knowledge of theory to the small but excellent book by E. W. H. Selwyn, *Theory of Lenses* (Chapman and Hall).

Image formed by a pinhole

If we start with the fact that light travels in straight lines, it is relatively simple to understand why a small hole, such as a pinhole, can be made to form an image of light reflected from objects placed in front of it. From each part of the object small bundles of rays are isolated by the pinhole and form small discs of light on a white surface, film or ground glass placed at a distance behind the pinhole in the manner shown in fig. 2.1, thereby forming an inverted image of the object.

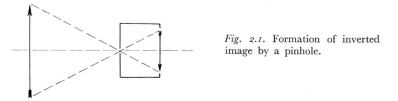

Fig. 2.1. Formation of inverted image by a pinhole.

The brightness or luminosity of the discs will be proportional to the intensity of the light reflected from various parts of the object. Such an image is of little practical use in photography, but it can be used to explain certain aspects of the use of lenses. For example, if we remember that the 'drawing' or formation of an image by a lens remains the same even if it is stopped down to a pinhole, it is fair to think of any lens as just a pinhole when it is only the perspective of the picture which is in question.

The size of the picture will be fixed by the camera frame, and all that we can do to alter the perspective or geometry is to move the pinhole to different distances from the film (focal plane). If the pinhole is close to the film we shall get a large part of what is in front of the camera projected on to the film and if it is a long way away only a small part of the scene will be projected on to the film – see fig. 2.2. The first pinhole can be called a 'wide-angle' one because there is a wide angle between the rays which reach the corners of the frame, and the second pinhole a 'narrow-angle' one. From this it can also be seen that the scale

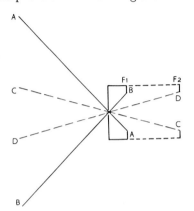

Fig. 2.2. The angle of the pinhole varies with the film distance. With the film at F1 it becomes a 'wide-angle' pinhole and with the film at F2 a 'narrow-angle' pinhole. The same situation applies to lenses.

of the image is directly proportional to the distance of the pinhole from the focal plane and that by doubling the distance we shall double the scale of the image. Ignoring the question of focus, which does not arise in the case of a pinhole, the scale of the image also varies directly with the distance of an object from the pinhole for any fixed distance between the pinhole and the focal plane, see fig. 2.3.

Fig. 2.3. The scale of the image formed by the pinhole varies directly with the distance of an object from the pinhole for any fixed distance. With the object at a fixed distance, the scale would also vary directly with the distance of the film from the pinhole.

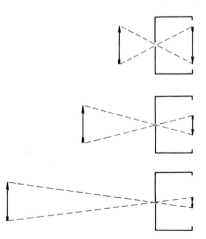

Image formed by a lens

In practice, a pinhole admits far too little light to be of use to the photographer, and even with a pinhole of the optimum size, the sharpness of the image is well below the requirements of acceptable definition. The answer, of course, is to use a lens in place of the pinhole, the purpose of the lens being to collect or admit a larger amount of light from each part of the object and concentrate or focus it on to the focal plane. An image of reasonable sharpness and very much greater brightness can, in fact, be achieved by a simple lens of meniscus design consisting of a single piece of glass. However, on the grounds of sharpness over the required picture area, the size of the opening through which light is admitted is still relatively small. To obtain still better definition and at the same time to make use of still larger apertures it is necessary to make use of two or more lenses, and often as many as six or seven in a large-aperture anastigmat lens.

To understand how lenses operate and why they are often of complicated construction, we need to know something about the wave motion of light. Light waves are of the same kind as those sent out by the B.B.C. to operate radio or television receivers, that is to say, they are electro-magnetic waves, but very much shorter in wavelength. The electric force in the wave changes from a maximum value, at the crest of a wave, down to zero, then changes direction by 180° to reach the same value as at the previous maximum and oscillates continuously in this way as shown in fig. 2.4. The distance between adjacent crests in fig. 2.4 is

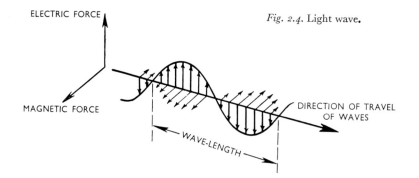

ELECTRIC FORCE

Fig. 2.4. Light wave.

MAGNETIC FORCE

DIRECTION OF TRAVEL OF WAVES

WAVE-LENGTH

only 1/2000 mm., but this is not so small as to be unimportant as we shall see later. The second thing that is important is that these light waves travel more slowly in glass than in air. The ratio of the velocity in air to the velocity in glass is the same as the refractive index, and can vary with the composition of the glass. This is a very important fact in the design of lenses.

If we accept these two propositions, then we can easily understand the way a simple lens works. Every minute bit of some scene will be sending out waves of light – if it were not so we could not see it. Let us consider a tiny bit of the scene directly opposite the lens. It will be sending out waves in such a way that the crests will lie on continuously expanding spheres centred on the spot from which they originate. A stone thrown in a pond will produce a similar effect but in one plane only. These spheres are technically termed wave-fronts. As soon as the wave-front enters the lens, which it will do first at the centre of the lens, it will be slowed down, and it is easy to see that the curvature of the wave-front can be reversed – see fig. 2.5. The wave-fronts therefore then tend to converge to a

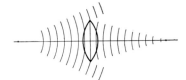

Fig. 2.5. Wave-fronts from a point source passing through a simple lens.

point and produce there a strong electromagnetic oscillation, that is to say a bright spot. In other words the lens focuses an 'image' of the bit of the scene we have been considering. The same kind of thing happens for every bit of the scene covered by the lens, which thus forms an image of the scene, turned upside down and reversed left to right.

To proceed any further we need some way of estimating the electro-magnetic disturbance at any given point ahead of a wave-front. The trick of doing this was suggested three centuries ago by Christian Huygens and is now referred to as Huygens' Construction. We imagine the wave-front divided up into tiny little

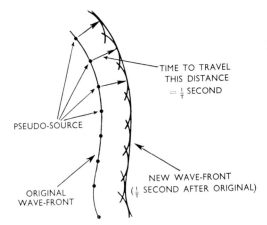

TIME TO TRAVEL
THIS DISTANCE
$= \frac{1}{T}$ SECOND

PSEUDO-SOURCE

NEW WAVE-FRONT
($\frac{1}{T}$ SECOND AFTER ORIGINAL)

ORIGINAL
WAVE-FRONT

Fig. 2.6. Construction of one wave-front from another by the Huygens' principle.

bits and each one we regard as a source of light. They have to be special kinds of sources (pseudo-sources shall we say?) because the light from a wave-front does not go backwards, but they still maintain the essential property of emitting waves. So now to imagine what happens at the focus we think of waves travelling through the region of focus from each pseudo-source. In fig. 2.8a we have represented crests of waves by a full line and troughs by broken lines. Only three sets of waves are shown because the diagram becomes unintelligibly complicated

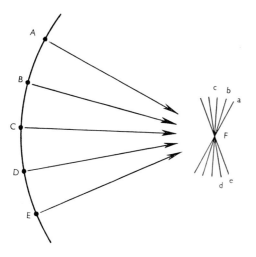

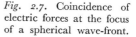

Fig. 2.7. Coincidence of electric forces at the focus of a spherical wave-front.

with more. The set represented by vertical lines is that which comes from the centre point of the wave-front while the set which slopes downwards from left to right comes from the lowest point on the edge of the wave-front and the remaining set from the uppermost point. At the point indicated by the arrow *A* three crests coincide so that the electric force is a maximum there. At *B* two troughs coincide with one crest, and the electric force at *B* is therefore one-third as great as at *A* and in the opposite direction. Somewhere in between at about *C* the electric force is at zero. When all the waves from all the points on the wave-front are added together it turns out that the image consists of a bright centre spot surrounded by rings as in fig. 2.9. If the aperture of the lens is opened up from that shown in fig. 2.8a to that in fig. 2.8b the inclinations of the waves to the axis are increased and the image shrinks. We can now see that if a lens designer wants an image to be sharp he will arrange that the wave-fronts coming out of a lens from any given object point will be a sphere centred on the image point, fig. 2.7. For then all the electric forces at the image point in the wave-fronts arising from all the pseudo-sources will be at their maximum values and in the same direction, so that they all add up and produce the greatest possible intensity of illumination. In other words he will have concentrated the light in the most effective fashion possible.

Lens aperture

Now if we go back and imagine our sets of three wave-fronts to come from lenses of different apertures, fig. 2.8a and 2.8b, we see that the greater the convergence – the bigger the aperture – the smaller will be the central patch of light. This leads to the conclusion that the more we stop down a lens the worse the definition

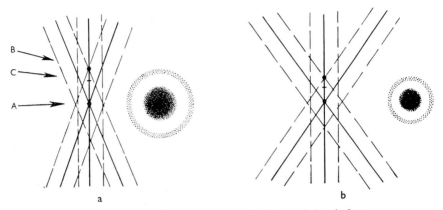

Fig. 2.8. Influence of convergence on coincidence of electric forces.

will become. This is true in practice if the lens is giving the best definition that is theoretically possible. But of course real lenses do not give the best definition that is theoretically possible. Firstly the lens designer cannot make the emergent wave-fronts exactly spherical, at least at full aperture, and secondly, a lens which is not focused exactly (and it cannot be so focused for every part of the subject if the subject has any depth) cannot be expected to give first class definition.

We are now in a position to consider why it is practically impossible to design lenses which make every emergent wave-front exactly spherical. To begin with let us consider what happens to a wave-front from a very distant source of light, so small that it might be thought of as a mere point of light. We might, for instance, take a star, since it is of interest to astronomers who need the most perfect image formation they can get. By the time a wave-front reaches the earth it will be flat. Then imagine it striking a block of glass the front surface of which is hemispherical. We can use Huygens' construction to find out how the wave-front changes shape as it travels along. If the distance from one position to another is small, then most of the effect at any point in the second position comes from the pseudo-source immediately behind the point and if we draw a series of small curves each centred on the original wave-front, the second wave-front is simply the curve which touches all the small circles as smoothly as it can – fig. 2.6. By applying this construction as the wave-front proceeds through the glass (allowing for the fact that light travels at about two-thirds its velocity in air) then by the time the wave-front is all in the glass, we find that it has a shape similar to that shown in fig. 2.10. In fact instead of being spherical the wave-front has turned up sharply near its edge. We may imagine the wave-front to be a spherical one with a distortion superimposed upon it roughly in the form of a saucer, namely, very nearly flat in the middle and rising more and more steeply

Fig. 2.9. The image of a point source of light formed by a lens will show a small disc of concentrated light surrounded by alternate dark and light rings as represented in this illustration.

towards the edge as shown in fig. 2.11a and 2.11b. Now the spherical wave-front is what we want, and the saucer-shaped addition is what causes the image to be less well defined than it should be. It is the outer parts of the wave-front which cause the distortions near the focus of the wave-front.

If a 'stop' to limit the wave-front is placed near the hemispherical surface, these outer parts of the wave-front are cut off and the definition at the focus is much improved. This is, fundamentally, why stopping down a lens normally makes the image sharper. The saucer-shaped addition which we have been speaking of is said to introduce 'aberration'. Now it turns out that whatever the curvature of the surface of the glass or the distance of the light source (always assuming it to be a point on the axis), or whether the light source is in the glass or outside, or whether the wave-front is converging as it meets the glass, the aberration (the unwanted addition to the required spherical shape) is always saucer-shaped. Sometimes it is a shallow one and sometimes deep, sometimes it is the same way up as shown in figs. 2.10 and 2.11, sometimes it is the other way round, but it is always of essentially the same shape.

So far we have considered only one object point, namely, on the axis of the lens. In real scenes there is only one such point, all others being situated off the axis. Now in all camera lenses there is a stop which is never very far from the surfaces of any of the components and this, in effect, means that none of the aber-

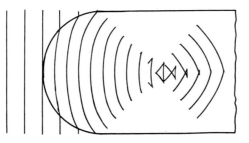

Fig. 2.10. Refraction of plane wave by block of glass with a hemispherical surface.

ration 'saucers' which get through the lens are complete if the object point we are considering is off the axis. For example, if we put a stop in fig. 2.10 anywhere but on the centre of the curvature of the front surface of the block of glass we get the situation in fig. 2.12, so that instead of a saucer as in fig. 2.11b, we get only the bit within the dotted line circle. What the lens designer does in principle is to suppose first of all that his lens is very much stopped down, so that all the aberrations are negligible, since then he is only considering the flat middle portions of the 'saucers'. Then he can trace the wave-fronts through the lens and find the points at which the wave-fronts strike the surfaces of the elements of the

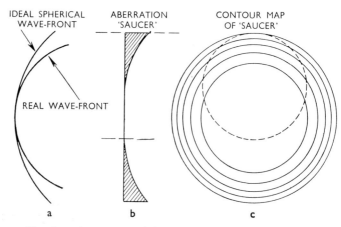

Fig. 2.11. The aberration saucer and the selection of a section of it by the lens stop.

lens. This trace enables him to determine how deep the various aberration saucers are and what bit of each gets through the lens when the stop is again opened up. The shape of the wave-front issuing from the lens can then be found by making up a contour map of each and adding them up together. The aim is to choose such a design for the lens that some of the saucers are the right way up and some upside down, and of such depths that when added all together they come out flat. Then he is left with his basic wave-front which is spherical and focuses as near as can be got to a point.

Fig. 2.12. Selection of a section of a wave-front by a stop. Compare this with fig. 2.11.

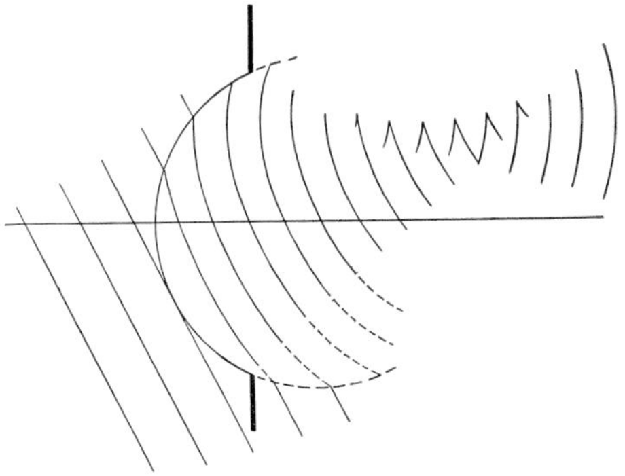

Lens aberrations

It is not necessary here to go any further into the theory of lens aberrations. The name and very often the price of a lens is usually a reliable indication of the degree to which they have been minimized, and practical tests with an unknown lens are the simplest way of testing its definition. In designing and making lenses the general policy is to aim at an acceptable level of definition at the full aperture of the lens. This means there are still residual aberrations. Now if such a lens is stopped down a little bit from its full aperture some of the wave-front is cut off and always a bit from the wave-front where distortion is usually most serious. The effect of stopping down is therefore to make the wave-front more nearly spherical and the lens thus gives better definition. At first sight we might expect the lens to give better and better definition the more it is stopped down, but as already shown, when the lens is perfectly corrected the definition gets worse as the lens is stopped down. Now after stopping down for, say, two stops the wave-fronts might well be, for all practical purposes, spherical; with the result that up to that point there is an improvement in definition, after which the definition would deteriorate.

Lens design

The reader who has thus far followed these very much simplified arguments will now have some idea of what the lens designer is up against in meeting the demand for sharp pictures. Camera lens design is one of the more specialized jobs, requiring a very unusual capacity for interminable calculations. It has to proceed by setting out a design and calculating what the image is like, changing the design a little, calculating again, and so on.

The minimum number of component lenses with which all the more important aberrations can be eliminated is three separated ones. This is the fundamental basis of the famous Cooke triplet invented by Dennis Taylor. The Tessar is rather similar but with one component made of two glasses cemented together. Such lenses give excellent definition for apertures of f/4 and are commonly used on medium priced 35 mm. cameras with apertures up to f/2·8. If better definition or larger apertures are required then more components and different constructions are required. With fewer components than three it is not possible to correct all the aberrations. All that can be done is to reduce the aberrations as far as possible and then stop down the lens until definition is adequate. This is what is done with the single lens of a box camera.

Focal length

The distance at which a lens forms a sharp image of a very distant object – usually said to be at infinity – is normally termed the focal length of a lens. This distance is measured from the rear nodal point of the lens to the focal plane. This point, also known as the principal point, usually lies near the lens diaphragm and may be considered the optical centre of the lens. A notable exception to this rule is the telephoto lens in which the rear nodal point lies some distance *in front* of the lens so that its effective focal length may be several times the distance between its physical centre and the focal plane. Telephoto lenses are commonly used on 35 mm. and other small cameras to avoid the bulkiness or size of normal long-focus lenses.

As a rule the focal length of a camera equipped with a fixed lens, or the 'standard' lens of a camera designed for interchangeable lenses, is roughly equal to the diagonal of the picture-taking size of the camera. We thus find a camera of $6\frac{1}{2} \times 4\frac{3}{4}$ in. format equipped with an 8 in. lens as the standard, one of $3\frac{1}{4} \times 2\frac{1}{4}$ in. a lens of 4 in. and a 35 mm. camera taking 36×24 mm. pictures with one of 40 to 50 mm. This gives an angle of view, based on the diagonal of the picture, of about $45°$. Lenses of shorter than standard focal length giving a wider angle of view or those of longer focal length (often of telephoto design) giving a narrower angle of view may be fitted as required to cameras designed for interchangeable lenses. The choice of focal length is discussed in Chapter 5.

f/number

We have already discussed the lens aperture and the 'stopping down' of a lens in relation to definition. With many simple cameras this aperture is fixed, though the recent tendency, due to the increase in film speeds, is to provide one or two additional stops of smaller size so as to reduce the amount of light admitted by the lens. With the majority of camera lenses the size of the aperture can be varied by means of an iris diaphragm much in the same way as the iris of the eye can change its size to allow for intensity changes or to extend near focusing accommodation. It has been common practice for a great length of time to calibrate the size of the lens aperture as the ratio of its optical diameter to its focal length. Such a ratio is known as the f/number, and lenses of the same f/number may be taken to admit the same amount of light irrespective of their focal length. Intermediate diaphragm sizes differing in area by a factor of 2 are usually engraved on the lens mount in the series $f/1 \cdot 4$, $f/2$, $f/2 \cdot 8$, $f/4$ and so on to as small as $f/64$ for lenses of long focal length. An alternative series based on $f/1 \cdot 6$, $f/2 \cdot 2$, $f/3 \cdot 2$, $f/4 \cdot 5$ and so on has been commonly used with lenses made on the Continent, but has now been discontinued in favour of the former series. It may be noted that the light-passing capacity of a lens is inversely proportional to the square of the f/number and consequently that larger f/numbers indicate a stopping down of the lens or reduction of its light-passing capacity.

While the f/number system suffices for most practical purposes as a common factor in exposure data, there was for a while a movement to introduce an alternative system known as 'T' stops. The 'T' stands for the actual transmission of a given lens and takes into account the absorbtion, reflection and flare factors of a multi-component lens. The effect of lens coating, however, see page 46, is to reduce surface reflections, and the grounds for the 'T' stop system have become less important.

There is a tendency in small cameras to utilize the variable diaphragm of the lens principally as a means of controlling exposure, and in many cases automatic – or partially automatic – control is effected by coupling a photocell device with the aperture control. However, the aperture has an important function in determining the depth of field over which planes of the subject are recorded in sharp detail by the lens.

Depth of field

The distance at which a critically sharp image is obtained at the focal plane varies with the distance of the object from the lens. As we have seen, for an object at infinity this distance corresponds to the focal length of the lens. As the object distance becomes appreciably less the plane of critical sharpness extends beyond the focal length and a sharp image at the focal plane is obtained by moving the lens forward. This is known as focusing the lens. This lens extension increases rapidly for objects at distances less than 20 times the focal length, being equal to the focal length for an object at twice the focal length. In this case the scale of the image is equal to that of the object, see page 158. We shall be discussing methods of focusing in a later chapter and at the moment only concern ourselves with the existence of depth of field. As we have already seen, the image of an extremely small point of light takes the form of a small disc even in the case of a theoretically perfect lens. With real lenses this disc is larger depending on the extent to which aberrations are present. However, we have now to consider that the eye itself is not a perfect lens nor the retina a perfect image receptor. Thus at a given viewing distance, the eye will accept discs up to a certain diameter as points, or in other words an image formed of discs or circles of confusion not exceeding a certain size as a sharp image. Now it can be seen from fig. 2.13 that points nearer and farther from one which happens to be critically focused by a lens will appear as larger discs of confusion since they are brought to a focus farther from and nearer to the focal plane. In so far as these larger discs are still accepted by the eye as sharp points either in a print or a projected picture, they represent a certain depth of field. Indeed it will be appreciated that without such a depth of field we should have the greatest difficulty of seeing objects in depth.

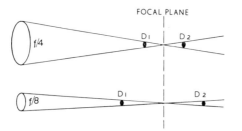

FOCAL PLANE

Fig. 2.13. The relative depth of focus, greatly exaggerated, shown by the discs D1 and D2, which may be considered acceptably sharp in the image. It can be seen that the narrower cone of rays given by the smaller aperture, provides the greater depth of focus. Depth of field is similarly greater.

It is customary to base depth of field calculations on the supposition that the diameter of the disc of confusion must be less than 1/1000 of the focal length of the camera lens. This in turn is based on the fact that the average eye can just distinguish 100 lines to an inch at a viewing distance of 10 in., and that to obtain normal viewing perspective a photograph should be viewed so that it subtends the same angle as the taking lens of the camera. This means that a photograph taken with a 10 in. lens can be viewed as a contact print at 10 in. while one taken with a 2 in. lens should be enlarged 5 diameters for the same viewing distance. It will be evident from this example that the size of the disc of confusion in the larger negative taken with a 10 in. lens can be five times larger than that of the small negative taken with a 2 in. lens. But the weakness of this 'mathematical' approach to depth of field is that photographs are not necessarily viewed at the correct viewing angle, nor do the dimensions of the photograph necessarily give any clue to the distance at which it should be viewed. Thus a $7\frac{1}{2} \times 5$ in. print could be a $\times 5$ enlargement of the whole of $1\frac{1}{2} \times 1$ in. negative, and therefore correct for viewing at 10 in., or it could be a $\times 10$ enlargement of a portion $\frac{3}{4} \times \frac{1}{2}$ in. in area which should in theory be viewed at 20 in. Clearly in the latter case the disc of confusion would have to be based on 1/2000 of the focal length. To some extent this is taken into account in calculating depth of field tables for miniature cameras. A further weakness of the usual calculations for depth of field arises when wider or narrower angle lenses are used, since the prints are likely to be viewed at the same distance as those taken with a lens of normal angle.

A more realistic approach can take in to account the fact that provided a photograph is reasonably sharp we do not have, at the moment of viewing it, any reference standard for sharpness other than the photograph itself. It is difficult for example to stop to consider critically whether or not one ought to be able to see the lines of mortar between bricks in a distant building. But if a photograph contains sharp and unsharp regions then we can and do immediately compare them. Questions of depth of field are not therefore really so much concerned with absolute measurement of definition as with the relative differences between parts of the picture which are in focus and those which are not.

From a practical standpoint it is interesting to note that since the angle of the cone of rays formed by a lens is inversely proportional to the f/number of the aperture, the depth of field increases with the f/number or as the lens is stopped down. Thus the relatively small aperture of the box camera lens permits acceptably sharp photographs to be made without the need of any lens adjustments over a distance range of about 6 ft. to infinity.

Depth of field diminishes as the scale of the image formed by the lens becomes greater. This can be related both to the distance of the object in front of the lens and also to the focal length of the lens. Thus as the lens-to-object distance diminishes, depth of field diminishes, and hence the need for more careful focusing for close-ups. It can also be seen that since the scale of the image for a given lens-to-object distance is directly proportional to the focal length of the lens‘ that depth of field diminishes as the focal length increases. It is this fact which gives the miniature camera the advantage of greater depth of field since the image formed by the relatively short focus lens is much smaller in scale than that taken at the same distance with, say, a 5 × 4 in. camera employing a lens of four or five times the focal length. The fact that the negative or transparency made with a miniature camera is later enlarged to give a print or screen image of the same scale does not affect the depth of field since this is a characteristic of the image formed in the camera. Depth of field as it applies to close-ups is discussed in Chapter 11.

Lens movements

We can think of a lens as having an axis or imaginary line passing through the centres of the spheres of curvature of the surfaces of its various components. In the normal way this axis passes through the centre of the picture frame of a camera and at right angles to the focal plane. In the large majority of small hand cameras the lens is fixed in this relationship with the focal plane, the only possible movement being along the axis for the purpose of focusing. However, in the majority of larger cameras, particularly those designed for studio and technical use, the panel on which the lens is mounted can be moved both vertically and horizontally in a plane parallel to the focal plane, and in many cases also tilted. Such movements, often in conjunction with tilt or swing movements of the focal plane, provide a valuable means of adjusting the field of view of the lens, of adjusting perspective and of changing the planes in which depth of field is effective. Such movements normally require the use of a lens of wide covering power, corrected to give acceptable definition outside the normal angle of view and so mounted as

45

to avoid vignetting (loss of illumination due to partial cut-off by the lens mount). One of the more commonly used movements is that known as a rising front since it frequently overcomes the necessity to tilt a camera upwards in order to include the top of a tallish building. Tilting, even in a small degree, causes the verticals of the building to converge upwards, an effect which gives the building the appearance of toppling over backwards. Because we know the walls of a building are vertical we tend to see them as such. But in a photograph the effect seems unnatural, largely because we notice the tilt in comparison with the vertical edge of the picture. By means of a rising front the camera can be kept vertical and the lens moved upwards until the top of the building is within the picture frame of the camera. This usually has the added advantage of reducing an excessive area of foreground which results when a camera having a fixed lens is used at a greater distance in order to extend its field of view. Similar corrections can be made with a swing back, in this case the lens being tilted and the converging verticals corrected on the focal plane. This sort of correction can, of course, also be done on the enlarger, but it is clearly more convenient if it can be done in the camera and is essential in the case of a transparency which is to be viewed in its entirety. The use of lens and camera movements is dealt with in later chapters.

Absorption, reflection and dispersal of light

As already noted earlier in this chapter in dealing with the light-passing capacity of lenses, not all the incident light arrives at the focal plane to form an image, some being absorbed by the glass, depending on its thickness and composition, some being reflected from its air-to-glass surfaces, and some being dispersed by particles of dirt and dust. The amount of light absorbed is relatively small, being only 0.5 per cent per 1 cm. thickness of glass. Surfaces reflections are much more serious and for a lens having 8 air-to-glass surfaces, account for a loss of about one third of the incident light which is roughly equivalent to $\frac{1}{2}$ stop. However, it is not the loss of light that matters most. Reflections from internal lens surfaces create inter-reflections, often of light outside the angle of view of the picture area, and some of this light falls on the focal plane causing some degradation of the image and loss of contrast. It is for this reason that a lens hood is a most desirable lens accessory, especially when the subject area has adjacent areas of strong brightness, as when making exposure against the light. Strongly localized inter-reflections caused by bright light sources are known as 'flare' spots and often take the form of halos or distorted shapes of the lens diaphragm.

Dirt on any of the lens surfaces tends to cause further degradation and loss of contrast through the dispersal of light. The remedy is obvious but is often neglected or overlooked, particularly in the case of enlarger and projector lenses.

Lens coating

It has now become common practice to coat the air-to-glass surfaces of multi-component lenses as a means of reducing the effect of inter-reflection within the lens and to some extent reducing the overall loss of light due to reflection.

However, the practical effect is to improve image contrast rather than increase the 'speed' of the lens. The improvement of contrast arises in the areas of low brightness which naturally suffer mostly from the effect of flare. Lens coating is based on the phenomenon of light interference already referred to in the previous chapter in connection with structural colours. The thickness of the layer is usually adjusted to give maximum transmission in the green-yellow region of the spectrum which explains why the residual reflections from the front surface of a coated lens usually appear bluish or purple. However, variations in the transmission of the coating, especially with complex lenses, are liable to produce slight colour casts in a colour transparency. This is hardly likely to be noticed unless the results of two differently coated lenses are directly compared, as when using interchangeable lenses.

Subject movement and exposure time

So far we have considered the image formed by a lens without reference to time. The act of seeing is a continuous one, or at least appears so, whereas a photograph is the result of a certain period of time which can range from as short as one millionth of a second to several hours. Assuming the object being photographed and the camera are both stationary, then the duration of the exposure time will not affect the form of the image except in terms of the amount of light action on the film. Thus under-exposure will result in failure to record the image adequately, or over-exposure loss of sharpness or graininess. However, we shall be dealing with this aspect later and for the moment will concern ourselves with the effect of movement of either the subject or camera during exposure.

Shutters

The shutter of a camera is the means whereby the duration of light action can be controlled. At its simplest it need consist of no more than a lens cap when the duration of exposure exceeds 1 second or when the source of illumination itself, as in the case of flashbulbs, is of brief duration. In the case of hand cameras and most technical cameras some form of mechanical shutter is fitted either as an integral part of the camera or as part of the lens unit. In simple cameras the shutter may take the form of a piece of metal containing an opening which flicks past the lens under spring-loading to give an 'instantaneous' time in the region of 1/100 to 1/25 sec. With more elaborate hand cameras and many technical cameras the shutter is usually of the diaphragm type taking the form of a number of blades pivoted around the lens mount which open and close under spring tension to give a range of speeds from 1 sec. to as little as 1/1000 sec. The speeds are usually graduated on a factor of 2 giving a series of 1, 1/2, 1/4, 1/8, 1/15, 1/30, 1/60, 1/125, 1/250 and 1/500 to keep in step with the f/number series. An earlier series included a rather more arbitrary spacing with such speeds as 1/5, 1/10, 1/25 and so on and was, in effect, regularized to enable the lens diaphragm stops to be linked with the shutter speeds in reciprocal values – see Chapter 10.

Although a diaphragm shutter is usually situated near the centre of the lens axis, where the convergence of rays usually reaches its apex, it may also lie behind the lens in the interests of lens interchangeability. The Retina Reflex III camera has such a shutter, permitting a range of lenses from 28 mm. to 200 mm. to be used. However, the more usual type of shutter for small cameras having interchangeable lenses is that known as a focal-plane shutter. As its name suggests, the shutter occupies a plane very close to the focal plane of the camera and usually takes the form of a flexible roller blind which opens the whole picture area at slower speeds (1/20 or longer) and is reduced to a slit for faster speeds, the time of exposure in this case depending on the speed of travel across the focal plane and the width of the slit. It may be observed here that although such a shutter is more efficient at fast speeds than a diaphragm shutter when both are used at fairly large apertures (at such speeds the time taken for a diaphragm shutter to open fully and close again becomes a significant factor in the total exposure time) the image of a fast moving object, such as a racing car, may show some distortion – see Chapter 5. In general the simpler mechanism of a focal-plane shutter permits speeds as short as 1/1000 sec.

Other types of shutters occasionally to be found on still cameras include the sector shutter, usually of the rotating type in which the duration of exposure is determined by the speed of rotation, and louvre shutters which somewhat resemble the structure of a venetian blind. Various types of sector shutters are used with cine cameras, where a succession of intermittent exposures is required.

Image blur

Returning again to the image of a point source which moves relative to the lens during the time the shutter is open we shall find that instead of a small disc, the image takes the form of a thin line when recorded by the film. An image, made up of such light tracks, occurs when 'time' exposures are made of the star-bursts of a rocket or the lights of street traffic at night. Concentric and eccentric designs can also be made by recording the motions of a small gyrating light source. By making several recordings through differently coloured filters, pleasing patterns known as harmonographs can be made.

In an ordinary subject the presence of image blur due to a small amount of movement may not be so easily recognized. When using a hand camera it is frequently caused by camera shake or a jerky movement in pressing the shutter. The inexperienced photographer often attributes the slight loss of sharpness to a poor lens. Indeed many photographers using electronic flash for the first time are surprised by the crispness of definition given by a lens which has been previously used entirely for handheld snapshots. The explanation is that the effective exposure time for electronic flash is in the region of 1/1000 sec., whereas most photographers use 1/60 sec. for handheld camera exposures outdoors.

The amount of image movement recorded in a photograph depends on a number of factors: (a) speed of movement (b) direction of movement (c) the scale of the image and (d) the duration of the exposure time. Indeed it is a matter of simple mathematics and geometry to work out the required shutter speeds for confining image movement to a disc of confusion which will appear sharp to the eye, using, in fact, the same standard as that used for depth of field calculations. The table below gives shutter speeds for this purpose.

SHUTTER SPEEDS TO OBTAIN SHARP IMAGES OF OBJECTS IN MOTION

Approx. Speed in m.p.h.	Typical Subjects	Distance of Subject from Camera								
		25 feet			50 feet			100 feet		
		Direction of movement relative to lens axis								
		90° ⇄	45° ⤢	0° ↕	90° ⇄	45° ⤢	0° ↕	90° ⇄	45° ⤢	0° ↕
2–3	Swimmer Pedestrian	1/125	1/60	1/30	1/60	1/30	1/15	1/30	1/15	1/8
4–6	Children playing Horse walking	1/250	1/125	1/60	1/125	1/60	1/30	1/60	1/30	1/15
8–15	Average runner Cyclist Horse trotting	1/500	1/250	1/125	1/250	1/125	1/60	1/125	1/60	1/30
20–30	Skating Horse racing Athletics	1/1000	1/500	1/250	1/500	1/250	1/125	1/250	1/125	1/60
40–60	Motor-car Speed-boat Train	* 1/1000	1/1000	1/500	1/1000	1/500	1/250	1/500	1/250	1/125
80–120	Fast train Racing car Aircraft take-off	* 1/1000	* 1/1000	1/1000	1/1000	* 1/1000	1/500	1/1000	1/500	1/250

* Sharp pictures may be obtained by swinging the camera in the direction of movement.

But the effect of movement is not simply a matter of calculations: a completely sharp image in the photograph of a subject that was clearly in motion at the time of photography usually gives an unnatural 'frozen' effect. Some degree of image movement or blur is occasionally desirable, particularly in the movement of water, 'action' photography generally, and in cases where it is desired to emphasize movement – an effect sometimes known as 'fluid motion'.

Movement compensation

Anyone who has sat looking from a train window at the apparently fast moving objects along the side of the track will know that sharp images can be gained for brief moments by the ability of the eyes to follow through some point of interest. Thus the completely blurred image of the sleepers of an adjacent track can momentarily be eliminated by a rapid swing of the eyes in the direction of movement. This method of obtaining a sharp image of a fast object such as a racing car is known as swinging or 'panning' the camera in photography. The blurring effect of movement due to swinging the camera is then transferred to stationary objects in the background, an effect in keeping with the idea of speed.

High speed photography

The sensitivity of early photographic plates was extremely slow and involved exposures of several minutes even in strong sunlight. At the same time a lens of f/5·6 was considered a large aperture lens, and no artificial light sources comparable to those in common use today existed then. Portraits, for example, required the use of a head rest, and the interiors of buildings such as churches which were both dimly lit and required the use of a small lens aperture, required exposures of several hours.

The immensely increased speeds of both films and lenses, and the invention of high-efficiency light sources now makes it possible to record images far beyond the capacity of the human eye both in duration and brightness. Thus, on a time base, photography has greatly extended the range of motion study, both in still photography by permitting us to 'freeze' extremely fast movement in single images, and by high speed cine photography whereby a succession of single images are projected very much more slowly than they were taken. The development of stroboscopic discharge lamps has also made it possible to record successive stages of movement, each critically sharp, in one photograph.

However, not only can we 'expand' the time base with high speed cine photography, but we can reverse the process by taking pictures at normal or longer taking speeds and then projecting them at fast speeds. This speeding up of the time has proved a popular source of humour in the cinema but also has valuable applications as, for example, in the study of the growth of plants.

In more general photography, and particularly when using colour materials, the development in recent years of easily portable electronic flash units has greatly extended the range of subjects indoors and out which may be photographed with both sharp detail and satisfactory colour balance.

Eye and camera

In regard to image formation, there are both similarities and differences in the optical characteristics of the eye and a camera. Although the lens of the eye may be likened to a single element camera lens, it has the unique quality of variable curvature on both surfaces. This enables it to change its focal length (dioptric power) according to the distance of the object being viewed – a process known as accommodation. Normal vision in a young adult extends from about 8 in. to infinity and in a child to as close as 4 in. However, with increasing age near-accommodation decreases and it is usual for older people to wear glasses for reading. Defects in vision include hypermetropia (long sight) and myopia (short sight), where in the former accommodation is restricted to distant objects and in the latter to very near objects. Abnormal inequality of curvature in the lens of the eye is called astigmatism.

Unlike the camera lens which is required to cover a flat focal plane of fairly wide angle, acute vision in the eye is restricted to a small area of the retina known as the macula lutea and in particular to a small depressed central part of it, the fovea centralis, which contains only closely packed cones and subtends an angle of about $\frac{1}{2}°$. The high resolving power of the eye lens is thus confined to an extremely narrow angle at the centre of its field. This will become obvious to the reader who pauses to observe a line of printed type critically: at normal reading distance each letter can be examined separately. Due to the fact that the eye is continually scanning a much wider field of view, satisfactory detail is seen over a wide field of view. In addition, mental processes based on experience supply detail which may not, in fact, be seen at the moment of observation. This explains why we are not normally aware of the 'blind spot' in the retina – the region devoid of receptors where the nerve fibres from all over the retina collect to enter the optic nerve.

We have already seen earlier in this chapter how the lens of a camera deals with geometric perspective in regard to horizontal and vertical parallel lines. The brain deals rather differently with the images received via the eye, tending to impose what may be called 'parallel' constancy so that we see the lines of a tall building as parallel unless we are very close to its base. This applies also to shapes, forms, colours, brightnesses and other attributes of a subject.

In addition, we normally have the use of two eyes or what is known as binocular vision. This enables us to see objects at close and moderately close distances as solid objects having depth as well as height and width. A similar effect can, of course, be obtained in stereo-photography, but in the normal way photographs are based on a single image. Our perception of depth is by no means confined to stereoscopic vision or binocular parallax. Motion parallax, whereby when we change our viewpoint there is a greater displacement of the image of near objects, is probably equally important, and in addition there are many other 'clues' to depth even when an observer closes one eye and stands motionless. The most important of these is the convergence of parallel lines which is the basis of geometric perspective. Another clue is that of shadows which vary in shape, size and direction according to the nature and position of the light source. In the assessment of large distances, the scattering effects of aerial haze – often known as atmospheric perspective – provide useful though often misleading clues to the relative distance of the features of a landscape. Other clues are based on the known size of familiar objects, loss of detail, colour (e.g. so-called advancing and receding colours) and brightness. Many of these clues are effective in a photograph though none is so effective as when viewing an original scene. However, by exaggeration and distortion, painters and photographers are able to gain effects of equal value in pictures of only two dimensions.

3

Colour Materials and Processes

MODERN colour photography has a relatively short history, for it is little more than a hundred years ago that Clerk Maxwell projected the first colour photograph based on the additive mixture of three primary colours. Nevertheless the production of a 'true' colour process was the goal of earlier workers, and from the latter half of the last century until the present day has engaged and still engages the attention of increasing numbers of technicians and scientists. A detailed history would show far more failures than successes, but in the present book we have space to mention only a few of the more important mile-stones.

Although Maxwell is usually credited with the first colour photographs, it is fair to mention that Edmund Becquerel obtained in 1848 a reflected reproduction of the colours of the spectrum by projecting a solar spectrum on to a plate coated with silver chloride containing free silver, though only after a prolonged exposure. As he discovered no means of fixing this image, the plates had to be kept in the dark and could be viewed only for brief periods. This process was probably a forerunner of one later developed by Lippmann based on interference phenomena.

Three-colour processes

But the real basis of colour photography undoubtedly rests on the trichromatic theory of vision which Thomas Young emphasized in a paper published in 1801; however it was not until fifty years later that this theory was seriously investigated by the German physiologist Helmholtz, and it was to prove the propositions of Helmholtz that Maxwell constructed his famous colour box, a type of spectroscope with which he produced the first colour triangle, thereby laying the foundations of modern colorimetry. Maxwell demonstrated that all colours, except spectral colours and others of very high saturation, could be reproduced by adding various proportions of the three primary colours. It was to demonstrate this that he engaged the photographer Sutton to make photographs using blue, green and red filters which he then projected through filters of similar colour to produce a single three-colour image on the screen. Unfortunately his demonstration was much in advance of colour sensitizing and the photographic material used by Sutton was completely insensitive to green and red light. The fact that images were obtained through the green and red filters was explained by R. M. Evans in 1961 as being due to the sensitivity of the material to the ultra-violet radiation which was reflected by the subject and transmitted by the filters. The success of the demonstration was thus based on a coincidence which happened to fit the theory.

Maxwell was not alone; the Frenchman, Charles Cros, working independently, published a paper on additive three-colour synthesis in 1867, and two years later, another Frenchman, Ducos du Hauron, also working independently, published descriptions of several methods of colour photography by both additive and subtractive three-colour methods. In the latter respect, du Hauron may be considered the father of modern colour photography, which is now based entirely on subtractive colour synthesis. But like many inventors, du Hauron's ideas were far in advance of technical developments, and remained so in spite of a life-long devotion to the subject of colour photography, during which he foresaw in fundamentals almost every process which has since been applied.

Yet another Frenchman, Gabriel Lippmann, demonstrated in 1891 a method of producing colour photographs by a system based on light interference. Drawing on the work of earlier physicists, he employed a very nearly grainless emulsion to record the effect of stationary light waves formed by placing the surface of the emulsion against a bath of mercury, the exposure being made through the glass base. The stationary waves were produced by the interference of incident and reflected waves, and after processing the plate, the separations between the various silver layers in the emulsion corresponded to various regions of the spectrum. By viewing the image so formed by reflected light with the plate again placed against a bath of mercury, the original colours of the subject were reproduced. In a way the Lippmann process applied Newton's theory that all the colours of the spectrum were needed to compose a colour image that would be acceptable to the eye. Apart from the complications arising through the need of a backing mirror, a Lippmann photograph offers the further disadvantage in that it can only be viewed over a very narrow angle, and the silver chloride collodion type emulsion is extremely slow. Nevertheless the process produced excellent colour photographs comparable in brilliance and colour reproduction to present-day three-colour processes.

Additive processes

It was the application of the principle of additive three-colour mixtures that was first to prove commercially successful in the form of the Autochrome plate introduced by the Lumière brothers in 1907. The system was based on the use of adjacent filters of extremely small size and closely spread beneath the emulsion, the filters being of violet, orange and green starch grains dispersed over the surface at random. By exposing the plate through the glass, the image consisted of small patches or discs each recording roughly a third of the spectrum. When processed to give a positive image (reversal process), a colour image of similar colours to the original was obtained by viewing the photograph by transmitted light. The process produced excellent results and numbered among its early users George Bernard Shaw and A. L. Coburn. A description of the process in a special Colour Photography supplement of *The Studio* published in 1908 showed both admiration and alarm aroused by the new medium. A brief extract of this description of the first practical colour process is, perhaps, not without interest today, when we take so much of colour photography for granted.

'An exquisite automatic delicacy resulting in an image of unyielding exactness – that, then, is the physical basis of the Autochrome process; and it is our task to find what manner of aesthetic structure it is possible to erect on such a base. And when we examine the case for Autochrome in this bare way, picked clean and reduced to its simplest elements, two decidedly ominous circumstances begin to thrust themselves forward. For we find in the first place that the "exquisite automatic delicacy" is of such a jealous nature that it becomes the stern enemy of all other delicacies. And we find, in the second, that the "unyielding" exactness of the image is veracious in that fanatical way which is really a kind of fierce falsehood, that the image is truer to Nature than Nature is true to herself, so implacably precise that it is in effect a distortion of itself.'

But we should hardly be so enthusiastic or alarmed in our reception of it today. Not only were the Autochrome plates of slow speed, but the resulting photographs were rather dark owing the the very high absorption of light by the starch grains even in the highlights of the subject.

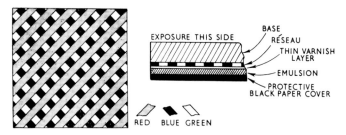

Fig. 3.1. Diagram showing the arrangement of the réseau and a cross section of Dufaycolor film.

Nevertheless the screenplate process, as it became commonly known, had a surprisingly long run and materials of this kind were still in use forty years after the introduction of the first Lumière plates. In fact the first screen-plate process was patented by du Hauron in 1868, and the first plates to be manufactured were those of Joly in 1895, in this case the filters being produced by machine-ruling of coloured ink lines on a glass surface previously coated with gelatin. Identically ruled taking and viewing plates were issued but the process failed because of the impossibility of obtaining emulsions of uniform sensitivity and the difficulty of maintaining good contact between the surfaces of the screens and the photographic plates, since, unlike the Lumière plates, the filters were separated from the sensitive material itself.

The most successful of screen-plate processes was that which was marketed under the name Dufaycolor, materials for which were still being manufactured

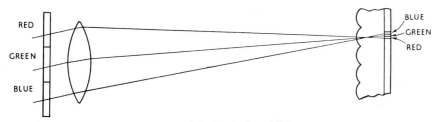

Fig. 3.2. Diagram of the lenticular additive process.

up to a few years ago. It was of the combined type, the screen or réseau of blue and green squares with red lines being printed on the film base. A thin layer of protective varnish was then applied before the emulsion was coated, this in turn being protected with a layer of black paper – see fig. 3.1. Exposure was made through the film base and the film reversal-processed to produce a colour transparency. Owing to the transparency and fineness of the réseau an image of satisfactory brilliance and definition could be produced for normal transmitted light viewing or projection. However, the absorption of light by the filters was still a considerable disadvantage in the case of small photographs and the appearance in 1935 of a subtractive colour process (Kodachrome) made its ultimate end inevitable.

A rather different application of additive three-colour synthesis was that known as the lenticular process, which was first suggested in 1896 by Liesegang. The idea was to use a filter over the camera aperture consisting of three strips of transparent material, blue, green and red. A plate filled with tiny holes was to be placed in front of the sensitive plate, behaving in effect like a multi-holed pinhole camera, each small image containing a small part of the total subject as seen through each of the three filter bands. The positive image formed in this way was then to be viewed in a similar but reversed optical system.

Some years later, Berthon patented a similar process, but instead of pinholes he suggested lenses embossed on the surface of the film, see fig. 3.2. As can be seen from this diagram, light reaching the camera lens is divided into blue, green and red bands, and the rays from a small area of the subject are brought to a focus to give tiny images of the three filters under each of the embossed lenses. Each small area of the subject is therefore recorded in terms of its blue, green and red content. The film is developed to give a positive image and is projected through filters similar to those used over the camera lens. The small embossed lenses focus the light from the small areas of the image which have densities corresponding to the blue, green and red sections of the filter, and the projection lens focuses an image of the film on to the screen. The first commercial film based on the lenticular process was marketed by Kodak in 1928 as 16 mm. cine film and was called Kodacolor. The film was later discontinued in favour of Kodachrome film, and the name Kodacolor is now applied to a negative colour film.

Subtractive processes

In these processes colours are obtained by superimposing dyed images. The earliest, described by du Hauron and Cros, involved the use of relief images of gelatin tissues. It was first necessary to make separation negatives, namely, black-and-white negatives of the subject made separately through blue, green and red filters respectively. The negative made with the blue filter was then used to expose a film of gelatin coated with a yellow colouring matter to form a yellow positive, the negative made with a green filter used to form a red positive, and the negative made with a red filter used to form a blue positive. The three positives were then superimposed in register. Similar techniques were developed by Vidal in 1872 and Marion in 1873. However, the exposure of the bichromated gelatin required several hours.

Another worker, E. Howard Farmer, discovered that, when finely divided silver, gelatin and a soluble bichromate are brought into contact with each other, the bichromate is reduced and the gelatin-bichromate combination becomes insoluble. Later, Manly combined these ideas to develop a process which in modified form became known as Trichrome Carbro. As a method of producing colour prints Carbro was long held to be the best process available. A modified version of the process was used by D. A. Spencer in the commercial production of Vivex colour prints during the 1930's, achieving a remarkable standard of excellence.

The idea of using relief matrices produced by the hardened gelatin technique for transferring dyes was first suggested by Sanger-Shepherd and Bartlett in 1902. A later variation making use of the differential absorption of dyes according to the amount of exposure given to the gelatin appeared under the name Pinatype. A vital ingredient in dye transfer, an 'acceptor' which would mordant or fix dyes, was first applied by F. E. Ives, who did a great deal of work with relief-image formation.

The modern equivalent, the Kodak Dye Transfer process, is described later in this chapter and its use in Chapter 32.

Other processes which have been applied with varying degrees of success are dye toning (commonly applied to monochrome photographs), dye mordanting and dye bleach processes. But it was the discovery and application of dye-coupling processes which prepared the way for modern colour materials.

Fischer in 1912 found that certain agents when added to a *p*-phenylenediamine developer solution caused the formation of a dye image as well as a silver image. The dye image, in fact, resulted from the coupling of this added substance with the oxidized developer, and it was given the name coupler. Although Fischer suggested the use of these couplers in multi-layered films, it was many years before technical advances in the production of colour-sensitized emulsions and in the use of couplers made possible a commercially successful colour process. It was the work of Mannes and Godowsky which resulted in the introduction in 1935 of Kodachrome film, a reversal colour film intended for users of 35 mm. still cameras and narrow-gauge cine cameras.

Modern subtractive colour processes

After this short historical survey of colour photography we can now look more closely into the nature of modern colour films. All films used for general colour photography are of the tripack subtractive type, that is, they have three separate emulsion layers coated on the same base. One of these is used to record the blue content of light passing through the lens, one the green content and one the red content. Owing to the inherent sensitivity of photographic emulsions to the blue region of the spectrum, the blue-sensitive layer is normally the top layer, where it receives the total light passed by the lens. Beneath it there is a filter layer (yellow in colour) which absorbs the blue region of the spectrum while freely transmitting green and red. The middle emulsion layer, which is sensitive to blue and green, therefore records only the green region of the spectrum, while the bottom layer, sensitive to blue and red, records only the red region.

In the case of a reversal colour film, the exposed film is first developed in a negative-type developer which converts the latent image to a black-and-white negative. The residual and undeveloped emulsion is then fogged (reversal exposure), and according to the type of film, developed in a coupling developer or in one which reacts with couplers in the emulsion layers themselves, so that dye images are formed in the three layers. The blue-sensitive layer forms a reversed yellow dye image becoming in effect a blue-absorbing filter which controls the amount of blue light passing through the image when the transparency is viewed with white light. The green sensitive layer forms similarly a magenta dye image, thereby becoming a green-absorbing filter, and the bottom layer cyan (blue-green) becomes a red-absorbing filter layer. Each layer therefore forms a dye image in the complementary colour to that to which it is sensitive and thus controls the transmission of its 'own' colour. The density or absorption of the dye image is related in reversal colour films to the residual silver; an area of the subject strongly emitting blue would produce a dense image in the blue-sensitive layer in the first development, leaving very little residual silver halide for the second development. Thus the density of the yellow dye would also be very small and, with the silver density removed, a very large amount of the blue light would be transmitted. At the same time the other two layers would be hardly affected in the first developer and the residual silver halide in each layer would produce a heavy deposit of dye, thus resulting in the almost total absorption of red and green. This particular area of the image would thus appear strongly blue in the photograph.

The developed silver images, along with any undeveloped silver halide still remaining in the film, are removed by bleaching and fixation, leaving only the three superimposed dye images. This fact gave rise to an early belief that such a colour photograph was entirely 'grainless' in the sense that a monochrome photograph is said to be 'grainy'; however, a residual grain effect can be seen in a greatly enlarged image.

A colour film intended for the production of colour negatives is of basically the same nature as a reversal film of the kind which incorporates couplers. The initial development produces both a negative image of silver and a negative dye image which is roughly complementary in colours to those of the original subject. When the film is bleached and fixed, only the dye image remains. As with a reversal film, each layer controls its own colour, but in terms of negative or reversed transmissions, so that a strongly blue area in the original subject appears as a deep yellow. When printed on a colour print paper of similar characteristics, very little exposure takes place in the blue-sensitive layer, while the green-sensitive and red-sensitive layers are fully exposed. Thus, when the print is processed, very little dye is formed in the yellow layer and the magenta and cyan dyes form heavy deposits. Viewed in white light this area of the print appears strongly blue. We may note here in passing that there is no basic difference, except in density, between the image of a transparency and that of a reflection print on a white opaque base. In the former case the light passes through the image only once while in the latter it passes through twice – once on the way in and once on the way back. Indeed a very over-exposed transparency placed in contact with a sheet of white paper takes on the appearance of a print.

Couplers

The dye images contained in a colour photograph are obtained by the reaction of agents known as couplers with the oxidized developer. The most satisfactory dyes from the point of stability are those formed in developers based on p-phenylenediamine compounds. A disadvantage of most of these compounds is that they sometimes cause a severe rash on the skin. Continued contact with such developers does not create immunity, but tends rather to increase sensitivity.

A large number of compounds have been found which act as couplers to form dyes in the colour-development process. However, the required characteristics of a coupler in addition to its colour formation and stability of the dye, may include such factors as its solubility, the insolubility of the dye produced, and the capacity of the coupler to diffuse through an emulsion layer. For example, the Kodachrome process makes use of a series of coupling-development steps, each developer containing an appropriate coupler. The couplers must therefore be soluble in the developer solution and also diffuse freely through the gelatin, so that the dye images may be formed in the appropriate layers of the film. On the other hand, couplers which are incorporated in the emulsions layers themselves must be of such a nature that they do not 'wander' from one layer to the next. In the Kodacolor process, which employs couplers in the emulsion rather than in the developer, this is achieved by first dissolving the coupler in an oily substance, which is then dispersed in very fine particles in the emulsion. In this way the couplers are prevented from wandering from one layer of the film to another. During the development the oxidation product of the developing agent dissolves in the oily substance and reacts with the coupler to form a dye within the protective liquid. In other colour films the same effect is achieved by 'attaching' large molecular groups to the coupling molecule. The nature of these 'anchors' is such that they immobilize the coupler without preventing the required dye formation.

In certain colour processes, couplers are used which are themselves 'coloured' and whose colour is destroyed when the coupler reacts with the oxidized developer to form a dye image. Such couplers are known as 'coloured couplers'. When development takes place two images are formed, the first consisting of the dye image formed by reaction with the oxidized developer and the second consisting of the residual coupler. Such couplers are used in the Kodacolor process as a means of correcting unwanted features in the absorption character-istics of the dye images. This use is discussed in Chapter 23.

Dye images

Ironically, one of the most important requirements of a colour photograph is that all the greys (from white through to black) should appear grey, or in other words have a zero colour saturation. While any set of three dyes that absorb roughly the blue, green and red regions can be adjusted to give greys for a given illuminant, they may not still look grey when the illumination is changed. To be unaffected by illumination changes, a grey must absorb or reflect equally all wavelenghts of the spectrum and is then known as a non-selective grey; the choice of dyes is therefore limited to those which will produce approximately non-selective greys, for these only do not change appreciably when the illuminant quality changes. These changes in greys are not as serious for photographs viewed by projection as for colour prints viewed in normally-lit surroundings. In an attempt to meet the requirements for a non-selective grey there is a temptation to choose dyes which have a low saturation at fairly high concentra-tions, but this limits the range of colours which can be produced by mixtures of the three dyes.

Each colour process is in fact something of a compromise and the slightly different colour rendering of different materials reflects this compromise on the part of the film manufacturer. Continued progress in the production of dyes in recent years has resulted in a very high standard of reproduction.

Kodak colour films

The range of Kodak colour films is a wide one and provides for the requirements of both the amateur and professional photographer in the fields of still and cine photography. Data of individual films likely to be of interest to the reader are given in Chapter 33 at the end of the book and only the more general characteristics will be dealt with in the present chapter.

Broadly speaking, Kodak colour films fall into two categories: that of Kodachrome, in which the couplers are in the developers, and that which includes Ektacolor, Kodacolor, Ektachrome and Eastmancolor films, in which the couplers are incorporated in the emulsion layers.

Kodachrome process

The film is composed of three emulsion layers on the same base, the lowest being red-sensitive, the second green-sensitive and the third blue-sensitive. The blue-sensitive layer is separated from the other two layers by a yellow filter layer. The film has a removable black backing which serves as an anti-halation layer. It is removed physically during processing. After exposure in the camera the film is developed in a black-and-white developer of normal type to give three superimposed silver images. The film is now exposed to red light so as to expose all the residual silver halide in the red-sensitive layer, and then developed in a cyan-forming developer. Then it is exposed to blue light which affects only the top blue-sensitive layer, since the yellow filter layer is still present. Development in a yellow coupler developer follows. Finally, the film is fogged and then developed in a magenta-forming developer. All the silver and the yellow filter layer are bleached out and fixed, leaving a positive colour image. An earlier and more complicated process involved the controlled bleaching of unwanted cyan and magenta images.

The complicated nature of the Kodachrome process makes it impracticable for user processing and the selling price of the film therefore includes the cost of processing in all countries except the U.S.A. The processing of Kodachrome film is undertaken by Kodak, and in the U.S.A. by independent laboratories as well.

The image produced by Kodachrome film is notable for its high definition, consistent colour rendering and relatively high colour saturation.

Ektachrome process

Films of this name are also designed for reversal processing, but as the couplers are coated in their respective emulsion layers only one stage of colour development is necessary. The arrangement of the emulsion layers is similar to that of Kodachrome film but with an anti-halation layer which is removed chemically during processing. The exposed film is first processed in a black-and-white developer to form a negative silver image. The residual silver halides in all three layers are then exposed to white light and then processed in a colour developer which produces both a silver and dye image in each layer. The silver images formed by both developers, and also the yellow filter layer and the anti-halation layer, are then bleached and fixed to leave a positive colour image. The film is intended for processing by the user and is therefore sold without processing rights. The processing of Ektachrome films is, however, also undertaken by a large number of independent laboratories throughout the world.

Ektacolor, Kodacolor and Eastmancolor films

Although basically similar to Ektachrome films in having the couplers in the emulsion layers, the couplers are of the coloured type, the colour of each being destroyed during the development in proportion to the amount of dye image formed. This results in the formation of a negative image in developed dye, at the same time leaving a positive image composed of the residual coloured coupler, and, of course, a negative silver image which is bleached and fixed along with the unused silver halide and the yellow filter and anti-halation layers. The positive images composed of residual couplers counteract the effects of overlapping absorptions of the negative image dyes and lead to greatly improved colour reproduction in prints. The presence of these residual coloured couplers gives the negative an orange colour cast. Note: Eastmancolor has a jet backing (like Kodachrome) which is removed mechanically, not chemically.

Kodacolor Film, first introduced in 1942, was intended for amateur use and made use of ordinary couplers. At a later stage (1943) an additional layer was incorporated to produce a positive silver-image mask which to some degree corrected brightness errors introduced by unwanted absorptions of the cyan and magenta dyes. In 1948 Kodacolor was again modified to correspond in character to Ektacolor film, which had been introduced the previous year as a sheet film for professional photographers.

Eastmancolor negative film is basically similar to Ektacolor but with characteristics adapted for motion picture photography. However, it is also suitable for the production of 35 mm. colour negatives intended for filmstrip production.

Colour-separation negatives

Black-and-white negatives made from original subjects, or from Kodachrome or Ektachrome transparencies, via suitable Wratten colour-separation filters can be used for photomechanical reproduction and also for preparing matrices for such processes as Carbro and Kodak Dye Transfer. In the latter process the negatives are printed on to matrix films, which are developed in a tanning developer and washed in hot water to give relief images. These are soaked in the appropriate dye solutions and transferred in register on to a premordanted paper. The process still offers a method of making colour prints of excellent quality at low cost and without elaborate equipment. See Chapter 32.

61

General characteristics of reversal films

The eye accommodates itself easily to changes in the colour quality of illumination when viewing an everyday scene but does not do so to a colour photograph. It is therefore necessary to adjust the colour sensitivity of films intended for exposure with certain artificial light-sources, so that the colour rendering approaches that obtained with a film balanced for daylight and exposed with unobscured sunlight. Man is primarily a creature of daylight and consequently accepts light of this quality as a kind of standard. As the processing procedure for a reversal film does not normally permit any kind of adjustment to the colour rendering of the transparency, it is necessary to make such adjustments either to the relative colour sensitivity of the emulsion, or by means of a filter to the light entering the lens. The relative sensitivity of a film is known as its colour balance, and a filter used to adjust the composition of the light, a correction or light-balancing filter. Both methods are commonly employed when exposing reversal films.

Taking noonday sunlight in a clear sky when the sun is well above the horizon as a standard for 'daylight,' we find the majority of reversal films balanced for 'daylight'. Such films are generally known as daylight-type reversal films, and may also be referred to as Type D, or, if of German origin, Type T (Tageslicht). Exposed with an artificial light-source such as a photoflood lamp, the colour rendering appears far too yellow and it is necessary to use a pale blue filter over the camera lens, which absorbs some of the red light, in order to obtain a satisfactory colour rendering. The yellowishness becomes even stronger if the film is exposed with ordinary tungsten light and still more filtration is needed. However, certain colour films are also available with a colour balance adjusted to one or more of the artificial light-sources commonly used by photographers. Kodachrome film, for example, is available with a colour balance suitable for exposure with photoflood lamps run at 3,400°K. It is described as Type A. At one time it was also available colour-balanced for clear flashbulbs (colour temperature around 3,800°K.) with the description Type F. On the other hand Ektachrome Sheet Film (primarily intended for professional photographers), and High Speed Ektachrome Film are available with colour balance for photopearl or colour-controlled studio lamps of 3,200°K. with the description Type B.

The question of colour balance is dealt with more fully in a later chapter since at the moment we are only concerned with the nature of reversal films. What has been said of colour balance applies also to the overall density of the image, namely, that the nature of reversal processing does not normally permit any adjustment for variations in exposure. This is tantamount to saying that there is not such thing as 'exposure latitude' with reversal films, although in practice some variation in overall density of the image is permissible, though to nothing like the same degree that is permissible with a negative-type film, where adjustments can be made in printing.

In order to obtain well-saturated colours certain reversal films have employed emulsions of fairly high contrast with the result that the separation between normal well-lit areas of the subject and those in the shadow tends to be too great. However, films of this nature give excellent results with moderate lighting contrast, and are superior to films of lower contrast under very low or zero lighting contrasts (flat lighting), since they give a higher colour saturation.

General characteristics of negative films

The problem of colour balance with negative colour films is simpler in some respects, as the printing stage allows considerable adjustment to colour rendering by means of filters placed in the printing light. For this reason negative films are usually restricted to one 'type', only adjusted in colour balance to an illuminant of 'mean' colour temperature such as clear flashbulbs. This is the case with Kodacolor film, which can be exposed without a filter in daylight or with flashbulbs. Nevertheless broad adjustments to colour balance at the time of exposure may be made by means of correction filters of the kind used with reversal films. This is, indeed, recommended in the use of both Kodacolor and Ektacolor films when used by the professional or an amateur who intends to make his own colour prints.

Owing to the lower contrast of negative films and the possibility of adjusting the amount of exposure given to the print, negative films offer a reasonable exposure latitude, equivalent to 3 or 4 stops and more with subjects of low contrast. However, reciprocity effects are more troublesome with colour materials in their effect on speed and contrast, and for this reason we find two 'types' of Ektacolor film. The first, known as Ektacolor Professional Film Type S, is designed for exposure times of 1/10 sec. or shorter and is colour-balanced for use with daylight and electronic flash, and the second, known as Ektacolor Professional Film, Type L, is designed for exposures of 1/10 to 60 sec. and is balanced for lamps of 3,200°K.

Printing and duplicating materials

Ektacolor and Kodacolor negatives are preferably printed on their companion material Ektacolor Paper, which is balanced specially for negatives embodying coloured-coupler masking. The arrangement of the emulsion layers differs from that of Ektacolor film, the blue-sensitive layer being coated first, then followed by a green-sensitive layer and with the red-sensitive layer on top. This arrangement gives a sharper image. The paper thus contains no yellow filter layer. This is made possible by the fact that the blue-sensitivity of the bottom layer is very much greater than the residual blue-sensitivity of the two upper layers. The emulsion surface has a fairly high gloss and is coated on a medium-weight paper base. The same type of emulsion is available on a clear base as Ektacolor Print Film for making positive transparencies from colour negatives.

Duplicating materials for production of duplicate transparencies may take the form of a reversal film giving direct transparencies and used in conjunction with filters to correct for deficiencies in colour balance, or an internegative colour film producing negatives from which either transparencies or prints can be made.

4

The Nature of Colour Photographs

WE CAN describe a colour photograph as the record, in dyes, of an image formed by a lens. Under certain viewing conditions this image can appear in all respects identical to a real scene, as, for example, when a colour slide is projected on to a white screen in a darkened room, when the impression can be that of viewing an actual scene through a window. Even when the photograph takes the form of a small print, we tend to view it as a likeness of mirror-like accuracy. Hence such phrases as 'the camera cannot lie', 'a photographic likeness', and 'photographic memory'. While we are all aware that man-made drawings and paintings are subject to inaccuracies, to deliberate distortions and refinements, in short, to what is known as 'artistic expression', we are inclined to regard a colour photograph as something impersonal, a mechanical reproduction that can be duplicated a million times if need be and hence an object of no unique and intrinsic value such as may be attached to a man-made painting. Indeed, its value lies almost entirely in the attributes least admired in a painting: a photograph is relatively cheap and easy to make, it bears the stamp of accuracy, and if lost or damaged can usually be replaced at small cost.

Modes of presentation

The popular conception of a photograph is that of the print where the image is viewed against a white paper base. The popular term for it is a colour snap. It is something that can be carried in the wallet, stuck in an album, or in larger sizes mounted and framed for display on the mantlepiece or china cabinet. The fact that modern colour processes, both of the additive and subtractive type, first took the form of reversal colour films from which the end product was a small transparency, did much to revive interest in the projection viewing of a photograph among enthusiastic amateur photographers. But such photographs had

---

Plate 1. Portrait in profile taken with late afternoon sun. This has given a rather warm colour rendering to the flesh tints. On the other hand the neutral tones of the statue strongly reflect the blue sky thus emphasizing the 'warmth' of the sunlight. The use of a long focus lens has made it possible to throw the statue slightly out of focus and to destroy all detail in the background. *Ektachrome transparency by Jack M. Oakley.*

Plates 2 and 3. Basilica Santa Trinità di Saccargia, near Sassari, Sardinia.

Plates 4 and 5. Village inn from the model village of Beconscot, Beaconsfield.

little more than novelty interest to the man in the street and did little to change his conception of a 'real' photograph as a paper print, even though it was only a black-and-white image. Also the variable nature of the colour rendering between one make of film and another, and often between films of the same make, detracted somewhat from the authenticity or realism of the colour photograph. The 'realism' of a black-and-white photograph was in fact preferred in many cases, and similar reactions were found in the cinema when the first colour movies were shown.

It was not until colour prints on paper became generally available, first as direct reversal prints from transparencies and later by a more conventional negative-positive process, that the colour photograph began seriously to challenge its monochrome equivalent as the normal mode of photography. And thanks largely to the gigantic army of box camera users, we are today in possession of simple and reliable colour processes for producing satisfactory colour prints. Indeed there are few people now remaining who would not prefer a colour print to one in black-and-white, and the continued large-scale use of black-and-white materials can be attributed largely to the greater cost of colour prints.

The colour print offers the great advantage that it can be viewed in the same way as any other object. It can be presented as a small print for the casual inspection of relatives and friends, whether at home, in the train or at the village pub. Properly mounted and framed, an enlarged print can become an ornament in the same way that any other picture can become an ornament. Indeed, though we do not think of them as such, most of the pictures we hang on our walls are photo-mechanical reproductions of paintings, not actual paintings. Frequent use is now made of gigantic prints in the form of murals, and a large part of advertising display material takes the form of colour prints or photo-mechanical reproductions of original colour photographs.

Projection

The viewing of photographs by projection is hardly less important. Motion picture photography could not have been developed without it. The use of prints for this purpose has indeed never progressed beyond the stage of 'What the butler saw' and other dramas still occasionally to be found on seaside piers for the entertainment of holidaymakers.

Plates 2 and 3. The two views of the basilica were taken an hour before sunset. The distant view was receiving direct sunlight and shows the yellow quality of the lighting. The second view, taken while the sun was obscured by a thin cloud, shows a more balanced lighting. Kodachrome II Film, exposures 1/125 and 1/60 sec. respectively, both at f/8.

Plates 4 and 5. The left hand version was exposed with direct sunlight and the strong lighting contrast has resulted in loss of colour and detail in the shadow areas. The second version with a small cloud obscuring the sun has given uniform detail and colour. Such lighting, namely with the sun obscured with small broken cloud, is often the most suitable for subjects in built-up areas. Kodachrome II Film, exposures 1/125 sec. f/8 and 1/60 sec. f/5·6 respectively.

Photos: E. S. Bomback.

67

The projected image, by virtue of being viewed in darkened surroundings offers a number of very real advantages compared with a print viewed in surroundings of normal illumination. The image appears more brilliant and the colours more saturated, since there is no standard of reference outside the picture area. As the screen image occupies a fairly wide angle of view and also represents the prevailing illumination, the eye more readily adapts itself to the quality of the projector illuminant, and as long as changes of colour balance from one slide to the next are small, considerable overall variation in colour rendering can be tolerated by the viewer during the course of viewing a number of slides. In the field of amateur photography there is the additional advantage that the screen image is more likely to be viewed at an angle equal to that of the taking lens, thereby obtaining correct viewing perspective, than is the case with small colour prints which would have to be viewed at 4 or 5 in. from the eyes to obtain the same effect. Psychologically there is the advantage of less distraction, since the screen picture becomes the principal object of interest, and there is little doubt that an identical series of subjects will be viewed with greater enjoyment on the screen than as prints enlarged sufficiently for normal viewing distance. A large screen picture permits a much larger audience to view and react to the same picture at one time, if we except for the moment the existence of very large-size prints of poster dimensions. Also a large screen picture, even when viewed at a distance which would subtend the same angle as when viewing a small print at a few inches, always *seems* larger for the simple reason that it is known to be a large picture.

These many advantages are much appreciated by the enthusiastic amateur photographer to whom the acquisition of a projector is no more costly than the acquisition of an enlarger, and the business of preparing for projection far less complicated than preparing the kitchen for a printing session. But for the man in the street, unequipped with a projector, a small transparency compares far less favourably with a postcard-size print, which he can at least view without the aid of a magnifier.

Large transparencies

A third mode of presentation is that of the large transparency, 10 × 8 in. or even larger in dimensions, which is illuminated from behind to give an image of great brilliance and sparkle. It is necessary that the illumination be uniform and of sufficient intensity to avoid degradation by the general lighting. Even with the use of fluorescent strip-lighting, the depth of the lighting unit tends to make it unsuitable for wall display in the way a framed print can be hung as a picture. It is, however, ideal for shop-window display, for exhibitions, museums and the like, where the depth of the unit is not important and the general illumination not excessive.

A rather similar method of presentation is that of back-projection, though this method involves still greater depth even with the use of a short-focus projection lens. The screen can be ground glass or an acetate material having a matt surface, such as Kodatrace. With an automatic projector successive pictures can be displayed at pre-set time intervals. Back-projection is commonly used in film and television studios as a means of obtaining a realistic outdoor background inside the studio.

Stereo-photographs

Presentations based on some form of stereo-photography are usually of novelty value, since they involve special viewing or projection equipment. True stereo-photography involves taking two photographs of the subjects, simultaneously if there is any movement in the subject, with two lenses which are separated laterally by a distance approximating to that of the human eyes. The two photographs, either in print form or as illuminated transparencies, are then viewed in a device which enables the left eye to observe the image taken with the left lens of the camera and the right eye to observe the image taken with the right lens of the camera. The effect is that of realistic spatial separation of the various planes of the subject. Similar effects can be obtained with the use of two projectors and polarizing filters – see page 250.

Stereo-photography can provide valuable records of surgery, archaeological excavations, topographic surveys and the like, where an accurate indication of depth is important.

How we look at photographs

An interesting and very detailed treatment of the nature of a colour photograph and the way we perceive form, light and colour in it has already been undertaken by Ralph Evans in his book *Eye, Film and Camera in Colour Photography*, and it is not proposed here to create more than an awareness on the part of the reader of the complexities involved in the apparently simple act of looking at a colour photograph.

Anyone who has undertaken black-and-white printing will be aware that the apparent density of the print image is strongly affected by the intensity level of illumination by which it is viewed. Thus print images which appear very satisfactory in the light of a bromide safelight turn out to be thin and lacking in contrast when viewed with much stronger tungsten lighting and even more so when viewed in direct sunlight. To some extent, therefore, the density of the print image must be adjusted to the level of illumination by which it will normally be viewed.

Adaptation of the eye to both the intensity and colour of the illuminant is governed largely by the angle of the photograph, and a very large print viewed so that it occupies nearly the whole field of view can provide adaptation conditions equal to, or even greater than, those of a projected transparency occupying a smaller angle. Adaptation usually extends also to the subject matter of the picture and we tend to see the colours we expect to see. This can be demonstrated by placing a pale blue filter over the lens of a projector while a slide is being viewed. Although the effect is immediately noticed, it rapidly wears off and the colours again assume their normal character. A similar effect takes place when viewing slides of average subject matter which are somewhat off colour balance.

A further factor is that of simultaneous contrast, whereby the tone and colours surrounding the picture influence both the tone and hue of the colours in the picture. This can be seen by viewing a print against white, grey and black borders, or by photographing an object against a number of differently coloured backgrounds. See plates 67, 68 and 69.

Another contrast effect, that known as successive contrast, occurs when two pictures are viewed in succession, and, for a few moments at least, the second picture is viewed with the eye already adapted for the first picture. This effect is important in the editing of a series of slides, and also when arranging colour prints in an exhibition. However, in the last case, if two pictures are viewed side by side, with the eye taking in both at the same time or at least darting rapidly back and forth, adaptation tends towards an intermediate colour balance. Thus we can get a condition where a picture of 'perfect' colour balance can be made to appear slightly off balance by being placed adjacent to one having a distinct colour bias. To a large extent this can be overcome by the use of a large white border, and under this condition it is possible to view the picture, given normal illumination and surroundings, in its true colours with a very high degree of 'impartiality'. It is this capacity for appraising colour rendering which makes first-quality prints considerably more exacting to produce than transparencies intended for projection viewing.

Turning to the question of object size and scale, we have to take into account the fact that a photograph, as an object localized in space, presents a number of problems to the viewer which must be solved, consciously or unconsciously, in making it conform to some established concept of reality. This is particularly applicable when viewing a small print.

It is normal to view a photograph squarely and to assume, unless there are clear indications otherwise, that the camera was used in a similar position in relation to the subject. Where, however, the camera has been tilted by a small amount the effect with a subject such as a building having parallel verticals is some degree of convergence. Such a photograph viewed on the assumption that the camera was held squarely makes the building appear to lean backwards. If the camera has been tilted by an amount large enough to be obvious to the viewer, he is able to interpret the photograph as an 'angle' shot.

Similarly with distance: judgement of object distance, as we have seen, rests partly on binocular vision and partly on a variety of what may be called depth clues. In viewing a photograph, which depicts the subject in two dimensions only, we have to rely entirely on depth clues and where some or all of these are absent we are left to draw deductions, sometimes completely wrong, of the distance and hence the true size of an object. In general, we assume that the size of an object, in the absence of any other clues, bears some relation to the amount of space it occupies in the picture area. Naturalists and others wishing to depict the size of an object usually include a ruler or some common object of fixed dimensions such as a coin or matchbox. However, even the latter item can be misleading since although the vast majority of matchboxes are of roughly the same dimensions, giant matchboxes are also obtainable and could be used by some practical joker to make an unknown object appear smaller than it actually is. Also we have the case where a familiar object, such as a vegetable marrow, has a 'normal' size which would tend to be applied to a photograph of a prize marrow of very much exaggerated dimensions if it were depicted against a perfectly plain background. However, with the same marrow supported in the embrace of its proud owner, we should at once perceive its true dimensions. Indeed, the fact that we tend to reconstruct the objects seen in a photograph as we think they should be, rather than what they are, makes possible a whole series of 'tricks' based on the use of models in place of very much larger objects. In films this is commonly applied to ships and aircraft to depict conditions such as storms and fires which would be otherwise impossible to photograph, and many a film depicting outdoors scenes has been made entirely inside a large studio by means of mirror and back-projection effects.

It is interesting to note in passing that portrait photographers have long since known that a higher than normal viewpoint of the lens helps to shorten a rather prominent chin while a low viewpoint helps to improve one that is receding.

Depth perception in a two-dimensional photograph depends somewhat on the extent to which the observer is aware he is looking at a photograph. This explains why the image of a projected transparency, being far less obviously a photograph, shows greater depth than the same picture viewed as a small print. One of the conditions of stereo-photography is that the photograph itself should disappear as an object, hence the fact that particles of dust on the surface of a transparency, a grainy image or zones of unsharpness can seriously impair the effect by making us aware of the existence of the photographic image.

Perhaps the most important factor in depth perception, apart from binocular vision, is geometric perspective. The photographic lens draws geometric perspective on a flat plane exactly on the lines of the classical perspective of the artist. The image of all parallel lines, except those perpendicular to the lens axis, will converge to some point inside or outside the picture frame. Lines parallel to the lens axis meet at a point where the axis cuts the film plane – the so-called vanishing point. All other systems of parallels will meet at a point where a line parallel to them from the lens would cut the film plane.

However, to obtain the same perspective as that given by a lens – and hence the correct perception of depth – it is necessary to view a photograph with the eye placed at a point which corresponds with the position of the lens when the picture was taken. Only in this position will the subject be seen point for point as the lens has drawn it. With contact prints this distance can be taken as the back focal length of the lens; but if the photograph has been enlarged, the distance then becomes the focal length times the magnification. However, as we have mentioned earlier in connection with depth of field, pictures are liable to be viewed at a variety of distances, and the size of the print or screen pictures is often not related to the focal length of the taking lens.

The size of the image of an object depends on its distance from the eye or camera lens and increases rapidly at closer distances. For example, in viewing two objects one at 5 ft. and one at 100 ft. and then moving forward by 2½ feet, the image of the nearer object is doubled while the more distance object remains almost unchanged. However, in viewing a photograph, any change in the viewing distance changes the size of all objects by the same amount. Thus in viewing a photograph at a distance less than that for correct perspective, the more distant objects are seen too large, while in viewing a photograph at a distance greater than that for correct perspective, nearby objects become too large.

The first error is far less frequent than the second and occurs when a photograph made with a long-focus lens is viewed at a distance more in keeping with a lens of standard focal length. News reel and television shots of race horses approaching the camera, but taken from a long distance with a telephoto lens, show the rear horses as if kicking the heels of the winning horses, yet as the course swings round to give a side view, it can be seen that there is often as much as 50 yards between them. This effect is known as diminished perspective. The opposite effect, exaggerated perspective, is one of the commoner faults of amateur photographers in attempting portraits at close distances.

Illumination

We come next to the part played by illumination as it appears in the original scene and in the photograph. To simplify what is, in fact, a very complex situation, let us start with a single light-source in an otherwise unlighted studio. The position of the light relative to the subject and camera determines the size and direction of shadows and these shadows form a valuable clue to the shape and depth of the subject. In addition, any reflections from the surface of the object will give a clue to the nature of the surface, whether it is glossy, smooth or rough. The same object lit with highly diffused illumination reaching the subject from all directions at the same intensity level will greatly reduce these clues, giving the impression of a flat object having no characteristic texture or surface. See colour plates 13 and 14.

The angle at which a directional light-source strikes the subject can enhance or falsify the character of the surface. Direct, frontal lighting may show nothing of the texture but enhance the colour and pattern on the surface: strongly oblique lighting will exaggerate surface texture, possibly to an extent that makes it unrecognizable and also conceals colour and pattern. See colour plates 15 and 16.

Objects having transparent properties rely very much on the existence of surface reflection. A sheet of clear glass deprived of reflections ceases to exist visually, though the existence of a window frame may tell us that it is there. In the absence of any indication of glass by way of a frame, it is not impossible to attempt to walk through a door consisting entirely of a heavy sheet of plate glass.

With regard to the colour of a glossy surface, its apparent colour saturation will be greatly diminished in highly diffused illumination, since in this case some percentage of white light will be reflected unchanged at whatever angle the surface is viewed. The mixture of white light and the characteristic colour of the surface is then likely to be taken as the true colour of the object. Photographed with strongly directional light at an angle which eliminates surface reflections, the colour will at once appear more saturated. See colour plate 14.

The true colour of a surface is often modified by coloured light reflected from adjacent surfaces. In cases where the source of such reflected light is not apparent in the photograph, the modified colour of the subject may be taken to be its true colour. Areas of the subject in shadow are more likely to be affected by reflected light and it may be noted that artists perceive this effect far more readily than an untrained observer. Some interesting applications of the colour mixtures possible from the inter-reflections of coloured metallic foils are discussed in Chapter 16. See colour plate 32.

The intensity level of illumination depicted in a photograph is inferred rather than seen, and to some extent this applies also when viewing an actual scene. For example, daylight illumination may range from as high as 10,000 foot-candles with strong mid-day sunlight to as low as 100 foot-candles on a grey overcast day. Still further down the scale, accepted levels of artificial lighting can be as low as 1 foot-candle. Since a decrease in illumination is accompanied by a decrease in our ability to perceive brightness differences, the intensity level of illumination has an important bearing on both our perception of an actual scene and its presentation as a photograph. For example, at high intensity levels a brightness ratio of more than 1000:1 is perceived, while under conditions of dark adaptation we can distinguish no more than a 2:1 brightness ratio. In fact colour vision no longer functions at a level below $\frac{1}{2}$ foot-candle and objects take on a dark blue appearance.

With a camera, the brightness ratio of a subject remains constant and is entirely independent of the level of illumination. Thus given adequate exposure a moonlit scene will not only show a normal brightness range, but the same colour rendering as a photograph made with sunlight. See colour plate 76. This may be understood better if one accepts the fact that moonlight is, in fact, reflected sunlight. To obtain the effect of a moonlit scene it is far easier to expose a daylight scene through a blue filter! In other words, a photograph must present a perceived rather than an actual range of brightness and colour, and must also take into account the nature and intensity of the illumination by which it will normally be viewed. This usually entails adjusting the image for daylight, though if prints are to be viewed with some kind of artificial lighting the photographer should duplicate this illumination when judging the quality of a print.

One of the problems confronting the photographer is the limitation in brightness range imposed by the photographic medium itself. Brightness ratios

73

of 1000:1 may be experienced and ratios of the order of 250:1 are fairly common. Except in the case of a transparency viewed over a bright illuminator, considerably lower brightness ratios apply to a photograph. In an attempt, therefore, to depict a scene of high brightness ratio, such as when shooting into the light, the photographer is faced with some kind of compromise: the photograph can either record the highlights and sacrifice the shadows, or record shadow detail and accept 'burnt out' highlights. One of the major considerations in lighting a subject for colour photography is that of working within the limited brightness range of the material. The practical aspects of this form the basis of Chapter 8, but it is interesting to note at least one commonly met example of the misleading effect given by a photograph. We may take the case of a landscape seen at sunrise or sunset accompanied with brilliantly lit colour cloud effects. The eye perceives both the lower brightness of the landscape and foreground, and the much more brilliant colour of the sky, but a photograph exposed to obtain the best rendering of the sky – the feature of the scene which in fact prompts the taking of the photograph – will depict the foreground more in keeping with its appearance at night.

The problem of portraying the nature of the illumination of an object is undoubtedly one of the most interesting to the photographer who has graduated from the snapshot stage. To a large extent it has to do with the reproduction of brightnesses 'brighter' than white. A typical example is that of a yacht with white sails and the sparkle of reflected sunlight from the water. To be acceptable in a photograph the white sails must appear as white as the white border surrounding the print, but as this is also the maximum whiteness obtainable with a print, the sparkle of the water can be no 'whiter'. This problem resolves itself in the case of a projected transparency, since there is no reference standard of white and the observer is free to decide what part of the object is white and what part is of a higher intensity. It is this characteristic of a projected transparency that gives it its peculiar charm compared with a print viewed in surroundings of normal illumination. However, the effect is not inherent in the transparency but rather the way in which it is viewed. A print so exposed as to render the whites in tones slightly darker than areas of higher illumination can give the same effect as a transparency if viewed with a spotlight in dark surroundings since there is then no outside reference to what we consider to be 'white'.

One other illumination effect is worth noting here, namely, that of non-uniform illumination such as is commonly encountered in interiors. For example, we tend to see the walls of the average living room lit with windows on one side only as being of roughly uniform tone and colour. Measurements with a light meter may well show reflected-light differences as great as 16:1. This brightness-constancy effect can have disastrous consequences for the unwary photographer, since the recorded image is governed by the actual brightness differences – not those perceived. The ability of the eye to adapt to the image of a print is far less than in the original scene, though it increases when viewing a projected transparency.

Colour balance

We can conclude this chapter with some further mention of colour balance as it affects the viewing of a photograph. It has long since been pointed out by Evans and others that even if a perfect colour process could be produced giving colour rendering identical to that of the original scene, it would not necessarily produce the most acceptable colour photographs. One has to take into account that a photograph is normally a small area viewed out of context, and not only lacks the contrast effects of its normal surroundings but is subject to contrast effects from different surroundings, whether those of a normally lit sitting room or the more 'favourable' surroundings of darkness when the photograph is viewed by projection. We have to take into account both the level and spectral quality of the illumination by which the photograph is viewed and its effect on the eye. These and many other factors make the achievement of good colour balance something in the nature of a trial-and-error task both on the part of the film manufacturer and the photographer using his material. Over and above this we have to allow for such factors as 'artistic' expression, and personal taste. Anyone who is a member of a photographic society which specializes in colour will know how diverse opinion and taste in colour balance can be. On perhaps an even more elevated plane, anyone interested in the technique of painting will appreciate even more fully the extent to which pictorial representation can depart from reality.

5

Cameras and Lenses

A MANUAL of colour photography would not be complete if it did not include some discussion of equipment used in making colour photographs. Clearly the most important item is the camera, for many photographers the only piece of equipment needed to produce colour photographs. However, it would be misleading to pretend that the exposure of modern colour films requires a camera which is basically different from, or superior to, one suitable for black-and-white photography. Indeed if we begin with the understanding that a modern colour film is basically the same as a panchromatic film in its behaviour inside the camera, it becomes fairly obvious that the same piece of apparatus can be used with either material with equally good – or equally bad – results. This applies to most applications of a camera, pictorial and technical, though as we shall show later the needs of colour film, particularly reversal colour film, call for camera features which may often be dispensed with in monochrome photography.

Basic camera

The basic essentials of a camera are the lens, the shutter, the viewfinder or focusing screen, a dark-slide or film holder for sheet film or a film transport mechanism for roll or 35 mm. film. These components are incorporated within the camera body, which acts as a light barrier to protect the light-sensitive film.

Few instruments vary so much in their shape, size and design as the camera. However, it is possible to classify cameras into two broad groups: those designed for professional and technical use which are for the most part functional, and those designed for amateur use in which functional value is to a greater or lesser degree sacrificed for consideration of cost, simplicity of operation, portability and appearance. Needless to say there is considerable overlapping in the two groups, and many small cameras originally designed for the amateur have developed into elaborate and costly camera 'systems' which are used as much by the professional as the amateur. The choice of a camera, irrespective of the status of the photographer, should of course depend on the use to which it is to be put. For example, anyone interested principally in architectural subjects would be correctly advised to choose a camera with a rising and falling lens panel and possibly other camera movements: he would be ill-advised to purchase a camera, even one with an elaborate interchangeable lens system, if it lacked these features. On the other hand the portrait photographer will be chiefly interested in the use of longer than normal focal lengths, and perhaps the occasional use of wide-angle lenses (when photographing groups). In this case, an interchangeable lens system is probably the most important feature, and considerations of size and format a matter of convenience or personal taste. The studio worker, tackling display sets and a variety of technical subjects, will need the maximum amount of camera movements and a camera of the monorail type – see fig. 5.1. In this,

Fig. 5.1. Monorail camera.

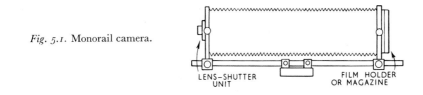

both lens and film plane are freely adjustable and the 'body' is nothing more than a flexible bellows. The press photographer requires ease of operation, usually a fast lens and fast shutter speeds, and for many subjects, such as sports events, long-focus lenses. Here again, size may be a matter of convenience or preference, though there has been a steady swing towards miniature cameras of $2\frac{1}{4} \times 2\frac{1}{4}$ in. and 24 × 36 mm. formats. The naturalist in search of wild-life subjects usually requires extra-long-focus lenses, but if his interest lies in small creatures, such as insects, the ability quickly and accurately to frame and focus at very close distances would be a major requirement. For photomicrography nothing more than a camera body with focusing screen and film carrier is needed, since the microscope itself provides the image. When we come to what might be called 'general purpose' photography the choice of camera becomes even more a matter of convenience and personal taste, and we can include here the vast army of amateur photographers who are chiefly interested in the souvenir kind of photograph. It is in this field that miniature reflex and automatic cameras are becoming increasingly popular. Finally we come to the man in the street – the camera owner with no special interest in photography as a hobby in itself – who makes occasional use of his camera for family snaps and picturesque views taken on holiday. For the most part the simple box camera – or its most un-boxlike modern equivalent – fits the bill.

Technical and view cameras

It is fitting to start a discussion of cameras with the stand or view camera, not only because it still represents traditional design extending back more than a century, but because it embodies features, usually lacking in smaller cameras, which can play an important part in the formation of an acceptable photographic image. An excellent example of such a camera is the Kodak Specialist 3 camera intended to accept either half-plate (4¾ × 6½ in.) or 5 × 4 in. film holders with an interchangeable adaptor back. It is equally suited to both monochrome and colour work. The camera, shown in fig. 5.2. is of the monorail type, the front and rear portions being independently movable on the monorail. The monorail is held by a separate adjustable bracket which provides the means

Fig. 5.2. Kodak Specialist 3 camera for ½-plate or 5 × 4 in. films or plates. It offers a full range of camera movements.

for supporting the whole camera on a tripod. The normal extension between lens and focal plane is from 4 to 14 in., and this can be extended a further 10 in. with an extension frame. Thus with a 'standard' lens of 8 in. (203 mm.) focal length, a magnification of up to ×2 can be obtained, and still greater magnifications by using lenses of short focal length or with low power supplementaries. The lens normally recommended for general purposes is the 203 mm. Kodak 'Ektar' lens f/7·7 which is mounted in two 'halves' on either side of a Prontor SVS shutter with a speed range of 1 sec. to 1/300 sec. and brief time (B). The shutter is kept open for viewing and focusing by use of a self-locking cable release and the shutter set to 'B'. This lens gives excellent coverage and high definition. The lens panel is easily removed, and with the spare lens panels available any suitable lens can be mounted for use with the camera.

Lens and camera movements include a rising and falling front, tilting front and back, cross front and cross back, and swing front and swing back, all of which movements can be locked. In addition to the standard sheet film and plate holders, it is possible to adapt the camera for use with 120-size roll film. For this format, giving a 6 × 9 cm. picture, the 203 mm. lens then makes an excellent long-focus lens for portraits or small studio sets. A reversible back enables the format to be changed from vertical to horizontal as required by the nature of the subject.

Technical cameras of similar monorail design include formats from 12 × 10 in. to one intended for 35 mm. film. Other types of collapsible 'base-board' design and 9 × 12 cm. and smaller formats include Linhof cameras and the excellent M.P.P. Micro-Technical camera of British make, see fig. 5.3.

Fig. 5.3. M.P.P. Mk VIII Micro-Technical camera.

There are, of course, many excellent pre-war studio cameras in existence, and some, such as the Gandolfi cameras, are superb examples of the art of the cabinet maker. While the original lenses and shutters of these cameras may no longer be suitable for colour photography, a modern lens of the between-lens shutter type may be all that is required to bring the cameras up-to-date, though perhaps they may not have quite such a wide range of movements as are now offered.

Fig. 5.4. Retina Reflex III camera, a precision 35 mm. camera which is ideal for the professional wishing to use 35 mm. colour film.

Miniature cameras

The term 'miniature' is perhaps most commonly applied to cameras based on 35 mm. width perforated film similar in dimensions to that used for 'standard' cine-photography, but it is convenient to apply it to hand cameras generally taking pictures of areas less than 6 square inches. It therefore excludes $3\frac{1}{4} \times 2\frac{1}{4}$ in. rollfilm cameras – few of which are now being made, but includes all cameras taking pictures of $2\frac{1}{4} \times 2\frac{1}{4}$ in. and smaller. The table below gives the various formats of cameras based on 120 (and 620), 127 and 828 rollfilms, 126 cartridges and 35 mm. film cassettes.

Picture Size		Number of Exposures	Film Size
cm.	inches		
$1\cdot8 \times 2\cdot4$	$\frac{3}{4} \times 1$	72	36 exp. 35 mm. Cassette
$2\cdot4 \times 2\cdot4$	1×1	50	36 exp. 35 mm. Cassette
$2\cdot4 \times 3\cdot6$	$1 \times 1\frac{1}{2}$	36	36 exp. 35 mm. Cassette
$2\cdot8 \times 2\cdot8$	$1\frac{1}{8} \times 1\frac{1}{8}$	20	126 Cartridge
$2\cdot8 \times 4\cdot0$	$1\frac{1}{8} \times 1\frac{5}{8}$	8	828 Rollfilm
$2\cdot8 \times 4\cdot0$	$1\frac{1}{8} \times 1\frac{5}{8}$	16	127 Rollfilm
$4\cdot0 \times 4\cdot0$	$1\frac{5}{8} \times 1\frac{5}{8}$	12	127 Rollfilm
$4\cdot0 \times 6\cdot5$	$1\frac{5}{8} \times 2\frac{1}{2}$	8	127 Rollfilm
$3\cdot5 \times 6\cdot0$	$1\frac{1}{2} \times 2\frac{1}{4}$	16	120 or 620 Rollfilm
$6\cdot0 \times 6\cdot0$	$2\frac{1}{4} \times 2\frac{1}{4}$	12	120 or 620 Rollfilm
$6\cdot0 \times 9\cdot0$	$2\frac{1}{4} \times 3\frac{1}{4}$	8	120 or 620 Rollfilm

It will be seen that on the basis of size there is considerable diversity, but there is even greater diversity in design. Any attempt to classify miniature cameras can therefore only profitably take the broadest lines. We can, for example, divide miniature cameras into two kinds from the point of view of film packing and film transport, namely rollfilm and 35 mm. film. We can also divide cameras into those of fixed lens design and those having interchangeable lenses. Another logical division is that of reflex and non-reflex cameras. In addition there are a number of established 'camera systems' involving a basic model for which there is a range of lenses, adaptors and various accessories to cover almost every conceiveable application of a camera in both pictorial and technical photography. Typical of such systems are the Contarex, Exakta, Leica and Retina cameras – all based on 35 mm. film. Finally we have cameras primarily intended for the non-technical user – automatic and semi-automatic cameras, 'simplified cameras' using symbols rather than numerical values for the exposure controls and focusing scale, and last, but by no means to be discounted, box-cameras (cameras having a simple, fixed-focus lens and one-speed shutter).

Interchangeable-lens cameras

One of the disadvantages of small format cameras is the need to make the fullest use of the picture area, especially when making direct reversal transparencies. With a camera having a fixed lens it is only possible to adjust the image size to fit the picture frame by moving nearer to or farther from the subject. Not only is this frequently impracticable, either due to obstacles or lack of space, but even when it is possible it may often be undesirable. Some mention has already been made of distortion arising from too short a lens-to-subject distance and in later chapters we shall have much to say about the application of lenses. One of the principal objects of an interchangeable lens system is to allow the image size to be adjusted independently of the subject distance. Perhaps the ideal system, and one which is already making its appearance in still photography, is the use of a variable-focus lens of the type commonly used in motion picture photography

Fig. 5.5. Kodak Instamatic 500, a camera employing simplified cartridge loading.

and known as a 'zoom' lens. Its function in the latter case is often that of making a subject appear to approach or recede from the camera, rather than to give a specific angle of view: a uniformly high degree of correction is therefore not needed at intermediate foci. Used for still photography, however, such a lens must give equally good definition at all focal lengths. At present such lenses designed for still photography are both expensive and bulky and there is much to be said for choosing two or three first-class lenses of fixed focal length. Variable-focus lenses are especially valuable for making small transparencies.

An alternative, though limited, system of obtaining different focal lengths with a camera having a fixed lens-shutter unit is the modern 'convertible' lens, whereby the focal length is changed by substituting the normal front component of the lens with one giving a wider or narrower angle. Such lenses offer the advantage of retaining a between-lens shutter but the interchangeable components are usually equally as costly as a complete lens. A similar, though much inferior system is that of lens 'converters' which are commonly available as a means of increasing the effective focal length by 70 or 80 per cent. With cameras having a full bellows movement of the lens, it is also possible to use single positive or negative lenses to shorten or lengthen the effective focal length. However, positive supplementaries are more commonly used to extend the near focusing distance with hand cameras having only a limited amount of focusing adjustment.

Modern interchangeable lenses are usually 'matched' to give the same colour rendering when making transparencies, see page 177.

Shutters

Although we have already mentioned shutters in a general way it is worth considering in some detail certain differences in efficiency and convenience between diaphragm and focal-plane shutters. The former is almost universally employed with cameras of fixed-lens design, and in this case takes the form of a between-lens shutter such as the Compur or Prontor shutter. In a few cases, notably the Retina Reflex III camera, it is placed immediately behind the lens, where it is, perhaps, a little less efficient, but offers an advantage over the focal plane shutter in the use of electronic flash. However, the essential difference in performance between the two types of shutter is that the diaphragm shutter exposes the whole film area simultaneously at all shutter speeds, whereas the

---

Plate 6. Chemical plant. A polarizing filter was used to darken the sky and obtain maximum colour saturation of the orange cap on the nitrogen tank and surrounding equipment. The negative was made with Ektacolor Film, Type S, using a 4 × 5 in. view camera. The verticals were kept parallel in the negative by use of the rising front and swing back. The Ektacolor print from which the present reproduction was made involved no special printing difficulties. It was made by W. G. Gaskins, during a three-month scholarship course in the U.S.A. provided by Kodak Ltd. to selected photographers.

Plate 7. Amalfi, Italy. A strong haze gives a useful indication of distance and for this reason is often referred to as atmospheric perspective. The excessive blueness that sometimes accompanies it can be reduced with a Wratten 1A filter.

Plate 8. Bruges, Belgium. The strong feeling of depth in this picture is due to geometric perspective – the converging of parallel lines towards a vanishing point. The exposure was made with hazy sunlight on Kodachrome Film.

Plate 9. The feeling of depth arises as much as anything from the viewer's knowledge that a boat is characteristically much longer than it is wide. The impression of length has been exaggerated by choosing a close viewpoint.

Photos: E. S. Bomback.

focal plane shutter only does this for the slower speeds. At faster speeds it takes the form of a slit which moves across the film, exposing at one instant only a strip of film and which takes anything from 1/20 to 1/30 second to expose the whole frame. At these speeds it is therefore impossible to make exposures with an electronic flash unit, as its light only lasts for 1/500 second or less. Herein lies the principal advantage of the diaphragm shutter. On the other hand, a diaphragm shutter loses efficiency at faster speeds, and as fast shutter speeds and large apertures are normally used together, the inefficiency is allowed for in the

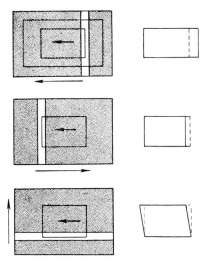

Fig. 5.6. Diagrams to show distortion of a moving image with a focal-plane shutter. The first shows elongation when the image movement is in the same direction of travel as the slit; the second when the slit travels in the opposite direction producing a shortening of the subject; the third when the slit travels upwards at right angle to the direction of movement. This distortion is eliminated with camera swing or panning.

shutter calibrations. But with a very fast film such as High Speed Ektachrome, used in bright light, the fast shutter speed is used at a small aperture that increases the overall efficiency. In this case a $\frac{1}{2}$-stop less exposure than that theoretically calculated is recommended in the film instructions.

When fast shutter speeds are employed to obtain sharp images of fast moving objects, the time taken for the narrow slit of a focal-plane shutter to travel across the film may be sufficient to introduce noticeable distortion of the kind shown in fig. 5.6. The shortest speed of most diaphragm shutters is only 1/300 or 1/500 second compared with 1/1000 second with a focal-plane shutter.

Reflex cameras

We have already mentioned the large mirror-reflex, but with small cameras the reflex principle has been applied in two different ways. Firstly there is the true mirror-reflex which shows the actual image formed by the taking lens, and secondly there is the twin-lens reflex having a separate viewing lens usually situated immediately above the taking lens and having the same focal length – see fig. 5.7. This latter system suffers from the disadvantage of parallax, and even when some form of automatic compensation for parallax is introduced over the focusing range of the camera, the actual viewpoint of the viewing lens is still a different one. At very close distances special lenses must be fitted over the viewing

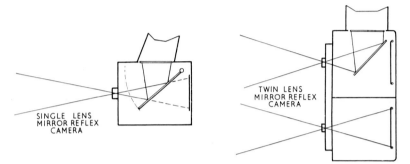

Fig. 5.7. Arrangement of a single-lens mirror reflex camera and a twin-lens mirror reflex camera. The former is entirely free from parallax.

lens, as for example the Rolleipars intended for use with the Rolleinar lenses. Also the image, in common with the normal mirror reflex, suffers from lateral inversion, making it a little difficult to follow subjects which are moving across the field of view. Twin-lens reflex cameras are most commonly made in $2\frac{1}{4} \times 2\frac{1}{4}$ in. format, though the principle has also been applied to 35 mm. cameras.

The single-lens reflex viewer was first applied in 35 mm. format in the Exakta cameras, a simple magnifier being used to give sufficient detail to the image for focusing. The first step towards the modern eye-level reflex made its appearance from East Germany as the Contax-S, later renamed the Pentacon. By means of a penta-prism the image was directed to the back of the camera so that it could be viewed through an eye-lens. As the result of four mirror reflectors (three within the prism) – see fig. 5.8 – the image is presented as it would appear to the naked eye. The popularity of the eye-level reflex was established by two between-lens shutter models, the Contaflex and the Retina Reflex cameras. Today there are a score or so models and in one form or the other it is probably the most popular type of camera among professionals and keen amateur photographers. Not only does it offer complete freedom from parallax at all distances, but it can also be focused visually with any lens or combination of lenses, and at the same time it gives a proper impression in scale of the subject as it will be seen projected or presented as an enlarged colour print.

However, the eye-level reflex camera is not without its disadvantages, though of a minor nature. Firstly, many such cameras permit the subject to be viewed only at maximum lens aperture. This makes for a brilliant image but also shows the minimum depth of field, a fact which may lead the unwary photographer to overlook unwanted detail in the background, which will, of course, be rendered very much more sharply at normal working apertures of f/5·6 or f/8. Secondly, the glass prism appreciably increases the size and weight of the camera, thereby sacrificing something of the portability of a miniature camera.

Automatic cameras

The term 'automatic' usually applies to a camera embodying a photo-cell device which adjusts the lens aperture and sometimes the shutter speed according to the amount of light falling on the photo-cell window. In some cases the act of winding the film on or pressing the exposure button provides the major motive power for adjusting the aperture, in others, the adjustment is made by turning a knurled wheel until a pointer in the viewfinder window (or elsewhere) lies between two datum points. In some models a warning device appears in the viewfinder when there is insufficient light for photography. Such cameras are designed chiefly for the non-technical photographer, but may be useful to the press-photographer or photo-journalist operating under variable lighting conditions on occasions when the rapid recording of events may be more important than the pictorial quality.

One of the weaknesses of exposures based on reflected light is that the total light received by the photo-cell may not be representative of the object or area being photographed. This is discussed fully in Chapter 9, but with automatic cameras the situation may be aggravated by the fact that the 'answer' given by

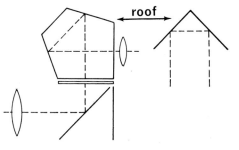

Fig. 5.8. Single-lens reflex with pentaprism and eye-lens. The roof embodies two surfaces at right-angles which rectify the lateral reversal of the mirror. Altogether the image is reflected four times.

the photo-cell may include too much sky or too much foreground. The former being a strong light source tends to cause under-exposed results, and the latter when in the shadow, rather too much exposure. However, in general, automatic cameras do produce remarkably consistent exposures.

Camera systems

Typical of the versatility of miniature cameras is the system which has been built up from the original Retina camera introduced in 1934. This original Retina, the first folding camera based on 35 mm. film, was notable for its compactness and modest price, and ran into several increasingly ambitious models before the outbreak of war. However, it was not until production was re-started in 1946 that the present Retina camera system began to evolve. Based originally on cameras having a fixed lens-shutter unit, many of the early accessories were designed to overcome the restriction of such a camera for close-ups, copying and photo-micrography: in 1954 the first convertible lens system was introduced giving a wide-angle interchangeable front component of 35 mm. focal length and a narrow angle lens of 80 mm. With it were introduced special viewfinders and focusing aids as well as a prism stereo-attachment. From this followed the first Retina Reflex camera, and still later an interchangeable lens system based on a 'behind-lens' diaphragm shutter – fig. 5.9. At the present time a range of focal lengths of from 28 to 200 mm. is available. More recently there have appeared automatic models, and it is safe to assume that the system will continue to expand.

Fig. 5.9. Retina Reflex III with interchangeable lenses of 28, 35, 50, 85, 135 and 200 mm. The camera is shown fitted with a 50 mm. lens.

Picture size and format

It may be felt by some readers that the true distinction between the professional and amateur photographer rests in the size of picture taken by the camera, and that the larger the picture the more 'professional' is the photographer. While it is true that many professional colour photographers do much of their transparency work in 8 × 10 in. and occasionally even larger sizes, and use a 4 × 5 in. camera for much of their colour negative work, few would hesitate to use a smaller format if it served their purpose better. A more valid distinction between the two kinds of photographer is that the professional usually has to satisfy a client, whereas the amateur need satisfy no one but himself.

The logical choice of camera size is one related to the kind of work to be done. The professional photographer wishing to sell colour transparencies is likely to do much better if, in addition to having the right kind of subject matter and skill in lighting and presenting it, he can present his transparencies in a size large enough to be viewed comfortably, without magnification, over an illuminator. Ideally this means a transparency of at least 8 × 10 in. in size, though sizes as small as 4 × 5 in. may still be appreciated without special viewing devices. An alternative to using a large camera is to make enlarged transparencies either directly from small colour negatives or via an inter-negative from smaller transparencies. Carefully done there need be no appreciable shift in colour balance, though depending on the degree of enlargement some loss of sharpness must be expected. This would be negligible in enlarging a 4 × 5 in. negative to 12 × 15 in. but would involve more than 12 times magnification from a 35 mm. transparency.

However, recent trends in the production of high definition colour films, which are only available to the small camera user (for example Kodachrome II film), help in some measure to strike a balance between, say, a 35 mm. camera and one of 4 × 5 in. format. But there is still the disadvantage that scratches, finger marks and dust are far more disastrous in a small negative or transparency than in a large one. Indeed, one of the perils of submitting small negatives to an editor or publisher for approval, disregarding any prejudice that may exist over their size, is that they can easily be damaged by careless handling. The hazard is even greater in loaning small transparencies for block-making, where the need for trimming and the handling necessary for making separation negatives, and frequent inspection during etching and proofing, make it very difficult even for careful operators to avoid some degree of damage. The same amount of damage to a 8 × 10 in. transparency would hardly be noticed.

The 35 mm. camera undoubtedly comes into its own when the photographs are intended for projection viewing. Larger sizes involve larger projectors but offer nothing by way of superior definition under normal viewing conditions.

Finally, from the amateur's point of view, the factors of cost and convenience are likely to be all important. The occasional prospect of selling a photograph is hardly sufficient reason for lugging about a large technical camera with bulky dark-slides, and with a 500 per cent increase in cost per exposure.

6

Light-sources

LIGHT by which we see or by which we take photographs may be described by the general term 'illumination'. In character and intensity it can range from sunlight to candlelight, the latter still being a major source of artificial illumination in some 'under-developed' countries. However, although we may perceive differences – even small ones – in changing from one kind of illumination to another, the sensation is usually short-lived, and the eye adapts itself to the new illumination while the mind turns its attention to the act of seeing or observing the objects which reflect the illumination. Because of this, we tend to overlook differences which are important to photography, and may attribute variations in colour balance, due to differences in the quality of illumination, to other causes, such as the film or the way it has been processed.

The characteristics of illumination which have to be taken into account by the photographer are; its spectral composition; its intensity and, in the case of artificial light-sources, distance from the subject; its direction relative to the subject and camera position; whether beamed or diffused, and if beamed, whether the rays of light are parallel or focused; its duration in the case of flashlight; and if more than one light-source is present, whether they are of the same or different spectral quality. These characteristics must be allowed for, or in some way controlled, if the photographer seeks to obtain a certain standard of colour balance or some specific lighting effect. The fact that many amateurs obtain very pleasing results every once in a while – and without quite knowing why – by shooting haphazardly under all conditions of lighting is of little use to the professional who must guarantee acceptable results on every assignment. Doubtless, part of the fun of colour photography is the unexpected success which often finishes up as a prize-winning picture, and gains the photographer far more credit for skill than he really deserves.

Major light-sources

We can divide illumination into two main categories: daylight illumination having its source directly or indirectly from the sun, and artificial illumination. The term 'daylight' includes clear sunlight with varying amounts of light from the sky; varying degrees of veiled sunlight due to haze, mist or cloud; totally diffused light from an overcast sky or a restricted area of blue sky (i.e. subject in the shade); early morning and late evening sunlight which is yellower than normal sunlight; and, lastly, daylight which finds its way through windows and doorways, and is more generally known as interior daylight. Artificial light-sources may be divided into two classes: those of a continuous nature and those of brief duration known broadly by the term 'flash'. Continuous-burning sources include incandescent lamps (e.g. tungsten filament lamps), arc lamps, fluorescent and discharge lamps (e.g. strip-lighting) and light sources such as oil and gas lamps, and candles which are of very limited interest to the colour photographer. Flash illumination may be that obtained from bulbs containing combustible material and, far less frequently now, from magnesium ribbon or powder, or the distinctly different illumination obtained from electronic flash units. All these kinds of illumination may be used at some time or another by the colour photographer and it is therefore useful to know something of their characteristics. However, before dealing with specific light-sources, we must first deal with the general characteristics of illumination.

Spectral composition and colour temperature

By measuring the energy in the spectrum of a light-source at various points and plotting these values against wave-length we can obtain a curve showing the distribution of energy or spectral composition of the light-source. Taking noon-day sunlight during the summer as an 'ideal' form of white or colourless light, we can compare the spectral curve of this with that of northern skylight and with that of an ordinary tungsten lamp intended for household illumination – Fig. 1.4 – page 21. The curves are plotted so that the relative energy in the brightest region of the spectrum is roughly the same: the curves thus show the relative energy distribution for roughly the same amount of visual sensation. The curve for northern skylight in the northern hemisphere shows a preponderance of blue radiation, which is due to the fact that dust and water particles in the atmosphere scatter the shorter wavelengths to a greater degree than the longer wavelengths. A tungsten lamp, on the other hand, shows a preponderance of red with a relatively low emission of the shorter wavelengths. Exposures made with a film balanced for sunlight thus show a somewhat bluish colour rendering when exposed by light from a blue sky, and a distinctly yellowish rendering when exposed by tungsten lamps unless appropriate light-balancing filters are used.

However, such curves are of limited interest to the photographer and it is customary to express the colour quality of illumination in terms of its colour temperature. Strictly speaking, colour temperature applies only to the spectral emission of a black body heated in a furnace, but it can be applied to tungsten filament lamps, and with varying degrees of accuracy to other light-sources having a continuous spectrum.

Colour temperature is usually expressed in degrees Kelvin (°K.), sometimes known as the 'absolute' scale of temperature, in which 0°K. equals minus 273°

Centigrade ($-273°$C.). Visible light, a dull red in colour, is emitted at a temperature of about 750°K., becoming a cherry red at 1,000°K. and yellow at 1,500°K. Enclosed in a glass envelope filled with an inert gas, a tungsten filament can be heated to a temperature of 3,400°K., though at such a temperature the lamp has a comparatively short life. Ordinary household lamps run at roughly 2,800°K., and have an average 'life' of 1,000 hours. Lamps designed for commercial and professional colour photography are designed to run at 3,200°K. – a compromise which gives a mean life of 100 hours. However, not only does the light become 'whiter' at higher colour temperatures, but the total light emitted by the filament also increases by a large amount, and it was for this reason that Photoflood lamps were first introduced for amateur photography indoors. For example, a No. 1 Photoflood consuming 275 watts has about half the light output of a 1,500-watt studio lamp. A more stable tungsten filament lamp with a colour temperature of 3,400°K. is that known as the quartz-iodine lamp. Iodine vapour keeps the lamp from darkening and it therefore gives constant brightness and colour temperature throughout its life.

As a rough guide to the selection of colour films and correction filters, it is possible to allocate colour temperature to the full range of light-sources used for colour photography. These values are given in the table below:

APPROXIMATE COLOUR TEMPERATURES FOR COMMON LIGHT-SOURCES

Light-Source	Colour Temperature °K.
Candle	1,900
Tungsten filament lamp 100-watt	2,840
,, ,, ,, 250-watt	2,900
,, ,, ,, 1,000-watt	3,000
Projection lamp 500-watt	3,200
Photopearl lamp 500-watt	3,200
C.P. studio lamps 500 to 10,000-watt	3,200
Photoflood lamps No. 1 and 2 ⎫	
Quartz iodine lamp ⎭	3,300 to 3,400
Clear flash bulbs	3,800
White flame carbon arc	5,000
Direct sunlight – early or late in day	5,000
,, ,, – at sunrise or sunset	2,000 – 4,000
Average noon sunlight	5,400
,, ,, ,, plus clear blue sky light	6,500
Electronic flash units	6,000 to 7,000
Overcast sky	6,800
Light from clear blue sky	12,000 to 27,000
'Daylight' fluorescent lamps	About 6,500*

* It is not possible to assign an accurate value to fluorescent sources because they do not have a strictly continuous spectrum.

The Mired system

The filters required to modify the colour temperature of light-sources can be conveniently predicted by using the reciprocal of the colour temperature multiplied by 1,000,000. This is known as the 'mired' value. The conversion table given below shows the mired values for a range of colour temperatures.

Mired Values of Colour Temperatures from 2,000°—6,900°K										
°K	0	100	200	300	400	500	600	700	800	900
2,000	500	476	455	435	417	400	385	370	357	345
3,000	333	323	312	303	294	286	278	270	263	256
4,000	250	244	238	233	227	222	217	213	208	204
5,000	200	196	192	189	185	182	179	175	172	169
6,000	167	164	161	159	156	154	152	149	147	145

It is also possible to allocate mired-shift values to light-balancing filters designed to effect changes in the colour temperature of a light-source, the shift-value of the filter being roughly the same, irrespective of the initial temperature of the light-source. A filter which lowers the colour temperature is said to have a positive shift-value and one which raises the colour temperature a negative shift-value. Values for the Wratten series of light-balancing and conversion filters are given in the table below. Filters may be combined, their mired-shift values then being added or subtracted according to their positive or negative value.

Mired-shift values for Wratten Light-balancing Filters and Conversion Filters												
No:	85B	85	85C	81EF	81C	81B	81A	81	82	82A	82B	82C	80B
Mired-Shift:	+149	+130	+99	+53	+35	+27	+18	+10	−10	−18	−32	−45	−130

Colour temperature meters

Instruments designed to measure colour temperature are commonly based on the use of a photo-cell which indicates the relative proportions of blue and red light emitted by a light-source. When properly calibrated, these can be useful for working with tungsten lamps, but may sometimes be misleading when applied to daylight photography. Some exposure meters also embody a device known as a 'colour finder' consisting of two narrow strips of coloured card mounted on the side of the meter. As the colour of the light falling on the colour patches changes, different parts of the two strips match visually, thus giving a rough indication of the colour temperature.

Nature of illumination

The most notable characteristic of clear sunlight is that its rays are for all practical purposes parallel. The shadows cast are therefore same-size silhouettes of an object when projected on to a background at right angles to the direction of sunlight. Beams of parallel light can, of course, be produced optically, but spotlights are normally adjusted to give slightly divergent beams when used for the stage or the studio. Searchlight beams used for air warfare and the lanterns of lighthouses also give very nearly parallel illumination. However, sunlight plus the light from the sky gives a mixture of parallel and diffused (multi-directional) lighting, the relative amounts of each varying with the presence of haze or mist. The light from either a blue or a totally overcast sky is diffused and does not produce discernible shadows unless the light reaching the subject has been severely restricted, such as in a narrow street with tall buildings or when coming through a window. Daylight, whether direct sunlight or light coming from the sky, may be considered as coming from an infinite distance and is therefore unaffected by the inverse square law of light propagation in terms of terrestial distances. This fact, plus the tendency of the eye towards brightness constancy, often leads the amateur to overlook the diminution of illumination when using artificial light-sources.

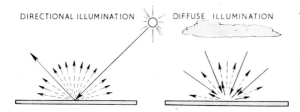

DIRECTIONAL ILLUMINATION   DIFFUSE ILLUMINATION

Fig. 6.1. Most surfaces reflect part of the light falling on them unchanged; this occurs at one angle with direct lighting, but at all angles with diffuse lighting, so that no matter how a surface is viewed in daylight its colour is mixed with some white light.

Apart from the important difference in the presence or absence of shadows, directional lighting gives an appreciably higher colour saturation, both visually and photographically, to the appearance of coloured surfaces. The reason is that most surfaces reflect part of the light falling on them unchanged. With diffused daylight illumination, some of this white light will be reflected at all angles so that no matter how the subject is viewed, the actual colour of the surface will be desaturated with some portion of white light. With strongly directional light the reflected light will also be more or less directional and, except when viewed at the angle of reflection, the colour of the surface retains its full saturation, see fig. 6.1 and plates 13 and 14.

Yet another characteristic of light of interest to the colour photographer is polarization. This is dealt with more fully in a later chapter, but it is worth noting that light reflected from polished non-metallic surfaces is strongly polarized at an angle of about 34° to the reflecting surface – the effect diminishing at smaller or greater angles – and also blue sky light coming from a direction at right-angles to a line between the camera and the sun. Thus by means of a polarizing filter such reflections can be partly or totally eliminated, and the colour of the sky darkened, under some conditions, to a tone almost equal to the night sky. By using a large polarizing screen over a light-source, polarized light can be created artificially. When all other means of eliminating reflections have failed, such light used with a polarizing filter over the camera lens can be useful in copying oil paintings having a very irregular surface.

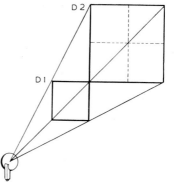

Fig. 6.2. The diagram shows how the light from a point source falling on a surface at right angles to its direction varies inversely with the square of the distance to the surface. The intensity of light at D1 is 4 times as great as at D2 which is at twice the distance.

Inverse square law of light propagation

The intensity of illumination falling on a flat surface at right-angles to the direction of light from a point source is inversely proportional to the square of the distance of the surface from the light-source. This is shown diagrammatically in fig. 6.2. Although the inverse square law applies strictly to a point source, it can be applied to photographic lamps generally, except when these are used with an optical system as in the case of spotlights or projectors, or when used with a polished metal reflector designed to 'focus' light at an average working distance. Exposure calculations when using tungsten lamps in normal reflectors can be based on this law, which also forms the basis of the flash factors or guide numbers used for flash-light. As the light transmitted by a lens is inversely proportional to the square of the f/number at which the lens is set, it is possible to multiply the distance of the flash lamp from the subject by the f/number to obtain a constant. Thus the f/number for any other distance is found merely by dividing this constant or guide number by the new distance to find the necessary f/number to allow for the effect of the inverse square law.

Daylight

Although it is usual to regard daylight as a single light-source, it is better for the colour photographer to treat daylight as a dual light-source composed of sunlight and light from the sky, which are different both in colour quality and intensity, and also differ in nature, sunlight being directional and light from the sky being diffused. Depending on atmospheric conditions (haze or cloud) the two sources of light may be more or less mixed, becoming one very large diffused light-source when the sky is completely overcast. Indeed the variable nature of daylight is both the delight of the amateur pictorialist and the bane of the professional on some routine outdoor assignment. Reversal colour films intended for exposure by daylight are balanced for illumination composed of direct sunlight with the sun well above the horizon plus light coming from a blue sky. For this reason photographs taken with the sun at a low angle (early or late in the day and in winter) appear rather too yellow, while those taken in open shade with the subject lit with blue sky appear rather too blue. The colour rendering with an overcast sky may also appear on the 'cold' side, but this is partly due to the lack of contrast and the fact that diffused light causes some colour desaturation. Under certain other conditions which cannot be visually detected the presence of an excessive amount of ultra-violet radiation will also give a bluish colour rendering. This may occur on a clear day after a heavy fall of rain, near large areas of water, and also at high altitudes (6,000 ft. or more).

Strong direct sunlight from a clear blue sky is by no means an ideal illumination for colour photography except for views of a general scenic nature or when the sun is behind the camera so as to give mainly frontal lighting. Taking the sun as the main light with illumination from the sky as a subsidiary or fill-in light for the shadows, the lighting ratio actually present may be as great as 7:1, which is considerably in excess of the lighting ratio of 2:1 generally desirable for portraiture outdoors. This can, of course, be overcome in local areas by the use of reflectors or fill-in flash, but for outdoor portraits strong sunlight still offers the serious disadvantage of being too dazzling to the eyes. The presence of strong haze or even a very thin cloud layer provides a far more manageable quality of lighting, and is considered by most professional photographers, and particularly those undertaking fashion photographs, as the ideal form of daylight. For portraits of children and small still-life sets the same effect can be obtained under conditions of strong sunlight by interposing one or more layers of muslin or cheese-cloth between the subject and the sun. See colour plate 13.

Interior daylight in a room having large windows on two or more sides may also be usefully employed for portraiture and still-life subjects, though for professional work it is usually simpler to employ some form of artificial lighting, since it is more easily controlled and can be used at any time of the day or night.

Practical aspects of using and controlling daylight are dealt with in the next three chapters.

Electronic flash

As the colour quality of electronic flash closely approaches that of daylight, it is logical to deal with this kind of lighting next, although it is of comparatively recent introduction into the photographer's range of light-sources. The first practical application of gaseous discharge tubes as a powerful illuminant of extremely short duration can be credited to Prof. Edgerton, and the first commercially available unit of this type was marketed by Eastman Kodak in 1939 under the name Kodatron Speedlamp. Some use was also made during World War II of electronic flash units for air reconnaissance at night. However, the first application of electronic flash was chiefly in scientific and technical research, advantage being taken of the extremely short exposure times possible. Indeed, the first general use of electronic flash was rather that of the novelty of 'stopping' movement, and photographs of cats leaping, glasses shattering on impact with a stone floor, and ballet dancers suspended in mid-air were its chief products.

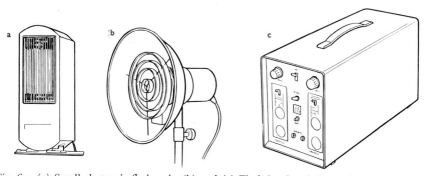

Fig. 6.3. (a) Small electronic flash unit. (b) and (c) Flash head and electronic power unit for feeding a number of such flashheads.

However, following the lead of Kodak, a number of firms specializing in electronic equipment began to make portable units, and because the extremely short exposure times created problems of reciprocity failure, the duration of the flash was extended to the region of 1/1,000 sec., a speed amply short enough for most photographic purposes. More recent developments have led to a considerable reduction in the size and weight of the power units needed to feed the discharge lamp, and the use of nickel-cadmium batteries with mains charging units has reduced running costs to negligible proportions. In other words, development has catered for both professional and amateur requirements, and there is now available a wide range of such units from very small single units, in keeping with the needs of the small camera user, to powerful units capable of feeding four or more flash-tubes for studio work. See fig. 6.3.

Most of the flash-tubes in use are those filled with xenon gas, and emit light

97

of roughly 6,000 to 7,000°K. – namely, closely approaching the quality of sunlight plus the light from a blue sky. With some lamps, particularly when new, the colour rendering tends to be a little bluish, but this is easily offset with a filter, such as the Wratten No. 81A, which absorbs a small amount of blue light. Some lamps, such as those of the Mecablitz series, embody a filter so as to obtain a closer match to direct sunlight.

Although the initial cost of an electronic flash unit is much greater than that of the flash unit needed to fire a combustible flashbulb, it offers certain advantages which amply repay the extra cost to the photographer able to make frequent use of flash. Indeed, one of the advantages accrues from the mere possession of the unit: as it costs practically nothing to produce a flash there is far more opportunity to learn how to apply this form of light and hence make use of it as a light-source on numerous occasions where one might otherwise make do with existing light, less favourable for successful results. Thus, with outdoor portraits taken with direct sunlight there is often a temptation to dispense with reflectors as a means of illuminating shadows, whereas the possession of a portable electronic flash unit, once the technique of fill-in flash has been mastered, offers the simplest method of obtaining a suitable lighting balance (see page 132). Another example is that of the close-up photography of flowers and insects, where the use of small apertures, even in strong sunlight, requires exposure times too long for a hand-held camera or for subjects which may be moving. At the comparatively short distances needed to cover the area of the subject, even a small electronic unit is many times more powerful than sunlight and delivers its light in something like 1/1,000 sec.

Our second advantage has in fact just been mentioned, namely the 'speed' of the flash. Many photographers using electronic flash for the first time are apt to be astonished at the crispness of the definition in portraits and close-ups made with electronic flash, owing to the elimination of camera shake and subject movement and for this and other reasons, many portrait photographers now use this type of lighting for all their studio work. A third advantage is that it can be freely mixed with daylight, and, for the photographer wishing to do both indoor and outdoor photography on the same type of film, enables him to adopt daylight-type film for all work without the need of correction filters. Since the range of colour films balanced for daylight usually exceeds those balanced for artificial lighting, he will also have a wider choice of colour film.

The major disadvantage of electronic flash, which it holds in common with combustible flashbulbs, is that the effect of a particular lighting arrangement cannot be seen until after the film has been exposed and processed. This can be overcome by some form of pilot lighting system such as that described on page 190. One warning is not out of place at this stage. Many small units embody a visible or audible signal to indicate when the condensers are recharged for firing. In most cases such signals occur when there is only a 75 per cent charge and it is advisable to wait a few seconds to be sure of obtaining the full light output of the unit.

It is customary to rate the light output of an electronic flash unit in terms of joules, the joule being equivalent to one watt flowing for one second. Units designed for operating a number of tubes and primarily intended for professional studio photography range from 200 to 2,000 joules, while smaller, portable units range from 30 to 200 joules. However the capacity in joules is not an exact indication of the effective light output, and different units having the same electrical output may vary considerably in light emission and coverage, the latter depending to a large extent on the design of the reflector. Most units are also issued with a booklet giving guide numbers or flash factors for a range of film speeds. These should be taken as a guide only, and each and every unit should be 'calibrated' by practical tests to establish the best flash factors under different conditions of use (see also plate 72). It is perhaps worth noting that recent increases in the speeds of colour films have made the small-capacity unit of, say, 50 joules fully adequate for use as a fill-in flash and also as the main light for subjects occupying a fairly small area. In general, however, when used as the main light-source, a larger unit of 120 to 250 joules, and designed to operate two or more lamps, is desirable.

Flashbulbs

In the early part of the present century flash photography was achieved with the use of magnesium powder or ribbon – a somewhat perilous process for the photographer and something of a shock to his sitter. Flash became more popular and controllable when the combustible material was placed inside a glass envelope and ignited electrically. Recent developments in flashbulb manufacture have produced smaller and more efficient lamps – a pack of six 'mini-flash' bulbs taking little more space than a box of matches – yet each capable of producing the effective light-output of 40 Photoflood lamps at an exposure time of 1/25 sec. In the interests of economy the smaller sizes of flashbulb, AG1, No. 1 and No. 5, have dispensed with a metal cap and make use of projecting electrodes which fit into the flash unit, itself often no bigger than a matchbox when the reflector has been collapsed. However, these small bulbs and more particularly the small reflectors supplied with the flash unit are chiefly intended for flash snapshots. For maximum efficiency a reflector of at least 4 in. in diameter should be used with a No. 5 bulb and one of 5 in. for larger bulbs.

Flashbulbs are of two types: those with clear glass envelopes giving light of approximately 3,800°K., and those with blue-coated envelopes designed for use with daylight-type colour films, either for fill-in flash with sunlight or as a main light-source. Owing to the moderate speed of many colour films, flashbulbs offer a convenient means for exposures indoors or, at night, outdoors. And it was for this reason that certain colour films, such as Ektachrome Type F, were specially balanced to permit the use of clear flashbulbs. However, the increased efficiency of blue-coated bulbs tends to make these films unnecessary.

Flashbulbs differ substantially from electronic flash tubes in the way they deliver their light output. Whereas the discharge tube produces its total light output immediately its circuit is closed and in a time of not much more than 1/1,000 sec., the combustion of a flashbulb takes roughly 1/30 sec. or 30 to 40 millisec., the first 12 to 15 millisec. being needed for the combustion to reach a useful light output (half-peak) and a further 5 millisec. to reach peak output, after which the combustion diminishes in the manner shown in fig. 6.4. Thus the

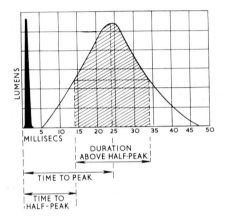

Fig. 6.4. Light-output curve of typical Class M flashbulb. The steep curve to the left represents electronic flash.

useful light output occupies a time of about 25 millisec. or 1/50 sec. some 12/15 millisec. after the lamp circuit has been closed. This makes it necessary to use a delay mechanism in the shutter release when exposures shorter than about 1/30 sec. are used with a diaphragm shutter – the so-called 'M' synchronization. Flashbulbs can, however, be used with 'X' synchronization (i.e., that intended for electronic flash) with exposure of 1/30 sec. or longer. A further complication arises with the use of a focal-plane shutter in that the shorter speeds usually involve the use of a narrow slit which moves across the focal plane, the total time required to expose the whole surface of the film being in the region of 1/30 sec. To enable short exposure times to be used it is necessary – except with miniature focal-plane cameras – to use a Class FP flashbulb in which the combustion is controlled so that light-output is maintained above the half-peak level for at least 25 millisec.

Plate 10. Fashion study. Unusual settings and backgrounds often provide a means of enhancing the subject. The subject has been lit with a broad area of floods with a key light to the left of the camera to provide a slight modelling of the coat. It is of interest to note the apparent blueness of the window in the background: this is in keeping with visual effect when the eyes are adapted to tungsten lighting. *Ektachrome transparency by Jack M. Oakley.*

Plate 11. Wet fish.

Plate 12. Half-wet pebble.

Plate 13. Diffused lighting.

Plate 14. Directional lighting.

Plate 15. Frontal lighting.

Plate 16. Oblique lighting.

A third class of flashbulb, Class S, still available as the PF 100, involves a longer delay before reaching peak output, usually at least 30 millisec. To obtain its maximum light-output it is therefore necessary to use the shutter at 1/15 sec. or longer. The PF 100, the PF 60 (Class M) and the PF 45 (for focal-plane shutters) are fitted with E.S. caps and may be fired directly across a mains circuit. This offers the advantage that a pilot lighting system can make use of the same sockets. In this case the bulbs are fired by a mains switch with the camera shutter open.

Tungsten lamps

Until recently, tungsten filament lamps of 2,000 watt and greater have been the mainstay of studio work, both in still and motion picture photography. The decline in their use can be attributed in the case of still photography to the availability of electronic flash units. Furthermore, colour films are on the whole relatively slower than black-and-white films and the large amount of tungsten light needed to light even a small set to obtain a level of illumination suitable for reasonably short exposure times often makes it more convenient to use flashbulbs or electronic flash for still photography. Nevertheless, tungsten lighting offers, in comparison with daylight, the advantage of a controllable and predictable light-source and the advantage of continuous light-output in comparison with flash.

As we have mentioned earlier in this chapter, tungsten lamps can be conveniently classified for the purpose of colour photography in terms of their colour temperature – see table on page 92. Thus household lamps range from 2,600°K. for a 25-watt lamp to 2,900°K. for a 250-watt lamp. However, the low light-output of these lamps in respect of the requirements of colour photography has made it preferable to balance colour films of artificial-light type to the higher colour temperatures of the more efficient studio lamp (3,200°K.) and the still more efficient Photoflood lamp (3,400°K.).

Plates 11 and 12. Specular reflections from the wet surfaces of the fish emphasize their 'wetness' but at the same time destroy much of the colouring. On the other hand the wet area of the pebble, photographed to avoid reflections, reveals much more of the colour and pattern of the surface.

Plates 13 and 14. The subject was chosen as having both glossy and matt surfaces and is shown lit with both diffused and directional sunlight. The diffused sunlight was obtained by placing a large screen of several layers of fine muslin between the subject and the sun. Surface differences are more apparent with directional light and there is also a higher colour saturation.

Plates 15 and 16. A piece of fossil-bearing rock is shown photographed with frontal illumination (on the left) and strongly oblique lighting (on the right). The frontal lighting records the colour and pattern but gives little clue to the nature of the surface: with side-lighting it is possible to see that the fossils have been eroded more than the surrounding sand-stone and form small hollows. It can also be seen that the surface of the rock is curved.

Photographs on Kodachrome II Film by E. S. Bomback.

103

Photoflood lamps

The high efficiency of Photoflood lamps is obtained by over-running the filament, a fact which considerably shortens the life of the lamp, but makes it an excellent light-source for occasional indoor work. For colour work of critical quality the effective life of a No. 1 Photoflood is halved, since it tends to blacken and discolour after the first hour's burning. Similarly the No. 2 lamp is good for only 3 or 4 hours, though in both cases the lamps are still suitable for lighting backgrounds or other areas of the subject where the colour rendering is not critical. However, the life of both lamps may be extended, in terms of the number of exposures made, by operating them with a switchboard which enables the lamps to be run in series during the arrangement of the lighting and then in parallel for the actual exposure. A suitable switch system is given in fig. 6.5.

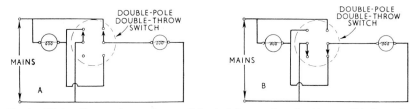

Fig. 6.5. Wiring diagram for a series-parallel switch for two photoflood lamps. (A) shows the switch position for full light output, (B) for reduced output.

Photofloods are available with either a B.C. or E.S. cap and may therefore be used in domestic lamp-holders for special effects in home portraiture. For example, a tall lamp-stand could be fitted with a Photoflood lamp if it is to be included in a portrait as the 'natural' source of light for someone reading a book. However, these lamps give off a large amount of heat – a No. 2 Photoflood is equivalent to a small electric heater of 500 watts – and should not be used in enclosed lamp shades. In normal use the efficiency of the illumination is greatly increased by using a large reflector of satin-finished aluminium. For use in the small studio the Kodalite Twin Assembly shown in fig. 6.6 is ideal for the use of two No. 2 Photoflood lamps. It is designed to throw an even flood of light without the need of extra diffusers. A smaller, home-lighting unit is available for use with No. 1 Photofloods. Photoflood lamps are also available with internal reflectors, and their higher cost may often be off-set by the possibility of dispensing with conventional lighting stands embodying a reflector.

The colour temperature of 3,400°K. will only be achieved if the lamps are run at the specified voltage, and fluctuations in the line voltage due to peak demands or an overloaded domestic supply may lead to unsatisfactory colour balance. Thus for critical work it is essential to employ some kind of voltage regulation, since a 10-volt drop in a 240-volt supply at the lamp socket reduces the colour temperature by about 50°K. and the light-output by about 15 per cent.

Typical characteristics of Photoflood lamps are given in the table below.

PHOTOFLOOD LAMPS

Colour Temperature 3,400 °K.						
Type	Watts	Cap	Nominal Efficiency Lm/watt	Average life (hours)	Dimensions	
					Length	Diameter
No. 1	275	B.C. or E.S.	29	2	110 mm.	60 mm.
No. 2	500	E.S.*	30	10	160 mm.	80 mm.

* Available with B.C. cap 200 to 250 volt only.

Photopearl and Colour-Controlled lamps

These lamps are less efficient in light-output but are considerably more robust than Photoflood lamps in terms of their burning life. The colour temperature of the Photopearl and lamps of similar type (Nitrophot, etc.) ranges from 3,100°K. to 3,200°K. These lamps are rated at 500 watts and with a nominal efficiency of 21 lumens per watt give approximately two-thirds the light-output of a No. 2

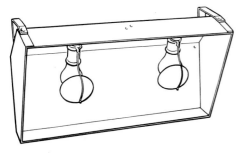

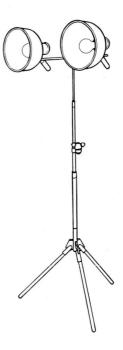

Fig. 6.6. Above: Kodak Studio Lighting Unit Model 2.
Right: Kodalite Twin Assembly for No. 2 Photoflood lamps.

Photoflood lamp. Since their burning life is in the region of 15 to 25 hours, they provide for the serious amateur a far more economical light-source than the Photoflood lamp. In addition they are far more stable in colour temperature and somewhat less dazzling to the eyes when used for portraiture. These lamps may also be obtained with internal mirror reflectors for use as broad spotlights.

Colour-controlled studio lamps of 3,200°K. are available in a wide range of wattages and are designed to meet the needs of the professional still and cine photographer. A typical range of these lamps is given in the table below.

COLOUR-CONTROLLED STUDIO LAMPS

Colour Temperature 3,200°K.						
Ref. No.	Watts	Volts	Cap	Finish	Average Life (hours) Low volt	High volt
CP/1	275	240, 250	B.C.	Pearl	5 to 8	
CP/2	500	115, 230, 240, 250	B.C. or E.S.	Pearl	25	15
CP/3	1,000	115, 230, 240	G.E.S.	Pearl	30	20
CP/4	1,500	115, 230, 240, 250	G.E.S.	Pearl	50	25
CP/12	2,000	115, 230, 240, 250	Bi-post	Clear	50	
CP/13	5,000	115, 230, 240	Bi-post	Clear	75	
CP/14	10,000	115, 230, 240, 250	Bi-post	Clear	100	

Quartz-iodine lamps

These lamps have a tungsten filament that burns inside a quartz envelope, and contain iodine vapour to keep the bulb from darkening, thereby allowing the lamps to maintain constant brightness and colour temperature throughout their life. Those intended for photographic illumination have a nominal life of from 12 to 15 hours and when run at the specified voltage give a colour temperature of 3,400°K. These lamps thus offer a very suitable light source for studio work with Kodachrome II Film, Type A, when consistently good colour rendering is important.

Household and other tungsten lamps

As can be seen from the table on page 92, household lamps vary slightly in colour temperature according to wattage with an average around 2,850°K. These lamps, used with suitable light-balancing filters, are quite suitable for lighting small sets – still life, table-tops, etc. – where they can be placed close to the subjects, but are not suitable for portraiture except of the available-light variety when using a high-speed colour film and a large aperture lens. However, such lighting is also encountered in shop-window displays, restaurants and other public buildings and may yield satisfactory results with or without a light-balancing filter with a Type B colour film. Theatre floodlighting and spotlights range from 2,900°K. to 3,100°K. and give excellent results with Type B films without a filter. Coloured lighting effects may permit the use of any type of colour film, though the best results may be given with a Type B film.

Fluorescent lamps

These lamps, which usually take the form of strip-lighting, provide a highly efficient and relatively cool light-source suitable for illuminating large areas with soft uniform lighting. Basically this type of lamp is a low-pressure mercury-vapour discharge tube generating ultra-violet radiation, and contains fluorescent phosphors which convert the ultra-violet to visible light having almost a continuous spectrum. Such lamps are available in a variety of colour qualities, and in large stores and public buildings are often used in more than one variety to give a more pleasing kind of lighting. The variety known as 'daylight' is of roughly 6,500°K. in colour temperature and gives reasonably satisfactory results with a daylight-type colour film and a CC30M filter. It also forms a useful illuminant for viewing large transparencies by transmitted light.

Discharge lamps

These are commonly used for street illumination either as sodium discharge lamps, which emit a monochromatic yellow light in the form of a double line in the spectrum at 589 mμ, or high-pressure mercury-vapour lamps, which emit a number of spectral lines. Neither are suitable as light-sources for colour work. A form of high-pressure mercury-vapour lamp, which is enclosed in a Woods glass (glass dyed with nickel oxide) envelope, emits only the near ultra-violet in the region 360 mμ and is used to illuminate fluorescent materials, such as those used for stage effects in variety theatres. These can be photographed with a fast daylight-type colour film using an ultra-violet-absorbing filter over the camera lens, so that only the visible light is admitted.

Coloured light-sources

Any 'white' light-source can be converted into a coloured source by interposing a coloured filter between the light-source and the subject. If the whole of the light illuminating the subject is to be coloured the filter can, of course, be placed over the camera lens, see page 232. However, for local colour effects on part of the subject or background it is usually preferable to use a spotlight or, for small subjects, a slide projector. Larger light-sources can be covered with sheets of coloured cellophane or plastic sheet. Coloured stage-lighting, neon signs, and other existing coloured light-sources may be photographed successfully with either daylight-type film or film which is balanced for artificial light. Various applications of coloured lighting are discussed in Chapter 16.

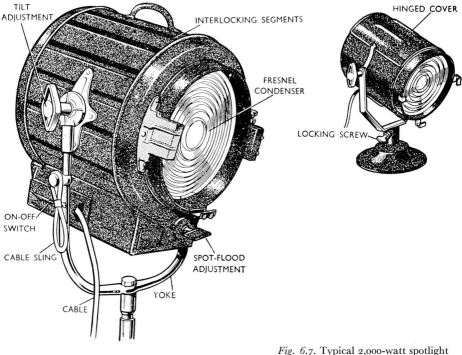

TILT ADJUSTMENT

INTERLOCKING SEGMENTS

HINGED COVER

FRESNEL CONDENSER

LOCKING SCREW

ON-OFF SWITCH

CABLE SLING

SPOT-FLOOD ADJUSTMENT

YOKE

CABLE

Fig. 6.7. Typical 2,000-watt spotlight and a small version for a 250-watt lamp.

Lighting Equipment

The sun as a light-source is already fixed in its location for any given time of the day and the only additional equipment needed for local control can either take the form of fill-in flash or some form of reflector board. Depending on the area of shadow to be covered, a reflector board can be as small as a pocket handkerchief for close-ups or one of several square feet for full-figure portraits. The most efficient reflector is one with a smooth metallic surface (it can be made of aluminium foil such as that supplied for kitchen use), but, as this can be almost as dazzling as the sun, one with a broken or printed metallic surface is preferable for portraiture. A white matt surface gives a highly diffused form of lighting, but the board must either be very large or placed fairly near the subject. Two long bamboo poles and a few yards of muslin or cheese cloth are all that is needed to provide an efficient diffuser for a local area of sunlight.

Artificial-light equipment requires the use of lamp stands and lamp reflectors, if these are not already provided with the lamp, as in the case of electronic flash equipment. Stands of the telescopic type capable of being raised to heights of 8 ft. or more are essential to a well-equipped studio. Each lamp should preferably have its own stand, though combination lights, such as the Kodak Studio Lighting Unit Model 2, can be suspended from the ceiling, see fig. 6.6. Large banks of lamps for general lighting are available commercially or can be made up in the workshop to suit particular requirements. This form of lighting used with spotlights for key and back-lighting effects provides excellent illumination for general studio work. Diffusers can take the form of large frames covered with muslin or translucent plastic sheet for use over the area of the lamp reflector. Hoods or funnels for restricting the area of lighting are available with some lighting equipment but anyhow are easily improvised. See fig. 6.8.

Spotlights, although fairly costly pieces of equipment, are by far the most serviceable and versatile form of photographic lighting. By means of a Fresnel-type condenser lens, the spotlight can be adjusted to give either a broad or narrow beam of strongly directional lighting, and with various diffusers, filters and other devices a whole range of other lighting effects. A small spotlight of 250 watts may be all that is needed as a back-light in portraiture, but one of 1,000 or 2,000 watts is desirable for use as main lighting. Fig. 6.7.

With a large number of tungsten lamps some form of distribution panel is needed for connecting lamp cables to the mains. For colour work it is useful to have a voltmeter incorporated, and some kind of voltage regulator. Thus, if fluctuations are known to occur, it may be preferable to operate with lower-voltage lamps employing a suitable rheostat to adjust the mains voltage to that required by the lamps. A distribution panel built in the form of a trolley will enable individual lamp cables to be shortened and thus reduce the danger of accidents. Finally it is advisable to check that the total consumption of the lamps does not exceed the capacity of the mains socket.

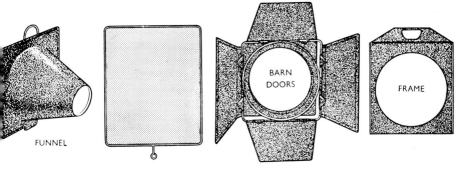

FUNNEL

DIFFUSER

BARN DOORS

FRAME

Fig. 6.8. Light accessories of this kind may be improvised.

7

Colour Balance and Correction Filters

AN EXACT reproduction of the colours of the original subject would seem to be the primary requirement of a colour photograph, but even supposing such an achievement were possible, the probability is that the colours would not *appear* to be identical with those of the subject. Painters have been aware of this in their own field for centuries, but it is comparatively recently that research workers in colour photography and the more experienced photographers have come to appreciate something of the complexity of colour reproduction. Leaving aside the technical difficulties of producing a 'perfect' colour film – perfect not only in its initial sensitivity to the image formed by the camera lens but also in the absorption characteristics of the dyes, which are later formed to produce the photographic image – there remains the fact that the eye does not view a colour photograph in the same way that it views the original scene. The more important reasons for this have been given in an early chapter, but it is useful to recapitulate those directly concerning colour balance.

Behaviour of the eye

Firstly, the eye tends to adjust its sensitivity to the prevailing illumination, and within seconds of changing from one kind of lighting to another, as for example from daylight to tungsten lighting, will usually accept the new light as 'white' or colourless. No such adjustment is made with a colour film, which is, of course, fixed in its colour sensitivity. A correction can be made, as we shall see later, by modifying the colour of the light reaching the film either by placing a filter over the camera lens or between the light-source and the subject. However, in viewing a photograph, the eye does not adjust itself to the same extent as when viewing the original scene, and, depending on the nature and size of the photo-graph, the quality of illumination by which it is viewed and the colour of adjacent surroundings may, in fact, make adjustments which are contrary to achieving a satisfactory colour balance in the photograph. Even when the viewing conditions are 'ideal' as when viewing a projected transparency in a darkened room, the eye does not adjust itself to the same extent as when viewing an original scene, and an exposure made with tungsten illumination using a film balanced for daylight will still appear too yellow, though not by the same amount as a small colour print viewed with daylight coming through the windows.

But there is another aspect worth noting, the area of a subject contained in a photograph is normally only a portion of a much larger scene, and when viewed with different surroundings may take on a different appearance. This in part explains the apparently high colour saturation obtained when viewing a transparency by projection in a darkened room, and also to the changed appearance of a subject which in its original setting was surrounded by a large area of contrasting colour.

The problem of achieving a correct colour balance in a small colour print is far greater, since it can be viewed in a wide variation of illumination – often of mixed quality – and in the most diverse surroundings. Fortunately those people chiefly interested in small colour prints are often the least critical and exacting.

Standards of colour balance

It will soon become evident to anyone seriously interested in colour photography, particularly if he is a member of an enthusiastic colour club, that 'ideal' colour balance or colour rendering is ultimately a matter of personal taste. One reason is that we can become used to a particular nuance of colour rendering which is given by the film we mostly use, and tend to judge photographs taken with other brands of film against this standard. A second reason may be that we view our own colour prints in a particular quality of illumination and in certain surroundings, while we view photographs taken by other photographers under quite different conditions, so that even prints of identical colour rendering appear different.

Unfortunately there is no impartial standard for assessing colour balance because, even if the colours were measured with a colorimeter, there could be a bias on the part of the observer, and furthermore the values would not necessarily apply to the 'ideal' required for visual viewing. This does not mean that a representative panel of viewers each presented with a number of variations of the same subject could not provide a mean verdict as to which version was the most acceptable: but the verdict would only apply to that particular subject and viewing conditions. The experienced photographer over a period of time inevitably collects a number of photographs which in his opinion are of first-class colour balance. If he makes a practice of submitting photographs to exhibitions and competitions and is fortunate to obtain regular awards, he has the further evidence that other 'experts' agree with him, and in this way can make a yard-stick for himself.

Conversion filters

Kodak colour films, as we have seen in the previous chapter, are produced in a number of different colour balances with the object of providing films for the principal light-sources used by amateur and professional photographers.

However, not every 'type' of colour balance is available in any one kind of film: Kodachrome film, for example, is available as 'Daylight' and Type A (balanced for photofloods), Ektachrome as 'Daylight' and Type B (photopearl and other lamps of 3,200°K.). However, it does not follow that the lack of a Type A version of Ektachrome film makes it unsuitable for exposures with Photoflood lamps or that the lack of a Type B version of Kodachrome film, means that it cannot be exposed with 3,200°K. lamps. Both these combinations will produce satisfactory results by using a suitable conversion filter over the camera lens, see table page 115. Indeed far greater differences can be accepted, and artificial-light films generally can be exposed with daylight by using one of the conversion filters supplied by Kodak. The Wratten No. 85 allows Type A Kodachrome to be exposed with daylight, the No. 85B serves the same purpose for Type B Ektachrome and Type L Ektacolor films. Owing to the fact that the artificial-light version of Kodachrome film is faster than the daylight version, the effect of the Wratten 85 filter is to reduce it to the same speed as the daylight type. With other artificial-light films the appropriate daylight conversion filter involves only about 2/3 stop loss of speed. Many experienced users of Kodachrome film prefer to use the Type A version with a Wratten 85 filter for all their outdoor photography on the grounds that it gives a more acceptable colour balance. This is not entirely a matter of personal preference, because the Wratten 85 filter also acts as a ultra-violet-absorbing filter, whereas daylight Kodachrome film exposed without a filter tends to produce somewhat bluish colour rendering under lighting conditions containing an abnormal amount of ultra-violet radiation. This is more noticeable with some lenses than others. Furthermore, if one wishes to work with one 'type' of film for both daylight and artificial-light exposures, it is clearly an advantage to use Type A film, since Kodachrome II daylight-type film converted for Photoflood lighting by means of a Wratten 80B filter then has only about one-third the speed of Kodachrome II Film Type A – see Chapter 33. However, it is interesting to note that full conversion of daylight films for various qualities of artificial lighting is by no means essential or always desirable for certain kinds of subjects. This became apparent with the introduction of High Speed Ektachrome Film as a daylight version only. Its extra speed was in fact as useful for available-light photographs after dark as for weak daylight or fast action shots. But by using the full correction required for tungsten lighting of 2,850°K., the effective speed of the film is reduced by 60 per cent. Indoor snapshots using an 80B filter, although slightly yellowish in colour rendering, are in fact more in keeping with the idea of domestic lighting, and even exposures made without a filter are reasonably acceptable, and certainly better than nothing when it is essential. The yellowishness is more acceptable if an actual light-source such as a reading lamp is included in the picture, and becomes less acceptable with more formal portraits, since in this case the viewer of the photograph tends to revert to the whiteness of daylight as a standard of lighting.

The need for a conversion filter with a negative colour film depends to a

Wratten No. 80B filter for exposing Daylight
Type film with Photoflood lamps

Wratten No. 85 filter for exposing Type A film
with daylight

Wratten No. 85B filter for exposing Type B film
with daylight

Wratten No. 85C filter for exposing Type F film
with daylight

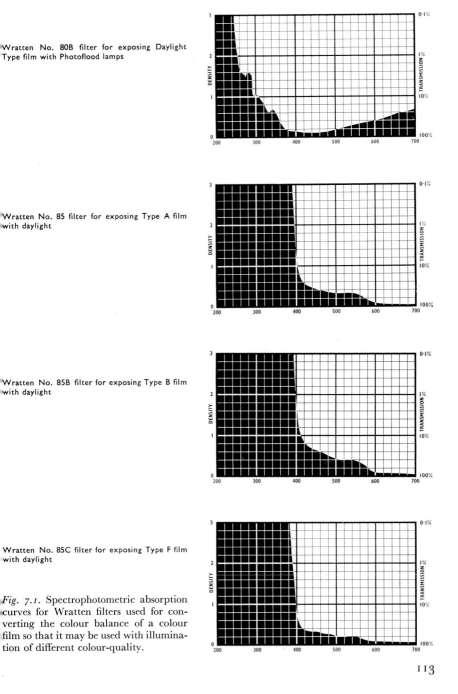

Fig. 7.1. Spectrophotometric absorption
curves for Wratten filters used for con-
verting the colour balance of a colour
film so that it may be used with illumination of different colour-quality.

large extent on the kind of printing the colour negatives will receive. Thus only one type of Kodacolor film is at present available, with a colour balance adjusted for clear flashbulb illumination (3,800°K.). However, the film can be exposed with daylight without a filter when prints are to be made by a laboratory equipped with automatic printers, but a filter is helpful, though not essential, if the prints are to be made by the film user.

Ultra-violet-absorbing filters

Daylight-type films occasionally require the use of an ultra-violet-absorbing filter to restrain the effect of excessive ultra-violet radiation on the blue-sensitive layer of the film. Such radiation is scattered by the atmosphere and in conditions of strong haze gives rather more blue in photographs of distant scenery than is normally visible to the eye. At high altitudes, where the atmosphere is 'thinner' and clearer, a greater amount of ultra-violet is reflected from the subject, being particularly noticeable in shadow areas on snow and light-coloured buildings. Rather similar effects can occur at low altitude after a heavy downpour of rain, the bluishness being particularly noticeable on wet sand and asphalt roads. However, with low-level sunlight, excessive blueness on horizontal planes of the subject is often a reflection of blue sky-light. Generally speaking, ultra-violet radiation seems to be more in evidence near large areas of water.

Kodak Ltd. provide two ultra-violet-absorbing filters: the Kodisk Haze filter, whose absorption is restricted to ultra-violet, and the Wratten 1A (Skylight) filter, see fig. 7.2, which also absorbs a tiny amount of green light and appears a faint pink in colour when held against a sheet of white paper.

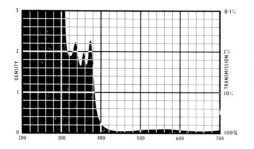

Fig. 7.2. Absorption curve for Wratten No. 1A filter. This filter is similar to the Kodak Skylight filter.

The use of the Skylight filter for all landscape photography is open to objection on the grounds that it suppresses natural atmospheric perspective. Nevertheless some photographers make a practice of using it for all outdoor photography with daylight-type film. As already mentioned, no additional ultra-violet-absorbing filter is needed when using an artificial-light film with a daylight correction filter such as the Wratten 85.

Neither the Kodisk Haze nor Skylight filter requires any increase in exposure. Practical applications of these filters are given in Chapter 12.

Light-Balancing filters

The Wratten series of light-balancing filters is designed to make adjustments in the colour temperature of tungsten lamps when it is not possible to operate the

CONVERSION OF COLOUR TEMPERATURE TO 3,200°K

Colour Temperature of Source in °K	Filters Required	Exposure increase in Stops*
2,490	82C + 82C	$1\frac{1}{3}$
2,570	82C + 82B	$1\frac{1}{3}$
2,650	82C + 82A	1
2,720	82C + 82	1
2,800	82C	$\frac{2}{3}$
2,900	82B	$\frac{2}{3}$
3,000	82A	$\frac{1}{2}$
3,100	82	$\frac{1}{3}$
3,300	81	$\frac{1}{3}$
3,400	81A	$\frac{1}{3}$
3,500	81B	$\frac{1}{2}$
3,600	81C	$\frac{1}{2}$
3,850	81EF	$\frac{2}{3}$

CONVERSION OF COLOUR TEMPERATURE TO 3,400°K

2,610	82C + 82C	$1\frac{1}{3}$
2,700	82C + 82B	$1\frac{1}{3}$
2,780	82C + 82A	1
2,870	82C + 82	1
2,950	82C	$\frac{2}{3}$
3,060	82B	$\frac{2}{3}$
3,180	82A	$\frac{1}{2}$
3,290	82	$\frac{1}{3}$
3,510	81	$\frac{1}{3}$
3,630	81A	$\frac{1}{3}$
3,740	81B	$\frac{1}{2}$
3,850	81C	$\frac{1}{2}$
4,140	81EF	$\frac{2}{3}$

* These figures are approximate. For critical work they should be confirmed by practical test, specially when combinations of filters are used.

lamps at the correct colour temperature for the film. They have an absorption affecting two primary colours, the Wratten No. 82 filters are bluish and raise the colour temperature, and the Wratten No. 81 series are brownish and lower the colour temperature, see page 115. As can be seen from the table, the changes effected by each set of filters are in steps of about 100°K. Thus the No. 81 filter converts 3,300°K. tungsten light to 3,200°K. (the colour temperature required by Type B colour films) and the No. 81A converts 3,400°K. (Photoflood light) to 3,200°K. At other colour temperatures the change will be in steps greater or smaller than 100°K. and the correct filter is then found by trial and error. The table gives some indication of the changes effected by these filters for conversion of tungsten light-sources to either 3,200°K. or 3,400°K.

The Wratten Light Balancing filters also serve as conversion or correction filters to enable colour films to be exposed with either Photoflood lamps or those of 3,200°K. The Wratten No. 81A enables Type B Ektachrome and Type L Ektacolor films to be exposed with photofloods: the 82A enables Kodacolor films to be exposed with photofloods and the 82C to be exposed with lamps of 3,200°K. Added to the Wratten 80B, the 82A filter enables daylight films to be exposed with 3,200°K. lamps. The Wratten No. 82 filters may also be used on the basis of trial and error for exposing with ordinary tungsten lamps, theatre and display lighting generally, with artificial-light films balanced for higher colour temperatures. The Wratten No. 81 filters may prove useful for correcting any undesirable bluishness when exposing with electronic flash. However the Wratten 1A (Skylight) filter may also serve this purpose.

Colour-Compensating filters

These filters provide a graduated range with absorptions in one of the three additive primaries red, green or blue (and therefore appear cyan, magenta or yellow in colour respectively) or one of the three subtractive primaries, cyan, magenta or yellow (in which case they appear red, green or blue respectively). For convenience the filters are coded by the initial letter of their colours and are graduated in six densities in each colour. The peak density of each filter is indicated by the two digits following the filter designation – CC – and is measured at the wavelength of maximum absorption. The range of Kodak Colour-Compensating filters plus an indication of the increase in exposure needed is given on the facing page.

The CC filters have a wide range of uses in colour photography both in the exposure and duplication of transparencies, and also in the colour printing of Kodacolor and Ektacolor negatives, when the filter has to be placed between the negative and the paper. An alternative series of filters – the Kodak Colour Printing filters (CP) – is available for use in enlarger lamphouses between the light-source and the negative, see page 296. The uses of CC filters include the following:

(1) To make changes in the overall colour balance of results obtained with colour films

(2) To compensate for deficiencies in the spectral quality of light by which colour films may be exposed, for example, fluorescent lighting

(3) To compensate for batch-to-batch variation of professional colour films where critical standards of colour balance are required

(4) To adjust the colour balance errors arising through reciprocity effects

(5) To adjust the colour of the light-source when making duplicate transparencies from Ektachrome or Kodachrome originals

(6) Bound up with a colour slide to correct undesirable colour bias

(7) As viewing filters to determine the correction which may be needed when making Ektacolor prints from Kodacolor negatives.

Filter factors

The absorption of light by filters necessitates an increase in exposure, though in some cases the absorption is so small as to have a negligible effect. Where a change is recommended in film speed when using a conversion or correction filter, the information is given in either 'stops' or 'factors'. If filters are combined, the exposure increases for each must be added together when they are expressed in stops (as in the table below); if the increases are expressed as factors they must be multiplied together (as in the table on page 122).

'KODAK' COLOUR-COMPENSATING FILTERS

Peak density	Yellow series (suppresses blue)	Exposure increase in stops	Magenta series (suppresses green)	Exposure increase in stops	Cyan series (suppresses red)	Exposure increase in stops
0·05	CC 05Y	–	CC 05M	$\frac{1}{3}$	CC 05C	$\frac{1}{3}$
0·10	CC 10Y	$\frac{1}{3}$	CC 10M	$\frac{1}{3}$	CC 10C	$\frac{1}{3}$
0·20	CC 20Y	$\frac{1}{3}$	CC 20M	$\frac{1}{3}$	CC 20C	$\frac{1}{3}$
0·30	CC 30Y	$\frac{1}{3}$	CC 30M	$\frac{2}{3}$	CC 30C	$\frac{2}{3}$
0·40	CC 40Y	$\frac{1}{3}$	CC 40M	$\frac{2}{3}$	CC 40C	$\frac{2}{3}$
0·50	CC 50Y	$\frac{2}{3}$	CC 50M	$\frac{2}{3}$	CC 50C	1

Peak density	Red series (suppresses blue and green)	Exposure increase in stops	Green series (suppresses blue and red)	Exposure increase in stops	Blue series (suppresses green and red)	Exposure increase in stops
0·05	CC 05R	$\frac{1}{3}$	CC 05G	$\frac{1}{3}$	CC 05B	$\frac{1}{3}$
0·10	CC 10R	$\frac{1}{3}$	CC 10G	$\frac{1}{3}$	CC 10B	$\frac{1}{3}$
0·20	CC 20R	$\frac{1}{3}$	CC 20G	$\frac{1}{3}$	CC 20B	$\frac{2}{3}$
0·30	CC 30R	$\frac{2}{3}$	CC 30G	$\frac{2}{3}$	CC 30B	$\frac{2}{3}$
0·40	CC 40R	$\frac{2}{3}$	CC 40G	$\frac{2}{3}$	CC 40B	1
0·50	CC 50R	1	CC 50G	1	CC 50B	$1\frac{1}{3}$

Reciprocity law failure and colour balance

Colour films are normally adjusted to give correct colour balance at an exposure time of 1/50 sec. and for practical purposes the reciprocity law of time and intensity holds good over an exposure range of 1/1,000 to 1/10 sec. Exposure times shorter or longer may involve some failure of the reciprocity law, causing both loss of speed and a shift in colour balance. The latter will be appreciated when it is remembered that we are dealing with films having three distinct emulsions, which may react somewhat differently to reciprocity effects. In practice, reciprocity effects are more likely to be encountered with the use of longer times, as for example in photomacrography, where lens extension and the need for a small lens aperture may together call for exposures exceeding 60 sec. Corrections for this can be made on the basis of trial and error using filters such as those of the Kodak CC range. See also page 142.

Polarizing filters

These filters consist of a polarizing medium in sheet form which takes the form of a layer of minute rod-shaped crystals parallel to each other: this layer has the power of polarizing light and also of controlling the intensity of light which is already polarized. To understand the phenomenon of polarized light it is necessary to know that light waves vibrate at right-angles to the direction in which the light is travelling and usually in all possible directions in the manner shown in fig. 7.3. When light passes through a polarizing filter, waves vibrating in only one plane are allowed to pass, and if, for example, the structure is oriented in a vertical plane, then only the vibrations in a vertical or near vertical plane

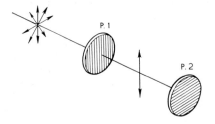

Fig. 7.3. Light waves usually vibrate in all planes at right-angles to the direction of travel. Passing through polarizing filter P1 it becomes plane-polarized vertically, then by a second polarizing filter P2, with its polarizing axis horizontal, the light is almost totally absorbed.

will be transmitted. If we now place a second polarizing filter in the path of this polarized light so that the structure is in a horizontal plane, this light will also be absorbed. However, the intensity of the polarized light can be varied by turning the filter about its own axis, maximum transmission occurring when the structure coincides with the plane of polarization.

Polarized light occurs naturally, the two most important sources from the photographer's point of view being light reflected from non-metallic surface

Plate 17. Two views of an Italian village taken from the same point. Above at 9 a.m. and below at 6 p.m. Clear sun with a slightly hazy sky remained constant and the differences may be chiefly attributed to the direction of the lighting. *Kodachrome II transparencies by E. S. Bomback.*

Plate 18. Taken at an altitude of 7,000 ft. without filter.

Plate 19. The same subject but with a Wratten No. 1A filter.

Plate 20. Taken with a Wratten 1A filter over the lens.

Plate 21. The same scene with a polarizing filter plus 2 stops more exposure.

Plate 22. Subject arranged in front of window and showing strong specular reflections.

Plate 23. With a polarizing filter adjusted to eliminate the reflections plus 3 stops more exposure.

Photos: E. S. Bomback.

such as glass, water, glossy paints, foliage and polished wood, where the maximum degree of polarization takes place at an angle of about 34° with the plane of the surface and diminishes to zero at 0° and 90°, and secondly, light from a clear blue sky at right angles to the direction of the sun diminishing to zero at 0° and 180° from the sun – see figs. 7.4 and 7.5.

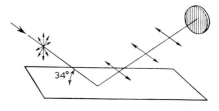

Fig. 7.4. Light reflected from a glossy non-metallic surface is strongly polarized at an angle of about 34° with the surface, and can be almost totally absorbed with a polarizing filter.

By using a polarizing filter such as the Kodak 'Pola' screen over the camera lens it is possible to control the amount of polarized light reaching the film, non-polarized light being partly transmitted as polarized light and partly non-selectively absorbed by an amount equal to a neutral density filter of 0·4. This absorption necessitates an increase of about 1½ stops in exposure. Thus in the case of specular reflections, those coming from an angle of about 34° can be totally eliminated, while others at greater or smaller angles are partially eliminated. With polarized sky-light the effect of prohibiting the polarized light is to darken the colour of the sky. It will also reduce the effect of haze mainly because of its polarizing properties, and also because it absorbs ultra-violet radiation.

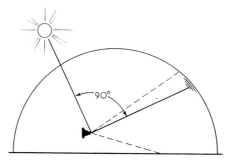

Fig. 7.5. Light from a blue sky is strongly polarized at an angle of 90° to a line between the sun and the camera. The effect of a polarizing filter is to darken the blue of the sky.

With colour photography the use of a polarizing filter may yield a substantial increase in colour saturation through the partial or total elimination of reflections, notably those caused by blue sky light. Examples of the use of polarizing filters are given on the facing page, plates 21 and 23.

8

Since the visual effect of a polarizing filter is very similar to its photographic effect, the best effect from any given viewpoint can be determined by rotating the filter while observing the subject until the correct position is found. The filter is then placed over the lens in this position. With a single lens reflex camera this can be done with the filter already placed over the camera lens.

Neutral-Density filters

These filters are non-selective and are used when it is desired to reduce the amount of light entering the lens by a definite ratio. For example we may wish to use a particular lens aperture under lighting conditions which require a smaller aperture even at the shortest shutter speed. This can easily occur when using High Speed Ektachrome film for outdoors under widely different lighting intensities. While a small aperture is often an advantage for 'grab' shots and candid portraits, since the greater depth of field allows for rough guesses in the focusing distance, more selective portraits benefit from a large aperture. By using a neutral-density of 0·9 it becomes possible to increase the aperture by 3 stops.

Kodak Neutral-Density filters are given in the table below and provide a range of filters from 0·1 to 2·0. Greater densities can be obtained by adding two or more filters together. Combinations can, if desired, be cemented together between glasses to form a single filter.

KODAK NEUTRAL-DENSITY FILTERS

ND. Filter No.	Density	Percentage Transmission	Factor
ND. 0·1	0·1	80	$1\frac{1}{4}$
ND. 0·2	0·2	63	$1\frac{1}{2}$
ND. 0·3	0·3	50	2
ND. 0·4	0·4	40	$2\frac{1}{2}$
ND. 0·5	0·5	32	3
ND. 0·6	0·6	25	4
ND. 0·7	0·7	20	5
ND. 0·8	0·8	16	6
ND. 0·9	0·9	13	8
ND. 1·0	1·0	10	10
ND. 2·0	2·0	1	100

Care and handling of filters and available forms

Kodak filters for photographic use in both the Wratten series and others, such as the 'CC' series, are available as unmounted gelatin squares, or in certain cases as gelatin cemented between glass of various qualities. The gelatin filters are lacquered for protection against damp and minor finger-marks, and used with reasonable care are quite suitable for experimental work and occasional use as correction or conversion filters. Inside its sealed envelope the filter is located in a paper folder one surface of which is printed with circles of various diameters to facilitate cutting. With lenses which may be taken apart, it is usually possible to place the filter inside the lens, otherwise some kind of mount, preferably with a deep recess, can be used to hold the filter in front of the lens. When quick changes between one filter and another are required in experimental work, an improvized mount having a slot of the kind shown in fig. 7.6 is easily made. If retained as squares the filters can be handled by the corners. Care should be taken not to handle the area used in front of the lens and also to protect it from moisture drops (rain, etc.). Dust should be removed with a fine anti-static brush. For experimental work concerned with colour balance, gelatin filters may be mounted between lantern-slide cover glasses for protection. This method is also suitable if filters, such as those of the 'CC' series, are to be used principally for viewing.

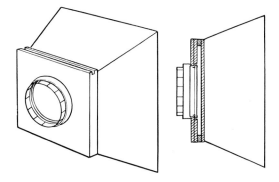

Fig. 7.6. Mount for holding 2-in. gelatin filters based on a Kodak Lens Attachment. It can be made from stout cardboard.

Mounted filters are obtainable in the following forms:

'*A*' *quality glass* – specially selected optical flats of the highest quality and recommended for work requiring maximum definition, especially when using long-focus or large-aperture lenses.

'*B*' *quality glass* – plane-parallel glass of sufficient accuracy for general photographic work.

'*Cine*' *quality glass* – specially selected 'B' glass of the highest quality.

Non-photographic quality glass – glass free from blemishes and suitable for visual work or use in front of light-sources.

Mounted filters in 'B' and 'Cine' quality glass are available from stock or may be ordered in a range of 'Kodisk' attachments and also with rim mounts. Filters in 'B' quality glass, but unmounted, are also available in 2 and 3 in. squares and in circles of 50·8 mm. either from stock or to special order.

Glass-mounted filters should be cared for in the same way as a lens, and should be stored in a dry place, as moisture can penetrate the gelatin at the edges and force the sandwich apart. Prolonged exposure to light should also be avoided, since, as with all dyes, the dyes used tend to fade.

8

Lighting Balance

ONE OF the principal technical difficulties of photography is that of representing in an acceptable manner the brightness or luminosity range of a subject which exceeds the recording capacity of a print. This is the more difficult – and complex – with colour photography, not only because the film has a more restricted exposure scale, but because satisfactory colour saturation is obtained over a comparatively narrow 'tone' range only. With lighter tones, colours tend to becomed 'washed-out' and at darker tones obscured with grey. To some extent the tone range of a colour print is extended if it is viewed in direct sunlight, the darker tones then becoming more luminous. This is also the case if a print is viewed by strong artificial light against a dark background, since it then more nearly approaches the luminosity of a projected transparency. Indeed one of the reasons why colour slides are so often preferred by the serious amateur is the much greater brightness range they offer when projected under ideal conditions. This greater brightness range extends as much to the highlights as it does to the darker tones and it becomes possible to represent brightnesses 'brighter' than white, as for example the sparkle of reflected sunlight on the sea as compared with the while sails of a yacht. It explains also why colour prints made from colour slides, which owe their attractiveness to strong lighting contrasts, are often disappointing.

However, this limitation affecting the print and to a lesser degree the colour slide need not be the cause of dissatisfaction or dismay on the part of the novice. On the contrary, it can offer a challenge to his skill and ingenuity, since in spite of these restrictions it is nevertheless possible to convey an effective impression of subjects of great brightness range. In fact the skill or artistic ability to achieve this is probably the most cogent argument that can be directed at painters and art critics who insist that photography is no more than a mechanical process of reproduction. There are, of course, many other valid arguments in support of photography as a form of artistic expression, but they are not relevant to our present chapter.

Brightness or luminosity range
This can be defined as the ratio of the lightest and darkest tones of the subject, and as a simple and convenient example we can take the black print on the white

paper of this book. Let us suppose the paper reflects 95 per cent of the light falling on it and the black print only 5 per cent: the brightness ratio is therefore 19:1. In this case, assuming the illumination is uniform, the brightness ratio is a characteristic of the subject and the subject can be described as one of 'high contrast'. If we make a drawing on a sheet of grey paper having a reflectance of 15 per cent, using white crayon with a reflectance of 45 per cent, then the subject brightness ratio is 3:1 and the subject can be described as one of 'low contrast'. At this stage of our discussion it is useful to note that differences in hue can present equally strong 'contrasts' and it is in this respect that colour photography differs essentially from black-and-white photography. Thus we may obtain a strong contrast by using red letters on a green background even though the two colours may have the same luminosity, and the brightness ratio is therefore zero. In a colour photograph this colour contrast is recorded, but in a black-and-white photograph the two colours would appear the same tone of grey, assuming that we use a well-balanced panchromatic film. However, we shall return to this aspect a little later.

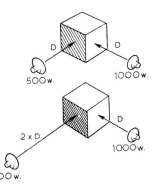

Fig. 8.1. Diagram to show the variation of lighting ratio with lamp wattage and distance. The upper cube shows a lighting ratio of 1 : 2. With the 500-watt lamp removed to twice the distance the ratio becomes 1 : 8.

If we now take a three-dimensional object such as a white cube placed edgewise, as in fig. 8.1, and light one side with a 500-watt lamp and the other with one of twice the wattage, both lamps being at equal distances from the surfaces they illuminate, we shall have a brightness ratio of 2:1. In this case we may also refer to it as a 'lighting ratio' of 2 : 1. By moving the smaller lamp to twice the distance, thereby reducing its intensity at the surface of the cube to one quarter, we shall increase the brightness or lighting ratio to 8 : 1. Alternatively if we paint this surface of the cube with grey paint having a reflectance only 25 per cent of that of the white surface keeping the two lamps at the same distance, we again obtain a brightness ratio of 8 : 1, but in this case it is the product of the tonal difference of the subject and the lighting ratio. If in addition to the grey surface we also move the smaller lamp to twice the distance, we shall build up a brightness ratio of 32 : 1.

From this it can be seen that the inherent brightness range of a subject in any one plane of uniform illumination remains constant, but may vary in different planes of illumination depending on the lighting ratio. In conditions under which there is complete control of lighting it is also possible in some cases to reduce the inherent brightness range. Thus in the simplified case of the cube with one surface white and the other grey, if the position of the two lamps is reversed, the grey surface being illuminated with twice the intensity of light, then the subject brightness range is reduced to 2 : 1. In normal subjects it is, however, unusual to find such a simple tone arrangement, the range from light to dark tones being distributed at random in all planes of the subject. Fortunately, subjects of average brightness range are within the recording capacity of a print and with plenty to spare in the case of colour slides. There is thus still some recording capacity left for variations in the intensity of lighting or, to put it more simply, in light and shade.

Lighting contrast

Unlike black-and-white photography, which depends a great deal on the interplay of light and shade, colour photography offers the very important contrast between one hue and another. This makes it possible to present a satisfactory picture at a brightness range of 1 : 1 and with uniform or completely 'flat' lighting. Such a subject, correctly exposed, can depict very satisfactory colour saturation in all regions of the spectrum. It is for this reason that 'colourful' subjects lit with frontal sunlight are usually the most admired by the casual viewer. It also explains why painters tend to make far more use of the interplay of colours than of light and shade.

The difficulty of depicting both colour and tonal difference does not arise until we begin to add the effect of light and shade. In other words it is the lighting contrast that is both the bane and delight of the outdoor photographer. To see why this is so, we must first decide what lighting ratios are acceptable with the more important classes of subject. To start with an extreme case, that of photographing a flat original such as a painting, we require completely uniform lighting. For portraits, flowers and close-ups generally, where the rendering of small differences or subtle shades of colour is important, a pleasing photograph may be obtained with a lighting contrast as low as $1\frac{1}{2}$: 1, with a ratio of 3 : 1 as the maximum desirable amount. With architectural subjects, where shape and form is often of greater interest than colour or detail, light ratios of 6 : 1 and greater may be acceptable. For certain kinds of indoor portraiture making use of window lighting or other so-called available-light sources, far greater lighting ratios can be tolerated if certain essential features are adequately illuminated, as for example, a profile or outline with the subject mainly in silhouette. The same applies to *contre-jour* subjects generally, though these are usually far more acceptable in a transparency than a print.

These lighting ratios take into account the fact that shadows appear more luminous in an original scene than in a photograph, and therefore to obtain an equivalent effect it is necessary to light the subject at a lower lighting ratio than would appear desirable. For this reason, until experience has been gained in the recognition of a suitable lighting balance, it is necessary to calculate or measure the lighting ratio.

Basis of lighting

A sound knowledge of lighting is without question the principal ingredient in successful studio photography, and although it is useful to read books on the subject based on the experience of other photographers, it is only by systematic, practical exercises in the use of lighting that the student can hope to become expert in the technique. While these lighting experiments need not deter the student from enjoying the more casual use of photography as a hobby, they will in the long run greatly increase the enjoyment of photography as a creative art. Of the various sources mentioned in the previous chapter, tungsten lamps of the photopearl type are probably most suitable. Although more expensive than photoflood lamps, their greater stability and much longer life make for better control and long term economy. Two such lamps with suitable stands and reflectors are sufficient to begin with. A third lighting unit either in the form of a small spotlight or a 250-watt reflector spotlamp will be useful for experiments in back-lighting.

Main or Key lighting

We are accustomed to the idea of a single main light-source in the form of the sun and also the idea of its light coming from an overhead direction. A single main light-source casts only one set of shadows, and their direction gives a direct indication of the position of the main light. Obvious though this may seem, it is worth stressing that by observing the angle of the shadows in a photograph it is possible to determine where the main light was placed.

Directional lighting is usually classified by the angle it makes with an imaginary line between camera and subject. Assuming we are lighting a sphere, this angle determines the extent of the shadow area in a photograph. If the light-source is strongly directional and parallel as with sunlight, or very nearly so as in the case of a focused spotlight, any shadow cast will be dense and have a sharp outline. On the other hand if the area of the light-source is relatively large compared with the subject and is also quite near the subject, the shadows will be diffused at the edges over an area called the penumbra and the total area in partial or total shadow will be larger. The use of still larger areas of main lighting, such as when using a small bank of lamps, carries this diffusion a stage further, but a similar effect may be obtained with a single light-source by the use of a diffusing screen of fairly large diameter placed between the lamp and the subject. Still greater diffusion can be obtained by directing the light-source on to a large reflector board (or wall) having a white matt surface. In this case the shadows may hardly be discernible, though it should still be obvious that the subject is lit more from one direction than any other.

As we pointed out in an earlier chapter, shadows are one of the 'clues' by which we perceive depth and solidity in a three-dimensional object, and since a photograph normally lacks binocular depth, the controlled use of shadows, often referred to as the 'modelling', can be a valuable means of representing the shape and roundness of a subject.

The direction or angle of the main light-source may be governed by the nature of the subject, the particular lighting effect it is desired to create, and the personal preference of the photographer. Perhaps the most common angle is one of about 35° in both a horizontal and vertical plane, see fig. 8.2, but it is far better for the student to try for himself a range of angles with a variety of different subjects.

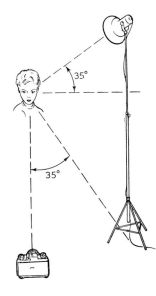

Fig. 8.2. A useful position for the main light is at a level of about 35° above the subject and an angle of 30-40° to the lens axis.

Supplementary or fill-in lighting

It is possible to light the subject with a single light-source and control the density of the shadows either by means of diffusers or reflectors. Indeed the effect desired may be achieved by using a single shaft of sunlight coming through a window, or a focused spotlight, as for example when the *motiv* of the photograph is the shadow rather than the object itself and also when it is desired to emphasize the texture of a surface rather than its colour. But in the case of portraits and other subjects where both modelling and colour are desired, then the shadows must be softened or lit to an extent which gives a lighting ratio of 3 : 1 or less. A simple and very satisfactory arrangement is that shown in fig. 8.3 where a single light-source is placed so as to illuminate one plane of the subject as well as a reflector which directs part of the light on to the shadow areas. The efficiency

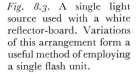

Fig. 8.3. A single light source used with a white reflector-board. Variations of this arrangement form a useful method of employing a single flash unit.

and effect of such a reflector depends on the nature of its surface, its size and distance from the subject. For example, a mirror will duplicate the quality of the main light-source and in the case of parallel light such as that of sunlight, will very nearly duplicate its intensity. However, with an artificial light-source the intensity of the reflected beam from a mirror follows the inverse square law of light propagation, see page 95. A polished metallic surface such as aluminium foil has in less degree the characteristics of a true mirror, and further diffusion at some sacrifice of efficiency will be obtained with a metallic surface having a satin or broken surface. Reflectors of coloured foil may also be useful for special lighting effects, see page 234. Totally diffuse light will be obtained with a matt-white surface, but to be effective the width of such a reflector must roughly equal the distance at which it is placed from the subject. Because of its large reflecting surfaces a room having white-washed walls makes an ideal 'studio' for a single light-source, for example, a single flash unit. The student is strongly advised to explore all possible angles of lighting making use of a single reflecting surface.

The use of a single light-source in a moderate-size room having walls of light colour (preferably white or light grey for colour work) may in itself create sufficient reflected light to be able to dispense with any additional reflector board, particularly if the lamp is placed well away from the subject. For small subjects a small tent may be used to similar effect, see pages 223 and 226.

But, of course, we shall soon exhaust the limitations of a single light-source, and greater manœuverability of the main light is possible when a second lighting unit is available as a supplementary or fill-in light. But at the same time this creates a danger of conflicting lights and double shadow effects. One way of avoiding this is to employ the second light-source as nearly as possible in line with the lens axis, thereby reducing any shadows to a minimum. Such an arrangement is shown in fig. 8.4 where two lamps of equal wattage and distance from the subject are placed one at 45° to the subject and one immediately behind and slightly above the camera. This arrangement also makes the maximum use

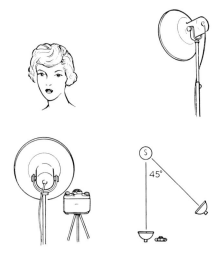

Fig. 8.4. A simple application of two lamps of equal wattage at an equal distance from the subject, which provides a lighting ratio of 1 : 2. The lamp near the lens axis acts as a general 'fill-in' light without casting shadows, while the second lamp acts as the main light.

of the total wattage of the two lamps and automatically provides a lighting ratio of 2 : 1 which is appropriate with a subject such as a portrait. The fill-in light may also take the form of a bank of lights or a single light with a diffuser so placed as to provide general frontal illumination. In this case the main light may be placed in any desired position. However, it is usually preferable to establish the location and effect of the main light before considering the need for additional fill-in lighting. If, from measurements with a light meter or previous experience, some additional illumination is needed for the shadows, it can be applied with a second lamp, preferable used with a diffusing screen, so placed that its light is restricted to the shadows. The ratio of this lamp with the main light can be roughly calculated on the basis of the inverse square law or an exposure meter may be used to measure the levels of illumination, see page 143. Care must be taken to avoid a second set of shadows, though if these only appear on the background, it is possible to eliminate them with a slightly different viewpoint or by increasing the distance between subject and background. If the background is to be lit separately or is of a fairly dark tone, the problem does not arise.

Back-lighting effects

Distinct from main lighting is the occasional use of controlled back-lighting (usually placed well above the subject) for providing outline and catch-lights in the hair, and subjects such as flowers, still life studies, close-ups of insects and the like. While a spotlight makes the ideal source, a reflector spotlamp or even a 250-watt household lamp well-hooded (see fig. 8.5) may be used as substitutes. With colour photography the intensity of this light should only be a little greater than that of the main light (far less than is permissible with black-and-white photography), otherwise these highlights will be 'burnt-out'.

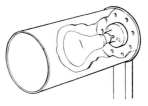

Fig. 8.5. A large cylindrical tin used as a hood for a 200-watt reflector spotlamp for use as back-lighting or hair-light. Holes in the base provide ventilation.

Lamp distance and covering power

As we have been discussing artificial light-sources it is important always to bear in mind the inverse square law of light propagation, since the eye has the tendency (unfortunate in photography) of equalizing brightness differences. This is particularly likely to occur with illumination falling on a background some distance behind the subject, the background appearing to be as well lit as the subject. However, a few simple calculations will demonstrate the extent of background fall-off. Let us suppose the main light is placed fairly close to the camera axis at a distance of 6 ft. from the subject and that it is also used to light a background a further 4 ft. away, i.e., a total distance of 10 ft. By squaring the two distances we get a lighting ratio of 100 : 36 or roughly 3 : 1 between the subject and background. If the background is required to be of the same lightness as the subject, it is clearly necessary to employ additional lighting for the background. It is worth noting that with a greater lamp distance, but the same relative positions of subject to background, the lighting ratio would be less. Thus with the lamp at 10 ft. from the subject the ratio becomes 196 : 100 or roughly 2 : 1. In some cases this might be acceptable.

This problem does not, of course, arise with sunlight outdoors or with a spotlight focused to give a parallel light beam. However, when a fairly large area of background requires to be illuminated, two well-shielded flood lamps, one on either side of the subject, will provide uniform illumination. Other methods of lighting a background are dealt with in Chapters 14 and 16.

Lamp reflector characteristics

The purpose of fitting a reflector behind a lamp is to increase the amount of light directed on to the subject, and a good reflector will more than double the effective illumination. However, certain flash units employ a polished metal reflector of such a shape as to concentrate the maximum amount of light at the most usual working distance. In this case they may be less efficient at other distances and even produce a central 'hot-spot'. Certain tungsten lamps, including Photoflood lamps, are available with internal reflectors and do not need an additional reflector. However, a large reflector is often preferable and its initial cost is soon offset by the purchase of cheaper non-reflector type lamps.

Reflectors for colour work should be of aluminium, preferably with a satin finish. White-painted reflectors are less efficient and tend to discolour. Multiple-lamp units and strip-lighting units may be lined with aluminium foil (which has first been crumpled) or painted white.

Sunlight as a main source

We can now return to the problem of sunlight or, to be exact, sunlight plus light from the sky, for in clear weather daylight consists of two different sources of light, one of strongly directional lighting and the other presenting a wide area of diffused lighting. Ignoring the difference in nature and colour quality, the ratio of intensity between the two light-sources varies from an extreme of 7 : 1 on a very clear day with a deep blue sky, to almost 1 : 1 in conditions of very strong haze or thin cloud which all but obscures the sun. An average ratio on a clear summer day in northern latitudes such as the British Isles is 5 : 1 and is considerably in excess of the ideal ratio for portraiture. But it offers another serious disadvantage, namely, that of causing dazzle to the eyes. For this reason it is often preferable to have the subject face away from the sun and use a reflector or fill-in flash to light the shadows. A reflector board presents no particular difficulties except perhaps that of locating it where it is most effective, but many photographers appear to have difficulty in applying the correct amount of fill-in light when using flash. For example, it is not uncommon to find the 'shadow' area of the subject almost as well-lit as the sunlit area, or parts of the subject which should naturally be in deep shadow unaccountably well-illuminated. In some cases the fill-in light is allowed to cast shadows of its own, thereby making it obvious to the viewer that some additional light-source has been used.

All Kodak colour films designed for daylight contain a simple guide for using fill-in flash in the instruction leaflet packed with the film. This information is also contained in the data sheets which form Appendix I of this book. However, there is another approach to the problem of achieving a proper lighting balance, namely, that of making use of the guide number given for calculating the flash exposure in a moderate-size room having reasonably light walls and ceiling. The same guide number used for outdoor photography at night would give at least 1 stop under-exposure owing to the absence of reflected light from walls and ceiling. Used for the shadow area of a sunlit subject it gives roughly 1 stop under-exposure and a lighting ratio of about 2 : 1. All that is necessary, then, is to divide the guide number by the lens aperture being used to find the distance at which the flash should be fired from the subject. If, in practice this is ound to be too much fill-in, the light can be further reduced by increasing the flash distance, or, if this is not convenient, by using a diffuser in front of the flash lamp. Lacking a proper diffuser, a clean pocket handkerchief placed in front of the lamp will reduce the light by about half.

Restricted daylight – outdoors and indoors

Extreme lighting contrasts may be encountered in narrow streets and alleys, under archways and balconies and other restricted locations which are partly lit with sunlight but otherwise receive little or no light from the sky. This applies also to interiors receiving an area of sunlight from a window. Here again the eye tends to equalize or at least substantially decrease brightness differences and it requires the impartiality of a light meter to appreciate just how great the actual brightness differences are. Such measurements may reveal a lighting contrast as high as 32 : 1 from readings taken off a grey card placed, firstly, to receive direct window light and then in a corner remote from the window. Although the lighting contrast will be lower when the window receives only light from the sky, it may still be in excess of the recording capacity of a colour film.

There are a number of solutions to this problem of excessive lighting contrast. Firstly, it is possible to confine the field of view to an area comparatively evenly illuminated, as for example in portraiture by placing the subject so as to receive direct light from a window. Reflectors may be used to illuminate darker areas, or if there is a broad shaft of sunlight, this may be used indirectly by means of a large reflector. One or more layers of muslin over a sunlit window will give a softer and more manageable lighting. Some form of supplementary lighting may be used, e.g. blue flashbulbs, and electronic flash. Interiors with light-coloured walls are generally more suitable for indoor portraits, and anyone planning a daylight studio should paint the walls and ceiling white. Practical aspects of indoor portraits with daylight are dealt with in Chapter 14.

Lighting Balance and Exposure

We have deliberately ignored reference to exposure in this chapter until now, because to a large extent 'correct' exposure pre-supposes a suitable balance between light and shade. Indeed the experienced professional, and particularly in the field of motion picture work, thinks in terms of lighting rather than exposure, and very often lights his scene to a constant exposure level. However the 'mechanics' of exposure and methods of assessing exposure are dealt with in the next chapter.

9

Assessment of Exposure

THE OVERALL sensitivity of a film intended for exposure in a camera i
commonly known as its 'speed', though various other terms, such as 'exposure
index', 'meter rating' and the like are or have been applied in attempts to find
some more specific definition. However the term 'speed' has recently received
official recognition by both the British Standards Institution and the American
Standards Association, and we may therefore use the term without reservation
Various methods have been devised for specifying the speed of black-and-white
films and each method has its own numerical values for expressing the speed
Indeed since Hurter and Driffield began their pioneer work in the sensitometry
of photographic materials towards the end of the last century, few aspects of
photography have received more attention. The system devised by these two
workers enjoyed the longest use and was not finally abandoned until the 1930s
when working conditions made the H.D. system outmoded and the steadily
increasing sensitivities of photographic materials made 'H & D' numbers
unwieldy. Today they would be far more so, and to express the speed of a modern
'high speed' film would require five digits, e.g. the H & D speed of Royal-X Pan
film would be of the order of 40,000. During the 1940s a semi-international
speed system was devised using the term 'exposure index' and based on a
fractional gradient criterion, which is itself related to practical camera tests to
establish the minimum exposure to give an acceptable print, (British Standard
1380 : 1947). The British Standards Institution employed primarily logarithmic
exposures indices, and the American Standards Association primarily
arithmetical exposure indices, though both standards permitted the use of both
kinds of speed scales. The former indices are expressed with the abbreviation
B.S. log, and the latter, which have perhaps become better known, with the
abbreviation ASA or ASA/B.S.

Speed system for colour film

However, the ASA exposure indices seem to suffer from the same defect a
H & D numbers, for we have already reached the stage where four digits are
needed to express the speed of the existing high-speed black-and-white films
For this and other reasons a new additive system of speed numbers has put in it.

appearance. This system differs from the former in that the criterion is based upon a fixed density above fog, the development conditions being arranged to yield a fixed contrast. However, these additive speed values are a development of the exposure value system which we shall be dealing with later in this chapter. Each number represents a factor of 2, and a difference of, say, 4 in speed values represents an arithmetical difference of $2 \times 2 \times 2 \times 2$ which equals $\times 16$ in speed. Kodak have already introduced these numbers in the instruction leaflets packed with colour films as a speed value following the stroke after the ASA speed number. Thus the speed of Kodachrome II is given as $25/3°$, the first number being the ASA arithmetic speed and the second the additive speed value.

But in fact until 1961 none of these speed systems applied to colour materials and the first attempt to give ASA speeds for reversal colour materials was embodied in the American Standard PH2-21-1961. Because of this B.S. or ASA exposure indices or speed values have been given in the form of settings suitable for use with exposure meters and automatic camera settings. At the most, speed numbers are merely means of defining the actual sensitivity of a film and could be determined with sufficient practical accuracy with a range of test exposures and the cost of a single spool of film.

What really matters to the photographer is that a particular film such as Kodachrome has a constant sensitivity to light, and that given a certain amount of light, or exposure to light, will produce a transparency of excellent projection quality. This, in fact, is what is meant by 'correct' exposure. Owing to the adaptability of the eye to different intensity levels, the non-technical user may not always realize that the sensitivity of a colour film is a fixed characteristic.

Subject brightness range and exposure

The brightness range of an average outdoor scene may be assumed to be of the order of 30 : 1 or in terms of a logarithmic exposure scale to $1 \cdot 3$ log. E. As the exposure scale of a film exceeds this amount, it is possible to record the total brightness range over a certain range of exposures and this range is referred to as the exposure latitude of the film. The exposure latitude falls with increasing brightness range and at higher ranges the available exposure scale may become fully absorbed by the brightness range of the subject. With still greater brightness ranges the film will be incapable of recording the total range. This is shown diagrammatically in fig. 9.1 for a typical panchromatic film. The situation is less simple for a negative colour film since it embodies three separate emulsions, one making a record of the blue image, one the green image and one the red image. Typical curves of a film exposed with a neutral scale are shown in fig. 9.2, from which it may be deduced that it has a latitude of about $0 \cdot 9$ log. E which is equivalent to three stops. This in fact is born out in practice with a film such as Kodacolor. In other words negatives receiving up to three stops more than the minimum 'correct' exposure will still give an acceptable print. The position with a reversal colour film is far more complex because the process embodies both the negative and the positive stage and offers no means of adjusting the overall negative density to a required positive density. In this strict sense of the term 'exposure latitude', a reversal film may be said to have no exposure latitude at all. Thus if we expose a negative colour film to a standard subject colour prints of roughly equal density could be obtained from negatives exposed over a range of 4 successive stops, for example, f/4, f/5·6, f/8 and f/11. With a reversal film transparencies of equal density demand the same exposure.

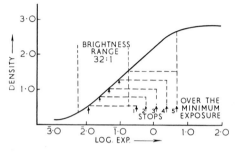

Fig. 9.1. Characteristic curve of typical negative film showing the region of the exposure scale used by a subject-brightness range of 1 : 32 (equal to log. 1·5). It can be seen that up to five stops over the minimum exposure can be given while still accommodating the brightness range on the useful portion of the curve.

However, this does not mean that a reversal film cannot tolerate deviation in exposure, but rather that some variation in overall density is acceptable depending on the subject and the method of viewing the transparency. With subjects of average brightness range, this kind of exposure latitude can be said to amount to 1 stop under-exposure and ½ stop over-exposure. However, as we have already seen, a transparency viewed by projection is able to reproduce a greater range of brightnesses than a print, and it therefore allows a wider choice in subject brightness range. It is one thing for a negative to record a greater-than-average brightness range and quite a different thing to reproduce this in the print. In black-and-white photography there are various ways of tackling this problem. We can develop the film to a low gamma (contrast), we can print the negative on a 'softer' grade of printing paper, or we can resort to shading o. dodging while exposing the print – holding back the lighter areas of the negative so as to obtain more exposure through the denser portions. Only the latter method is as yet available to the colour worker, and this only if he makes his own prints, see Chapter 25. But as we have shown in the previous chapter the correct approach is to adjust the brightness range of the subject before making the exposure, and this of course, holds equally for reversal films.

Plate 24. The shadows cast on a landscape by broken cloud tend to appear darker in a photograph than to the eye, assuming the exposure has been adjusted for the sunlit areas. In the example given, a moment was chosen when the shadows formed a natural 'frame' for the village.

Plate 25. The back-lighting effect has given an otherwise unspectacular landscape a remarkable feeling of depth. The sun was in fact shining through a hole in the clouds and with a wider angle lens the picture would have been more effective.

Plate 24. South Harting, Sussex.

Plate 25. Landscape in Provence.

Photos: E. S. Bomback.

Plate 26. Morning alarm
The reward for bein,
woken early was a fin
back-lit subject in whicl
the shadow patterns giv
depth and interest to th
picture.

Plate 27. At Whipsnade. Th
back-lighting shows up th
form and texture of th
antlers and the fine ey
lashes. The loss of colour i
the shadows can be judge
from the portion of the bac
in full sunlight.

Plate 28. Drying fish. Take
against the light the tran
lucent nature of the subje
loses nothing by way
colour. Flowers and oth
translucent subjects a
also suitable for this trea
ment.

Kodachrome transparencies
E. S. Bomback.

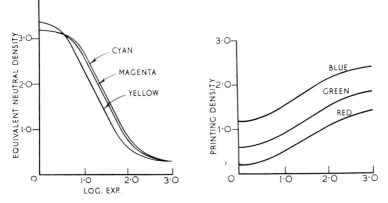

Fig. 9.2. Typical characteristic curves of a reversal colour film, and a negative colour film incorporating a coloured coupler. The high blue and green densities are due to the colours of the couplers.

Correct exposure

We have arrived at the question 'What is correct exposure?' For a black-and-white film the answer is fairly simple: minimum correct exposure is the least exposure which will permit a print of excellent quality to be obtained. Further exposure increases the density of the negative and with it graininess of the image, light dispersion within the emulsion (at the cost of definition) and the printing time. Such a criterion can be used for a negative colour film, with the reservation that some degree of over-exposure is preferable to under-exposure. Thus in a case where an accurate assessment of the subject brightness is impossible, it is wiser to give a somewhat fuller exposure rather than run the risk of under-exposure. Indeed the time-honoured rule for exposing black-and-white negative material, namely, expose for the shadows, holds good for colour negative materials providing the shadows are not too dense.

With reversal films, correct exposure depends somewhat on the use to which a transparency is to be put, whether intended for viewing, photomechanical reproduction, the making of duplicates and so on. If intended for viewing on an illuminated panel, the desirable overall density will also depend on the intensity of the viewing panel and the level of the surrounding illumination. Similarly with projection viewing; the density of the colour slide may be chosen to suit particular viewing conditions. In general, transparencies intended for reproduction or duplication benefit from $\frac{1}{2}$ stop less exposure than that desirable for normal projection viewing, especially when using a high-wattage projector for home viewing.

What we have just said applies to 'average' subjects: the level of exposure for subjects which exceed the exposure scale of the colour film, and to some extent subjects having a low brightness range, will depend on the kind of effect

139

sought by the photographer. In the first case – high brightness range – there is, theoretically at least, no specific level of correct exposure. We may take the case of a landscape at sunset where the camera field of view includes some objects in the foreground against a vividly lit and colourful sky background. We are able in an actual scene to appreciate both detail and colour in the foreground objects as well as the brilliance of the sky, but photographically the brightness range exceeds the recording capacity of the film, and the most we can do is to record a part of the brightness range. Since it is usually the colours of the sky which we most desire to capture, it is logical to base the exposure on the sky in such a way as to obtain the maximum saturation of colour in this region of the subject. By doing so we inevitably under-expose the foreground, but since it is æsthetically acceptable to have a dark foreground, and may in fact be preferable, the restriction imposed by the colour film is not a serious one. In general this applies also to *contre-jour* (against-the-light) subjects. However it is instructive to make a series of exposures of such a subject at intervals of 1 stop, based on a mean exposure. It may well be found that exposures 1 and 2 stops greater than the mean, and 1 and 2 stops lower also give acceptable, though different 'versions' of the subject. In the case of a sunset the results may well cover apparent stages of a normal sunset taken at, say, intervals of 5 min.

A similar range of possible exposures also exists with a subject of low brightness range, particularly if it is rich in colour contrasts. We can in fact 'create' a subject having a very low brightness range such as that in plate 73, which relies mostly on its colour contrasts. In this case the range of possible exposures may exceed 5 stops, the effect of decreasing exposure being to increase both density and colour saturation. But since the three emulsion layers may react somewhat differently to differences in exposure, the relative colour values may also vary, see page 118.

Although reversal colour films have little exposure latitude, it does not follow that they are difficult to expose with subjects of average brightness range and with certain 'standardized' forms of lighting, such as sunlight and flash when the direction of the light is within 45° of the lens axis. The reason is that the exposure is based on the lighter tones of the subject – the highlights rather than the shadows. Given constant illumination these tones remain roughly constant, and it is the darker tones that will vary according to the lighting contrast. Any attempt to base exposure on the shadows, as when using negative materials, will usually result in over-exposed, burnt-out highlights.

Exposure controls

Exposure is the product of a certain intensity of light acting on the sensitive silver halides of the emulsion for a certain length of time. Thus we have the simple equation:

$$Exposure = Intensity \times Time$$

It was discovered very early in the history of photography that the density obtained for any particular film and developing process was a function of the exposure, independent of the actual intensity and time. This became known as the reciprocity law of Bunsen and Roscoe and is the basis of exposure control by means of a variable lens aperture and variable-speed shutter. Actually, it has since been established that this law does not hold good for every emulsion, but we shall deal with this a little later. For the moment it is sufficient to note that an exposure resulting from 1 unit of light for 1/10 sec. will produce the same density as one resulting from 10 units of light for 1/100 sec.

We have therefore two means of controlling the amount of light action on the film, which as we have seen requires to be a constant – or very nearly so – for a reversal colour film of any given speed. The intensity of light reaching the film may be controlled in one of three ways:

(1) By means of a variable lens diaphragm
(2) By means of a neutral-density filter
(3) By changing the level of illumination

The lens diaphragm offers the most convenient method, and for manual control is calibrated in 'stops' or f/numbers based on a factor of 2. The f/number itself is the ratio of the optical diameter of the lens to its focal length, and represents a constant light-passing capacity for all lenses, irrespective of their focal length – except for the loss of light by absorption and reflection, which can be abnormally high in complex lenses. Except for the maximum aperture, which may occasionally give an irregular value such as f/3·5 or f/1·9, f/numbers usually follow the series f/1·4, f/2, f/2·8, f/4 and so on to f/numbers as 'small' as f/64, depending on the focal length of the lens. An alternative series once in vogue on the Continent and therefore to be found on many pre-war lenses differs from this by about 1/3 stop – f/1·6, f/2·2, f/3·2, f/4·5, f/6·3 and so on.

The diaphragm control of a lens may be fitted with click stops at each full f/number setting, or, with shutters embodying an exposure value scale, with click stops at ½ stop intervals. Cameras embodying a semi-automatic or fully-automatic exposure control normally make use of the lens diaphragm to compensate for differences in subject brightness and may dispense entirely with f/numbers.

One disadvantage of using the lens diaphragm as an exposure control is that it may sometimes be better employed as a means of controlling depth of field (see page 43). Assuming that it is not possible or convenient to make the adjustment in terms of the time of exposure, then we can resort to the use of a neutral-density filter. These filters are non-selective in their absorption and are available in a range equivalent to adjustments of 1/3 stop up to a density of 1·0 – see page 122.

The third method of controlling the intensity of the exposure is often possible when using artificial light-sources. An increase in intensity to enable a larger stop to be used may be achieved either by increasing the total wattage or by reducing the lamp-to-subject distance: the reverse effect is obtained by increasing the lamp distance or reducing the wattage. With simple cameras having a fixed lens stop and shutter speed, photography is restricted to a very limited subject brightness unless either of the last two methods is possible, or, with very much lower brightnesses, 'timed' exposures can be given.

The second variable in the exposure equation is that of time and most cameras make provision for this by means of a variable-speed shutter. The available speed range varies somewhat with the type and 'vintage' of the shutter. Thus the current series for diaphragm shutters of the Compur or Prontor type is based on a factor of 2 – 1, 1/2, 1/4, 1/8, 1/15, 1/30, 1/60, 1/125, 1/250 and 1/500 sec. Previously a somewhat irregular series was used which included 1/2, 1/5, 1/10, 1/25, 1/50 and 1/100, the change to a uniform series being made with the introduction of the exposure value system. In this the lens diaphragm and shutter speed controls are reciprocally coupled to give a constant exposure, as for example in the following combinations:

f/2	f/2·8	f/4	f/5·6	f/8	f/11	f/16	f/22
1/500	1/250	1/125	1/60	1/30	1/15	1/8	1/4

The appropriate exposure value is obtained from a table or from the scale of an exposure meter, and is then set on an exposure value scale on the shutter. The exposure value system uses a series of numbers – 1, 2, 3, 4, 5, 6, etc. – each of which represents a factor of 2. In exposure assessment the system takes into account the 'light value' or overall brightness of the subject and the speed of the film. Each number defines a level of exposure which can be obtained with various combinations of aperture and shutter speed. For example, an E.V. of 13 gives the combinations:

1/15 at f/22, 1/30 at f/16, 1/60 at f/11 and so on.

The new additive speed system provides a speed number which, when added to the 'light value' of the subject, gives the exposure value.

Reciprocity failure

The interchangeability of the factors of intensity and time holds good for the normal range of intensities, and for colour films it is usual to adjust the balance of the film for an exposure time most likely to be used with a specific kind of light-source. Thus, daylight films are balanced to give their rated speed and best colour rendering at 1/50 sec. Loss of speed may occur with considerably longer or shorter exposure times needed to compensate for differences in intensity. Normally the photographer is only concerned with lower-than-normal intensities, which may result in loss of speed. To compensate, it then becomes necessary to increase the exposure time beyond that required by the reciprocity law. A typical set of curves illustrating reciprocity law failure is shown fig. 9.3.

Aids to assessing exposure

These may take the form of guides and exposure tables such as those given in the instruction leaflet packed with Kodak colour films, see also table on page 147, or somewhat more elaborately as exposure calculators which embody a greater range of variables, and simplify arriving at the final answer, a typical example being the Johnson's Exposure Calculator. Used with reasonable care such aids to exposure will yield a high percentage of successful exposures. Their weakness lies in the difficulty of specifying different intensity levels of daylight with such terms as 'Hazy Sun', 'Cloudy-bright', 'Cloudy-dull' or, with artificial light, in allowing for differences in the efficiency of lamp reflectors. A more positive aid is

Fig. 9.3. Typical reciprocity curves in which log. exposure is plotted against log. intensity for different densities. The situation is more complicated with colour film since there are three different emulsion layers.

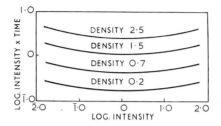

that based on the use of a light-measuring meter, in its photographic form more commonly referred to as an exposure meter. Such an instrument makes use of the electric current generated as the result of light action on a photocell – the current generated being proportional to the intensity of light falling on the cell. The current is measured by a micro-ammeter and the scale of this is calibrated in units of light (as in the case of the Weston Master meter), in exposure values, or in some cases purely arbitary numbers which are then applied to a calculator embodied on the meter. When such meters are built into the camera on a semi-automatic exposure basis the deflection of the needle is merely related to a datum point, the movement of a wheel necessary to bring the needle on to the datum point being coupled directly to the lens diaphragm. With automatic cameras the actual needle may be replaced by a self-adjusting stop or similar device which adjusts the exposure according to the amount of light received by the photocell.

Use of exposure meters

The most common method is to direct the meter 'window' towards the subject so as to measure the total reflected light. Such a reading is known as a reflected-light reading and works well in practice providing certain precautions are taken. The reflected-light method relies on the fact that the light reflected from an average subject receiving mainly frontal lighting is roughly the same. However, if the distribution of light and dark tones departs radically from the average, as for example when a relatively small, light-toned object is set against a dark background, the reading is representative more of the background than the object of principal interest and the meter would indicate too much exposure. A reverse arrangement of tone would result in too little exposure, and this may also happen when the acceptance angle of the meter is greater than that of the lens and includes a large area of sky-light. In these circumstances it is preferable to take outdoor readings with the meter tilted some 10° or 15° downwards. It may also happen that the meter reading has been influenced by a large area of dark foreground (as when standing in the shadow of a building to take a scene which is in full sunlight), and in this case leads to over-exposure.

The danger from occasional errors of this sort tends to be greater with semi-automatic and fully-automatic cameras, since the tendency is to rely on the setting given by the meter while viewing the subject through the viewfinder (where in fact the needle and datum point for the meter may be situated). In the case of a subject posed against a background of widely differing tone, it is necessary to take the reading near enough to exclude most of the background, or to rely on a reading taken from a substitute surface.

Fig. 9.4. White or grey card used in front of subject, facing the camera lens, as a means of obtaining a meter reading. Care must be taken to avoid any shadows from meter or hand falling on the card.

The use of a key-tone or grey card is often preferred by the experienced worker as it is less open to error. A card having a reflectance of 18 per cent or 1/5 that of a perfectly white surface is very suitable for colour work with reversal films. This can be obtained by trial-and-error measurements with a light meter of a selection of grey cards. The card should have a matt surface (to avoid the possible danger of specular reflections off a shiny surface) and be large enough to permit he meter to be held at a distance sufficient to avoid its own shadow being thrownton to the card. A size of 10 × 8 in. is suggested, and for convenience of carryin g it may be cut in half, width-wise, and hinged with adhesive plastic tape so that it can be folded and carried in the pocket. The reading should be taken with the card held as nearly in front of the subject as possible and facing at right angles to the camera, see fig. 9.4. A white card may be used in a similar way (a clean pocket handkerchief will do for lack of something better), but in this case the reading will represent only the highlights of the subject and it is necessary to increase the indicated exposure by 4 to 5 times depending on how 'white' the substitute surface is. This is equivalent to an increase of about 2 stops. If a succession of white-card readings is to be made, it may be more convenient to reduce the speed setting for the film being used to 1/5. For example, if Kodachrome II were being used, the speed scale of the meter may be set to 5 ASA instead of 25 ASA: in this case the white-card reading can be used without further modification.

A rather different method of using an exposure meter is that of reading the light coming from the principal source of illumination, pointing the meter *towards* the location of the camera from the point of view of the subject. When using a reflection-type meter it is necessary to fit a special diffuser over the window, which has the effect of cutting down the light reaching the photocell to about 1/10. Such a method goes by the name 'incident-light' reading, and has been both commended and disparaged by the expert. It is commended on the grounds that the reading gives a true indication of the intensity of light falling on the subject, and disparaged on the grounds that it takes no account of the reflection characteristics or overall tone of the subject. Perhaps the best compromise to the meter user is to take both a reflection and incident light reading with a subject of unusual tone distribution.

With subjects of greater-than-normal brightness range it may be useful to take two reflected-light readings, one of the brightest tones and one of the darkest. A compromise exposure can then be made at a mean level. Indeed, an exposure meter may be as useful for achieving a correct lighting balance, as for assessing the correct exposure level.

Calibration of exposure meters

While the manufacturers of exposure meters take care to see they are properly adjusted when leaving the factory, like all delicate instruments they are liable to damage or maladjustment in the course of time. Any new meter or newly-acquired second-hand meter (now commonly acquired as a built-in component of a camera) should be checked against a reliable meter or, failing this, against recommendations given in the exposure guide packed with a colour film. Should there be some disagreement between the exposure guide and the meter on an average subject in sunlight, it is almost certain to be the meter at fault, and a few test exposures are recommended giving 1 and possibly 2 stops more and less than that indicated by the meter. Should in fact the meter given consistently high or low readings, then the error can be adjusted by changing the speed setting. For example if the meter indicates 1 stop more than is necessary, the ASA setting can be doubled, and for Kodachrome II Film a setting of 50 ASA used in place of one of 25. With an automatic camera such an error will not be apparent until after the first film has been exposed and processed.

Exposure photometers

A photometer is an instrument for measuring light intensity, and usually functions by comparing the intensity of the light to be measured with a standard intensity of known brightness. One of these instruments designed specifically for the needs of the photographer concerned with critical lighting problems is the S.E.I. Photometer. This instrument permits the user to determine the brightness of small areas of the subject by comparison with a small internal light-source which is itself maintained at a constant output by means of a photocell 'zero adjuster'. By a system of neutral-density filters it is possible to take readings over a brightness range of a million to one.

Trial-and-error exposures

In spite of every kind of exposure aid yet made available to the photographer, there remain certain kinds of subject or lighting conditions which can only be satisfactorily resolved by the time-honoured method of trial-and-error. This method is sometimes referred to as 'bracketing exposures' and is based on the principle of giving one or more exposures at 1 or ½ stop intervals greater and less than an exposure made at the estimated correct exposure. The number of exposures given and the intervals between the exposures depend very much on whether the estimate is based on a meter reading, some kind of existing guide, such as that in the table below, or is merely an inspired guess. Thus in dealing with the finer aspects of lighting and colour rendering in *contre-jour* subjects, two additional exposures one at 1 stop more and the other at 1 stop less than the mean exposure indicated by an exposure meter would be sufficient. On the other hand, in establishing exposure conditions for first experiments in photo-microscopy, a much larger range would be needed, though it would be cheaper to establish the approximate exposure level with a black-and-white film of similar speed rating.

It is usually well worth the expenditure of extra material to make such trial exposures whenever undertaking work of an experimental nature, whether it be of a technical kind or purely 'artistic'. If transparencies are to be made for both projection and duplication (and also reproduction) bracketed exposures at ½ stop intervals will supply both needs. Other aspects of exposure are discussed in later chapters dealing with the application of colour photography.

SUGGESTED EXPOSURE AT NIGHT

Times in seconds based on lens aperture of f/2·8

Subject	32–40 ASA	64–80 ASA	125–160 ASA
Brightly-lit street scenes	1/2	1/4	1/8
Neon and other electric signs	1/15	1/30	1/60
Well-lit shop windows	1/8	1/15	1/30
Floodlit buildings	4	2	1
Interiors such as milkbars, departmental stores, etc.	1/8	1/15	1/30
Average domestic lighting – fairly close to lamp	1/4	1/8	1/15
Circus ring, theatres with brightly-lit stage ..	1/15	1/30	1/60
Bonfires, campfires, etc.	1/15	1/30	1/60

Note: It is preferable to photograph street scenes, floodlit buildings, bonfires and other outdoor subjects of a similar nature at dusk while there is still sufficient daylight to give some detail to the background.

146

DAYLIGHT EXPOSURES WITH SHUTTER SPEEDS OF 1/100 – 1/125 sec.
(Exposure values are given in heavy type)

Film	Type	Speed ASA*	Bright or Hazy Sun (distinct shadows) See Note 1	Weak Hazy Sun (soft shadows)	Cloudy Bright (no shadows)	Cloudy Dull or Open Shade
			EV	EV	EV	EV
Kodachrome II Kodachrome II	Daylight Type A with No. 85	25/3°	13 f/8	12 f/5·6	11 f/4	10 f/2·8
Ektachrome E–3	Daylight	50/4°				
Ektachrome – X Kodachrome – X Kodacolor – X	Daylight Daylight Daylight or Flash	64/4° 64/4° 64/4°	14 f/11	13 f/8	12 f/5·6	11 f/4
Ektacolor Professional	Type S	80/4·5°	15 f/16	14 f/11	13 f/8	12 f/5·6

WITH SHUTTER SPEEDS OF 1/200 – 1/250 sec.
(with focal-plane shutters use ½-stop larger aperture at f/6·3 or smaller)

High Speed Ektachrome	Daylight	160/5·5°	16 f/16	15 f/11	14 f/8	13 f/4·5

* ASA figures in degrees are speed values for new additive exposure system.

Notes:
(1) In bright or hazy sun with subjects on light sand or snow give ½ to 1 stop less than for average subject.
(2) Dark scenes (foliage, clothing, etc.) give ½ stop more. Light scenes and distant views give ½ stop less.
(3) Nearby subjects, side-lighting or back-lighting give ½ to 1 stop more.
(4) Restricted shade (in narrow streets) give 1 to 2 stops more than open shade.
(5) Winter in the U.K. and similar latitudes give 1 stop more.
(6) Period between 1 and 2 hours after sunrise and from 2 to 1 hours before sunset give 1 stop more.

10

Pictorial Aspects of Photography

IN CONSIDERING the pictorial aspects of photography it is necessary first to distinguish between the photograph that attempts accurately to depict the original scene, person or object – and from a technical viewpoint this is by far the most difficult to achieve – and the photograph that endeavours to create some effect, either by way of suppressing some parts of the scene, by characterization in a portrait (usually by some technique of lighting), or idealizing or glamorizing a person or object through association with some intrinsically attractive or desirable situation. In the first case we are concerned with truth and fact: in the latter only half-truth, the rest being imagination or fantasy. Nowhere better than in the field of advertising can we find more potent examples of the use of effect, or more skilful examples of the photographer's art. And it must be admitted that to a major degree the advertiser has become the principal patron of the arts. This is meant in no derogatory sense since we have only to cite the case of British Railways to realize how many painters have been given the chance to 'interpret' and perhaps idealize the British countryside. It is perhaps worth noting that the greater freedom of the painter to omit unwanted detail indeed to glamorize reality, has put the photographer at a disadvantage in respect to this particular 'client'. The needs of the country-dweller for a telephone, electricity and television take little account of the problems of photography.

It is instructive for the student intending to make a profession of photography to make a frequent and systematic study of glossy magazines, as much for the photographs employed for advertising, as those of a purely editorial nature. Indeed even the latter may be found to be connected indirectly with advertising since the cost of making and printing colour illustrations often exceeds the editorial budget.

One of the most commonly used methods of enhancing the value of a commodity is to associate it with the most desirable assets of society. Feminine beauty clearly ranks highest on the list, and skill in portraiture may often be as important as the ability to photograph a tablet of soap, a camera, or a car. 'Gracious living' in a society based on tradition and the stately homes of England comes a good second best and may be applied equally to brands of food, cigarettes or drinks. But we can safely leave it to the reader to compile his own lists

148

dding merely the hope that the colour illustrations of the present book may be
s best advertisement.

Decorative photography

ncreasing use has been made in recent years of photo-murals, often of a scale
arge enough to suggest an actual countryside. It may well be that with the
increasing availability of colour print materials, much more use will be made of
the decorative kind of photograph. Colour photography already has a major
take in the field of calendars, Christmas and greeting cards, postcards and the
rochures of travel agencies. And some very fine child and animal portraits are
to be found on the boxes of well-known brands of chocolates and biscuits. But so
ar, little advantage has been taken of the more abstract possibilities of photo-
raphy, partly because abstract art is considered a field of the painter, and partly
ecause photographers themselves tend to be recorders of existing themes rather
han creators of original designs.

Portraiture

t is probably in the field of portraiture that photography has achieved its greatest
ppeal and highest distinction. And this, moreover, in terms of black-and-white
ather than colour photography. No manual artist can hope to compete with
he lightning speed of a camera or draw with such linear accuracy as that of a
ens. Before the advent of photography it was only the more wealthy who could
fford to commission a portrait: today it is difficult to escape the privilege, even
f it be no more than a passport portrait. Standards and 'fashions' in photographic
ortraiture have varied a great deal in the hundred odd years it has been
ractised, though it is interesting to note that very fine work was done towards
he end of the last century at a time when the equipment and materials were still
elatively crude. Colour photography is perhaps still too young to have developed
ny distinctive styles except in the field of 'glamour' portraiture connected with
he film industry and fashion world. Being a more realistic medium it is also more
ifficult to impose a distinctive and personal style or finish to the photograph.

Pictorial photography

Undoubtedly the greatest attraction of colour photography is that it offers a
relatively simple medium for anyone with the urge to create pictures but neither
he flair nor time for using paints. In an age when the creative urge is becoming
teadily more frustrated, photography has grown increasingly popular as a hobby
or people of all ages and professions. This indeed is the true amateur photography, the taking of pictures for the satisfaction it gives to the photographer and
he pleasure it can give to others. For the most part such photography takes the
orm of 'capturing' or recording scenes or objects of natural beauty, and to a
arge extent this is also what the painter has done – at least until it became
apparent that the camera could do as well or better. The 'art' of such

149

photography is basically one of selection, of choosing the right lighting conditions, of fitting the chosen subject matter into the format imposed by the camera. In this sense a photograph embodies an element of personal expression which varies with the taste and feeling of the photographer. It is in this field that colour photography has opened new vistas, has removed, as it were, the monochromatic spectacles of black-and-white photography and revealed nature in its full richness of colour. It has been said that the painter Turner discovered the sunset and it is equally apt to say that the colour photographer has rediscovered it!

Exhibitions

The testing ground for the pictorial photographer who desires the judgement and approval of his fellow workers may begin in the local camera club and finish in international exhibitions such as those of the Royal Photographic Society or the Photographic Society of America. Recognition for outstanding merit is given to members of such societies in the form of associateships or fellowships, medals and certificates.

Aspects of pictorial composition

Much has been written about the rules of photographic composition. In simple language 'composition' is the fitting of the subject matter in the frame area of a picture. There is necessarily a strong personal element in the way this is done and the 'rules' are more often flouted than honoured. However, it is useful to mention some aspects of composition for the relative newcomer to photography. Firstly, the centre of interest of a picture should preferably not occupy the centre of the area it occupies. It can be somewhat to the left or right, and may appear more natural if there is some kind of 'lead-in' such as a road, path or low wall. With a landscape it is usually better not to have the horizon across a line dividing the picture into halves: depending on the nature of the subject, either the sky or the foreground may predominate. When the sea forms a large part of the horizon, it should be kept as level as possible at the time of photography, since later correction with a small transparency may prove difficult. In the same way the vertical lines of buildings should be kept parallel to the sides of the viewfinder. By tilting the camera upwards, even slightly, the verticals will converge, giving the building the appearance of 'leaning backwards'. Secondly, we can consider the lines and masses which give the subject or scene its characteristic shape. Lines need not necessarily be outlines, but may also take the form of lines connecting points of interest rather as a group of stars forming a constellation may be joined to suggest certain shapes. Vertical lines may help to suggest height, and horizontal lines width: strongly converging lines, due to perspective, will suggest depth. The imaginary lines joining points of interest may take various shapes such as circles, rectangles and triangles, the last shape being specially esteemed by the pictorialist. Masses may be suggested by tonal or colour differences and be contained by the outline of a building or other object. Masses may be said to balance each

ther, a larger mass of dark tone or weak colour being balanced by a small area
f bright tone or strong colour. This is perhaps rather a finer aspect of
omposition and it will help to make experiments with simple still-life subjects.
'his applies even more to so-called colour harmonies and contrasts, and it can be
xtremely instructive to photograph the same object against a range of differently
oloured backgrounds. There are, in addition, many theories of colour harmony.
)ne is that adjacent colours of the spectrum go well together, as also variations
1 tone of the same colour. Many systems have also been worked out for the
uidance of interior decorators, which may be interesting, if not actually helpful
o the colour photographer. Chief among these is the Colour Harmony Manual
ased on the Ostwald colour system, other systems of interest being the Munsell
nd Plochère systems. Many of the leading paint manufacturers also supply
1genious colour guides for the home decorator and at least one 'School of Colour
Photography' supplies differently-coloured cut-out components for attempting
xperiments in colour harmony.

Undoubtedly some people have a stronger feeling or 'eye' for colour than
thers. Those especially gifted in this respect, coupled with strong powers of
isualization, are likely to become painters of the compulsive type. Others less
ifted may still be drawn towards painting and may ultimately achieve almost
qual success by training themselves to see more objectively. Coming to the
ormal person, we all have a liking for colour, and there can be few more
bsorbing pastimes than making experiments in using colour through the
1edium of photography.

Colour values

'he term 'value' is used in the Munsell-colour system to mean luminance factor,
ut we use it here in a more general sense. Thus colours can be said to have a
trong or weak value, be warm or cold, advancing or receding and so on. The
)nger wavelengths, which are also those less easily scattered by the atmosphere,
1at range from red to yellow, are usually described as strong, warm, or advancing
olours. Red is used almost internationally for warning and danger signs, it is the
olour of blood, a colour to provoke both passion and fear. Orange and yellow, a
ttle less strong, have been found to be good 'sales' colours, and the choice of
ellow as a background colour for Kodak film cartons is not without reason.
)range and yellow are also associated with ripeness and maturity, with the
utumn, with sunrise and sunset. The shorter wavelengths, greens and blues,
1ay be described as weak, cold, or receding colours, Green is usually considered
he most restful colour, possibly because it is the colour of grass and foliage. Blue
eing most readily scattered is associated with the distance and receding planes.

However, certain colours react very strongly with each other to give strong
ontrasts, to many people discords rather than harmonies. A highly saturated
reen on a moderately saturated red background will assume a strong value, and
` both be highly saturated, a violent contrast. Generally speaking, colours

151

complementary to each other produce the strongest contrasts, and use may b made of this fact to create startling emphasis or to arrest the attention as in th case of advertising posters. Still greater colour saturation is obtained by usin fluorescent pigments or inks with the same object, the effect on the eyes bein rather similar to the effect of a strident hooter or noisy motorcycle exhaust o the ears.

Colours of moderate and low saturation (pastel shades) are the most restf and often the most pleasing in our surroundings. It is a matter of personal tast There are photographers who prefer a film which gives high colour saturatio and those who prefer one giving somewhat lower saturation. Some photograp ers, being specially interested in landscapes and plant life, may prefer a film f the rendering of its greens, while a portrait photographer is likely to be far mo interested in the rendering of reds.

Pictorial effects with colour

A strong yellow bias in the skin-rendering of a portrait taken against a fresh bl sky would suggest to most observers that it had been taken at sunset: indoo against a dark background, that it had been taken with firelight. These and eve most striking effects can be obtained by the use of coloured gelatines over one c more of the light-sources. Glass, porcelain, and other glossy surfaces can be mad to yield reflections of any desired colour, and the colours of a surface may b intensified or modified by the use of coloured lighting. Thus a white backgroun can be made to yield almost any desired colour merely by projecting light of th desired colour on to it. Taking the matter to an extreme, a white subject can b 'painted' with coloured light to suggest that the colours are a characteristi of the subject rather than the illumination, see plate 32. In principle there is n difference in the appearance of a sheet of red paper which strongly absorbs a other regions of the spectrum whether it be lit with white light or red ligh Neither would a sheet of white paper illuminated with red light appear an different. In all three cases it is the colour of the reflected light that matters.

The mixing of coloured light, whether with multi-light sources or by mear of successive exposures on the same frame of film can produce both unexpecte and startling results. Unexpected, for example, when we illuminate one side of white subject such as that in plate 53 with red light and the other with greer where the two overlap we find we have produced yellow, and on a white back ground behind the subject we find a green shadow on a yellow backgroun apparently cast by a red light, and a red shadow on a yellow background cast b a green light. There is, of course, no magic in this: we have already seen ho colour mixtures behave in an earlier chapter.

Yet more interesting effects can be obtained by the reflections from coloure metallic foils, blue on a red foil producing magenta, green on a blue foil produ ing cyan, and so on. Completely synthetic images can be obtained in this way an with a very high degree of colour saturation. These and other effects discussed i

Chapter 16, may occasionally be used to obtain special backgrounds, or from a pictorial point of view, abstract colour designs, see plates 32 and 73.

Differential focusing

This is typified by a contrast in sharpness between two planes of a subject, usually between the object of principal interest and those in the background. To be effective it requires a shallow depth of field, and unless working at very close distances, demands a lens of long focal length. When this condition is fulfilled, differential focusing may be applied very effectively in portraiture, with the eyes as the plane of critical focus, and may also be used to eliminate unwanted detail in an adjacent background. However, in the latter case it is often less satisfactory than with black-and-white photography if the background contains objects of contrasting colours and tones, since these are apt to appear as meaningless and distracting blobs of colour. Differential focus is occasionally applied with good effect to direct attention into an intermediate plane of the subject by leaving the foreground unsharp. Examples will be found in advertising photography where figures in the foreground, often with low-key lighting, are rendered moderately unsharp. This is in keeping with the true visual effect, though due to the narrowness of the angle of acute vision, we are rarely conscious that objects nearer than the one we are inspecting are more or less unsharp.

Image distortion

Diffusion effects, which from time to time have been much esteemed by the black-and-white worker, are generally less suitable for colour work, and in any case can usually be applied later at the print-making stage. Unusual and sometimes pleasing effects can be obtained by the use of coloured tulle or similar material some distance away from the lens. The effect of the screen on the contrast and colours of the subject can be controlled by the amount of light falling on the surface of the material facing the lens.

Optical distortions can be obtained by placing obscuring glass, which is available in a wide variety of surfaces, in front of the subject. It is occasionally used in portrait and figure work, but has interesting applications in creating abstract designs and in titling, see plates 33 and 73.

Multi-images and 'fluid motion'

Motion in still photography can be depicted in two ways: one by making successive exposures on the same frame of film, each exposure being short enough to produce a sharp image as for example when using a stroboscopic lamp, and the second by employing an open shutter technique to record the actual displacement of the image either as tracks, as in the case of fireworks, or as directional image blur which is useful to a limited extent in action photography or in larger amounts for pictorial effects with subjects such as dancers. Both forms have useful technical applications in time and motion study.

153

The use of double or multiple images on the same frame of film need not however, be restricted to motion effects. It can be used in portraiture (often by the use of a mirror) to display more than one aspect of the subject, or to obtain 'surrealistic' effects by combining incongruous objects in the same picture. Such effects may be done at the camera stage (often necessarily so with reversal films or at the printing stage. On occasions when only one light-source is available, the exposure of the film may take the form of successive steps using the light in different positions and at different distances. An electronic flash unit lends itself particularly to this technique, and even a small unit can be sufficient to illuminate a large interior by exposing successive areas. Multi-exposure are often effective in producing abstract designs, see plates 51 and 73. These and other aspects are discussed in Chapters 13 and 16.

Relief images and colour derivatives

Relief images may be obtained by combining a low contrast positive image made from a colour negative on black-and-white film with the negative, but slightly out of register, when making the print. The effect is to reduce brightness contrast and at the same time produce an outline effect in regions of marked tonal difference. Similar effects may be obtained by binding up a low contrast negative with a positive transparency.

Even more ingenious effects may be obtained by a process pioneered by Ralph M. Evans and published in the *Penrose Annual* for 1951 called Derivations from Colour Photographs*. Making use of a printing process such as that of the Kodak Dye Transfer Process (see Chapter 32), it employs various masking techniques to 'take the picture apart', recombining or omitting the various part as required or as taste dictates. By reducing brightness contrast to zero with a white-light mask, separation negatives can be made having colour difference only. Contour lines are recorded on high contrast film by the vertical displacement of the original and mask negative. The parts of the picture have thus been broken down into a highlight negative, a brightness negative, three separation negatives representing the colours, and a contour line positive. Matrices and further masks or positives can be made from any of these in any combination and the matrices can be dyed in any colour before transfer to the paper. The variations are thus infinite, and depending on the patience and imagination of the printer the final product may be so far removed from the original as to become a purely abstract design. An example is given on the facing page plate 29.

Similar effects may also be obtained using Ektacolor Paper and exposing with colours different from or complementary to those of the original negative It is a field of investigation still very wide open to the imaginative and ingenious technician.

* See Kodak Publication 'Colour Derivations'.

ate 29. Colour derivative. Although resembling a painting it has been derived from a normal
tachrome transparency by a process of making separation negatives and masks which are then
ed to make matrices for printers with the Kodak Dye Transfer Process. In this way brightness
ferences may be modified and colours changed according to the taste of the operator. The
hnique was pioneered by Ralph M. Evans of the Eastman Kodak Company.

Plate 30.

Plate 31.

Plate 32.

Plate 33.

Solarization

Certain emulsions, when exposed too heavily, reverse their tonal contrast in the brighter parts of the subject. As this effect was first noticed with exposures in sunlight (at that time the strongest light source available) it was given the name solarization. The word is loosely (and wrongly) applied nowadays to black-and-white materials, and to a limited extent to colour materials also, which have been partly developed, then fogged, then developed further, resulting in a partial reversal of image tones. So far such effects have achieved little more than novelty value, and similar effects in a more controllable manner can be achieved by making a high-contrast positive mask which embodies only the upper half of the brightness scale, and using this mask when making the colour print.

Other pictorial effects

The use of low- or high-key lighting is less effective with colour photography as in either case it leads to desaturation of colour. Unusual viewpoints, exaggerated perspective, magnification with small objects, bizarre subject matter, photomontage (a composite photograph based on parts of several photographs), distortions in colour balance, errors in exposure and anything else the photographer may have a mind to try are all capable of yielding useful effects. It is not what you do that matters (except perhaps to another photographer) but what you accomplish by way of a picture, for example, see plates 49 and 50!

Plates 30 to 33. Four different ways of presenting a porcelain figure based on lighting and background. In plate 30 a strongly coloured fabric was used as a background with a single spotlight from the side to give a profile shadow. In plate 31 an attempt has been made to suggest a bronze statue, greenish with verdigris. A large empty demi-john of green glass was placed between the subject and spotlight. Apart from imparting a greenish colour, it gives the effect of overhead sunlight filtering through foliage. Plate 32 makes use of coloured foil to produce reflections of colour lighting on the figure and inter-reflections on a sheet of blue foil used as base and background. Three 60-watt lamps were used to illuminate the foils. Plate 33 attempts to portray the figure in terms of modern art using hammered glass to distort the shape. The figure was lit with two slide projectors, one on each side of the subject and fitted with yellow and amber filters respectively. Blue foil was used for the base and mauve poster paper for the background. *Kodachrome transparencies by E. S. Bomback.*

157

Close-ups and Photomacrography

THE TERM 'close-up' is commonly applied to subjects photographed at close camera distances. For our purposes we may regard a close-up as a photograph taken at a distance less than 20 times the focal length of the lens and not less than twice the focal length, which, in fact, gives a scale of reproduction of 1 : 1 or a life-size image. Photography at scales greater than life-size is usually termed photomacrography. In this case it is not the camera-to-subject distance that is of particular importance, but the distance of the lens from the focal plane, or, in other words, the lens extension. Photography at greater magnification using a microscope is known as photomicrography, and, as it involves somewhat different problems, is dealt with later in Chapter 19.

Scale of reproduction

As we have seen earlier – page 34 – the scale of an image formed by a lens is directly proportional to its focal length. By doubling the focal length we double the image scale for the same lens-to-object distance. However, if we take the case of the 'standard' lens with a focal length roughly equal to the diagonal of the picture size of the camera, whatever this size may be, then prints or transparencies viewed at a distance to give proper perspective will all appear of the same scale irrespective of the focal length of the lens. This is, perhaps, more apparent if prints are made for a specific viewing distance, let us say of 10 in. A negative taken with a whole-plate camera fitted with a 10 in. lens would need no further enlargement, one taken with a quarter plate camera having a 5 in. lens would need a ×2 enlargement, while one made with a 35 mm. camera having a 2 in. lens would need a ×5 enlargement. However, if we disregard perspective and enlarge an area common to all three negatives by the same amount, the difference in scale between the three prints will now be proportional to the focal length of the taking lens. This, in fact, is what usually happens when using a camera having interchangeable lenses of different focal length, one reason for using a lens of more than normal focal length being to obtain a greater print scale.

The scale of reproduction in a photograph can be taken as the ratio of the linear size of the image to that of the original object, and also by the following equation:

$$\text{Scale} = \frac{\text{linear size of image}}{\text{linear size of object}}$$

The scale of reproduction of the image will be equal to the distance of the image from the lens divided by the distance of the object from the lens. Hence, when the two distances are equal in the case of a normal lens, the scale becomes unity or life-size. When the lens-to-image distance becomes greater than that of the object-to-lens, we get the scale of magnification from this formula. Or in terms of focal length and lens-to-object distances, we can say that the scale of reproduction is equal to

$$\frac{\text{focal length}}{\text{lens-to-object distance} - \text{focal length}}$$

both being measured in the same units of distance. When the lens-to-object distance becomes substantially greater than the focal length, as it does in general photography, the scale can be taken as the ratio between focal length and distance. For example, the image scale of a transparency taken 10 ft. from an object with a 2 in. lens is roughly 1/60. When the lens-to-image becomes greater than the lens-to-object distance, the scale of reproduction or magnification can be found by the formula:

$$\text{Magnification} = \frac{\text{lens-to-image distance} - \text{focal length}}{\text{focal length}}$$

This is the same as saying that the lens extension divided by the focal length gives the degree of magnification.

Lens extensions and effective f/number

Before leaving the subject of ratios it is necessary to consider what happens to the f/number. This as we know is the optical diameter of the lens divided into its focal length. If, however, we increase the lens-to-film distance in order to focus objects nearer the lens the effective intensity of light falling on the film becomes less. In the interests of critical exposure it becomes necessary to make allowances for this when the increase in lens-to-image distance exceeds the focal length by 1/10, or in other words when the scale of reproduction exceeds 1/10. If it is desired to find the effective f/number the following formula can be used:

$$\text{Effective f/number} = \text{nominal f/number} \times \frac{\text{lens-to-image distance}}{\text{focal length}}$$

However, it is usually easier to refer to a table such as that below, or, in the case of certain lens extension devices, to a scale of corrections engraved on the base.

159

SCALE OF REPRODUCTION AND INCREASE IN EXPOSURE
TO COMPENSATE FOR REDUCTION IN THE NOMINAL f/NUMBER

Scale	$\frac{1}{8}$	$\frac{1}{4}$	$\frac{1}{2}$	1	2	3	4	6	8	10	12
Exposure time at Inf. taken as 1 sec.	$1\frac{1}{4}$	$1\frac{1}{2}$	$2\frac{1}{2}$	4	10	16	25	45	80	120	160
No. of stops by which effective aperture is less than the nominal	$\frac{1}{3}$	$\frac{1}{2}$	$1\frac{1}{3}$	2	$3\frac{1}{3}$	4	$4\frac{1}{2}$	$5\frac{1}{2}$	$6\frac{1}{2}$	7	$8\frac{1}{2}$

Depth of field

For close-range photography depth of field calculations are more logically based on the ratio of the size of the object to the size of the image, than on the object to lens distance. The following formula, in which m is the ratio of object to image and d the diameter of the disc of confusion in the negative, gives the total depth of field.

$$\text{Total depth of field} = m\,(1 + m)\,2d\,(\text{f/number})$$

Thus, if the object is ten times as big as the image, d equals 1/500 in. and the f/number is 4 the total depth of field is:

$$\frac{10 \times 11 \times 2 \times 4}{500} = 1\cdot75 \text{ in.}$$

At close ranges it can be taken that the depth of field extends equally on both sides of the plane of focus. If it is desired to use a smaller disc of confusion the calculated depth of field becomes proportionately less.

It may be deduced from the above formula that depth of field is the same for any given scale of image in the negative irrespective of the focal length of the lens. The superiority of the short-focus lens as used on a miniature camera arises from the fact that the scale of the print image is normally achieved by a greater degree of magnification of the negative. For example a 1 : 1 object/image scale in the print may be obtained by making the negative at a scale of 1/5 and then enlarging 5 times. In this case the depth of field is that obtained when working at a scale of 1/5. On the other hand, a scale of 1 : 1 would normally be obtained at the negative stage using an 8 × 10 in. camera. Thus, at the same aperture the short-focus lens would show a greater depth of field. The table on page 161 gives the total depth of field for a range of object/image scales.

At scales greater than 3 : 1 the depth of field, as can be seen from the above table, becomes extremely small and it calls for direct visual focusing to select the plane of critical focus.

Depth of focus, on the other hand, becomes increasingly great, depth of field and depth of focus being equal at a scale of 1 : 1. With magnifications it is in fact easier to achieve a visual focus by moving the subject nearer to or farther from the lens, or, if the subject is fixed, the whole camera in relation to the subject.

TOTAL DEPTH OF FIELD IN INCHES BASED ON A DISC
OF CONFUSION OF 1/500 in.

Image scale	f/4	f/5·6	f/8	f/11	f/16	f/22	f/32	f/45
1/20	7·00	9·60	14·00	19·25	28·00	38·50	56·00	77·00
1/10	1·75	2·40	3·50	4·80	7·00	9·60	14·00	13·20
1/6	0·67	0·92	1·34	1·84	2·68	3·68	5·67	7·36
1/4	0·32	0·45	0·64	0·88	1·28	1·76	2·56	3·52
1/3	0·20	0·27	0·40	0·55	0·80	1·10	1·60	2·20
1/2	0·095	0·13	0·19	0·26	0·38	0·52	0·76	1·04
1/1	0·032	0·04	0·06	0·08	0·12	0·16	0·24	0·32
2/1	0·012	0·016	0·025	0·033	0·05	0·066	0·10	0·132
3/1	0·007	0·01	0·014	0·019	0·03	0·04	0·06	0·08

Lens-extension devices

With cameras having a fixed lens and rigid body it is not usual to be able to achieve a scale of greater than about 1/10. There are a few lenses such as those of the Makro-Kilar series which enable magnifications of up to 4 times to be achieved without any other attachment. Larger technical cameras are usually fitted with an extension bellows permitting scales of up to 1 : 1 or 2 : 1 to be achieved with the standard lens or greater magnifications when using lenses of shorter focus. With small cameras having interchangeable lenses it is necessary to fit either extension tubes, which are often available as an 'additive' series – see fig. 11.1 – or an extension bellows device such as that of the Novoflex. In some cases these extension devices are fitted with a reflex viewer to enable the image to be focused visually.

Fig. 11.1. Set of extension tubes.

Supplementary lenses

With cameras having a limited focusing range, an alternative approach to obtaining scales up to very nearly life-size is to increase the dioptric power of the lens by adding a supplementary lens. This, in effect, gives a combined lens of shorter focal length and the existing separation between lens and film therefore provides a greater effective lens extension than that provided by the normal focusing movement. The 'dioptre' is a way of expressing focal length as the reciprocal of the focal length in metres. Thus a lens with a power of 1 dioptre has a focal length of 1 metre and a lens of 50 mm. a power of 20 dioptres. For positive lenses it is customary to add a + sign and for negative lenses a — sign. The advantage of the dioptric system is that the total dioptric power of a combination of lenses can be found by adding their individual dioptric powers together (if positive) or by subtracting their dioptric power if a negative lens is added to a positive one. Thus if two +2 dioptre lenses are used together the effect is that of a +4 lens, and if the two are added to a +20 dioptre lens, the effect is that of a +24 lens.

However, it is more convenient for the photographer to know the actual focal length of a supplementary lens, since, with the camera lens focused for infinity, a subject at the distance of the focal length of the supplementary lens or lenses will be sharply focused at the focal plane, see fig. 11.2. With the camera

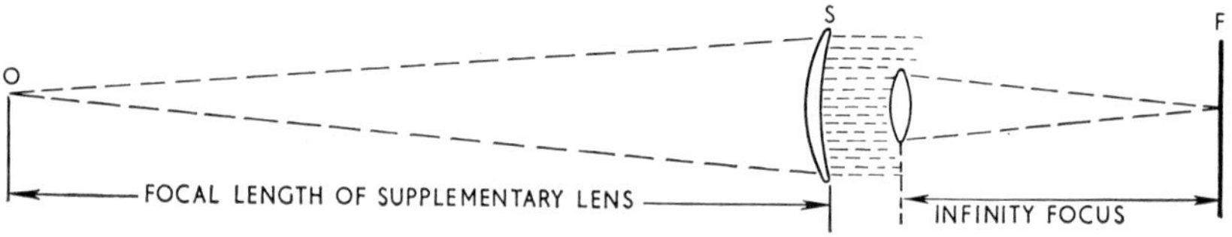

Fig. 11.2. An object O at a distance equal to the focal length of a positive supplementary lens will be focused with the camera lens set at infinity.

lens focusing movement, objects as closer distances will be brought into focus. The table below gives a guide to the focusing range of a series of positive supplementary lenses:

Supplementary lens			Distance of object from front surface of supplementary lens in inches					
Focal length			Focus setting of camera lens					
Metres	Inches	Dioptres	Inf.	20 ft.	10 ft.	5 ft.	3 ft.	2 ft.
1·33	52	+¾	52	43	36½	28	21	15½
1·00	39	+1	39	34	30	23¾	18¾	14¾
0·50	19½	+2	19½	18½	17	15	12½	10½
0·33	13	+3	13	12½	12	10¼	9½	8½
0·25	10	+4	10	9½	9	8½	7½	7
0·20	8	+5	8	7½	7¼	7	6¾	6¼
0·16	6½	+6	6½	6¼	5½	4¾	4½	4¼
0·10	4	+10	4	4	3¾	3¾	3½	3¼

Note: The above distances have been rounded off to the nearest ¼ in.

Supplementary lenses for close-up work normally consist of a single-element meniscus-type lens and should be used as near to the front surface of the camera lens as possible with the convex surface facing outwards. If a filter is to be used in addition to a supplementary lens it should be fitted last. Positive lenses of plano-convex or double-convex design are not suitable, as they introduce distortion into the image. Good quality spectacle lenses of up to +4 dioptres are satisfactory for normal work, but they should be of meniscus design and must not contain any correction for astigmatism. Close-up lenses of shorter focal length (greater dioptric power) should preferably be of achromatic design consisting of two elements cemented together. Typical of such lenses are those of the Retina 'R' series for reproduction scales of 1 : 4·5, 1 : 3, 1 : 2 and 1 : 1½. Even so, these lenses should preferably be used at smallish apertures to obtain critical definition over the whole field area.

Fig. 11.3. Retina Close-up Rangefinder with NI and NII close-up lenses.

Close-up lenses of +1, +2, and +3 dioptres are available in diameters to fit a wide range of lens mounts. However, the Kodak Portra lenses, and the 'N' close-up lenses designed for use with Retinette and Retina cameras are now only available as +1 and +2 lenses, since the effect of a +3 lens is obtained by using the two together. However, bearing in mind that every additional air-to-glass surface introduced into the optical path may reduce the optical perform-ance, even if only from dust or surface reflections, it is preferable to use a single lens of the required dioptric power rather than a combination.

The need to use a smallish lens aperture with supplementary lenses to obtain satisfactory definition over the whole field of view is rarely a disadvantage, since a small aperture is usually required to obtain adequate depth of field. Loss of definition at larger apertures occurs first at the edges of the field and may easily pass unnoticed if the subject occupies only the centre area. But when the subject consists of a flat surface such as a postage stamp or piece of fabric, and occupies the whole field of view, even a small loss of definition will be apparent. In such cases it may be preferable to work at f/11 or a smaller aperture. To some extent the need for small apertures is related to the focal length of the supple-mentary lens, and a +½ or even +1 lens such as the TI or TII lenses intended to extend the near-focusing range of telephoto lenses of Retina cameras may be used at full aperture without noticeable loss of definition.

One advantage of using supplementary lenses for close-up work is that the effective light-passing capacity of the lens (or lens combination) is still that indicated by the f/number of the camera lens. No exposure correction is therefore needed when using a supplementary lens for close-ups. On the other hand, if a positive lens is used as a means of reducing the focal length of a lens, with a camera which can be focused for infinity at this shorter distance, the effective aperture becomes greater than the nominal aperture. For example if a $+2$ lens is added to a camera lens of 10 in. ($+4$ D) the effect is that of a lens of $6\frac{1}{2}$ in. ($+6$D) and the effective aperture becomes roughly 1 stop greater than the nominal f/number:

$$\text{effective aperture} = \frac{f/8 \times 6\frac{1}{2}}{10} = f/5 \cdot 4$$

Parallax and framing devices

The problem of parallax is one peculiar to cameras which rely on some form of viewfinder independent of the camera lens. In other words it is associated with all small cameras except those of the single-lens reflex type. Depending on the position of the viewfinder, the image seen becomes increasingly displaced, with decreasing distance, in relation to that formed by the camera lens, such displacement being known as parallax, see fig. 11.4. With more 'advanced' cameras some

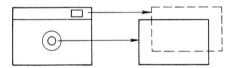

Fig. 11.4. At close distances the image seen in the viewfinder no longer coincides with that given by the lens.

form of parallax compensation is embodied in the optical system of the viewfinder (usually coupled with the focusing movement of the lens) over the normal focusing range of the camera. With simpler cameras the viewfinder may contain notches or broken lines to indicate the correction needed at distances between 3 and 5 ft. But the problem of parallax only becomes really serious at distances less than 10 times the focal length of the camera lens, and it then becomes necessary to employ some form of accessory viewfinder or framing device. A simple accessory to cover the distance range covered by the 'N' close-up lenses is that of the Retina Sports Finder, shown in fig. 11.5, which allows the 'peep-sight' to be set against a scale of distances. The same finder is, of course, also useful for action shots involving fast movement. However, there still remains the problem of determining the distance of the camera, and most devices include some form of focusing aid. For example the Retina Close-up Rangefinder, fig. 11.3, provides

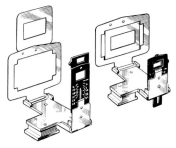

Fig. 11.5. Retina Sports Finder with parallax correction.

Fig. 11.6. Retina Ground Glass Focusing Adapter for Retina IIC and IIIC cameras.

both parallax correction and the means of placing the camera at the distance required by the use of NI, NII or NI+NII lenses at different focus settings of the camera lens. Similar devices are available for other cameras, some of which can be applied to an existing rangefinder system. In the case of the Rolleiflex twin-lens reflex camera, a special 'viewing' lens embodying both dioptric and parallax corrections is available. Other devices such as the Retina Ground Glass Focusing Adapter, fig. 11.6, for use with Retina IIC and IIIC cameras, offer the same accuracy in framing and focusing as a conventional view camera fitted with focusing back.

Field Frames

A field frame which indicates both the distance of the subject plane of critical focus and the field of view covered by the lens is undoubtedly one of the most effective aids for close-up work at scales of reproduction from about 1/4 to life-size. An excellent example of such an attachment is the Retina Close-up attachment shown in fig. 11.7. It provides for four scales of reproduction by means of different pairs of distance rods which fit into a holder attached to the base of the camera.

Fig. 11.7. Retina camera fitted with Close-up Attachment for use with the R series of Close-up lenses. Four sets of distance and spacing rods give the field for scales of $1 : 1\frac{1}{2}$, $1 : 2$, $1 : 3$ and $1 : 4\frac{1}{2}$.

The device is thus equally convenient for hand-held camera work or with a camera stand. It is ideal for the photography of live insects, flowers and other subjects encountered outdoors. Indeed such a device is equally convenient with a single-lens reflex camera since it makes for greater manœuverability of the camera. Field frames are not difficult to improvise and fig. 11.8 offers two suggestions for making one.

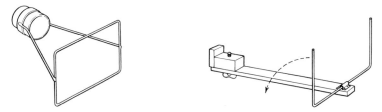

Fig. 11.8. Two suggestions for making a field frame. The first, for small subjects, is based on an extension tube; the second provides a base for mounting the camera and a folding wire frame.

Designed for copying rather than close-ups, the Retina Document Copying Stand – see Chapter 17 – is, in effect, a kind of field frame and can be used for this purpose when a larger field than that covered by the Close-up Attachment is desired. Also the 1 : 1 Copying Stand for the Retina III, which is intended for copying colour slides, may also be used for close-ups of stamps and the like.

Lighting for close-ups

It is not always appreciated that small objects can benefit as much by a skilful lighting arrangement as those of larger dimensions, and that the same general lighting technique as applied, say, in normal portraiture can be applied to a close-up study of a single bloom. However, many small creatures, such as birds and insects, possess not only fine structural detail but often display what are known as structural colours, namely those due to interference, diffraction and the dispersion of light (see page 21). These colours are often more favourably displayed in strongly directional light such as that of sunlight, and a small spotlight can therefore be very useful for indoor work. Surface structures and textures are often of special interest and these can be strongly emphasized by the use of a beam of light shining obliquely on the subject. With flowers and other semi-translucent objects strong back-lighting may also offer an interesting lighting arrangement.

In general, objects at very close distances call for somewhat fuller exposure than those at normal distances and initial tests with $\frac{1}{2}$ and even 1 stop more than the normal exposure will be worth making. This is in addition to any allowance that may be necessary by reason of lens extensions or for reciprocity failure. Indeed the latter may be particularly troublesome when magnifications of ×.

ıd greater are involved, since an exposure factor of $\times 25$ or more will be needed
ı compensate for the loss of intensity. Needless to say, small objects permit
rtificial light-sources to be used at much closer distances, and to some extent
ıis can be made to compensate for the smaller effective aperture. But sunlight,
ınfortunately, is a constant intensity at all distances, and is frequently inadequate
ı permit exposures short enough for a hand-held camera to be made at
ıertures of f/16 and smaller. However, it is in the field of outdoor close-ups that
ıe small electronic flash unit really comes into its own. Used at distances
ıetween 1 and 2 feet from the subject it will supply a lighting intensity much
reater than sunlight, and give an exposure time of 1/500 sec. or less, see plate 72.
Vith a small reflector board made from aluminium foil, a suitable lighting
ılance can be achieved with the flash unit placed in almost any position in a
ırcle drawn round the subject, except, of course, a position directly opposed to
ıe camera lens if the subject itself does not provide a screen, as when illuminat-
ıg a spray of blossom from behind. Electronic flash in the form of a ring tube
ıounted round the lens also provides the answer to the problem of uniformly
ghting specimens having a hollow interior, as for example botanical studies of
rumpet-shaped blooms, medical studies of operations, diseases of the mouth, and
ıe like. In the interests of lighting it may sometimes be preferable to use a longer
ıcus lens, since to achieve the same scale, the distance between subject and lens
rill be proportionately greater. Thus a 1 : 1 scale of reproduction with a 2 in.
ıns gives a lens-to-subject distance of only 4 in., whereas with a 5 in. lens the
ıstance becomes 10 in.

ackgrounds

'he very restricted depth of field with close-up work is often an advantage,
ınce unwanted detail in a background can easily be thrown out of focus merely
y moving the subject forward a few inches. On the other hand, detail in the
ıreground and immediate background only partially out of focus can be
ispleasing to the viewer of the photograph, since it distracts the attention from
ıe plane of critical focus. With moderate close-ups and using a small aperture,
ıuite distant objects may be reasonably sharp or, even worse, become meaning-
ıss blobs of light and colour. In such cases it is preferable to use an artificial
ıckground of uniform tone and of a colour in harmony or contrast with those of
ıe subject. For outdoor work in the garden or countryside a stout bulldog clip
ıtached to the end of a stick can be used to hold sheets of thin cardboard. A
ıange of several tones and colours can be carried in an artist's folder or a knapsack.

When a ground-glass screen is used to view the subject, it is usually necessary
ı use a large lens aperture to obtain sufficient image brightness for critical focus-
ıg. This is done automatically with many eye-level reflex cameras. On the other
ıand, the exposure is usually made at a very small lens stop in order to obtain
ıfficient depth of field. This can result in failure to notice undesirable back-
round detail, which, however, becomes all too apparent in the photograph.

12

General Aspects of Outdoor Photography

VARIABLE and unpredictable though daylight is, we must accept it for th majority of subjects outdoors since, except in a small way, there is no substitut As we spend the greater part of our waking life with daylight as the princip source of illumination, it is the standard upon which we form our judgment colour, and though we are able to adapt ourselves to other qualities of lightin we are usually conscious of the difference at the back of our mind. Thus we kno that tungsten light is yellower, and when we wish to judge the 'true' colours of subject, we usually examine it with daylight. It is because of this that colou photographs taken with artificial light are required to appear more as if take with daylight. However, this does not mean that we must always use 'rea daylight when depicting a subject outdoors. It has been pointed out by D. Spencer (Colour Photography in Practice) that 'daylight' quality portraits a more easily made with artificial light in a studio. But in spite of the large stud sets often used in film making, it is obvious that we can only photograph landscape with daylight. Even moonlight, though it appears of different colou quality from sunlight because of its much lower intensity (we become virtuall colour-blind), is no more than reflected sunlight, and appears so to a colour fil if given an adequate exposure, see plate 76.

Daylight

The great majority of camera users, if we include the very simplest types cameras, make very nearly all their exposures with daylight, occasional exposur with artificial light being restricted to flashbulbs. To the more serious amateu under no particular compulsion to deliver the goods on schedule, the variabilit of daylight is a major source of interest, and its unpredictability no more than a occasional frustration. It is also true to say that the majority of amateur colou photographers restrict their exposures to occasions when the sun is shining, an it is for this reason that daylight-type colour films are balanced to give their be colour rendering with clear noonday sunlight plus the light from the sky. B there are other reasons why so many photographers prefer sunlight, and for th most part pack their cameras away during the winter if they happen to live in countries such as the British Isles. One reason is the strongly directional nature of sunlight, which gives both light and shade effects, and a higher colour saturation. Indeed there are few people who would not prefer a sunlit landscape to one photographed under a heavily overcast sky. Sunlight is also the strongest form of daylight and thus permits shorter exposure times or smaller apertures. Finally, by restricting exposures to sunny conditions during the middle hours of the day, the problem of exposure is greatly simplified, and with average subjects hardly exists at all once the correct exposure level is known, since the lighter tones of the subject remain more or less constant and it is on these that the exposure is based. This fact explains the success possible in using a box camera having a fixed lens aperture and shutter speed.

One of the fascinating aspects of daylight photography is that one can spend half a life-time making exposures with it without exhausting all its possible effects with a colour film. That this should be so is not extraordinary when we take into account all the possible combinations of the variable factors of daylight. Firstly, there is the variation in the sun's altitude on a daily basis, starting with sunrise and ending in sunset: there is variation in altitude on a seasonal basis, whereby the sun reaches its maximum altitude at midsummer at noon and makes an increasingly lower arc as it approaches midwinter. This variation is for all practical purposes non-existent at the equator but becomes of increasing importance at greater latitudes. Then there are variations in atmospheric conditions due to haze, dust and mist, and even greater variation due to cloud, or, in more general terms, variations of cloud cover. In addition there are variations due to locality and altitude and situations where daylight itself is restricted by the nature of the surroundings, for example, open and restricted shade, sunlight through foliage, etc. See plates 17, 24, 25, 34, 35, 55 and 56.

And to these variations in daylight we must also add the seasonal changes in the colouring of grass and foliage which together make up the back-cloth of outdoor photography. How different the bare trees with their delicate tracery of branches and twigs from the swollen green mantles they wear in summer: how different the orchard in blossom in the Spring from its ripe maturity in Autumn! It is all too easy to become poetical when one has followed these seasonal changes year by year, each year recording a little more of the fascinating variations presented to the camera. Indeed, if it does nothing else, the pursuit of photography is a wonderful inducement to using our eyes. In search of the perfect composition, the perfect arrangement of the generous ingredients provided by Nature, we often scour miles of countryside, viewing this and scanning that, assessing the quality of the light, and as like as not, sitting on some cold hill-side for hours waiting for the right formation of clouds or the right altitude of the sun.

Except for the necessity to adjust the exposure to different brightness levels of daylight, it is possible to accept its other variables passively, making no attempt to compensate for differences in colour quality, excessive brightness range, ultra-violet radiation or any other characteristic which may be open to modification. We may, if we wish, restrict all our exposures to ideal lightir conditions, thereby achieving a collection of colour photographs all of rough. the same quality. On the other hand, if we have anything like an enquiring min we shall want to make a study of daylight and try to find exactly how a colou film behaves under different conditions and qualities of lighting. It is to this en that the following notes are written.

Sunlight

The sun is a powerful source of light coming from what can be considered to l an 'infinite' distance and reaching the surface of the earth after it has passe through the earth's atmosphere. Its actual colour temperature in outer space estimated to be between 6,000°K. and 7,000°K., but owing to the fact that pa of the blue light is scattered by the atmosphere, the direct sunlight reaching tl earth's surface at mid-day at the equator is only 5,400°K. if we exclude ligl reflected from a clear blue sky. This, in fact, is the case when we have a narro shaft of sunlight coming through a roof window or between the buildings of narrow street. But if we take the case of a horizontal surface in the open receivir both sunlight and the blue light from a clear sky, the effective colour temperatur is around 6,000°K., and it is to such a quality of light that daylight-type films a₁ balanced. Thus in the case of isolated sunlight we can expect somewhat 'warme results. However, when the sun passes through a substantially thicker layer ₄ atmosphere, as it does when it approaches the horizon – see fig. 12.1 – still mo₁ of the blue light is scattered and it becomes noticeably yellower. This indeed ca occur with the sun still well above the horizon, if the atmosphere contains a larg amount of moisture haze (mist), or smoky dust, such as is common in the wint₄ in industrial areas. On the horizon itself or in strong mist the sun appears orang or red in colour.

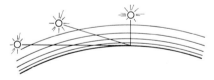

Fig. 12.1. Diagram showing the increase in depth of atmosphere as the sun approaches the horizon.

But in addition to a change in colour temperature, the intensity of sunligl also decreases as it approaches the horizon, owing to the scattering and absorptic by the thicker layer of atmosphere. Thus, while it is painful to look at the sun ₐ mid-day, it becomes considerably less bright on the horizon. In addition, if w were to measure the light reflected vertically from a horizontal plane, its brigh ness, even from a constant source, would decrease as the angle of incidenc decreases – see fig. 12.2 – such a surface receiving no light at all at an angle of 0°. We reach a position, in fact, at sunrise and sunset, when the principal illumination of a horizontal surface is that of blue skylight. Hence the very blue colour rendering of roads, water, and other level surfaces early in the day and late in the evening – see plate 36 and 37.

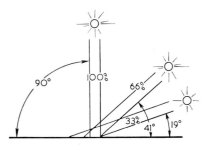

Fig. 12.2. Diagram showing how the brightness of a horizontal surface in sunlight varies with the angle of the sun above the horizon. For example the intensity of reflected light at 19° – allowing for the atmosphere – is only about one third of that with the sun overhead.

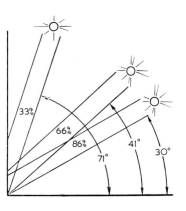

Fig. 12.3. Reflected sunlight from a vertical surface is normally at a maximum at an angle of about 30° above the horizon, allowing for the atmosphere.

But, of course, the average subject lies in various planes, some horizontal, some vertical and some sloping. Where, for example, the subject may consist principally of the facade of a building facing the sun, maximum intensity of sunlight (allowing for the effect of atmosphere) occurs when the sun is from 18° to 40° above the horizon, at which angle a horizontal plane would only receive about half the light. At the same time the vertical plane would receive less light from the sky, and might, in fact, receive more reflected light from a light foreground, at least in its lower regions, see fig. 12.3 All this may seem like splitting hairs, but it may well account for irregularities in colour rendering of neutral or delicately coloured areas.

The shaded parts of a subject which do not receive direct sunlight may vary even more in colour rendering and brightness, depending on how much light they receive from the sky and how much from other reflecting surfaces. If, as in the case of a horizontal plane shaded from sunlight, the surface receives light

171

from a very blue sky, then neutral tones will appear very blue and other colour will be modified accordingly – see Plate 77 – the colour temperature of the ligh being in the region of 20,000°K., and thus calling for as much correction as tha provided by a Wratten No. 85 filter. A vertical surface in the shade could wel receive most of its light from a blue sky, or if surrounded by a light foreground, mixture of light reflected from sky and foreground, or if the sky is screened with a roof, most of its light from the ground, see fig, 12.4. In a built-up area

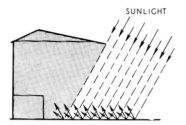

SUNLIGHT

Fig. 12.4. Sunlight reflected from a light foreground into an area of shadow takes on the colour of the foreground.

vertical planes are far more often illuminated by light reflected from adjacen walls receiving sunlight than from light coming from the sky. The shadows unless the buildings happen to be strongly coloured, thus appear far more neutra in tone. In the portrait of the two small girls facing page 280, plate 61, mos of the light came from sunlight reflected from the road and facing wall, an although in shadow has a 'warm' colour rendering. On the other hand green lawn would give a greenish colour cast, and yellow-orange sand o gravel, a distinctively warm colour rendering and so on. In the case of water which behaves rather like a mirror, we should expect to find a bluish colou rendering, as for a surface facing the sky.

On a clear day in the open and with the sun to one side of the camera, th subject is lit by two different light-sources. Any attempt to balance one will upse the balance of the other. It is this reason which makes the use of correctior filters for low-level sunlight of little practical value in general landscape photo graphy, since they tend to make the already bluish shadows still bluer. However when the sun is behind the camera (giving shadowless illumination) or is comin through a window or other restricted area, it becomes a single source of light an may be modified in the same way as any other light-source with a suitabl correction filter.

Plates 34 and 35. These examples of photo-reporting demonstrate admirably the value of colou photography in giving realistic impressions. There is frequently a need for the photo-reporter t work quickly and unobtrusively and a moderately long focus lens used with an eye-level refle such as the Retina Reflex Camera can be a most valuable asset. A lightly overcast sky presen the most favourable lighting conditions, as it is possible to shoot from any angle and without th need of fill-in flash (which invariably attracts attention). Both pictures were made with Koda chrome II film using an 85 mm. lens.

Plates *34 and 35*. Street scenes from a Sardinian village. *Photos: E. S. Bomback.*

Plate 36. Fisherman at dawn.

Plate 37. Water-melons.

Photos: E. S. Bombach

Before leaving the subject of the dual nature of daylight, we must not overlook those occasions when the sky is for the most part covered with broken white cloud which still permits clear unobscured sunlight to reach the subject. In this case the sky is more nearly like a large white reflector, which reflects the sunlight almost unchanged in its spectral quality. Subjects in the shade are rendered in very much the same colour as they would be in direct sunlight, except that the diffused light gives a somewhat lower colour saturation. See plates 3 and 5.

Overcast sky

The presence of a continuous cloud layer acts as a strong diffuser, and daylight then becomes a vast single light-source of totally diffused lighting. Subjects in the open receive roughly equal illumination from all directions and there are no shadows. The spectral quality of the light depends somewhat on the altitude and nature of the cloud layer or layers. A low layer of cloud merely 'mixes' the sun and sky illumination to give light of roughly the same colour quality as sunlight plus light from a blue sky. If the top layer of the cloud is very high the colour temperature more nearly approaches that of the sun outside the earth's atmosphere, since at heights much above 40,000 ft. relatively little light is lost by scattering, and the sky in fact appears almost black. With very thin, high-level cloud layers that only partially obscure the sun, the shadows will be relatively soft or luminous and of identical colour rendering to parts receiving partly diffused sunlight. This, as we have said in an earlier chapter, is probably the ideal form of daylight for portraits outdoors. See plates 2 to 4, 34, 35.

Mist and fog

We may regard mist and fog as kinds of cloud formation at ground level, and if one's 'ground level' happens to be a few thousand feet above sea-level, it will be a fairly common occurrence. The terms 'light' and 'heavy' mist, 'dense' fog, 'peasouper' and 'smog' indicate the density and in the case of the last two the addition of smoke. The effect is that of a diffuser which both disperses and reflects light from the light-source to the subject and from the subject to our eyes or a camera. Depending on its density and the distance of the subject, it reduces the clarity of the image and its contrast. At night, street lamps appear to have a halo or luminous sphere, and, as any car driver knows, there is often more reflected light from headlights than illumination of the road. To a large extent the photographic effect of mist and fog is similar to the visual, and by choosing a subject having a number of planes, the relatively steep difference in contrast and loss of detail may be used to pleasing pictorial effect. The 'secret' of such pictures is often the inclusion of some object of warm colour – red, orange or yellow – in the immediate foreground, as a 'key'. The presence of a light mist in wooded areas with the sun as a back-light has long been a favourite subject for the black-and-white photographer and is no less effective with colour film. As we have already noted, a strong haze can reduce the sun to an orange ball long before it reaches the horizon, although the general illumination of the scene may still be of normal daylight quality. On the other hand mist contaminated with smoke tends to produce rather an unpleasant yellow colour rendering, and the use of a pale blue filter may be worth while. The effect of a translucent mist commonly occurring in the early morning in the Spring and Autumn is far greater with the light in front of the camera than behind it. This also applies to atmospheric haze, see plate 7, 25, and 56.

Snow

A single snowflake is made up of minute and vari-patterned crystals of water, which under great magnification are as transparent as a thin layer of ice. But in the mass as a layer of snow the effect is that of a strong, non-selective reflector, hence, of course, its white appearance. However, owing to the effect of colour constancy (see page 28) it tends to appear white even when illuminated with light which differs distinctly from the accepted standard of whiteness. Thus snow shadows which strongly reflect the colour of the light falling on them seem grey in the original scene but may appear distinctly coloured in a photograph. The classic example is the effect of a clear blue sky which is frequently encountered in mountainous areas such as the Alps during winter. Critical viewing will make it possible to 'see' that the shadow is as blue as the sky, but it still comes as something of a surprise that the shadows appear so without effort when viewing a colour photograph. Indeed, there may well be some exaggeration in blue due to excessive ultra-violet radiation, invisible to the eye, but 'visible' to the colour film as blue light. Thus it can be advantageous to use an ultra-violet absorbing filter such as the Wratten No. 1A. This blueness can be all the more noticeable when the sun itself is approaching the horizon and hence tends to be somewhat yellowish in colour. Not only do the shadows tend to be larger but their blueness will contrast with the yellow of the snow. This effect will be partly destroyed if the exposure is on the full side, for then the sunlit snow will be recorded as clear film and the snow will then appear 'white'.

It is of interest to note how the exposure level can affect the colour rendering of a scene containing areas of white or near-white tones. Up to a certain point colour saturation increases with the density of the image, and with reversal film thus increases as the exposure is reduced. As in the case of a sunset mentioned in in earlier chapter, it is instructive to give a range of exposure of a snowscape at ⅓ stop intervals. From this it will be seen that fuller exposures tend to destroy much of the texture in the lighter tones of the snow, and it is very much a matter of personal judgment as to the best compromise between highlight tones and the impression of brilliance.

Ultra-violet radiation

Although we have already discussed this aspect of outdoor photography in an earlier chapter, it is worth amplifying certain points. Firstly, it is not always easy to predict undesirable effects resulting from ultra-violet radiation, and in some cases the photographer is apt to confuse the natural blueness of a distant scene, an area of water, or a horizontal plane receiving a large amount of blue light from the sky, with the effect of excessive ultra-violet radiation. Secondly, the amount of ultra-violet radiation reaching the colour film depends somewhat on the lens, some lenses of complex design giving a distinctly 'warmer' colour rendering than others. For this reason a series of lenses designed for use with one camera are usually 'colour-matched'. These remarks, of course, apply to the use of reversal films: no such fine adjustment is needed with colour negative film. Perhaps the most practical advice to the landscape photographer using reversal film is to make two exposures of subjects which depend on 'atmospheric' perspective, one with and one without a filter.

Use of long-focus lenses

In cases where a long-focus lens is used to produce a larger image scale of distant objects or features of a landscape, the resulting picture may appear both excessively blue and low in contrast. The explanation is fairly apparent if we look for it, since we have in effect reduced the apparent distance while retaining the characteristics of distant scenery. Although a Wratten No. 1A filter may help to reduce the blue, there is no way of increasing the contrast. This situation is less likely to occur with a normal or wide-angle lens since planes nearer the camera will be included in the picture, these being of increasingly normal colour rendering and contrast as they approach the immediate foreground. The blueness and lower contrast of the more distant planes then becomes a natural manifestation of distance or depth. It is for this reason that most landscape painters and photographers include some item of foreground interest. This, of course, should have a compositional function as well, and a figure may be included to 'balance' a more distant building. It is not always appreciated that more interesting effects can be gained with a long-focus lens by including an object or person in the foreground of the picture, as this diminishes perspective. Mountains, for example, can be made to appear more impressive by this trick.

13

Architectural Photography

THE PHOTOGRAPHY of buildings generally, and of architectural features both external and internal, has always provided professional and amateur alike with an interesting and satisfying challenge in the use of a camera. Although the use of colour films introduces some additional problems, the basic problem is still that concerned with geometric perspective and the preservation of verticals. It is a field of photography where the tools of the trade – camera and lenses – are of major importance, where the wise photographer puts aside the thought of convenience, and considers rather the usefulness of his equipment.

Choice of camera

We may perhaps simplify the choice by considering the kind of work we want to undertake and the sort of situations we are likely to encounter. Firstly, if we intend to use reversal colour films with the object of producing transparencies for photomechanical reproduction, it will be preferable to use a technical camera of at least 4 × 5 in. size with at least a moderate range of lens and camera movements, since there is little or no scope for later correction of converging verticals, and smaller transparencies provide little room for cropping if maximum image quality is to be maintained. On the other hand, if negative colour film is to be used, greater freedom exists at the camera stage, though at the cost of some

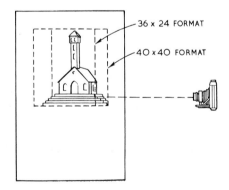

36 x 24 FORMAT

40 x 40 FORMAT

Fig. 13.1. Use of a large-format camera for obtaining small slides. The longer focal length becomes, in effect, a long focus lens for pictures of smaller format while at the same time retaining a normal angle of view. The diagram shows how tilt can be avoided by restricting the desired subject to the upper part of the negative area.

178

nconvenience when making the print. If small transparencies are wanted for ecture purposes, it may still be useful to use a larger camera since this permits cropping of the transparency, when, for example, rather too much foreground has been included in the picture in an attempt to avoid tilting the camera, see ig. 13.1. Thus a $2\frac{1}{4} \times 2\frac{1}{4}$ in. camera gives some scope for cropping to $1 \times 1\frac{1}{2}$ in. or superslide format, and a $2\frac{1}{4} \times 3\frac{1}{4}$ in. camera similar scope for $2\frac{1}{4} \times 2\frac{1}{4}$ in. or smaller slides. If our interest lies in architectural detail and decoration, we might get by quite well with a miniature camera equipped with interchangeable lenses, though there would still be occasions when some degree of rising front and perhaps some degree of swing in both lens and back would produce more satisfactory results. Finally, if we have no more than a pictorial interest in buildings and their decoration, we are always at liberty to choose those situations most favourable to the camera we are using, even if no more than a simple snapshot camera. Pictorially we are also free to choose any viewpoint or angle which will give an interesting effect.

Verticals

We have already pointed out in an earlier chapter (page 51) that one of the 'constancy' effects of vision is to see verticals as parallel lines even when the image formed on the retina, owing to looking upwards or downwards, contains some degree of convergence. In acute cases, as when standing close to a skyscraper

Fig. 13.2. It can be seen how a small amount of tilt upwards gives the effect of buildings toppling over. This has been avoided in the right-hand picture by use of a rising front.

179

or looking down from the roof of such a building we see the convergence quite naturally. However, the exact situation whereby we change from seeing parallel lines to seeing converging lines is not easily determined, since by making the effort we can see convergence in an original scene where we should normally see parallel verticals. However, the situation is much simpler when viewing a photograph and even a small amount of convergence is detected if the photograph is viewed squarely and takes the form of a picture inside a rectangle. To avoid this it is necessary that the axis of the lens be at right-angles to the vertical, or, if tilted, be compensated by an appropriate degree of tilt of the focal plane, see fig. 13.2. With a camera having no provision for front or back swing, this means that the lens must face squarely towards the vertical plane of the building. This in itself presents no problem unless the height of the building exceeds the available field of view, the camera being at ground level. Less common is the situation where the camera level is much higher, and the depth downwards exceeds the lower limit of the field of view.

There are a number of solutions to this problem. The simplest is to be able to apply a rising or falling lens movement, the lens itself being of wide-angle type permitting a larger field of view than that of the picture format. Thus we may imagine the lens forming a large circular image of wide field from which we can select the desired area by moving the lens up or down, see fig. 13.3. This method

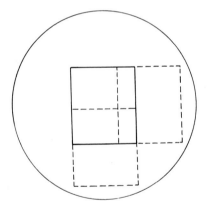

Fig. 13.3. The circle indicates the angle covered by a wide-angle lens in relation to the picture format of the camera.

only holds good if the lens gives adequate coverage and does not suffer from vignetting, to which effect reversal films are particularly sensitive. Secondly, we may, if conditions permit, increase our distance from the building, thereby reducing the image scale to a degree which permits the whole building to be included in the picture area without any camera tilt. In the case of reversal film this method suffers from the disadvantage of giving too large a foreground, if we are at ground level, or too much sky if we are working from a height. As we have said, by using a large camera we may resort to cropping, and because of the onger focal length of the lens, still finish up with an image that fills the picture area, see fig. 13.1. Or again, if conditions permit, we may choose a more central viewpoint so that the camera is more nearly level with the centre of the building. If we are able to change the focal length of the camera lens, two solutions are open to us depending on the available working distance. Firstly, we may use a wide-angle lens, thereby obtaining a smaller image, but at the same time rather more foreground or sky than we may want, or we may increase the camera distance by a substantial amount and use a long-focus lens, thereby maintaining the required image scale and with probably just the right amount of foreground or sky. In both these cases, however, we may introduce some apparent distortion in perspective, since the angular displacement of the print image may differ from that of the camera at the time of photography. We may also, of course, use a combination of two or more of these solutions, finding, for example, both a some-what higher viewpoint at a somewhat greater distance, and at the same time using a moderately longer focal length to compensate for the increased distance. One rather drastic solution open to the pictorial photographer is to reduce the distance and use a large angle of tilt so that the picture clearly becomes either a worm's-eye or a bird's-eye view.

Perspective

As we have already seen in an earlier chapter (page 71) a well-corrected lens gives very nearly perfect perspective provided that we view the image of the photograph at a distance which gives the same angle as that of the lens at the time of photography. If we view the image at a narrower angle we get the effect of exaggerated or 'steep' perspective, and this commonly occurs when using a wide-angle lens for photographing interiors. The effect is the more noticeable if the subject contains objects both near and far from the lens. One remedy is to choose a viewpoint which reduces the depth between the near and far planes. For example, the use of a wide-angle lens for panoramic views presents no such difficulty if the picture includes only distant features. In the same way the use of a wide-angle lens to photograph the façade of a building or the face of an interior wall presents no problems in perspective. On the other hand, this kind of distortion can be beneficial to the client who wishes to give the impression that a small room is, in fact, much larger.

The use of a long-focus lens for interiors is normally restricted to photo-graphing detail such as carvings and other ornamentation. Indeed, as we have shown earlier, a long-focus lens is usually preferable to the use of a normal-angle lens if, to obtain the required image scale, the latter lens must be used at very close distances. Used outdoors a long-focus lens will have the effect of foreshortening distance so that objects in the background – buildings or moun-tains – will appear relatively larger than when the subject is taken with a standard lens. This assumes that the long-focus lens is used at a greater distance to give the same image size of the object of principal interest in the foreground.

181

Lighting contrast

The highlight and shadow ratio on a clear day in the open is rarely excessive i the subject is a fairly large building, though the direction of light may itself be unfavourable at certain times of the day. For example, a side of the building facing south will receive frontal lighting during the middle hours of the day (ir the northern hemisphere) and more interesting light may occur earlier or late in the day. But in restricted areas undesirable shadows may be cast by nearby buildings, and the amount of light falling on shadow areas may be severely restricted at certain times of day. A study of the orientation of the building and its surroundings may suggest a more suitable time for a future visit, or since the altitude of the sun varies also on a seasonal basis a more favourable time of the year. Thus it may be found that the porch of a building, a portico or verandah i better illuminated in the winter when the sun is low at midday, than in the summer when it is almost overhead. A study of the lighting on some local building of merit at various times of the year can be very valuable to the architectura photographer. Naturally the traveller is often obliged to accept the lighting a any given time of day and date, but it frequently happens that, by making use o the early hours of daylight, he can steal a march on his lazier colleagues. For the same reason it may be better to plan a tour for the spring or autumn rather than the summer, gaining the additional advantage that adjacent foliage and vegeta tion will be more interesting.

A study of lighting in areas of narrow streets and tall buildings may revea that light reflected from one wall at a certain time of day strongly illuminates a facing building normally in deep shade. This is commonly the case in countrie with warm climates, where light-toned finishes to the exterior walls of building are favoured.

Lower lighting contrasts due to strong haze or a layer of cloud are far easie to handle with colour film but make for less interesting effects, since the shape and direction of shadows provide valuable clues to the structure and surface of a building.

Restricted viewpoint

Apart from the possibility of using a wider-angle lens when the camera distance is too short for a lens of normal angle, it may be worth considering whether a part of the building can be selected to represent the whole. This often makes for a better composition than a photograph of the whole building, which may involve including unwanted parts of adjacent buildings or which, in any case may not compose well in the picture area. It may also happen that windows o adjacent offices, hotels and houses offer a favourable viewpoint, the owners o which, courteously approached, will gladly give access, if not immediately, at some more convenient time. It may even happen that a restricted viewpoint can be turned to advantage, using some feature of a building in the foreground as a natural frame or device for excluding unwanted detail in the background.

182

Traffic

Passing over the danger of disregarding street traffic in search of the best viewpoint, it frequently happens that the early morning, as well as offering more favourable lighting, also solves the problem of traffic congestion. Car parks before office and shopping hours are frequently empty, and many vantage points become tenable. Though now of little practical importance to the colour photographer, it is of interest to recall that the photographer of fifty years ago with much slower materials was able to overcome the problem of traffic and pedestrians passing in front of the camera viewpoint by setting his lens at a small aperture and giving an exposure of several minutes. So long as he kept an eye open for loiterers, no trace of the passage of such temporary obstructions was recorded on the negative. This method may still suggest itself to the photography of buildings at night, making use of existing street lighting or flood-lights, though the lights of passing traffic may still prove troublesome unless very prolonged exposures are used, and these unfortunately will involve reciprocity failure.

Flood-lighting, extensively used in big cities during the tourist season, may also suggest itself as an alternative approach to the photography of famous buildings. It usually happens that the lighting has been skilfully placed to show up the more attractive features of the building, aside from the fact that it may isolate the building from unwanted surroundings. The enterprising photographer may well consider the possibility of photographing a smallish building by a number of well-placed flashbulbs. These can be fired successively with the camera on a tripod and the shutter uncapped just before each flash is fired. Bearing in mind that a flash factor of nearly 400 applies to the use of a PF60/97 for High Speed Ektachrome Film or a PF60 used with the Type B version, and a Wratten 81C filter, it will be appreciated that lamp-to-subject distances of 50 ft. and more can be effective at apertures of f/8. By using clusters of four bulbs the lamp distance can be doubled or the aperture reduced by two stops in the interest of depth of field. Flashbulbs or electronic flash can be similarly used for lighting interiors, the chief precaution being to avoid standing in such a position that the flash unit and its means of support are not between the camera and the area being illuminated. Cases have been reported where a large interior has been uniformly illuminated with the expenditure of 1,000 and more flashbulbs exposed over a period of several hours, or even with a large charge of flash powder!

Interior lighting

Much of the charm of photographs of architectural interiors in black-and-white lies in the use of existing daylight coming through windows and other openings, shafts of sunlight piercing the gloom of lofty naves, yet without loss of subtle tonal differences in the deepest shadow areas. However, such photographs are often a demonstration of the photographer's skill in the darkroom in the use of dodging and shading techniques. Lighting contrasts of well over 1,000 : 1 may be involved and are clearly outside the exposure range of a reversal film. This, however, does not mean that such effects of lighting are impossible with colour photography, but that they cannot be achieved solely with natural lighting. It is merely a question of lighting balance, namely of raising the level of interior illumination to something more nearly approaching that of sunlight. Perhaps this is more easily said than done if we want to preserve a completely natural effect, and some care must be taken in studying the directions from which supplementary lighting would naturally come and also to use strong diffusers to avoid false shadow effects.

However, in modern architecture the trend is towards uniform illumination by means of large window areas during the hours of daylight and equally uniform lighting from fluorescent lamps after dark. While this has simplified the photographer's task, it may still be necessary to use supplementary lighting with daylight, since what may appear to be uniform to the eye may not be so in a colour photograph.

The colour quality of the daylight reaching the interior will vary with the time of day, the orientation of the windows, weather conditions, possible reflections from adjacent walls facing a window, the colour of the glass, and, if curtains are present, the colour and nature of such curtaining. Unfortunately, the eye rapidly adapts itself to the prevailing light, and the lack of colour-balance in the photograph may be attributed to another cause. For example, many churches employ green-coloured glass in windows not fitted with stained-glass pictures. This may impart a greenish colour bias in tones that should appear neutral. A large area of window receiving blue light from the sky may similarly impart a bluish colour bias, and the two together may combine to produce a cyan bias. Such conditions can be noted by the observant photographer and, when using reversal films, corrected by using a suitable colour-compensating filter. If the quality and colour of daylight is variable and of questionable colour quality, it may be simpler to photograph interiors of moderate size with artificial lighting. Indirect flash-lighting using the ceiling or light-coloured walls as reflectors is often the simplest approach to obtaining the lighting quality of diffused daylight. This method often goes by the name 'bounced flash' – see also page 199 on its application in portraiture.

Sculpture, carvings and relief images

Daylight or existing artificial lighting is seldom the most appropriate for photographing the detail of a building. Naturally there are occasions when the sun may strike a statue or relief carving at the right angle, but even here some form of supplementary lighting may be needed to reduce the lighting contrast. However, distinction needs to be made between richly painted figures and decorations, which are often to be found in churches, and those of natural stone and wood. The former may be recorded best with almost flat lighting coming from the camera position, while the latter rely on the effect of light and shade to obtain the effects of solidity and roundness. Relief images, inscriptions and surface textures generally benefit from various degrees of oblique or side-lighting of a strongly directional nature, and although the sun may occasionally serve this purpose, a spotlight or flash unit is normally an essential accessory.

Stained-glass windows

The approximate recording of the colours of stained-glass windows presents no difficulty and a high degree of saturation can be obtained in colour transparencies, falling little short of reality when they are viewed over an illuminated panel. More accurate colour rendering will depend somewhat on the quality of daylight illuminating the window, the range of colours in the window, and the density of the colours. Direct sunlight behind a window, although pleasing to observe, gives a 'burnt-out' region in the photograph even when the actual ball of the sun is screened by intermediate stonework. However, a region of sky fairly near the sun gives an excellent form of illumination, intense enough to permit hand-held cameras to be used with a colour film of a speed as low as 32 ASA. Windows lit by a clear blue sky may take on a slightly blue cast if the colours of the glass are of a delicate pastel nature. In this case a Wratten No. 1A or 81B filter can be used. When the subject contains highly saturated colours, the warmer colours (red, orange and yellow) will scarcely be affected, whereas greens and blues may show improved colour rendering. Exposures can be based on a reading taken reasonably close to the window so as to take in a representative area of the window, but it is generally worth while to give one or two exposures above and below the indicated exposure to be sure of obtaining the best effect for transparencies intended for projection. The colour saturation will become less as the exposure is increased.

Normally the interior illumination of the building is insufficient to allow recording of detail of the adjacent wall if the exposure is such as to obtain the best saturation of the window. Supplementary lighting, such as blue flash-bulbs or electronic flash, can be used at from $1\frac{1}{2}$ times to twice the normal flash factor distance depending on the level of illumination required. It must be remembered, however, that the apparent brilliance of the colours in the window will be less effective if surrounded by lighter tones. When using flash, care should be taken that the angle at which the unit is fired does not cause a reflection from the glass into the camera lens.

The major problem of stained-glass window photography is normally one of location. Most windows are situated well above the floor level and to avoid tilting the camera involves using a rising front or some other camera movement. However, the photographer on tour equipped with a small camera and two or three lenses, may, with the help of the custodian or verger, gain access to galleries and other vantage points not open to the general public. It is, in any case, always advisable to obtain permission for photography inside public buildings.

14

Portraiture

ANY PICTURE depicting a likeness of the human face may be described as a portrait, and portraits of a sort have been a favourite subject ever since it was discovered how to make marks and lines on walls, skins, canvas and paper. And understandably enough, since the face is the stamp of each individual's personality – the principal outward sign of one's identity. As a subject, the face seems to lend itself equally well to line or continuous-tone treatment, to monochrome or colour. As long as certain aspects of its 'geography' are right, a few strokes of a pencil are enough to make it recognizable, when we are already familiar with the original. This is the art of the caricaturist. But in spite of our familiarity with faces in general and a few in particular, very few people have the knack of being able to draw – or paint – a convincing likeness. Thus until the advent of photography, the drawing and painting of portraits was in the hands of a relatively few artists. This monopoly ceased with the appearance of the Daguerrotype towards the middle of the last century.

In a sense, the camera brought realism and authenticity to portraiture: in another sense it discouraged and has well-nigh destroyed the art of portrait painting. To some extent the painted portrait still retains 'prestige' and snob value, but the less materialistic artists have sought refuge in forms of portrait intended, so we are told, to reveal the soul rather than the face. And certainly such styles, which make no pretence at a likeness, must be a great relief to artists lacking the ability to produce a convincing likeness. But if all photographs of the face may be described as portraits, the term is more generally reserved for calculated attempts by means of posing, lighting, and choice of background or setting, to present both a likeness and something of the character of the subject. The term 'posing' may here be taken to include the surreptitious approach of 'candid' portraits and various psychological approaches adopted with children and others to free them from camera consciousness. At any event it is in this sense that we use the term in the present chapter.

Much has been written on the subject of photographic portraiture, and there are inevitably differences of opinion between one author and the next. But in one respect most experts are in agreement, namely, that it is the most difficult and exacting of all branches of photography. This is because it demands great deal more than technical skill in handling a camera and the use of lighting: to be successful, the portraitist must be something of a psychologist, a student of human nature. Not only must he try to understand his subject, but to be successful professionally, he must try to see his subjects as they see themselves, and with children as they are seen by their parents.

Kinds of portrait

Omitting snapshot and identity portraits, both of which may yield the occasional masterpiece, we can broadly classify portraits into the formal kind, often of the type associated with ceremonial dress, uniform or robes of office; character studies, which can include carefully posed and lit portraits of actors and actresses, writers and politicians, the very young and the very old, and any face that happens to appeal to a photographer specializing in this kind of portrait; spontaneous or candid portraits of the type taken by photo-reporters and others interested in catching their fellow creatures unawares; glamour portraits designed to enhance sex appeal, often by association with luxury and expensive clothes, and fashion portraiture, which tends to idealize and impersonalize the face as a setting or foil for the clothes displayed; and family portraits which aim to depict their subjects with the most pleasing and amiable expressions.

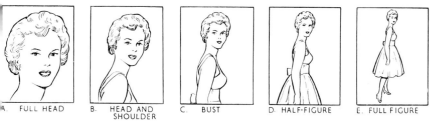

A. FULL HEAD   B. HEAD AND   C.   BUST   D. HALF-FIGURE   E. FULL FIGURE
                         SHOULDER

Fig. 14.1. Classes of portrait in relation to the extent of the subject included in the negative area (A) normally requires a lens of three times the standard focal length, (B) twice the standard focal length, while (C), (D), and (E) can usually be accommodated with a standard lens.

The portrait studio

While there is much to be said for the use of daylight for portraits – and we shall be discussing this later in the chapter – it is on artificial light-sources that the professional must chiefly rely, as much as anything for their constant availability and the degree of control they offer. The use of artificial lighting, however, presupposes some form of studio, even if the studio be no more than an adapted sitting room when taking informal portraits in the home. It is perhaps simpler to lay down the requirement of an ideal studio than to find such a room and to arrange it as it should be. However, without being too ambitious, it is fairly

187

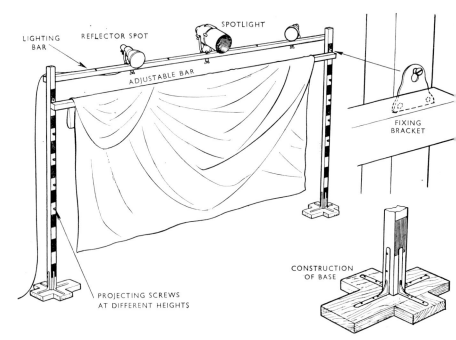

Fig. 14.2. Suggestion for a movable stand to hold background materials and lamps used for back-lighting. The side posts should be about 8 ft. high.

simple to determine suitable dimensions for the room. Assuming we wish to be able to tackle full figure portraits of the erect figure standing perhaps in a small 'set' having a field area of 8 × 6 ft. (this allows some headroom and foreground for an average figure), then the minimum camera distance for a lens of standard focal length (roughly equal to the diagonal of the negative size) is about 10 ft. If to this we add 5 ft. behind the lens for working distance and about the same distance behind the subject for backgrounds, the length of the studio should be about 20 ft. Although a width of 12 ft. would be adequate, better space for placing lights and for manœuverability would require 15 ft. A height of 10 ft. will be needed to allow for the vertical placing of lamps. Clearly the room could be larger to allow for longer focal lengths and increased background space. A somewhat shorter room would be suitable for half-length portraiture, the lens-to-subject distance being halved and something less than 5 ft. behind the subject. But it is usually desirable to maintain a camera-to-subject distance of not less than 10 ft. in the interests of acceptable perspective. In fact, a seated figure normally occupies a greater depth than a standing figure. Thus to fill the picture area comfortably would mean using a lens of nearly double the focal length. This is less important in making a negative since the required image can be obtained

188

ıy enlargement. For head-and-shoulder and large-head portraits, a lens of three ɔ four times the standard focal length would be needed to maintain this distance, nd in the case of transparency work it may be necessary to compromise by educing the camera-to-subject distance, though preferably not to less than 6 ft.

For colour work the walls of the studio should be painted with matt white ɔr light grey paint. The former gives higher reflecting power but may be lazzling to the eyes with high-efficiency tungsten lamps. While it is sometimes empting to think of a studio having a large expanse of window with the object ɔf making occasional use of daylight, the need to be able to black-out the vindow when using artificial light may far outweigh the advantage. In fact, it is ɔetter to think in terms of ventilation, when tungsten lamps are being used, in ʳiew of the large amount of heat they emit. Thus a small window can be ɔrovided with a shutter having a ventilating fan fitted into it. Some thought hould also be given to heating for the winter months, and an electric heater vhich can be switched off when not required is the simplest solution. A small lressing room off the studio is an ideal arrangement either for use as a make-up oom or for changing clothes. It should contain, among other things, a large nirror at chair level with illumination surrounding it, see fig. 14.3. Failing a eparate dressing room, a corner of the studio can be screened off for the same ɔurpose. But if nothing else, the studio should at least contain an adequate wall nirror.

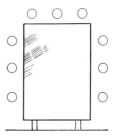

Fig. 14.3. A mirror for applying make-up should be provided with lamps as shown in the diagram.

Apart from lighting units and their ancillary equipment, a large wooden tand of the kind shown in fig. 14.2 will be useful for supporting backgrounds ɪnd lamps used for back-lighting and for lighting the hair. Alternative arrange-nents may suggest themselves, and, if the room is very high, something after the tyle of a theatre stage drop may be devised. Props by way of chairs, stools and he like should not be allowed to clutter up the studio and only those required ɔr the session should be in position.

It is convenient also if a small darkroom leads off the operating end of the tudio for loading plate-holders and storing lighting accessories, spare lamps, ɪnd the like. An ante-room, curtained off from the studio, is also desirable for ɔlients to relax in, should there be any delay in beginning the session. This should ɪlso be equipped with a mirror and be made as comfortable and attractive as ɔossible. Anything that encourages your prospective subject to relax, such as illustrated magazines, flowers or a few toys (when dealing with children), will simplify your job inside the studio.

Choice of lighting

We have already discussed the characteristics of artificial light-sources in Chapter 6, and it remains to be seen which of the two principal sources – tungsten lamps or electronic flash – is the more convenient and suitable for portraits. For tungsten lighting, colour-controlled lamps of 3,200°K. are both more stable and economical for regular use, lamps of the photoflood type being more suited to occasional use. In order to produce a reasonable level of illumination for a set of 8 × 6 ft. using colour films of from 40 to 64 ASA, three or four 1,000-watt floodlights will be needed for general lighting, with, say, two 500-watt floodlights for additional background illumination. A 2,000-watt spotlight will make a valuable key light and a 500-watt spotlight will serve for back-lighting or hair-lighting effects. In other words, we need from 6,000 to 7,000 watts of lighting to be able to use an exposure time of 1/10 to 1/30 sec. at an average working aperture of around f/5·6. We could use considerably more light, or, with the large apertures possible with small cameras, somewhat less light. However, from the point of view of electrical consumption, a power line suitable for supplying up to 30 amp. for 240-volt lamps (more than double this for 110-volt lamps) is vital. This may be compared with the few hundred watts required by electronic flash used with a pilot lighting system. Furthermore, the latter delivers its light in something like 1/1,000 sec. and thus eliminates the danger of exposures spoilt through subject movement – a very real danger with young children. On the other hand, the continuous nature of tungsten light enables a more realistic visual assessment to be made of a particular lighting arrangement, and also fine adjustments to be made to the position of lights and in the use of diffusers and reflectors. With experience, the pilot lighting system provided by the large electronic flash equipment may be used with similar effect, and in practice the professional portrait photographer tends to work to certain lighting arrangements of proved success. These may vary according to the age and sex of the subject – strong lighting effects for men, almost total diffusion for children, and so on – and also to his personal ideas on what constitutes good lighting. The greater ease of controlling and experimenting with tungsten lighting will usually appeal more to the student or the serious amateur for whom

Plate 38. This highly-finished studio portrait was taken with tungsten lighting and Ektacolor Film, Type L. Diffused lighting was used to give general illumination with two small spotlights, one each side and behind the plane of the subject, for modelling. Additional lighting was used for the background. The 8 × 10 in. negative was retouched with neutral and red pencils to remove facial blemishes, and further retouching was done on the Ektacolor print with a brush and Flexichrome dyes to remove an unwanted reflection on the nose and one catch light from each eye. The edges of the print were darkened slightly in exposure. The photograph was made by W. G. Gaskins, while taking the three-month scholarship course in the U.S.A. offered by Kodak Ltd. to selected photographers.

Plate 39.

Plate 40.

Plate 41.

Plate 42.

ach subject is a separate challenge to his skill and imagination, and, perhaps
nore important, for whom time is of no special account. On the grounds of film
hoice there are equally good films for both kinds of illumination.

Finally it should be noted that the lower lighting contrasts generally
esirable with colour portraits, particularly with women and children, are more
asily obtained by using electronic flash, indirectly making use of the white walls
f the studio and other reflecting surfaces, than by using diffusers with tungsten
imps. Generally speaking, an electronic lighting system consisting of a power
nit capable of delivering 500 to 1,000 watt-seconds or joules with from four to
ix flash heads (one adapted as a spotlight) provides ample illumination for the
ortrait studio.

Clothes and make-up

The photographer providing a service for personal and family portraiture may
ave little interest or control over the clothes and make-up, if any, of his clients.
Women tend to choose colours which are fashionable or which they imagine suit
nem best, and it may be difficult to do more than suggest 'quiet' colours and a
noderate application of make-up. On the other hand, the photographer has
omplete control over the tone and colour of the background, and a vivid colour
f dress can be made less disturbing by using a background of the same colour,
nough of a darker tone. This situation is also the same for the fashion photo-
rapher, since his task is to display the clothes rather than the model. But his
hoice may extend to both the setting and the model. The position is different for
ne photographer specializing in 'character' studies, 'glamour' portraits for
alenders, picture postcards and magazines, and, of course, also for the amateur
sing either his friends or professional models as subjects. In such cases the
hotographer may be in a position to choose the clothes and, if needed, the kind
f make-up to be applied to the model.

Plate 39. The high contrast given by strong overhead sunlight is acceptable in this portrait of a
ardinian peasant as being in keeping with the rugged features and the festive occasion. Had the
ubject been a young woman, fill-in flash would have been needed to give detail to the eyes.
rom a Kodachrome II transparency by E. S. Bomback.

Plate 40. The effect of overcast daylight has been obtained in the studio by the use of a large area
f diffused lighting. The umbrella suggests, however, that it has been taken outdoors.
Ektachrome transparency by Jack M. Oakley.

Plates 41 and 42. These two indoor portraits were made with flash bounced from a large reflector.
. similar lighting effect would result in using the light from a single window. However, with the
ortrait of the child, the exaggerated contrast which results from such unbalanced lighting has
een used to outline the profile. In some cases the effect may add interest to a portrait as being in
eeping with available light photography, in others it may be classed as the work of a novice who
as yet to learn the difference between the visual and photographic effects. In the portrait of a
oung woman a second reflector has been used to give an effect more in keeping with the visual
npression of illumination coming from a single window in a small room with walls of average
ones. Ektachrome transparencies by Jack M. Oakley.

12

It is difficult to give advice on the choice of colours in wearing apparel, though it should go without saying that too many colours should be avoided, and highly saturated colours, particularly in red and orange, used with discretion. Cyan and green, colours complementary to skin tints, should also be used with caution, since they may suggest an undesirable degree of pinkness in the complexion. The problem seldom arises with men, though dark blues, such as navy blue, may reproduce poorly with tungsten illumination. Lighter tones, including white for girls, are preferable for children, vivid splashes of colour being introduced by means of hair ribbons, toys and other accessories.

Make-up is normally associated only with women, but may be equally desirable with certain male subjects who suffer from a 'blue chin'. While the effect may be minimized if the subject has a close shave shortly before the portrait session, make-up may still be necessary to eliminate the 'shadow' that still remains and which may look like dirt rather than a dark beard.

With women, moderate make-up as worn for the street is equally suitable for colour photography. However, in a 'close-up' portrait, the make-up must be applied meticulously, since it is equivalent to inspecting a face from a close distance. Many professional photographers rely on the services of a make-up expert, and failing this it may be preferable to leave it to the subject to make any adjustments considered necessary. Children, the majority of men, and old people generally are seldom in need of any make-up. Diffused lighting is generally more favourable to the complexion that has lost its 'pristine' bloom than strongly directional lighting.

Posing and subject-photographer relationship

No one commissioning a portrait painter would object to being the subject of close observation at sessions extending over weeks and often months. Unfortunately, the knowledge that a camera can work with such instantaneous speed leads many people to suppose that five minutes should be ample time for a photographic portrait. With pre-arranged lighting a passport 'likeness' can be, and usually is, disposed of in little more than a minute, but then we neither desire nor expect a 'character' study from such a visit to the photographers. But it is difficult to be specific about the time needed to make a worth-while portrait since much depends on the subject and to some extent on the photographer himself. In some cases it may amount to no more than 'putting the subject at ease', in others almost the contrary may be true, and the subject may need to be provoked to take on the desired expression or mood. Professional models, like good actors and actresses, pride themselves on their capacity to produce whatever mood or expression is called for by the photographer. But it is on the photographer that the real burden lies, and it is profitable to consider some of the attributes of a good portrait photographer. We have already referred to some namely a liking for one's fellow creatures; the ability to identify oneself with the subject. In addition, if you are by nature a good listener, are tolerant, patient and understanding, someone who can inspire confidence and enthusiasm, are gentle without being timid, can accept defeat without becoming angry or sarcastic, have an 'eye' for a good composition and are a moderately good technician, it is worth considering photographic portraiture as a career.

The word 'posing' may suggest something rather formal, even unnatural, and is often used as a derogatory term in referring to someone we consider to be 'affected' or to put on airs and graces. But in the sense used by photographers it means placing the subject in a suitable position in relation to the camera, choosing a particular aspect of the face, arranging the arms and hands, and if a full figure portrait is being taken, the general posture of the figure and its relation to the background or setting. It could mean no more than telling the subject in which direction to look, or it could involve an elaborate, step-by-step preparation with pins and clothes-pegs if you are attempting a costume piece.

Some people have a natural grace and bearing, and unconsciously take natural and pleasing poses. This seems to apply especially so to the Latin and Oriental races. The Nordic races tend to be more stolid, more matter-of-fact, more unresponsive to natural feelings. As a nation the British take pride in concealing their emotions owing to a belief that it is a weakness to give reign to their feelings: the result is that there are few more awkward or self-conscious subjects to be found when it comes to facing a camera for something more than a passport photograph.

Posing is often much easier if the subject is given something to hold or something to do. Men are especially self-conscious about their hands, and a book, pipe or some collector's piece may offer an excellent solution, even if the hands are not included in the picture area. Directions generally should take into account that the subjects left and right are the reverse of the photographer and it is therefore better to use some other reference, such as 'Turn towards the door' or 'Keeping your head still, fix your eyes on my hand'. This latter direction – or something like it – is particularly useful since on being requested to look in a certain direction most people turn the head rather than the eyes. By making the subject look into the lens, the portrait will appear to look out of the picture no matter from what direction it is viewed. Generally speaking, it has the effect of giving the photograph an intimate and direct appeal. By having the eyes turned away from the lens, even by a small amount, the effect is to keep the subject 'inside' the photograph. This gives an impersonal effect more in the nature of a character study.

With young children it is often far easier to engage the attention and interest of the subject with some toy or the aid of an assistant who has 'a way with children' than to attempt giving verbal directions. Even if the child is old enough to understand them, it often results in promoting self-consciousness. Child 'specialists' have been known to resort to the most elaborate subterfuges, including a complete Punch and Judy show with the camera man hidden in the base! The photographer's task is then that of choosing the best 'natural' poses to make exposures, and the more generous he is in the use of colour film (herein lies the advantage of the small camera) the more successful he will be. However, children are often more at ease at home, and many photographers prefer to avoid operating in a studio. Indeed a photographer specializing in family portraits may be better off with a car than a studio.

Basic lighting plans

In suggesting a number of basic lighting plans, it is with the intention of encouraging the student to try them out for himself and from these to progress to the finer points of lighting. For this he will need a good-natured model, and preferably one who is used to working with the portrait section of a camera club. It is also advisable to keep notes of such experiments.

One of the simplest plans is the use of a single source of flood-lighting, well to one side of the camera and making a vertical angle of at least 30° with the horizontal plane of the camera, see fig. 14.4. The lamp should be placed well

Fig. 14.4. A simple lighting arrangement based on one flood-lamp and a large reflector or white wall.

back and so directed that it covers a large reflector placed as close to the subject as the angle of the lens will permit, with the object of throwing light into the shadows. It is preferable to have the subject facing, though not necessarily looking towards, the flood-light. This plan may be compared with outdoor lighting consisting of hazy sunlight with light coming from a whitish sky. By varying the nature of the reflecting surface, and, if a matt surface, its distance from the subject, a considerable range of lighting contrast may be obtained. The lighting unit, which may consist of a single lamp fitted with a light diffuser or a small bank of lamps, can be placed anywhere within a wide range of angles, the reflector being moved round to throw light into the shadows. If necessary, an aperture can be cut in the reflector to enable it to be used in front of the lens. As the angle of the lighting unit approaches full side-lighting, care must be taken to shield the lens of the camera from direct light. Simple though this arrangement can be, it is very suitable for photographing children, since it allows considerable latitude in the position of the subject and only involves the use of one cable or flash lead. If the subject has dark hair a small spotlight or well-shielded reflector spotlamp can be placed well above and somewhat behind the subject.

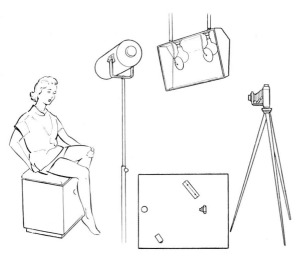

Fig. 14.5. Arrangement based on a broad flood-light near the lens axis with a spotlight to give high-lights or modelling.

The second plan consists of using a broad area of general flood-lighting to provide a high level of uniform illumination over the whole field of view, and a spotlight to introduce high-lights of slightly higher intensity than the general lighting – see fig. 14.5. The spotlight may be used over a wide range of angles but should be well above the plane of the camera. An additional spotlight may be used to obtain catch-lights in the hair. Here again the effect may be that of very delicate sunlight. The student may like to try this arrangement using photofloods and a 500-watt slide projector in place of the spotlight. The light from the projector may not exactly match that of the photofloods but can usually be corrected with a Wratten 81C filter in the slide gate. But remember that most slide projector lamps are designed to be burnt in a vertical position and should not be tilted at an angle exceeding 20°.

The third plan is based on the use of a spotlight as the main light-source with the object of gaining somewhat stronger lighting contrasts and is perhaps best suited to male subjects of the rugged type, though it may, of course, be diluted' to suit any subject. The position of the spotlight is determined without other lights being used and should be at a distance of at least 10 ft. for a head-and-shoulder portrait. The nearer the lamp is to the subject the greater the area of shadow, and excessive shadow areas are best avoided in colour work. By having the main light at the greatest possible distance, shadows may be so reduced as to need little by way of supplementary lighting. In this plan, supplementary lighting is provided with a single floodlight, see fig. 14.6. The lighting ratio can be varied with the distance of this lamp, measurements being made with a light meter from a matt white card.

In all three plans additional lighting may be needed for the background, depending on its distance from the subject, the tone rendering required and the distance of the main light from the subject. If a spotlight is available, it is possible to produce various shadow effects on a light-toned background, such as that shown in fig. 14.7.

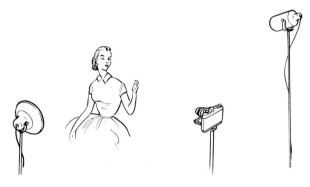

Fig. 14.6. A spotlight used as main light to give strong directional lighting with a small flood to act as fill-in.

The fourth plan, which is very suitable for portraits of children, is a variation of plan two, and is found very successful when using a medium-capacity electronic flash unit (120-200 watt-sec.) with provision for two flash heads. The light from one flash head is converted into a broad area of diffused lighting by placing a screen of translucent plastic fabric (of the kind sold for bathroom curtains and usually with a white pattern printed on it) between the lamp and the subject as shown in fig. 14.8. This gives an effect similar to light coming from a window. The second lamp is directed upwards to the ceiling, but at such an angle as to allow a little of the 'spill' light to fall on the subject with the object of providing catch-lights to the eyes and hair. If both walls and ceiling are white both lamps may be used indirectly, one towards a wall facing the subject and the second towards the ceiling. In a small room, such as a bathroom or nursery, one

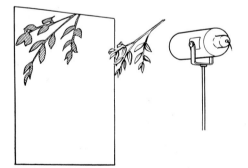

Fig. 14.7. Use of a spotlight to throw a shadow on to a background.

amp is sufficient, and it probably provides the best method for using a single flashgun. This method also goes by the name 'bounced' flash, and apart from producing a most delicate quality of lighting eliminates the problem of adjusting the flash-to-subject distance. Thus both subject and photographer are as free to move as in lightly overcast daylight without the need to adjust the exposure. The exposure level is best found by trial and error, but can be roughly based on half the normal guide number for direct flash.

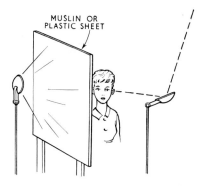

Fig. 14.8. A flash unit may be converted into a broad flood by placing a sheet of translucent plastic material between the lamp and the subject. In this arrangement a second flash unit is directed towards the ceiling as an indirect light source, allowing some spill light to fall on the eyes of the subject.

MUSLIN OR PLASTIC SHEET

Indoor portraits with daylight

There is always a hard core among portrait photographers who maintain that daylight from windows is the most satisfactory form of lighting for indoor portraits, and there is certainly something to be said for this point of view. Unfortunately, from the professional's point of view this can be something of a gamble with the weather, and during the winter the hours of useful daylight are very restricted. However, portraits taken in the home, and of subjects in authentic working backgrounds – craftsmen, artists and others – may of necessity involve the use of daylight, if not always as the principal light-source, then as a subsidiary source in the form of windows in the background.

The practicability of using daylight for colour work has been greatly increased in recent years by the general increase in the speed of colour films. It is also helped by the modern tendency in domestic and industrial building to make much greater use of windows, and it is not uncommon to find a sitting room with windows on three sides. In such a case daylight can often form the only source of lighting. Windows admitting direct sunlight may be controlled with muslin curtains, or the sunlight may be 'collected' on to a reflector board and redirected to a subject a little away from the window as a useful source of diffused light.

One of the minor problems of interior daylight is the variability of its colour quality. This can be due not only to the variability of the sky and the presence or otherwise of sunlight, but also to such influences as nearby foliage and grass lawns, the walls of adjacent buildings, window curtains and the interior decoration generally. Thus a shaft of sunlight falling on a bright red carpet can easily impart a reddish quality to the lighting. Low-level sunlight shining into a room may be strongly yellow, though it may not appear so. The use of correction filters may offset these effects when using reversal colour films if the overall quality is off-balance. Otherwise, in a case where local variations occur owing to light coming from more than one window, or because of reflecting surfaces, it may be preferable to restrict the light to one window, or perhaps remove or cover the offending cause of coloured reflected light.

When using artificial sources to supplement daylight, the colour temperature should correspond as nearly as possible to that of the daylight. For this purpose both electronic flash and blue flashbulbs offer satisfactory forms of supplementary lighting.

The chief problem with window daylight is often that of excessive lighting contrast, a state of affairs seldom appreciated by the untrained photographer owing to the visual effect known as 'brightness constancy' (see page 133). The only reliable guide to intensity variations is a sensitive light-meter. A suitable lighting balance may be achieved in a variety of ways: by using reflectors or supplementary lighting for the shadows, by reducing the intensity of light coming from one window with one or more layers of muslin, by placing the subject so as to receive more uniform lighting (in this case it may be necessary to take the camera outside and shoot through the door or open window), or by raising the general level of interior illumination by use of flash bounced off the ceiling.

Outdoor portraits

Given the right lighting conditions, nothing can be simpler or more 'authentic' than an outdoor portrait. Such conditions occur when sunlight is softened by strong haze, and also under a lightly overcast sky. With strong sunlight some form of fill-in light is usually desirable and can be supplied by means of reflectors or flash. Of the two, reflectors are less convenient to handle but easier to manage when it comes to achieving 'natural' results. Considerable care is needed with fill-in flash to avoid false lighting effects, even when the right degree of lighting balance is achieved. Undoubtedly the best way of obtaining competence in the use of fill-in flash is to acquire a small electronic flash unit and to make tests under all possible conditions. For the most part, these tests can be carried out with black-and-white materials if the cost of colour film has to be considered.

However, even when the right lighting conditions exist or have been created, a very high proportion of outdoor portraits fail to qualify as anything more than competent snapshots. The reason for this is the failure on the part of the photographer to choose a suitable background or setting, or, as is very often the case, to judge from results, that the photographer seems to be be unaware of the existence or nature of the background when taking the photograph. One reason for this is the very narrow angle of acute vision, but equally important is the mental process whereby we select and reject according to our interests. It is worth drawing attention to yet another difference between seeing with our two eyes and looking at a two-dimensional photograph. With binocular vision we ee in depth and it may be quite obvious (and unimportant) that there is a elegraph pole some distance behind the subject. But in a photograph it can ppear to be growing out of the subject's head. The normal adult eye can focus utomatically from as near as 8 in. to the far distance, but when focused on earby objects is no longer in focus for distant objects. Differential focusing to an ven greater degree can be applied photographically, but frequently the high evel of illumination outdoors calls for small apertures which, with short-focus enses, result in excessive depth of field.

All this adds up to the importance of developing what might be called ackground awareness. Indeed, it should be the first consideration in outdoor ortraiture: first find a suitable location, and other things, such as lighting, osing, viewpoint and so on will follow. Failing an ideal background, other nethods such as differential focusing, walls in deep shadow, doorways and rches looking into a dark interior and the like, may at least provide an unobtru- ive background. Indeed, it is not always appreciated that a blue sky makes an deal background for 'close-up' portraits, both the tone and colouring blending vell with the tones and colours of the subject.

The use of a long-focus lens, as well as providing better perspective, offers he additional advantages of greater capacity for differential focusing and a arrower angle of view. In this latter respect it is often possible to avoid un- vanted background features in the distance which would be included with a lens of normal angle.

15

Natural History

WE CAN distinguish between the naturalist who uses photography as a means of making records and the photographer who chooses natural history subjects because of their intrinsic beauty or because such subjects offer a challenge to his skill in tracking them down and 'shooting' them. The naturalist will be far more concerned with the accuracy of his record than its pictorial effect, and may frequently have little more than a utilitarian interest in cameras. Indeed, lacking the photographer's enthusiasm for the photographic process, he may frequently fail to make the best use of it. This chapter is therefore chiefly addressed to the naturalist wishing to make use of colour photography in his researches, and to some extent covers – in a more simplified manner – ground-work which has already been discussed in earlier chapters of this book.

The question of accuracy

The image formed by a high-grade photographic lens over its intended angle of view should satisfy the most exacting demands for definition if correctly focused and free from movement blur (either from camera shake or subject movement). The best definition can usually be expected at an aperture 2 to 3 stops below the maximum, any loss of definition at maximum being chiefly at the edges of the field. Depth of field, namely the depth over which the image will appear sharp, increases as the lens is stopped down. A common cause of unsharpness in photographs is that of camera shake, particularly when using a hand-held camera at shutter speeds longer than 1/100 sec., though it can occur in the hands of a careless operator at 1/100 sec. and shorter. Camera shake may also occur when using a small tripod at shutter speeds of 1/50 sec. to 1/4 sec. through neglecting to use a flexible cable release of at least 10 in. With many modern cameras exposures of stationary subjects at slow shutter speeds can be made without camera shake by using the delayed action device (usually indicated by 'V'). This can also help with hand-held camera exposures, though in this case the lever of the delayed release should only be set a small amount. A few experiments will indicate the amount needed. A second cause, usually detectable because of its local nature, is that of subject movement. Blooms on slender stems are set into motion with the slightest breeze, and insects, although stationary, may be moving

eir antennae or mandibles. The extent of such recorded movement depends on
e scale of photography, the speed and direction of movement, and the duration
 the exposure. It can be reduced or eliminated by careful observation of the
ecimen so that the exposure is made during a moment of complete rest, or by
ing a fast shutter speed. However, an electronic flash unit is probably the best
arantee of obtaining sharp images since it gives an exposure time of $1/500$ sec.
 less.

From the point of view of recorded definition, a film such as Kodachrome II
as no equal in 35 mm. and smaller film sizes. However, the use of larger format
ameras with Ektachrome, Kodacolor or Ektacolor films may give equally
tisfactory definition because of the larger image scale. On the question of
oosing between a reversal colour film (producing direct colour positives) and a
egative colour film (producing colour negatives from which positives are
inted) the advantage may lie with the reversal type since transparencies are
ore easily viewed under standardized conditions, are suitable for photo-
echanical reproduction, are ideal for lecture purposes and are the least
xpensive form of colour photography when only one copy is required. If
uplicates are required for educational purposes, it may be better to use a
egative-type film, and in the case of film-strip production, a film such as
astmancolor Negative film.

On the question of the accuracy of colour rendering – doubtless the big
uestion in the mind of most naturalists – there is no simple answer. It is a subject
hich has already taken up a large part of this book. To summarize, complete
ccuracy is impossible, nor is the degree of error a constant one even under the
ost standardized lighting conditions, since minor variations in colour balance
ay arise from non-standard processing, ageing of the film, small batch-to-batch
ariation of the same film, reciprocity failure, unfavourable climatic conditions
igh temperature and humidity) combined with unfavourable film storage
efore exposure, delay in processing after exposure, and, over a period of time,
ding of the dyes which make up the image. However, this does not mean that a
tisfactory standard of colour rendering is impossible with reasonable care in
oring and exposing colour films. In work of a comparative nature it is advisable
 obtain sufficient film beforehand of the same emulsion number (needless to say
hanges of the kind or type of film should be avoided) and to store the film in a
efrigerator until required for use. Film which has been stored in this way should
e allowed to reach the existing temperature before use, otherwise there is a
anger of moisture condensation on the surface of the film when it is unwound
side the camera. The use of a standard source of light, such as electronic flash
which also provides a constant duration of exposure) or flashbulbs, is an
dditional precaution. It may sometimes be worth while to include a neutral
rey scale at the edge of the field as an indication of the colour balance of the
hotograph. For specialized work involving unusual subjects or requiring a high
egree of accuracy or likely to extend over a longish period of time, it is advisable
 consult the Kodak Technical Advisory Department.

Unaccountable colour casts

In addition to the possible causes summarized above and dealt with more full in earlier chapters, the naturalist, by the nature of his locations, must occasionall look for other causes of unsatisfactory colour balance, often of a very simple kin but which may easily escape notice. Sunlight 'filtering' through foliage will ten to give a yellow-green cast, and small specimens receiving reflected light fro nearby foliage may suffer from a green cast. Reflections, generally from brightl coloured flowers, may be troublesome when photographing small creatures suc as insects in the field. If the source of the coloured reflection is included in th photograph the effect is understandable and acceptable. Specimens photograph ed under glass in a large greenhouse may also appear greenish if there are vin and creepers. Occasionally glass may be painted with a white-wash to deflec some of the sunlight away from the plants and this may become discoloured wit age. The colour rendering of flowers on display in a marquee may suffer in similar way if photographed with existing illumination. Irridescent colours see from an angle even slightly different from that of the lens may differ in th photograph or fail to be recorded at all. This can arise when using a 'close-up viewfinder device or field-frame, and is one good reason for using a single-ler reflex camera.

The visual effect of certain colours may differ appreciably from the photc graphic effect, owing to spectral differences in the response of the eye and th film. This commonly occurs, with blue flowers, the common bluebell and mornin glory being 'classic' examples. Both flowers indeed reflect some red light, a fac which becomes increasingly apparent as the morning glory fades during th course of the day. Subjects photographed through the surface of a rock pool ma appear strongly blue owing to reflections of the sky off the surface of the wate These are less likely to be noticed at the time if interest is centred solely on th specimens. The reflections may be 'killed' by holding a large board over th water at an angle which will cut out the reflection of the sky, or by means of polarizing filter if the camera is used at an angle of about $35°$ to the surface of th water, or a device such as that shown in fig. 15.1. Similar reflections off shin foliage caused by blue sky light may also be lessened by the use of a polarizin filter. The effect, if any, of the polarizing filter can be observed by rotating th filter in front of the eye: the position which gives the best effect is also the positio in which the filter should be used over the camera lens. Normally an increase c $1\frac{1}{2}$ to 2 stops in exposure is needed when using this filter. See plates 21 and 2

Flowers and plants in natural locations

In general, strongly directional lighting such as sunlight is ideal for obtainin both maximum colour saturation and the effect of depth from light and shade Almost equally good, but offering the advantage of being always available an completely under control in regard to direction, is electronic flash. As alread mentioned, the 'speed' of the flash eliminates the danger of image blur. A smal ortable flash unit is adequate for most situations, and if used at a distance of bout 2 ft. from the subject, allows apertures of down to f/22 to be used when naximum depth of field is required. When used with a camera having a dia-hragm shutter of the Compur or Prontor type, the shutter may be adjusted to a need fast enough to 'kill' any sunlight, or, if desired, at a speed which would alance the level of sunlight with the flash illumination. An example based on the se of Kodachrome II Film will demonstrate how this is done. Let us assume first nat the plant or flower is in sunlight but, because the wind causes the plant to nove, it is decided to make the exposure solely with electronic flash. Let us ssume the flash factor is 50, then with the flash 3 ft. from the subject a suitable vel of exposure will be obtained with the aperture set to f/16 ($50 \div 3 = 16$ pprox.). With sunlight only, the shutter would need to be set at 1/25 sec., but nce the effect of electronic flash remains the same at shutter speeds of up to /500 sec. (being in the region of 1/1,000 sec.) we can, by setting the shutter at /250 sec., reduce the sunlight to one-tenth of the flash illumination, in effect iminating it as a souce of exposure. If, on the other hand, we wish to use both nurces of illumination – the sun as a back-light and the flash as a frontal lumination of very nearly the same intensity – we can set the shutter to 1/25 c. and move the flash back to, say, 4 ft.

One of the major differences between flash illumination and sunlight is that ne sun is unaffected by the inverse square law of light propagation (see page 95) hereas the flash illumination will fall off steeply beyond the plane of the subject. hus, if the subject is in the open, and the flash is used as the only effective light-nurce, the background will appear as it would at night. This would present no roblem with a small plant growing on a rock face, and it may be hard to istinguish a flash photograph from one made with sunlight. The simplest remedy ith an extended background is to use an artificial background of uniform tone nd colour only a short distance behind the subject.

If the photograph is to be taken with the existing daylight, then certain ossibilities may present themselves for improving unfavourable lighting. If the in is shining but the plant is in the shade, it may be possible to direct sunlight n to the plant by means of a metal foil reflector or even a mirror. Alternatively may be possible to remove an obstruction – such as a branch or tall plant which causing a shadow to fall on the desired area. Finally, there remains the some-hat drastic remedy of digging the plant up and replanting it in a typical but nore favourably-lit location. In conditions of overcast sky or a shady location a Vratten No. 1A filter will give a warmer colour rendering.

ackgrounds

ature is a gardener on a grand scale and her effects are usually seen best at a istance. Seeds fall willy-nilly and plants vie for a place in the light: one has only o inspect a deserted garden or a tropical jungle to appreciate this. Unfortunately is seldom makes it easy to find the desired specimen growing in isolation, with e result that casual photographs often make it difficult for the non-technical observer to distinguish between the specimen illustrated and its surrounding and background. Indeed one of the weaknesses of books on natural histor illustrated by their authors is the failure to 'separate' the subject from its back ground so that it becomes clearly the centre of interest.

There are a number of approaches to this problem. One is differentia focusing, namely that of throwing the background out of focus. This is ofte easily achieved with close-range photography even at a medium aperture, but can be made even more effective by using a larger aperture, and still more wit a long-focus lens. However, the background should not contain violent difference of colour or light and shadow. Another method is to undertake a little judiciou 'photographic' gardening, removing unwanted material in the foreground – od spikes of grass, leaves and any other debris which may spoil the effect of th picture. The natural background may be considered essential to the record bu this does not preclude the selection of a viewpoint which excludes the mor 'fussy' detail. As with outdoor portraiture the sky is often the most satisfactor background for flowers of the tall-stemmed variety. A small pair of secateurs ca be a valuable accessory, permitting the painless removal of brambles, sma branches and other weeds having fibrous stems. A third method, alread mentioned in connection with lighting, is that of transplanting the specimen, an a trowel might also be added to the accessory bag. Finally, there is the use of a artificial background. See plates 27, 43, 44 and 45.

Scale

It is usually of interest to the naturalist to be able to determine the dimensions the original specimen from the photograph, and a common method is that including a scale or ruler. This can be stuck in the ground to indicate height laid to one side of the plant on the ground. If kept towards the edge of the field can be fairly unobtrusive and offer the advantage of showing the scale no matte what size the print is. By keeping it well to the edge it may also be trimmed off print or transparency required merely to illustrate a species or a variatio in colour. In any case, for book illustrations a 'key' dimension, such as th diameter of a flower, is best given in the caption. An alternative, though perhar rather more complicated method, is to measure the distance between lens an subject and, if more than one focal length of lens is used, to give the focal lengt of the particular lens used at the time of photography. From this it is possible calculate the scale of the negative image, see page 158. For small objects it often convenient to work at a fixed scale in the negative or transparency, an the scale of any picture can be obtained by multiplying the 'camera' scale by th degree of enlargement, see plate 45.

Wild animals and birds

The increase in the protection of wild life in various parts of the world has mad the 'shooting' of animals and birds with a camera almost as popular as it onc as to shoot them with a gun. In many ways it requires much more skill and ingenuity to obtain good shots with a camera, and it can certainly be equally dangerous if the animal happens to be large and unfriendly.

Obviously the first thing is to locate the desired subject, and having done this, to get within shooting range. For this there are a number of approaches and methods which call for both a knowledge of the habits of wild life and the application of lenses. For example, a knowledge of the feeding and nesting habits of birds would enable one to construct a 'hide' in the most favourable position, and a knowledge of optics the best focal length of lens to use. The indiscriminate use of long-focus or 'telephoto' lenses for subjects difficult to approach can result in false perspective and, for colour photography in particular, false contrast and colour saturation due to atmospheric haze. Hence the advisability of building a hide whenever possible. Remote-control exposure devices provide another solution. Having mounted the camera (perhaps a little camouflaged) near the entrance to an animal's lair, or a water supply known to be used by the desired subject, or a suitable 'bait' by way of food, the photographer retires to a distance with some form of remote-control shutter release, or, failing this, some form of trip release. Among remote shutter releases, there is the pneumatic type, which with a narrow plastic tube can be effective up to distances of 50 yards, the solenoid attachment operated by battery and cable or by a 'radio' control device of the type used by model boat and aircraft enthusiasts, and finally, and perhaps least satisfactory, a long string with some kind of lever arrangement to trip the shutter. Trip devices, to be set off by the subject itself, need to be highly sensitive for small creatures, and with large animals if directly connected to the camera may lead to damage to the equipment. The best kind are therefore of the solenoid type in which a thread or wire is made to operate a micro-switch. During the hours of darkness it is possible to make use of photo-cell devices which are based on the interruption of a beam of light causing a flash unit to fire.

One of the disadvantages of remote-control devices, whether operated from a distance or without any assistance by the photographer, is the difficulty of knowing if the subject is correctly placed in relation to the camera. With remote control releases it is usually possible to observe the location of the camera through binoculars. With trip devices it is often a matter of luck, since there is no guarantee that the desired subject will be the first to touch it off. Another disadvantage is that few cameras incorporate automatic film-wind mechanisms, a notable exception being the Instamatic 400 camera, which has a spring-loaded film wind and shutter re-tensioning mechanism. In this respect the movie photographer has a distinct advantage over the still photographer.

Long-focus lenses

The approach by means of a long-focus lens is most conveniently carried out with a single-lens reflex camera, thus enabling the photographer to frame and focus his subject directly. When he is working from a hide, a view camera is equally satisfactory, since once the camera has been set up a series of exposures can be made based on direct observations of the target. Small cameras designed for interchangeable lenses will need an accessory viewfinder indicating both the field of view and compensating for any parallax errors. At greater distances, the danger of parallax no longer exists and observation of the subject can be made with the aid of binoculars when lenses of very long focus are in use.

A precaution not always observed when using long-focus lenses is the increased risk of camera shake. Not only is a tripod desirable, but the shutter should be operated with a reasonably long flexible release. If there is no alternative to supporting the camera with the hands, then the shortest possible shutter speeds should be used. High-powered telescopic attachments, such as the Zeiss 8 × 30B Monocular, usually have a small effective aperture and if used for hand-held cameras require a film such as High Speed Ektachrome to achieve sufficiently short exposure times. In general, such attachments are not a good substitute for a long-focus lens of conventional design. The foreshortening of perspective typical of long-distance photography with long-focus lenses is not easy to avoid if the field of view includes a number of birds or animals of the same kind but at different distances. The effect is to convert a normally scattered flock or herd into a closely packed one, all of roughly the same size and sometimes appearing to be growing out of each other. The effect is not troublesome on open terrain or water when a single specimen or several specimens in the same plane are photographed. Such effects are not noticed in close-range photography, and may in fact give a more natural perspective than that obtained with a lens of normal focal length used at a closer distance. It is frequently pointed out that all focal lengths give the same perspective when the viewpoint is the same, but while this is true in a strictly optical sense, the apparent perspective in a photograph will only be accepted as true if the viewing angle is the same as that of the lens. In practice this is rarely so when using a long-focus lens for distant subjects otherwise there would be little point in using such a lens.

Insects and other small creatures

The use of a camera for close-ups and photomacrography has already been discussed in Chapter 11. For field work a small camera used with a field-frame

---

Plates 43 and 44. Both subjects have been taken with sunlight. The seed-head required the use of a +1 dioptre lens and was taken from a low viewpoint to make use of the sky as a background Exposure with Kodachrome II Film, 1/125 sec. at f/8. The three frogs, each clinging to one face of the cactus stem, required a +3 dioptre lens. A small mirror, held by an assistant, was used to direct sunlight on to the right of the subject. Exposure with Kodachrome II Film was 1/60 sec at f/11.

Plate 45. The subject was taken with an R1 : 3 close-up lens with the camera set to infinity. In this way the transparency represents a scale 1/3 life-size. The reproduction being a ×3 magnification therefore gives a life-size image. The colour of the background was chosen to contrast with the colours of the shells. Exposure made with Kodachrome II Film using electronic flash

Photos: E. S. Bomback

Plate 43. Seed-head of wild parsley against a sky background.

Plate 44. Trio of green frogs on a small cactus plant.

Plate 45. A life-size record of a typical range of colouring found on a variety of marine molluscs.

Plate 46. Underwater photograph at 20 ft. using electronic flash at a distance of 20 in. from the subject. Exposure with Ektachrome-X Film (no filter), f/16. Compare this shot with plate 47 of a similar subject at the same depth taken with the same film. Exposure (no filter) 1/125 sec. at f/5·6 by available light.

Plate 47.

Plate 48. Diver with underwater photographic equipment taken at a depth of 30 ft. with Ektachrome-X Film (no filter), 1/125 sec. at f/4. Suspended from the Rolleimarine camera housing is a large close-up lens. Locality of all three photographs, Giglio, Mediterranean. *Photos: Geoff Harwood.*

of the type shown in fig. 11.8 offers the most convenient solution to the problems of framing and focusing at very close distances, especially when dealing with live subjects. Such a device can be suitable for scales of reproduction of up to 1 : 1, but at still closer distances involving magnifications, the depth of field becomes so shallow as to require visual focusing with a reflex viewing screen, or, if the camera can be set on a tripod, a camera having a focusing back. However, unless very small insects are to be photographed, it may be better to restrict field photo-graphy to a range of scales provided by the four field frames of the Retina Close-up attachment – 1 : 4½, 1 : 3, 1 : 2, and 1 : 1½. These make use of colour-corrected supplementary lenses, the camera lens itself being set to infinity. No correction to exposure is needed as when using a normal lens at considerable extension from the focal plane. As it is usually necessary to use a lens aperture as small as f/22 to obtain adequate depth of field, a small electronic flash unit is virtually indispensable when using colour films of medium speed (64 ASA). At the sacrifice of some definition High Speed Ektachrome film will permit ex-posures of 1/125 at f/22 in sunlight. However, the maximum definition is usually of paramount importance to the naturalist in recording the extremely fine detail of his subjects. Thus the use of a film such as Kodachrome II with electronic flash is undoubtedly the best guarantee in this respect.

One advantage of working to particular scales in the negative or trans-parency is that the dimensions of the specimen can readily be calculated. It will be apparent also that, if a fixed reduction of, say, 1 : 2 is to be adopted, the field covered will be twice that of the camera format – in the case of a 35 mm. camera a field of about 3 × 2 in. For transparency work a larger format camera may, therefore, be needed. However, when working with a negative film it is often convenient to work to a smaller camera scale and enlarge the print image to the required scale, plate 45. This is also possible with transparencies intended for photomechanical reproduction, but less so for small transparencies intended for projection, since this involves using lenses of different focal length and masking the slides to different sizes if the screen picture is to be kept constant. There is also the additional advantage of working to a smaller scale for larger subjects, as the available depth of field keeps in step with the requirements of the subject.

The expedient of using dead specimens to simulate live specimens in natural surroundings is unlikely to commend itself to the naturalist, though it is frequently attempted by the amateur. Unfortunately such illustrations find their way into otherwise reputable books on entomology owing, no doubt, to the author being dependent on another source than his own for illustrations. If the only available specimen is a dead one, it is preferable to show it carefully mounted. By using a small spotlight it can be attractively lit and need in no way detract from the general quality of illustrations.

Marine subjects

The major problem is that of sky reflections off wet surfaces or shallow pools of water. If the sky is blue the effect will be to give the subject a strongly blue

211

coloration. This may occur to a lesser degree even in tidal areas which have become dry, owing to the ultra-violet radiation which seems to be more prevalent in coastal areas. This latter tendency can often be reduced with a Wratten No. 1A filter, but sky reflections can be more troublesome. As mentioned earlier, either a shield to protect the subject from the offending area of sky, or a polarizing filter may be tried.

Surfaces which have a matt texture give a much better colour saturation when they are wet, since reflected light is mainly specular, and on curved surfaces is seen as small spots of light which give a sparkle to the subject. Thus it is usually useful to wet the surfaces of rocks and shells before making an exposure unless the intention is to record the appearance of specimens left high and dry by the tide – see plate 12.

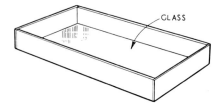
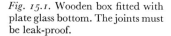

Fig. 15.1. Wooden box fitted with plate glass bottom. The joints must be leak-proof.

The problem of photographing subjects through a disturbed water surface (due to waves or wind) can often be solved by using a shallow box having a plate-glass bottom, see fig. 15.1. Such a device is commonly used by Mediterranean fishermen at night when fishing for squid and octopus. The glass must be well sealed to prevent leakage. Such a device also solves the problem of surface reflection with still water. For those who are willing to go paddling, a box-like construction with a glass front (something like an enormous lens hood) may be fitted in front of the camera to enable underwater photography to be carried out in shallow tidal areas, see fig. 15.2.

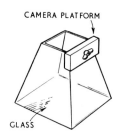

Fig. 15.2. With the camera fitted on this 'underwater' lens hood it is possible to photograph through shallow depths of water without distortion and surface reflections. It should be about a foot deep.

Underwater photography

Colour photography under water presents a number of problems not encountered in normal photography. Firstly, it is necessary to protect the camera in a watertight case, and, in making this, consideration must be given to the rapid increase of pressure with increase of depth – an underwater case designed for, say, depths of up to 15 ft. may fail at greater depths. The need to use a case presents secondary problems associated with the camera controls, which, with simple equipment, may provide little more than a means of releasing the shutter. Thus the exposure must be pre-set and the lens adjusted to the most likely working distance. More elaborate equipment providing full camera control is necessarily costly, but offers the great advantage of permitting a series of pictures to be taken under various lighting conditions and at various distances.

Secondly, the refractive index of water is different from that of air, being roughly $1\frac{1}{3}$ times greater. This explains why it is impossible to see clearly under water without goggles, or to use a camera under water except through a flat air-to-glass surface. Even so, this difference in refractive index has the effect of displacing the image in the manner shown in fig. 15.3 so that it appears larger by the ratio 4 : 3 or nearer by the ratio 3 : 4. The effect is that of using a lens of one third greater focal length and hence results in a narrower field of view and reduced depth of field. It is possible to offset this by using a special correction lens in conjunction with the glass panel so that the normal characteristics of the camera lens remain unchanged. Alternatively, to obtain the same angle of view, a lens of shorter focal length may be used.

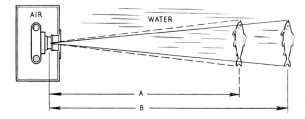

Fig. 15.3. Diagram showing the difference between the apparent (A) and the real (B) distance of an object under water. The lens must be focused for the apparent distance.

The difference in refraction also affects the focusing scale, and an object at an actual distance of 6 ft. would require the scale to be set at three-quarters the distance, namely $4\frac{1}{2}$ ft. If use can be made of a reflex viewer, focusing can, of course, be done visually.

Colour photography under water is complicated by the fact that water is coloured. The absorption of the red component of white light increases rapidly with depth, and this imparts a cyan colour to unfiltered reversal colour photographs. While this is not objectionable, when the intention is to convey an 'underwater atmosphere' to the photographs, see plate 48, the colour of the light must be corrected when making biological or geological records which require reasonably correct colour rendering. With reversal films this can be achieved in shallow water by means of Kodak Colour Compensating red (R) filters at the rate of 4 CC units per foot (per 0·3 metre) of light path (depth + camera—subject distance). For instance, with a subject 5 ft. deep at a distance of 5 ft. from the camera, the number of units required to give the necessary correction is $(5 + 5) \times 4 = 40$. In this case the filter to use is the CC 40R. Below approximately 20 ft. (6 metres) the density of the filters required makes the use of flash a more practical proposition.

At first sight it may appear that anything that is true for reversal films will also apply to colour negative films. This is true if the negatives are not to be printed on automatic colour printers or the Kodak Colour Enlarger. These work on the principle that all scenes integrate to a neutral grey, and negatives are automatically corrected to yield a print with equal amounts of the three dyes – yellow, magenta, and cyan. If an underwater negative, which has not had the full CC filter correction described previously, is printed using one of these machines, the print will have cyan highlights and red shadows owing to the severe under-exposure of the red-sensitive layer. This can be avoided if the printing is done in a normal enlarger, by adjusting the filter pack so that the shadows are reproduced as black with the minimum cyan filtration.

Flash units

The usual method of arranging flash units for underwater cameras is to incorporate the battery-capacitor circuit and the camera connections inside the case with only the two wires leading to the flashbulb being brought through the case. The bulb and flash-head can be exposed to the water without affecting efficiency. A suitable circuit is shown below, fig. 15.4. With a metal camera case only one wire needs to be taken through the case, the return path being through the metal. This one wire must, however, be insulated from the case and must be watertight.

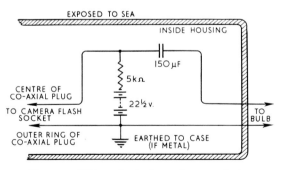

Fig. 15.4. Wiring circuit for underwater flash.

Except in very clear water, the flash should be as far as practicable from the camera, at least 2 ft. (0·6 metre), to minimize the glare caused by the flash lighting up the plankton and sediment close to the camera.

Underwater technique

The technique employed for underwater photography is completely different from that of normal photography. Both the diver and the camera will be virtually weightless underwater. While this is a very pleasant state for the diver, it does introduce problems of stability of the camera. A good strong frame finder is a great help in this respect; it can be braced firmly against the mask, greatly reducing the risk of camera shake. The majority of photographs will probably be taken on the bottom, and it is therefore an advantage to take down 3 or 4 pounds (about 1·5 kilogrammes) more weight than that required for neutral buoyancy. Also, as much of the weight as possible should be carried near the front of the diver's belt; this increases stability both when travelling horizontally and also when sitting on the bottom.

Exposure

Exposure under water can be determined with the aid of a normal exposure meter in a special case, in a preserving jar, or inside the camera case if there is room and sufficient visibility, as with a 'Perspex' case. This applies similarly with cameras having built-in meters having an unobscured view of the light reflected from the subject. Incident-light measurements tend to be unreliable, and the normal reflected-light technique should be used. Fully automatic cameras, in which the exposure is set by direct or servo control from a photo-electric cell, are very suitable for use under water. With colour film, exposure correction for depth will be automatic if the same filter is used over the camera photocell as is used over the camera lens.

In clear British waters (visibility 20-40 ft. or 6-12 metres), the following table of apertures can be used as a guide for both colour and black-and-white films rated at 50 to 64 ASA, with a shutter speed of 1/60 sec.

Depth	Over Light Sand	Average and in Open Water	Over Dark Rock or Weed
Down to 2 ft. (0·6 metre)	f/16	f/11	f/8
5 ft. (1·5 metres)	f/11	f/8	f/5·6
10 ft. (3 metres)	f/8	f/5·6	f/4
20 ft. (6 metres)	f/5·6	f/4	f/2·8
40 ft. (12 metres)	f/4	f/2·8	f/2
80 ft. (24 metres)	f/2·8	f/2	f/1·4

Flash – see plates 46 and 47.

To allow for the absorption of light, guide numbers have to be reduced according to the visibility. For example, in exceptionally clear water, guide numbers should be divided by 2. The following table may be taken as a guide.

Visibility	Factor by which the Guide Number should be divided
Greater than 40 ft. (12 metres)	2
20-40 ft. (6-12 metres)	3
10-20 ft. (3-6 metres)	4
5-10 ft. (1·5-3 metres)	5

However, some correction to colour may be needed. The following example will give some indication of the correction needed; 10 ft. (3 metres) of water plus a CC20M filter is about the same colour as the blue coating on flashbulbs Thus with daylight-type film a CC20M filter and clear flashbulbs, colour render-ing will be approximately correct at a distance of 5 ft. (the light travels from the flash to the subject and back again, a total distance of 10 ft.). At distances closer than 5 ft., blue flashbulbs and the approximate CC red filter – 4 units per foot (per 0·3 metre) of total light path – must be used for complete correction. At more than 5 ft., clear bulbs and red filters can be used.

When clear bulbs are used, the guide numbers should be calculated on the basis of the equivalent blue flashbulb using the visibility factors above. For example, High Speed Ektachrome Film used with a PF. 1B flashbulb has a guide number of 100 at 1/125 sec. With a visibility of 15 ft. (4·5 metres), this guide number must be divided by 4, giving an effective guide number of 25. With the subject at a distance of 2½ ft., an aperture of f/10 is indicated. However, this aperture must be varied according to the filter used. In this case it is the CC 20R – total light path of 5 ft. multiplied by 4, as shown on page 214 – which necessi-tates an exposure increase of 1/3 stop, see table on page 117 for other filter factors of CC filters.

16

Small Sets in the Studio

UNDOUBTEDLY one of the most satisfying fields of colour photography is to be found in the studio in composing and lighting a small set. The field is a wide one, and can be taken to include all photographs which fall under such headings as 'display photography', 'still-life', 'table-tops', 'colour abstracts' and so forth.

In general, small sets come within the sphere of close-up photography in respect of framing and focusing, the distance range being from a few inches to several feet depending on the field to be covered and the focal length of the lens. Unfortunately the majority of small cameras are ill-designed for such a working range, the viewfinder, separate from the lens, no longer showing the actual field of view covered by the lens, and the lens itself often a fixture and incapable of being focused at distances less than about 15 times its focal length. Though there are ways and means of adapting such a camera for close-ups, as we have shown in Chapter 11, there remains the absence of camera movements (vertical, lateral and tilt movements of lens and focal plane) and the still more important absence of a ground-glass screen.

The untrained eye tends to see objects for what they are, rather than in terms of the light and colour they reflect, or the kind of image that will result when a colour photograph is made. Indeed many people think of a camera as a kind of mechanical eye – a third eye – that records exactly what their own eyes see. This is true to some extent in the case of scenic subjects, buildings, and others which are a considerable distance away. But over the range of closer distances the difference between the eye and the camera lens becomes much greater. For example, by using the lens at a large aperture, the depth over which the various planes of the subject appear sharp can be very much restricted. In this respect the camera lens is very much more selective than the eye, which tends to accommodate itself automatically at closer distances, see plate 49. The local control of depth of field made possible by various camera movements is, of course, completely alien to natural vision. The effect of restricting depth of field on a particular subject arrangement can only be seen before a photograph is made when it is possible to view the image formed by the lens on a ground-glass screen. To take another example, the perspective or ratio of scale between objects near and far from the lens can, for a given picture-viewing angle, be controlled by the focal length of the camera lens. This is particularly relevant to close-range photography where with a short-focus lens the far plane of the subject could be, say, twice as far from the lens as the near plane, thus giving a scale ratio of 2 : 1, whereas when the same subject is photographed with a long-focus lens of 4 times the focal length (but used at a distance to keep the image scale of the near place the same) the scale ratio becomes only 5 : 4. This is shown in fig. 16.1. Here again it requires a ground-glass screen to appreciate the pictorial effect.

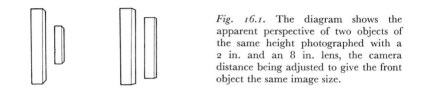

Fig. 16.1. The diagram shows the apparent perspective of two objects of the same height photographed with a 2 in. and an 8 in. lens, the camera distance being adjusted to give the front object the same image size.

Equally important is the effect of a ground-glass screen in destroying the sharpness of the aerial image formed by a lens (whether that of the eye or an optical viewfinder) so that it conforms more to the quality of the image reproduced by the grainy structure of a colour film or that of a half-tone reproduction. At closer distances the eye sees with a needle-like sharpness that tends to increase the reality of objects, an increase which is further reinforced by stereoscopic vision. For this and for other reasons it is usually impossible to visualize a collection of objects on a table as anything else but what they are. But put a camera in front of them, destroy this sharpness, restrict depth of field, change the perspective, select a given area, separate this area from its surroundings, 'interfere' with the nature of the optical image by means of diffusing screens and other devices, and apart from other changes that may occur through variations in the colour quality of the lighting or from variations in exposure, and the photograph may suggest little or nothing of the real objects from which it has been made. Most, if not all, this difference can be observed on a ground-glass screen.

Thus the ground-glass screen becomes the photographer's 'canvas' on which he composes his picture, and not until the image is satisfactory in all respects does the question of recording it arise, see, for example, plates 30-33 and 62-65.

The choice of camera therefore falls heavily in favour of one having a ground-glass screen, whether of the view type in which a reversed (upside down) image is seen at the back of the camera, or a reflex camera of the pentaprism type giving an image of natural size and the right way up. Since many subjects require camera movements, a 4 × 5 in. (or larger) technical camera may seem to be the best answer. However, the ease and economy with which successive exposures may be made with a 35 mm. reflex camera, such as the Retina Reflex III, makes it an ideal second choice when it comes to exploring variations in subject arrangement and lighting. Indeed, valuable though a ground-glass screen can be, the final pictorial effect can only be judged from the photograph itself.

Lighting

We have already dealt in earlier chapters with the more orthodox light-sources and their uses, and most of what we have said applies equally to the lighting of a small set, when the aim of the photographer is to record the colours of the subject as accurately as possible. Naturally, recommendations for studio lighting in the chapter on portraiture can be considerably scaled down in terms of wattage, not only because of the smaller area to be covered, but because the need for short exposure times to overcome possible subject movement rarely exists. At the same time it is necessary to maintain a reasonable level of illumination since the visual effect in both colour and contrast can be very different at low levels, reaching a degree of virtual colour blindness (scotopic vision, see page 26). If proper use is to be made of a ground-glass screen, the level of illumination may have to be considered in terms of the lens aperture, though in practice the use of small stops for increased depth of field does not present the same problem in visualization as the use of large stops for restricting depth of field. Thus is it normal to see all planes of the subject sharp, and if this is desired in the photograph it can as easily be assessed by direct visual observation. The fact that the viewfinder of the Retina Reflex III (and earlier models) only shows the effect of maximum aperture is therefore less serious than one might suppose.

The need for correct colour balance, and hence the use of lighting sources of the correct spectral composition for the type of colour film being used (and including various compromises by way of light-balancing and correction filters) raises an interesting and not wholly irrelevant side-issue on the choice between a reversal and a negative colour film. A reversal film normally requires that the balance between illumination and film sensitivity be accomplished at the camera stage, any further adjustment to colour balance in the transparency (which is the result of a standardized processing technique) being limited to binding up colour compensating filters either for viewing the transparency or making separation negatives for photo-mechanical reproduction. At first sight the situation appears to be different for negative colour films, since it is possible to introduce colour correction at the printing stage. But unless you happen to do your own colour printing or have the services of a specialist print finisher, the greater freedom in exposing colour negatives is something of an illusion, since the only standard a normal print finisher can work to is colour rendering as near 'life-like' as possible. In practice this allows a considerable element of personal choice. But when we come to the finer points of colour balance or to the realm of deliberate distortions, only the photographer himself is able to judge whether the desired effect has been achieved. It is thus, paradoxically, the film which offers the least control over colour balance, namely, a reversal film, that offers the best chance of achieving unorthodox effects. Given standardized processing and a high degree of uniformity in emulsion characteristics the image of the transparency is directly related to the original camera exposure.

To return to the question of illumination, for a wide range of pictorial effects the advantage clearly lies with continuous light-sources, the usefulness of

flash light-sources being limited to conventional lighting effects, situations callin
for indirect lighting (diffused lighting), occasions requiring very short exposure
and for effects based on multi-images. This does not mean that an electroni
flash system provided with efficient pilot lighting is unsuitable, but rather that
is needless outlay of capital and still would not offer the finer niceties of lightin
such as are possible when using continuous sources.

As we have said earlier, lighting can take one of two extreme forms; it ca
be strongly directional (specular) or totally diffused. In practice it is usually
blend in varying proportions of these two forms. However, whereas strongl
directional lighting can be readily converted into diffused lighting, the revers
is not true. Thus, apart from the possibility of using sunlight, probably the bes
source of directional lighting – the spotlight – is the most useful lighting unit t
work with. Two or three small spotlights of 250 or 500 watts, plus the sam
number of single floodlamps of 500 watts are sufficient for the most elaborat
lighting schemes, bearing in mind the use of reflectors, mirrors, diffusers an
other devices that can be applied to spotlights by way of filters, Pola screen
funnels, frames, barndoors and so on. But if a small slide projector does nc
already exist among the photographer's equipment, one of the spotlights shoul
take the form of a 500-watt slide projector, since it will cost little more than
conventional spotlight and, in spite of its limited lamp tilt, provide invaluabl
effects by way of backgrounds (front and back-projection) and the introductio
of certain coloured lighting effects.

The use of fluorescent lighting as a source of diffused illumination is not t
be recommended, since the visual and photographic effects can be very differen
But with this one exception, there is little restriction in the kind of light-source
that may at times be used. Ordinary household lamps of 150 and 250 watts, an
reflector spotlamps of the type used for shopwindow display, make an excellen
combination for the amateur not able to buy expensive lamps and equipmen
and since he will usually own a slide projector there will be few effects he cannc
obtain. Lamps of still lower wattage may prove useful, and low-voltage lamp
such as car headlamps, operated via a transformer or robust battery charge
may take the place of spotlights.

A studio staging

While it may be satisfactory to use nothing more than a table or bench as
working base, it can greatly assist operations to have at one's disposal a frame
work or scaffolding from which to hang backgrounds, support reflectors and smal
lamps, suspend objects which may be required to 'float', provide the means c
support for a glass base, a frame for a back-projection screen, or any sheet c
glass which may be used in front of the set. Such a scaffolding dispenses entirel
with the conventional table and may be used equally well in the studio or out
doors when it is desired to make use of daylight. The dimension of such a stagin
and the nature of its refinements depend on the working field likely to be required

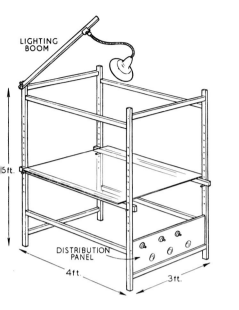

LIGHTING
BOOM

5ft.

DISTRIBUTION
PANEL

4ft.

3ft.

Fig. 16.2. A simple staging for small sets.

Fig. 16.3. A stand for supporting backgrounds and sheets of glass.

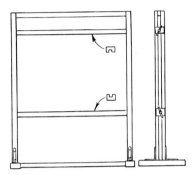

nd the ingenuity of the photographer. The example shown in fig. 16.2 is intend-
d to illustrate what we have in mind and may be adapted as the reader thinks fit.

In principle the stage consists of four corner-posts bolted to cross-arms at the
ase and the top. Additional cross-arms are adjustable in height and are kept in
osition with pegs or slots in the uprights. These cross-arms can be made from
otted wood with the object of supporting sheets of glass in a vertical as well as a
orizontal plane. Lighting units can be mounted in the base for use when a glass
ase is needed for photographing glassware or other subjects requiring light from
elow. Cross-supports on the top can take the form of expandable curtain wire,
ooden battens fitted with bulldog clips, or anything else that might suggest
self. By making a camera platform (as a detachable unit) to fit over the top, the
age may be equally serviceable for copying, making slide titles and making
bstract compositions based on multi-image effects, distortion effects through
ater and obscuring glass and other devices.

A much simpler frame suitable for backgrounds, a back-projection screen,
r for supporting glass in front of a set is shown in fig. 16.3. It may also be used in
onjunction with the stage to allow greater spacing for backgrounds.

Treatment of subject matter

One of the characteristics of good art is simplicity, and in photography simplicity
an often be interpreted as avoiding unnecessary detail and irrelevant material.
t is a mistake to assume that complexity or elaboration is a sign of maturity.

221

There is often a tendency for the novice to start with a simple idea and finish u
with a miscellany of ideas. This is sometimes due to a belief that every part of tl
picture area should contain something of interest, so that there is a temptation t
go on adding material until the object of principal interest becomes merely oı
of a number of objects, any one of which may attract the attention of the viewe
On the other hand, a stronger pictorial effect is often to be obtained solely by tl
choice of a background, the colour and texture of which is in keeping with tl
subject. Such is the power of imagination that even the simplest of suggestioı
can evoke the most startling reality. For example, there is no simpler way fc
suggesting that a subject is lit with sunlight than to throw a shadow of a lattic
window on the background – an effect which can be obtained very simply wit
some pieces of wire held in the beam of a spotlight.

One practical method of demonstrating the negative effect of over-elabora
tion is to take shots at various stages in building up a still-life or table-top set. J
will often be found that those pictures taken in the earlier stages are the moı
effective. In fact the picture that evokes the viewer's imagination will have fa
greater impact than one which leaves nothing to be imagined.

Glassware

Objects made from glass, whether as tableware or ornaments, have always had
special appeal to photographers both for the lighting challenge they offer, an
the delicate line and tone effects to be obtained with imaginative handling. Th
customary method of lighting plain glass in black-and-white photography :
simply to place it in front of an illuminated background, all light-sources in froı
of the subject being extinguished or screened. To eliminate all frontal reflectior
it may be necessary to place a sheet of black paper in front of the camera with
hole in it for the lens, see fig. 16.4. Glass having an etched or relief patter

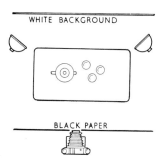

Fig. 16.4. Lighting arrangement for photographing glassware in 'outline' and without surface reflections.

requires a moderate amount of overhead or frontal lighting by way of fill-iı
An alternative approach is to use a dark background and light the glass from on
side with a spotlight. With colour photography it is possible to use coloureı
backgrounds and introduce outline effects from one side with a spotlight. B

lacing a coloured gelatine in the beam, the reflections may contrast in colour with the background, see fig. 16.5. Such effects can be very pleasing with glass animals. The use of coloured metallic foils as base and background may also commend itself to the photographer seeking colourful subjects for Christmas cards.

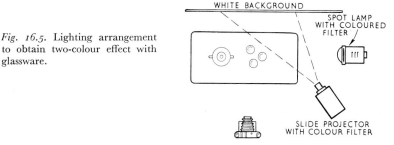

Fig. 16.5. Lighting arrangement to obtain two-colour effect with glassware.

WHITE BACKGROUND

SPOT LAMP WITH COLOURED FILTER

SLIDE PROJECTOR WITH COLOUR FILTER

Polished metal-ware

The usual technique is to place the subject inside a tent of white muslin so that it is lit with diffused light from all directions: a single spotlight to one side of the camera can be used to introduce highlights. Highly polished metallic surfaces have the characteristic of giving specular reflections of their own colour, and when photographing gold, copper or brass objects the highlights must be carefully controlled or they will be burnt out in the photograph, giving a false effect of white highlights.

A more imaginative treatment of large metal objects of brass and copper is to 'invite' reflections from nearby objects. Depending on the curves of the metal object, whether spherical, conical or cylindrical, various optical distortions will occur which provide additional clues to the shape of the subject.

Silver, aluminium, and tin, although very slightly different in appearance, are very nearly non-selective reflectors, and may all be used for that purpose in colour photography.

Textures and grained surfaces

The nature of a surface can be strongly emphasized by using directional lighting at a very acute angle with the surface. If the light is very nearly at zero degrees, even an apparently smooth surface such as a sheet of paper may appear as coarse-grained as a stucco wall. On the other hand, frontal lighting will record the colour and pattern and virtually eliminate texture. This applies similarly to diffused lighting, but in this case the colours will be somewhat desaturated.

The use of strongly textured backgrounds lit to reveal their character may prove useful for emphasizing the glazed surface of china or porcelain ornaments.

223

Fabrics

These materials introduce the aspect of texture, but certain fabrics such as satin shot-silk, and velvet rely equally on surface reflections. Indeed, satin in particula is a favourite material of the photographer because of the lustre of its surface Coarse linens, hessian and knitted fabrics are typical of those materials which ar recognized chiefly by texture. Cottons and many synthetic fibres present a mor or less matt surface, except under conditions of strongly directional surfac lighting.

On the subject of fabrics it may be worth noting that fluorescing compounc may have been used to make white garments 'whiter than white'. When thes are photographed with daylight or electronic flash, both rich in ultra-viol(radiation, the photographic result may possibly prove to be blue. The use of U.V-absorbing filter over the camera lens may not be effective in correcting thi since the 'damage' has already been done: in the studio it is necessary to plac the u.v. filter over the light-source. If the full effect of fluorescing colours required it is, however, necessary to restrict the light falling on the surface ■ ultra-violet radiation by using a filter such as the Wratten No. 18A or 18B c Wood's glass in front of the light-source (which must of course be rich in ultra violet), and a u.v-absorbing filter over the camera lens. The exposure level : best found by trial and error. Fluorescing colour effects are often used in th variety theatre, but may be of interest to the photographer looking for unusua effects.

Food

As a general rule, food must be reproduced as near 'life-like' in colour as : possible, or, perhaps, to put it more accurately, as near to what we conside wholesome food looks like. Experiments in the United States have shown tha guests invited to a dinner which included steaks dyed green, peas dyed blue an other anomalies, either suffered immediate loss of appetite or later ill-effects, th latter in spite of the fact that the dyes were harmless. The modern food industr makes considerable use of dyes in prepared foods, jams, sauces, etc., with th object of restoring both the colour of the food and the confidence of the prospec tive consumer. The photographer is therefore limited to lighting effects whic enhance the colours, e.g., the use of directional rather than diffuse lighting, wit perhaps the occasional use of filters to enhance an overall colour such as a rang of cheeses or a bowl of peaches which may otherwise appear on the pallid side.

Background effects

From a practical point of view the background must be large enough to cov(the field of view at the distance at which it is to be used and taking into accour the angle of view of the lens. Thus narrow-angle lenses present less trouble tha wide-angle lenses. It is usually advisable to be generous with the size of th background, since in making a small change to the camera angle it is easy t

verlook a small deficiency of coverage in a dark-toned background which may
rove difficult to eliminate in the transparency.

Unlike black-and-white photography, where the choice of background tone
usually dictated by the overall tone of the subject, the use of colour film
troduces an entirely different method of obtaining separation between subject
d background, namely that of difference in colour. However, it must be used
ith some understanding of the effect of colours, for though a blue background
ill appear to be farther away than an orange or red object in front of it the
verse is not necessarily true. Indeed many observers would see the background

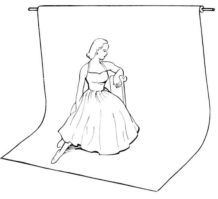

Fig. 16.6. Roll of background
paper used to eliminate the
'horizon' between wall and floor.

a foreground plane with the red object at a greater distance, as though seen
rough a hole. However, if the subject is lit in such a way as to give it solidity it
ill invariably appear to stand in front of a background of uniform colour, though
re again the apparent distance of the background may depend on the colour.
, however, we make the tone of the background darker, greater separation is at
ce apparent. The presence of shadows on a background, whether cast by the
bject or some object outside the field of view, will also strengthen the feeling of
paration, and at the same time provide the observer with a means of gauging
e actual distance.

The depth of colour in a background can conveniently be adjusted in
lation to the colours of the subject by varying the intensity of light falling on it.
nder-lit, a light blue would appear a medium or dark blue, and vice versa. The
lour may also be modified or enriched by using coloured gelatines over the
ght-source used for the background. Indeed the experimental worker with a
ide range of coloured gelatines of the type used for theatre stage-lighting effects,
ay prefer to work with a white background and create his background colours
sing a spotlight or slide projector. In modifying existing colours, particularly
hen electronic flash is used for lighting, some account of colour mixing must be
ken. Thus an orange filter will enrich a yellow or orange background, but a
ue filter may give it a grey appearance. An artist, in mixing paints, would
pect – and get – a green colour by mixing yellow and blue, but it should be

225

remembered that reflected colours under white-light illumination are as much characteristic of their appearance as the colour they absorb. A rich crimson is th result of almost total absorption of blue and green light and if viewed with filter of either of these colours would appear black.

Background materials

The choice of materials is almost unlimited, anything from corrugated paper t seal skin being possible. However, a range of plain materials in various colours including white, grey and black, is a basic essential. These may be of cotton o poster paper for small areas, or display paper, which is available in widths up t 9 ft., for larger areas. Both poster paper (3 ft. wide) and display paper are avail able in rolls and are useful when the 'horizon' between base and background i to be eliminated see fig. 16.6. To obtain maximum black in a background various types of flock paper are available. Such a material is usually necessar when multi-exposure images are to be made on one frame of film.

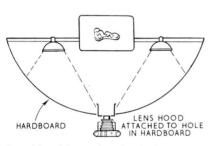

HARDBOARD

LENS HOOD
ATTACHED TO HOLE
IN HARDBOARD

Fig. 16.7. Sheet of thin hardboard painted white or covered with matt aluminium foil forming a semi-circular reflector in front of the subject. The camera, used through a hole, is fitted with a deep lens hood.

Considerable variety in design and colour has been offered in recent year by way of wrapping-paper sold in sheets 20 × 30 in. Various kinds of commercia wrapping paper and corrugated cardboard, hessian and sacking, plastic fabrics wallpapers, building materials such as masonite and insulating board ma suggest themselves from time to time. Masonite or hardboard, obtainable i sheets up to 8 × 4 ft., makes an ideal base for reflector boards, being painte either with matt white paint or covered with aluminium foil. Being flexible, i can be bent in a semi-circle for diffused lighting effects, see fig. 16.7. Specia papers for model-makers which give the effect of stone walls, parquet floorin

Plate 49. The idea of this table-top creation originated from the sight of a bunch of over-siz radishes hanging in a shop window. The same shop was able to provide a cucumber with a curve end. The components are held together with orange sticks. Thin plastic was placed over greenish blue paper to suggest water, and pieces of cotton wool were pinned to a blue background as th sky. The use of a 135 mm. lens with a Retina Reflex camera made it possible to throw th background slightly out of focus. The set was lit with a single No. 2 Photoflood placed high an well back from the subject to ensure uniform illumination. Exposure with Kodachrome II Film Type A, 1/8 sec. f/5·6.

Plate 50. The three tumblers, resting on upholstery canvas, were illuminated with a spotligh The camera was set up immediately above the subject.

Plate 49. Dyak war canoe.

Plate 50. Shadows from red tumblers.   Photos: E. S. Bomback

Plate 52.

Plate 51.

Multi-exposure effects using tri-colour filters.

Plate 53.

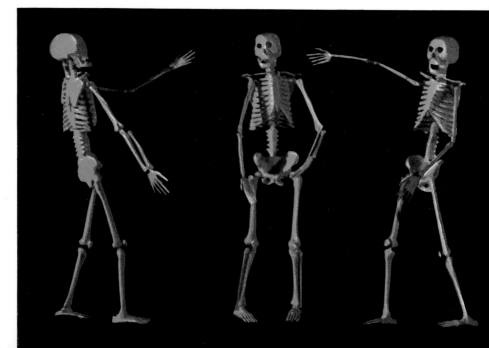

nd brick walls may also be useful in table-top work. There is a wide variety of
ther backgrounds, such as clouds, waves and so on which may be obtained from
nops specializing in display material. One of the best sources is Kettles, of
Iolborn, London, but most large cities contain such a supplier. Ingenious ideas
or backgrounds are often to be seen in the window displays of large stores, and a
isit to a friendly chief window dresser may be worth-while.

rojected backgrounds

The use of a spotlight to throw a shadow on a plain background is a form of
rojection, but this can be taken a stage further by using a slide projector to one
de of the camera to throw a normal screen picture on a white background. To
void light from the projector falling on the subject, the angle of the projector
lust be arranged so that it covers the required background area in the manner
nown in fig. 16.8A. For this reason a long-focus projection lens will be easier to

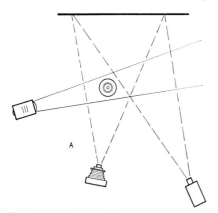

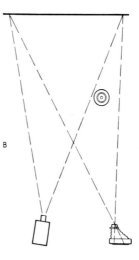

Fig. 16.8. The use of front projection can often
be arranged as in (A), but if perspective distortion
is to be avoided, an arrangement as in (B), using
the horizontal swing of the camera, can be used.

andle. Alternatively, if the subject has a simple outline it may be possible to
ick a small piece of black paper of similar shape on the slide in a position which

14

will make it coincide with that of the subject. If the photograph is to be made with a single exposure it will be necessary to balance the lighting on the subject with that of the projected image. But as will become immediately evident in arranging such a set, the lighting on the subject must not be allowed to fall on the background or the image brilliance will be greatly reduced. This usually involves using spotlights as side-lighting. However, the 'set-up' can be tackled in two stages involving two separate exposures on the same frame of film. Firstly, the subject is photographed with a sheet of black cloth or flock paper over the background, using any lighting arrangement that is desired, the exposure being adjusted in the usual way: secondly, the black material is removed and all lighting extinguished except from the projector, the exposure this time being adjusted to the screen image. Any appreciable difference in colour quality between the subject lighting and projector can either be corrected at this second stage by placing a filter over the camera lens or take the form of a permanent correction at the projector gate.

One disadvantage of front projection is the unavoidable angular displacement of the image, since even if one merely wished to copy the projected image it is impossible for the camera and projector lens axes to coincide. However, with a camera providing lens movements this may be overcome in the manner shown in fig. 16.8B.

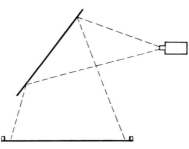

Fig. 16.9. Use of a large mirror to reduce distance of projector behind back-projection screen. The slide must be reversed laterally to allow for the reversal of the mirror.

However, back-projection is the more logical approach and is commonly used in motion picture sets where the nature of the subject makes it undesirable or impossible to use a natural background. Thus it would be pretty nearly impossible to photograph a convincing close-up of a boat-load of ship-wrecked people on a rough sea with a viewpoint at sea-level, since any adjacent boat would be far too unstable. It is a relatively simple matter to project a background of a rough sea with the boat on some kind of pivot which permits it to be rocked in various ways. Studio hands with buckets of water can do the rest. A satisfactory back-projection screen can be made by pinning a sheet of Kodatrace or matt celluloid on to a wooden frame. Any slide projector can be used, though, if the working space is restricted, it may be necessary to use a short-focus lens to obtain the necessary screen magnification. An alternative method is a mirror arrangement as shown in fig. 16.9. For single-exposure photography a 500 watt projection amp will match up reasonably with 250 watt spotlights. However, the chief problem is not that of screen brightness, since this is easily overcome by the two-exposure method already described for front projection, but that of uniform brightness, as there is always a tendency for the centre of the image to be brighter. There is no simple solution to this, though it is frequently possible to choose a subject for the background which has a darkish centre, or to arrange the subject so that it covers the 'hot-spot'. Another method is to avoid having the projector and camera axes in line and either the projector or camera can be set at an angle with the screen. A third and more satisfactory method, if regular use is to be made of back-projection, is to make up a 'correction' filter or transparency which absorbs some of the light at the centre of the field. Such a filter can be made photographically by 'copying' with reversal film a circular grey patch on a white background, the tone of which ranges from a nearly black core to light grey. Another method is to paint such an image on a piece of fixed-out film using a neutral retouching dye. A little trial-and-error will soon achieve the right density.

What has been said for frontal projection in respect of spill light from lamps used to light the subject applies equally to back-projection, but in this case considerable protection can be given by using a large cut-out screen of black paper between the subject and background as shown in fig. 16.10. The alternative method, in many ways far simpler, is the two-exposure system already described, see plate 65.

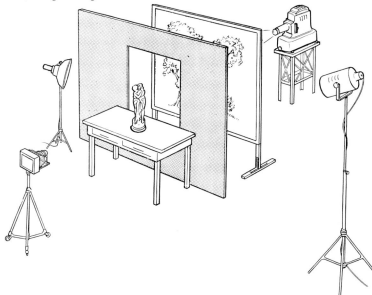

Fig. 16.10. By using a large opaque screen with a suitable aperture between the back-projection screen and the subject, it is usually possible to avoid any spill-light falling on the screen.

Apart from its more obvious uses of supplying a realistic or abstract back
ground, the latter being based on a suitably arranged mosaic of coloured
gelatines bound between two cover glasses and used at various degrees o
unsharpness, back-projection provides a method of experimenting with image
distortion of existing subjects and also for achieving pseudo-painting effects. As
the screen image is already in a flat plane, side effects due to the depth of an
actual subject are avoided. And since all the light comes from behind the screen
there is no trouble from reflections, and no problems of shading the lens from the
light that projects the image on to the screen. See plates 51 and 52.

Coloured lighting

It is perhaps useful to remind the reader that white light is a mixture of the
colours of the spectrum and that the three layers which make up a transparency
or print may be regarded as complex colour filters, so adjusted as to convert white
light (by subtraction) into an image of colours resembling those of the original
subject. Anyone who desires an instructive photographic pastime at the cost o
no more than a set of Wratten colour-separation filters, can try out the effect o
lighting a subject in three stages using a projector or spotlight in three different
positions, in each case using a different separation filter over the camera lens. As a
rough guide the green filter will need 4 times and the blue filter 16 times the ex
posure of the red filter to give a reasonable colour balance where the three light
sources overlap. If a white background is used to record shadows these will be
combinations of two of the primary colours. Thus the shadow cast by the green
spotlight will appear magenta as it will have received both red and blue light
the shadow of the blue spotlight will appear yellow (red plus green), while the
shadow of the red spotlight will appear cyan (green plus blue). Multi-colour
shadow effects may be effectively applied to titles made up with solid letters
    The purpose of a filter is to absorb certain regions of the colour spectrum. A
filter appears red when placed in front of a white light-source because it has
absorbed most of the green and blue regions of the spectrum: a yellow filter
appears yellow because it has absorbed a great deal of the blue region. Roughly
speaking we can say that a filter absorbs its complementary colour.
    Any material which, when viewed against white light, changes the colour
of the light may be used as a colour filter. Glass is perhaps the most familiar
material – in the form of stained glass windows, bottles, etc. – but thin sheets o
dyed gelatin or plastics are more commonly used in photography. For extreme
accuracy in sensitometry and other work liquid filters are commonly used. If a
filter is to be placed in the image-forming path of an optical system, e.g., in front
of a camera lens, with the object of modifying all the light reaching the colour
film, then it must be flat and free from blemishes and dust – see page 123. But if
the filter is merely required to modify a light-source then any transparent material
may be used. For example, a very wide range of colours is available as stout
celluloid sheets for theatrical lighting, but the very thin acetate material available

at stationers as wrapping paper in a fair range of colours provides a cheap method of modifying large areas such as windows. By using one or more layers, the density of the filter can be adjusted to any desired level.

In general, the use of coloured lighting is restricted to special effects in display work – usually as a form of back-lighting – or to table-top fantasies, titling and abstract designs. See plates 31, 32, 33 and 53.

Multi-exposures

Most photographers have at some time accidentally made two exposures on one frame of film. The result may even have been oddly amusing if the dark tones of one subject have coincided roughly with the light tones of the second subject. However, we are not concerned with accidental results but with deliberate effects obtained by making two or more exposures on the same frame of film.

We have already mentioned two reasons for resorting to this method of exposure in the present chapter in connection with front and back-projection, and in the use of a single light-source for multi-lighting effects. This latter application can be particularly useful to the photographer who is limited to one electronic unit or only one spotlight. The first exposure, for example, can be made with the light-source used as main light, the second as a fill-in, the third as background lighting and so on. Indeed, as we mentioned in Chapter 13, a whole interior can be uniformly illuminated by successive exposures with flashbulbs or electronic flash. It is, of course, necessary either that the room be otherwise dark or at least at a negligible level of illumination, if the shutter is to be kept open during the sequence of exposures, or if this is not possible or convenient, that the shutter be closed or a cap fitted over the lens during the interval between one exposure and the next. If the shutter is of the type that can be re-tensioned independently of the film-winding lever, a short exposure can be given when using electronic flash, but with short 'time' exposures it is usually simpler to have the shutter permanently open and the lens protected with a cap. With small cameras having a double-exposure prevention device, it is usually necessary to resort to some trickery to re-tension the shutter. Generally speaking, this can be done without appreciably shifting the film by pressing the rewind button when operating the film wind knob or lever. Before doing this, it is necessary to take up any slack film in the cassette by turning the rewind knob firmly but cautiously in the direction of the arrow, and, of course, without pressing the rewind button. Some photographers take the additional precaution of holding the rewind knob at the same time as operating the winding lever and keeping the rewind button pressed. This operation is extremely difficult with the camera mounted on a tripod – at least without moving the camera – and even then, if exact registration is required, there is still a danger that the film has been moved forward by the friction of the take-up spool, even if only a few thousandths of an inch, and with a small transparency enlarged ten times this can be disastrous. For this reason it is far better to use a lens-cap or have the room in darkness.

233

If multi-exposures are used to 'combine' two or more subjects, or aspects of the same subject, from different viewpoints or at different scales, or to repeat a given subject in the manner shown in plate 53, it is necessary to consider the effect of overlapping images both in respect of colour and density. A few examples will show what we mean. First let us take the case of putting two viewpoints of the same subject on a single frame of film. If the two versions of the subjects are both to be recorded in normal colour and density – in fact, as if a single exposure is to be made of two identical objects – it will be necessary to use a black background. Thus in making each exposure the only part of the film to receive any significant amount of light will be the area covered by the image of the subject. Assuming we could obtain a perfectly black background (one which absorbs all the light falling on it) and that the flare factor of the lens could be reduced to zero, we could go on using up the area of the background with as many separate images as could be fitted in without overlapping. But this is not possible in practice, since, even with the use of black flock paper and restricting the light falling on it to a minimum, we cannot escape some lens flare. But this is only likely to worry the photographer who wishes to make twenty or more exposures.

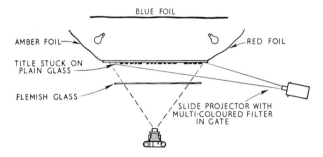

Fig. 16.11. Use of 'Flemish glass' to give letters of a title an 'artistic' appearance. A coloured foil with reflections from adjacent foils provides a background of highly saturated colours.

However, the moment we wish to introduce a background which reflects light we are confronted with the problem of overlapping images. If we take two versions of the same subject on different parts of the film, then each will receive an additional exposure due to the background, while the background will have received two 'doses' of the same lighting. This may not matter very much if the background is of dark tone and its colour does not conflict with that of the subject.

With normally coloured objects the problem of overlap is chiefly one of exposure. Where two equally bright areas overlap, the exposure is roughly doubled, and if this is to be the area of 'key' interest then the combined exposures must not be allowed to exceed the level required for 'correct' exposure. Thus two normally-lit areas to be overlapped should be given half the 'correct' exposure, or if to be of different densities in areas not overlapping, fractions such as $\frac{1}{4}$ and $\frac{3}{4}$, adding up to 1. More often, the overlap consists of a highlight area of one image overlapping a shadow area of another, in which case the exposure may be based on the normal.

If multi-image combinations are to be really effective careful planning is involved in lighting and pre-determining the positions of the various components. This will be greatly simplified if a large-view camera is used, as the positions can be pencilled on the ground-glass screen, otherwise it will be necessary to chalk positions on the working base in such a way that they can be readily seen in a low level of illumination and are not recorded in the photograph. If differences in scale are involved it will be necessary to note the different focus settings of the lens and any possible exposure corrections arising out of the inverse square law of light intensity, unless a spotlight is being used at a fairly great distance, or the lamp-to-subject distance is kept constant. All this requires something like a reminder list when it comes to making the exposures, since it is all too easy to spoil a lengthy session by omitting to allow for one of the variables.

Finally it must be admitted that multi-exposure effects are sometimes more easily made by combining single images from two or more negatives in a single print, or in the case of transparencies by binding up two and even three transparencies together. The latter method is frequently used for making title slides of a simple nature. See also plate 73.

Image distortion

Pictorial effects of novel and, at times, attractive nature can be created by photographing an object or simple geometric colour design through various kinds of obscuring glass. This kind of glass is available in a wide range of patterns and textures, some uniform, others of a random nature. The effect of such screens depends on the distance at which they are used from the subject, whether the subject has depth or is itself a flat surface, and the nature of the pattern and its scale of reproduction. As the effects can easily be observed on a ground-glass screen it is largely a matter of personal taste what effect, if any, one imposes on the image. Interesting effects can be obtained from water flowing down the surface of a sheet of plain glass, or if a horizontal plane is used, by shooting through a glass dish of water the surface of which is disturbed in some way.

One of the problems of using such screens is the difficulty of lighting the subject so as to avoid reflections on the uneven surfaces of the screen. An arrangement such as that shown in fig. 16.11 offers one solution for subjects in depth, but the use of back-projection (see page 230) is by far the most satisfactory approach. In this case the subject is photographed normally and the projected image re-photographed through the screen.

17

Copying

THE PHOTOGRAPHIC copying of documents in business and commerce by means of a camera using 35 mm. or 16 mm. black-and-white film has long been a widespread practice, since it affords a simple, accurate and bulk-reducing method of keeping records. Considerable use has also been made of photographic copies of rare manuscripts, books and other material likely to be of interest to students and others, which is either too precious to be made available in original form or too limited in printed form to be available at more than the larger reference libraries. Since the advent of modern reversal colour films, increasing use has been made of 35 mm. transparencies by leading art galleries as a means of providing copies of paintings and drawings, as reproductions of high quality and modest price, to art students and members of the public having a taste for such work.

The copying of flat originals does not differ essentially from ordinary colour photography and many of the problems connected with the framing and focusing of the subject have already been dealt with in Chapter 11. In fact the occasional copying of posters, guide maps, paintings on show in street exhibitions can be accomplished with as much facility as photographing a brick wall. The copy will be all the better for uniform lighting, but even this is not important if we merely want a simple record to include in a series of travel pictures. See plates 59 and 60.

But in the strict sense, copying an original implies producing an exact replica, accurate in detail, geometry, tone and colour, and in some cases preserving as nearly as possible the appearance of the surface texture. The dimensions of the original can, of course, be recorded as actual measurements, so that the scale of the photographic copy is not important except in so far as it may affect detail or some later process of reproduction based on the photographic copy. Thus in the case of a manuscript, so long as the scale of the original is large enough to provide clearly legible writing with a suitable degree of enlargement, the copy is satisfactory: but if the fine detail of, say, an etching were lost owing to copying at too great a reduction the copy would be unsatisfactory.

On the question of geometry it is necessary that the lens be free from such aberrations as distortion, astigmatism and transverse chromatic aberration. Special highly corrected process lenses designed for copying from flat originals

236

re sometimes referred to as 'apochromats', though in fact the majority of high-grade photographic lenses of normal focal length give satisfactory results at an aperture some 3 or 4 stops below maximum. The plane of the original must also be at right-angles to the lens axis, which in turn must be at right angles to the film plane. Many copying devices ensure this automatically, but if a camera is being set up in front of a vertical original, care must be taken to see that the edges of the picture frame, if there is one, are all parallel with the edges of the ground-glass screen when the image is centrally placed on the screen.

In black-and-white photography, originals are usually classed as being either of continuous tone or of line, the latter being treated as two-tone subjects, either black on white or white on black, and copied with high-contrast materials. With continuous-tone subjects the aim is to preserve the tonal relationship as accurately as possible, though with black-and-white copies of coloured originals some compromise is necessary owing to the fact that colours also have to be reproduced as 'tones'. No such distinction is possible when using colour films, coloured line originals may either be copied with negative or reversal colour films, or, if the negatives are required for photo-mechanical reproduction, as separation negatives using a material such as Kodak Separation Negative Film, see Chapter 31.

Colour rendering

Assuming that due precautions are taken to match the quality of the lighting to that for which the colour film is intended, or, failing this, to make such adjustments as are needed by means of balancing and correction filters (see page 112), how accurately can we expect to reproduce the colours of an original painting, or for that matter any colour picture? To anyone who may be hoping to achieve an exact colour rendering it will be disappointing to learn that none of the colour films at present available will give more than a close approximation of the colours as a whole. Those who have followed the earlier chapters of this book will already know that the dyes used in colour films are not perfect. The fact that surprisingly life-like results are obtained with a large range of 'natural' subjects is due to the skill of the film manufacturer in effecting a compromise in the colour rendering of the film. This is normally directed towards giving the best or most acceptable rendering of flesh tints and other familiar colours such as the blue of the sky, the greens of grass and foliage, and, of course, tones of neutral grey. So long as these key colours are within close limits of what we expect them to be, quite large deviations in other colours will pass unnoticed unless the subject is of particular interest. For example, the colour of a blue-green dress may be rendered almost green, but this error would only be noticed by the owner of the dress.

It is, in fact, chiefly when we are dealing with pigments such as those used in painting, printers' inks, and the dyes used in fabrics and colour photographs, that we are likely to encounter the greatest and often most unexpected deviations

237

in colour rendering. Furthermore, the difference is all the more apparent whe it is possible to compare the copy with the original.

However, the need for exact colour reproduction is chiefly likely to intere only the art connoisseur and student, and most people will be happy to have a approximation of the original colours. Even here it will be necessary to take som precautions if regular use is to be made of a camera for copying coloured original Certain colours, notably greens and blues, may show substantial shifts in a colou photograph, and quite different results may be obtained with different branc and types of colour film. This is quite apart from differences due to deviations i the colour quality of the lighting, the level of exposure and the exposure time. I is therefore an advantage to standardize all copying work using a suitable bran of film, the same quality of lighting, and as nearly as possible at the same intensit level, since in this way any deviations in colour will at least be reasonabl consistent. If copying is to be done with a reversal-type film such as Kodachrom II, Type A, it will be worth-while to experiment with colour compensating filte to arrive at the most acceptable compromise with certain subjects. With colou negative film such correction can be made at the printing stage, by making te prints which can be compared with the original under normal illumination.

Duplicate copies

If the intention of the photographer is to make a number of copies from the sam original in small transparency form, there are three possible methods. Firstly, h can make a single 'master' transparency of suitable quality for direct duplicatin on to another reversal film; secondly, he can make a colour negative; and, thirdl he can expose as many copies as are likely to be required directly from the origina after having established the most favourable exposure conditions. The fir method is the least satisfactory as it involves the deviations from two stages c copying, and in practice the deviations which arise from the duplication of transparency with another reversal film may be greater. An alternative metho that of making an internegative from the 'master' transparency would, in fact, b better in the case of an existing transparency, but in the normal way it is obvious preferable to adopt the second method, namely that of using a negative colou film in the first place. This method is undoubtedly the most suitable for producin duplicates which take the form of film strips, since a number of paintings or oth originals can be photographed successively under carefully controlled conditio to produce a strip of negatives. Such a set of master negatives can also be mad from existing transparencies, though here again it is clearly better to be able t work from the originals. In certain respects the third method is the most satisfac tory if the numbers of duplicates required is not excessive and can be reasonabl estimated in advance. In this case Kodachrome II Film is the ideal medium a there will be no deviations from duplicate to duplicate when they all receiv identical automatic processing. Each will have the quality of an original with very high degree of definition (this inevitably suffers slightly when a slide itse is copied) as well as good colour rendering.

lumination

'hough occasional copying work may be done using sunlight as the source of lumination, it is usually preferable to adopt some standard light-source such as ungsten lamps or electronic flash. In using tungsten lamps it is preferable to andardize on the longer-burning 3,200°K. lamps, rather than Photoflood type mps of 3,400°K., even though it means using a light-balancing filter with odachrome II Type A Film. Alternatively, quartz-iodine lamps of 3,400°K. aay be used, since these lamps maintain a constant colour temperature and rightness throughout their burning life. For critical work some form of voltage gulation is desirable.

Since, ideally, two lamps are needed to obtain uniform illumination, the se of electronic flash calls for a unit with two flash-heads of equal light output. y a double exposure it is, of course, possible to use a single flash head in two ositions, but this is scarcely likely to commend itself to the professional. The use electronic flash with a daylight-type reversal film may call for the use of a Vratten No. 81A (or stronger) filter to correct a bluish colour rendering. In some ases it may be advisable to use a U.V.-absorbing filter over the flashheads.

The usual lighting arrangement for copying is shown in fig. 17.1, the two mps being placed one each side of the original, making an angle of roughly 30° ith the surface. The lamps should not be placed too close to the subject and ould be of pearl or frosted type in satin-finish reflectors. Electronic flash should e used with a diffuser in front of the tube. If a large original is to be copied, nder tungsten lighting the uniformity of illumination should be checked with an xposure meter using a white card having a matt surface or incident light ttachment. However, uniform lighting of useful intensity level can be obtained om a single light-source such as a well-diffused spotlight placed well back from ιe subject. The use of a slide projector is open to the objection that the lamp lament often causes some unevenness of illumination.

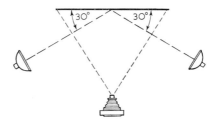

Fig. 17.1. Normal arrangement of lamps for copying a flat original.

eflections

'he lighting arrangement may have to be modified to eliminate surface reflections om originals, such as oil-paintings, which present an irregular surface. A 1itable solution may be possible by choosing a different lighting angle, but .iling this, the subject can be lit with polarized light, by placing Pola-screens in front of the light-sources and photographing the original through a polarizing filter, see fig. 17.2. The polarized light falling on the subject and reflected from pigments is depolarized, but the specular reflections remain polarized. Thus if the polarizing filter over the lens is set to a position which excludes this light the reflections will be totally eliminated. The use of crossed Pola-screens requires an exposure increase of approximately 10 times, but trial exposures based on 8, 10 12 and 16 times the estimated exposure without filters are recommended.

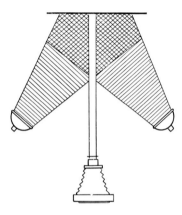

Fig. 17.2. Complete elimination of reflections on a subject such as an oil-painting by using polarizing filters over the light-sources and camera lens.

However, the total elimination of reflections may alter the character of painting by increasing the colour saturation and contrast compared with that apparent under normal viewing conditions. For this reason it may be better to allow some residual reflections, or, in cases where reversal film is being used reducing the saturation and contrast slightly by a controlled flash or fogging exposure equivalent to about 2 per cent of the normal image exposure. This may be made by placing a sheet of white matt paper over the original and repeating the same exposure with a neutral-density filter of $1 \cdot 6$ over the lens.

Small originals

When these measure 11×8 in. or less, the Retina Copying Stand shown in fig. 17.3 provides a convenient attachment for use with Retina cameras fitted with a 50 mm. lens and using a NII supplementary. With the camera lens set at infinity the copying stand is used with full-length legs covering a field of $8\frac{1}{4} \times 11\frac{3}{4}$ in. and with the lens set at $3\frac{1}{2}$ ft. with short legs to cover a field $5\frac{1}{2} \times 8\frac{1}{4}$ in. Still smaller originals can be conveniently handled with the Retina Close-up Attachment described on page 165 with the recommendation to restrict the aperture to f/11 and less. Very small originals such as postage stamps can be done to a scale of 1 : 1 with the accessory shown in fig. 17.4.

Fig. 17.3. Retina Document Copying Stand for originals up to 11 × 8 in. The glass pressure plate and lighting unit are optional extras.

When ordinary lens extensions are used for copying small originals, due allowance must be made for the increase of the nominal f/number. Factors for this are on page 160.

Transparencies

The copying of transparencies presents less difficulty in lighting, and the light-source necessary, used with a suitable diffusing screen such as flashed opal glass, can be either a tungsten lamp or an electronic flash unit. Fluorescent lamps, commonly used for viewing screens, should be regarded as unsuitable for copying except when making black-and-white negatives with the object of producing monochrome prints. The exposure level required and the need for compensating filters, are very much a matter of trial and error, though with a large trans-parency it is possible to take an exposure meter reading of a continuously illuminated image.

It does not follow that, if a transparency of correct colour balance is copied with the same film and with illumination of the same quality, the duplicate will have the same colour balance, since in reality the two subjects are quite different. Nevertheless, once a suitable correction has been established, reasonably consistent results may be expected from further work. If the colour of the original transparency is itself out of balance, further correction may be needed using filters complementary to the colour bias.

The copying of 35 mm. transparencies to the same scale has been made very simple by the 1 : 1 Copying Stand designed for use with Retina IIS and Reflex III cameras. A special slide attachment holds the slide in position while the camera with the attachment fitted is held in front of a suitable light-source, see fig. 17.4. Similar devices are available for certain other cameras of interchangeable lens design. An enlarger such as the Kodak Precision Enlarger may also be used for making same-size or enlarged copies of 35 mm. transparencies.

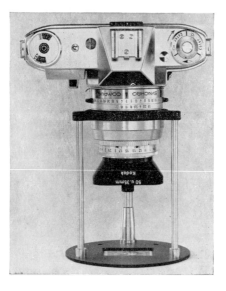

Fig. 17.4. Retina 1 : 1 Copying Stand for very small originals such as postage stamps. A slide attachment enables it to be used for copying 35 mm. transparencies.

Black-and-white copy negatives

Kodacolor and Ektacolor negatives are suitable for making black-and-white prints, using Panalure printing paper in place of ordinary bromide paper, though the latter will yield acceptable prints of a wide range of subjects. However, to obtain black-and-white prints from a colour transparency necessitates the making of a copy negative. A number of methods for making such a negative exist. Where only an occasional need arises and the quality of the print image is not critical, a photograph can be made of a projected screen image, placing the camera as near the optical axis of the projector as possible. The objection to using back-projection is that the screen is brighter in the centre, but if a correction filter of the kind described on page 231 has already been made for general back projection effects, this method will also produce a satisfactory image. Contact printing offers another method and can be useful for dealing with a number of small transparencies at one time by laying them as closely as possible, without overlapping, on panchromatic sheet film which is then covered with a heavy sheet of plate glass. This results in the negative image being reversed when the image face of the transparency is laid face down, but this can easily be corrected when making the print by having the negative reversed in the enlarger. The 'multiple' negative can be cut into convenient sizes for printing.

Direct optical printing is, however, the best method, large transparencies being copied with a camera, and small transparencies with a copying attachment such as that already described for the Retina camera. For maximum definition from 35 mm. transparencies it is preferable to enlarge the image as much as possible in the copy-negative stage, ideally making a copy negative of the print size required and making the print by contact. A convenient compromise is to enlarge the 35 mm. transparency on to No. 120 roll film, using a roll-film adapter of the type designed for plate cameras. Alternatively, sheet film may be used in film holders. In both cases it is necessary to devise some method of locating the film on the enlarger easel so that the image falling on the film is identical with that focused. This is best done with a block of wood whose upper face is the same height above the easel as the film inside the roll-film adapter or plate holder, and covered with a piece of fixed-out bromide paper. Locating pins on the easel will enable the film-holder to be kept steady while the sheath is withdrawn. Since it is necessary to use panchromatic film, all stray light from the enlarger must be carefully screened and the room must be in total darkness while making the exposure.

A film such as Verichrome Pan is ideal for the purpose, but as there is a tendency for copy negatives to become over-contrasty a somewhat curtailed development may be needed. The contrast may also be reduced by placing a diffusing screen over the condenser lens of the enlarger, and still further by removing the condenser altogether, using only a diffusing screen to obtain uniform illumination of the transparency. The transparency should, of course, be masked in the enlarger in the same way as an ordinary negative. It may also be worth-while to restrict the copy negative to little more than the exact area which is required in the print, since the additional enlargement at this stage is preferable to a greater degree of enlarging at the print stage.

Colour copy negatives

Small copy negatives from colour transparencies can be made with Kodacolor film loaded in a camera having a 1 : 1 copying attachment in the manner already described above for making black-and-white negatives. If the transparency is illuminated with tungsten light of 3,200°K., a Wratten No. 82C filter should be used over the lens. For making larger copy negatives, Ektacolor Sheet Film, type L, may be used with illumination of 3,200°K.

However, it should be noted that the coloured couplers in Kodacolor and Ektacolor films provide no correction for the dyes in the transparency, and if the negative is to be made specifically for printing on Ektacolor paper, masking of the transparency may be necessary. For this reason, it is preferable to use Ektacolor Internegative Film which is designed for making colour internegatives and copy negatives at exposure times of 1 to 16 sec. with 3,200°K. lamps without the need for supplementary masking. Such negatives can be used to make prints with Ektacolor paper or positive transparencies with Ektacolor Print Film. They can also be used to make black-and-white prints on Panalure paper.

18

Stereo-Photography

ONE OF the more important ways by which we perceive depth, results from having two slightly different views of an object, due to the separation of our eyes by a distance of about 62 mm. In the normal way the two images are 'fused' together in the brain giving the effect of solidity, though in moments of relaxation we are likely to become aware of the two images. The same 'trick' can be accomplished with two photographs taken with a camera having two lenses separated by this distance or the same camera used on a sliding base to take two views from positions 62 mm. apart. Some people are able to accomplish the fusion merely by looking at two smallish stereo-photographs while at the same time allowing the eyes to produce a double image. As soon as this second image overlaps the image of the adjacent photograph they 'snap' together and a realistic impression of depth is obtained. Anyone able to do this will still be aware of two vague images on each side of the 'solid' image, and this can be avoided by placing a sheet of cardboard between the two photographs, see fig. 18.1, so that each eye only sees its corresponding photograph. Devices for doing this, and at the same time allowing the image to be viewed at a suitable distance for normal perspective are called stereoscopes or stereo-viewers. With small transparencies it is necessary to view the two images with transmitted light and many viewers incorporate battery or mains-operated light-source. Colour slides may be viewed by projection, using a system based on crossed Pola-screens with a two-lens stereo projector.

The principal of stereoscopic images was known before the invention of photography, but the invention of photography made its application far simpler. Indeed stereo-photography became so popular in the latter part of the nineteenth century that few middle-class homes were without a stereoscope, and the search for a perfect stereo-system, for viewing both still and movie photographs, had

Plate 54. Portrait with fill-in flash. Using the sun as a back-light the flash has been gauged to illuminate the shadows to an extent that will appear 'natural' in the photograph. The example given shows very nearly the maximum acceptable amount and some photographers would prefer slightly stronger shadows. However, it depends somewhat on the nature of the subject and the purpose of the photograph. Had the subject been an ancient bargee, a good deal less flash would be preferable. *Ektachrome transparency by Jack M. Oakley.*

Plate 55. Spring.

Plate 56. Winter.

Photos: E. S. Bor

ted with colour photography in its attraction to people of inventive dispositions. Of the two, colour photography has made the best progress, for a simple and universally applicable stereo process yet remains to be invented.

The addition of binocular viewing in photography has never progressed very far beyond a novelty value in general photography, though in certain specialized fields the addition of a third dimension can be very valuable. One reason for its limited importance is that binocular vision is only one of a number

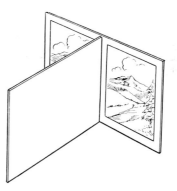

Fig. 18.1. Method of viewing stereo-pairs without the aid of an optical viewer.

ways by which we can appreciate depth, and though the one-eyed individual may have some difficulty in threading a needle, there are many other 'depth-cues' to be drawn on (see page 51). Furthermore, the effectiveness of binocular vision is limited to objects up to a distance of about 300 ft. so that in viewing a distant landscape the one-eyed person is at no disadvantage compared with a person with two eyes. It is, in fact, only at closer distances that binocular vision becomes really useful, a fact not always appreciated by the novice in stereo-photography. At the same time it is worth noting that the camera can be made to yield exaggerated stereo effects by increasing the separation of the two exposing lenses, a practice which is commonly made use of in aerial reconnaissance and photogrammetry.

Of its more specialized uses we can mention its application to commerce, providing a more realistic photograph of machinery and other goods; in education the third dimension can make the picture more convincing: in archaeology and survey work generally it can correctly depict spatial relationships; and in the field of medicine, photographs and films demonstrating surgical technique can be very nearly as good as an eye-witness view of an operation.

Plates 55 and 56. These two photographs are attempts to depict seasonal moods. The freshness and delicacy of spring has been depicted by shooting into the light to reveal the translucence of young foliage. Seen as a projected transparency the brilliance of the foliage is much more intense. The lower picture of marshland was also taken towards the light but with the sun veiled in mist. Such effects – in this case a warm sepia – are often unpredictable. Both exposures were made with Kodachrome film and reveal the remarkable versatility of this material.

Methods of making stereo-pairs

It is convenient to use the term stereo-pair in referring to stereo-photograph since although the term 3D has become very popular it can be taken to imply a actual third dimension – and attempts in three-dimensional portraits hav already been made.

There are three commonly used methods for making stereo pairs. Firstly any camera supported on a tripod or some kind of sliding base can be used t photograph two successive views of a stationary subject. This method offers th advantage that the base separation can be reduced from the normal for close-up or increased for distant objects. The second method is to use a device in front o the camera lens which divides the field into two aspects, such as the Retin Stereo Attachment and similar devices. As can be seen from the accompanyin diagram, fig. 18.2, prisms are used to achieve this effect. This method has bot

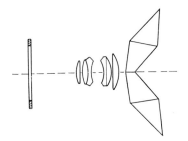

Fig. 18.2. Optical diagram of the Retina Stereo Attachment.

advantages and disadvantages, among the former being economy of film (bot pictures occupy one frame of film), simplicity of mounting – Kodak will retur such pairs in a 'ready-mount' with a centre masking strip – plus the possibility o photographing subjects in motion and using the camera for hand-held shots. O the debit side, only a vertical picture format is possible, and the effective angle o the lens is therefore halved. The third method is to use a stereo-camera, one i fact having two lenses separated by a distance of 62 mm. Many such camer have been made from time to time, the more advanced modern ones being base on 35 mm. film. Two picture formats are in common use, one based on the AS standard of 22·5 mm. width, and the other of European origin of 30 mm. widt The arrangement of the pairs is shown in fig. 18.3. Obviously such cameras a the most convenient to use for anyone wishing to specialize in stereo-photograph

Requirements of stereo-photography

The full effect of a stereo pair demands that the eyes lose awareness of t surface of the photograph and this requires that the images be free from surfa blemishes and dust, and contain no obvious grain effects. In addition, the imag should be sharp in all planes and have a normal gradation of tones, dense shado areas especially being avoided. Transparencies must be carefully exposed avoid loss of colour saturation owing to over-exposure, or loss of image brilliance through under-exposure.

In making exposures the camera must be kept laterally level, though moderate amounts of downward or upward tilt are acceptable so long as verticals are not too much in evidence. If they are, the same rule applies as in ordinary photography, and the remedy is to use a camera with a rising or falling front. The need for sharpness in all planes generally requires the use of small apertures, and this in turn may lead to camera shake and hence loss of sharpness if slower shutter speeds are used without a tripod, or insufficient care is taken when using a hand-held camera.

From a pictorial point of view the subject demands several planes of interest, the most effective zone of distances being between 6 and 25 ft. Subjects having only one plane of interest, apart from a distant background, tend to appear rather as 'cut-outs'. The effect of depth and solidity requires that some aspect of the depth of a rectangular-shaped object be seen. This means that frontal view-points of buildings and other subjects should be avoided, and a view including part of the side chosen. Binocular depth is then strengthened with the almost equally effective convergence of geometric perspective. For similar reasons it is preferable to avoid flat lighting, and well-balanced lighting effects used for normal colour photography are equally desirable for stereo-photography.

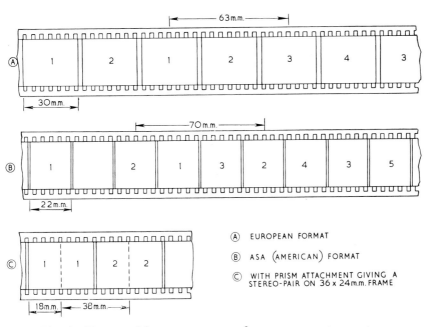

(A) EUROPEAN FORMAT

(B) ASA (AMERICAN) FORMAT

(C) WITH PRISM ATTACHMENT GIVING A STEREO-PAIR ON 36 x 24 m.m. FRAME

Fig. 18.3. Format and frame arrangements of 35 mm. camera stereo systems.

Indeed used with discretion both side-lighting and back-lighting effects may be applied.

Although stereo-photography can handle complicated subjects with more success than normal photography, it is still wise to avoid excessive or fussy detail. For example, the telegraph pole which may appear to be growing out of someone's head in an ordinary photograph will be seen as a more distant object, but it is still preferable to avoid it.

Close-ups of small objects

Stereo-cameras and attachments based on an image separation of 62 mm. are not suitable for making stereo pairs at close distances owing to increasing parallax which can reach a stage where one image is absent altogether. Certain 'close-up' attachments exist in which the lens distance has been greatly reduced and even a slight angle of convergence applied, such as results when we examine an object very close to the eyes. In the normal way stereo-photography of still objects and specimens can be done by using a sliding base having an adjustable stop which limits the degree of movement according to the distance of the subject. As a guide the 'base' movement when photographing an object at 3 ft. can be half the normal – or about 30 mm. – and at 8 in. to about 22 mm. At the same time the lens axis can be tilted slightly to centralize the image.

Stereo-projection

Given ideal conditions the most effective way of displaying stereo pairs is by means of polarized light projection. It requires either two projectors placed side by side, or a special projector having two lenses. If a prism attachment has been used with the camera, a similar projecting attachment may be used with an ordinary slide projector. It is also necessary to use a metallic surface screen, since other surfaces will depolarize the light on which the system depends. Pola-screens with the axes at right-angles to each other are used over the two projection lenses or prism attachment, and the observer views the screen with polarizing spectacles, the lenses of which are orientated so that the left eye is in the same polarizing plane as the projected image taken with the left lens of the camera (being at right-angles to the other image it prevents it reaching the eye) and the right spectacle lens is similarly orientated for its appropriate image and again excludes the unwanted image. Owing to the absorption of light by the polarizing filters – equivalent to a total neutral density filter of about $0 \cdot 8$ – it is necessary either to project smaller pictures or to use a higher-wattage projector. A thorough darkening of the room will also help matters.

19

Photomicrography

THE STEP from photomacrography to photomicrography is not a large one. Lower-power microscope objectives of 15 mm. and longer may be used directly on a camera with extension bellows or tubes for image magnifications of 10 or 20 times, and with further enlargement in the print or as projected transparencies yield final magnifications of 100 times and more. Basically a microscope is little more than an extension tube at the lower end of which is fitted the microscope lens or objective, and at the upper end an eyepiece which provides a further stage of magnification. If in place of the eye we allow this image to fall on a sensitive material, the result is said to be a photomicrograph.

While photomicrography may appear to be essentially a field for the scientist, many very beautiful effects can be obtained with colour film using crossed polarizing filters to photograph such subjects as crystal forms, synthetic fibres, and also features of small creatures such as the eyes of a fly or the scales on a butterfly's wing.

It is in the field of photomicrography that the small colour transparency, based on the use of 35 mm. film, has been accepted as a standard by the majority of workers. Small slides may readily be examined in a simple viewer or, when required for demonstrations and lectures, projected on to a screen. For the latter purposes colour slides are often preferable to the use of a projection microscope, which at the critical moment may fail to produce the required effect, and in any case frequently distracts the lecturer from giving his best attention to the audience.

Cameras and focusing devices

All the leading 'camera systems' based on 35 mm. film provide some form of microscope attachment. In some cases the camera is used without its lens, in others with the lens in place. Special attachments are also available from some of the leading microscope makers, which consist basically of a camera body for holding the film and some means of focusing the image. However, any camera which permits the lens to be removed can be readily adapted for use with a microscope and even cameras with a fixed lens may be made to serve the purpose.

Obviously a camera already fitted with a focusing screen, whether of the view type or single-lens reflex, is the easiest to adapt since it already provides a means for focusing the microscope image: with other cameras some kind of focusing adapter will be needed. This can take the form of a separate focusing viewer consisting of a tube having the same depth as the camera when placed in position over the microscope, see fig. 19.1. Thus, anything which is in focus on the ground-glass screen of the adapter will also be in focus at the focal plane of the camera. If it is desired to make exposures of live subjects or specimens which are unstable, as, for example, crystal formation, some kind of beam-splitting device must be incorporated for viewing and focusing at the side of the microscope. The Retina Micro Adapter is an example of such an adapter, see fig. 19.2.

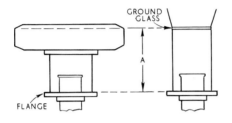

GROUND GLASS

A

FLANGE

Fig. 19.1. A flange fitted on the eye-piece of the microscope provides a base for a camera body or a focusing adapter.

With suitable lighting, exposures may be short enough to require an automatic shutter, but the use of one already fitted to the camera may be open to the objection of causing vibration at the time of exposure, and even at moderate magnifications vibration is fatal to image sharpness. One method of overcoming this problem is to mount the camera immediately above the microscope but supported on a separate stand. An extension tube from the camera extending some way over the eyepiece and lined with black flock paper will make an adequate light-trap for moderate room illumination. Another method is to use an automatic shutter in front of the light-source, opening the camera shutter on 'time' just before the exposure is to be made. In cases where it is necessary to make use of a camera shutter of the Compur or Prontor type (e.g. with the Retina Micro Adapter) it is preferable to avoid using the slower speeds from 1/ to 1 sec., should the exposure time fall in this range, by using a neutral-density filter in the illuminating beam so that a brief time exposure can be used. In this way any vibration caused by the shutter gear system will be avoided. Longer exposure times may involve some correction for reciprocity failure, but it is a choice between two evils. Needless to say, any set-up for high-power photomicrography should be on the most solid support and preferably on the ground floor of a building.

With cameras having a fixed lens, it is possible to obtain reasonably sharp results by a method known as 'infinity focus'. When a microscope is focused by a person with normal eyesight (or one wearing 'distance' glasses) at the same time as he observes some distant object with the other eye, the microscope emits light rays which are very nearly parallel and which may be sharply focused with the camera lens set to infinity. While this method is regarded as something of a makeshift by the serious worker, since the focus depends to some extent on the normality' of the eyesight of the person focusing the image, it may appeal to the beginner in search of nothing more than pictorial effects, since it involves no additional equipment. Other disadvantages of this method are the difficulty of centering the image and the fact that the microscope field will record as a small circle within the rectangular film frame. The size of the circle will depend on the magnification of the eyepiece. Anyone wishing to try this method should mount the camera on a firm support so that, when visual focusing has been effected, the camera can be moved over the eyepiece of the microscope accurately in line with the optical axis of the instrument. The front of the camera lens should be as close as convenient to the eyepiece, and any gap between them should be shielded to eliminate stray light. The camera lens should be set to infinity and at full aperture. The camera diaphragm offers no control over the intensity of light passing through the lens and may act as an obstruction.

Retina Micro Adapter

This attachment overcomes these disadvantages except for the reduced image size, though such images viewed in a transparency viewer or by projection are then seen at the same scale as when viewing the image in the microscope. Although specifically designed for use with Retina cameras, it is not difficult to apply it to other 35 mm. cameras. The adapter consists essentially of a mounting platform for the camera, and a mounting ring to connect the unit to the draw tube of the microscope. A beam-splitting eyepiece incorporated in the side of the adapter enables almost the whole field to be observed even when making the exposure. A graticule enables the image to be correctly focused. This attachment, mounted on a standard microscope, is shown in fig. 19.2.

Fig. 19.2. Retina Micro Adapter.

Illumination

The standard microscope has a sub-stage condenser system and swivelling mirror, so that light can be collected from a suitable source and directed and concentrated on to the under side of a specimen. Occasional use could be made of daylight coming through a window, but it is clearly preferable to use a constant light-source. Such lighting units are available from microscope manufacturers based on the use of 6-volt high-intensity lamps operated via a rheostat and transformer. It is necessary to obtain uniform illumination over the field area. Operated at correct voltage such a lamp delivers light of about 3,250°K., which is near enough correct for Type B colour film and can be balanced for Kodachrome Film, Type A, with a Wratten 82 filter.

Colour balance

However, it does not follow that the colour rendering will be all that is required even when the light-source has been correctly balanced for the type of film being used. A coloration in the condenser lenses or the optical system of the microscope as well as possible reciprocity effects if exposures exceeding 1 sec. are used, may require the use of colour-compensating filters. Preliminary tests will indicate in what direction, if any, the colour must be adjusted. Some guide can be obtained by viewing the off-balance slide through different compensating filters until one is found which gives the correct visual balance: this will make a good starting point for the next photographic test.

Any filters used should be placed in the light beam before it reaches the sub-stage, and it is therefore possible to give protection to gelatine filters by binding them between cover glasses.

Exposure

It is not possible to give any exact guide to exposure since this will depend on the light-source being used, the speed of the film, the numerical aperture of the microscope objective, the magnification of the eyepiece, any filters used, and the diaphragm setting of the sub-stage. The latter has to be adjusted to suit the objective employed, and in so doing it affects the image intensity – but the diaphragm must *not* be used to vary the intensity as this will adversely affect the image quality. A study of a more specialized book on the subject, such as *Microscopy* by E. R. Marten, is recommended. An exposure meter will give some guide, and initial exposure tests may be done with a black-and-white negative material such as Kodak Panatomic-X to save wastage of the more expensive colour film. This film, when developed in D-76 developer, is approximately the same speed as Kodachrome II Film, Type A. Some adjustment of the exposure may be needed according to the nature of the subject, but this is largely a matter of experience. In the same way, exposure meter readings which depend on an integrated reading may also need adjustment.

The Zeiss camera attachment for photomicrography can be supplied with a photo-electric tube with amplifier, and provides a light-measuring instrument of the greatest sensitivity, and is effective even at the low intensities encountered with polarized light.

20

Processing Colour Materials

THE PROCESSING of Ektachrome, Kodacolor and Ektacolor films, and Ektacolor paper does not present any special technical difficulties, nor does it require a high degree of skill. The required conditions are no different from the controlled processing of panchromatic films, though the various stages are more numerous. However, while black-and-white materials offer considerable latitude in processing, the same does not apply to colour materials. To appreciate why this is so it is necessary to remember that we are dealing with three distinct emulsions coated on the same base, each adjusted to give the required effect as the result of a certain amount of exposure to light of specified quality or colour temperature, and equally as the result of a certain amount of chemical treatment which we broadly label with the term processing. The main requirement, therefore, for anyone intending to undertake colour processing is the ability to carry out a somewhat lengthy sequence of operations with a high degree of accuracy.

Basic processes

Kodak colour materials fall into three groups in regard to processing: negative materials, which include Kodacolor and Ektacolor films for use in a camera, and Ektacolor Print film and paper for printing colour negatives; Ektachrome reversal films; and Kodachrome reversal films. This last group of films involves a processing procedure which is impracticable for the private user and for the commercial laboratory, and for this reason processing is undertaken by Kodak Ltd. A résumé of this process is given on page 60.

In the first group – negative materials – we have materials involving only one stage of development, namely, the production of a negative image in the case of camera films, and a positive image in the case of printing materials. In this single development stage, both silver and dye images are formed. The dye images are formed by the oxidation products of the developing agent reacting with 'couplers' in the emulsion and are therefore proportional to the amount of silver developed. By bleaching and fixation, the silver images, together with the residual silver halides, are then removed leaving only the dye images. Two processes are in current use: Process C-22 for Kodacolor and Ektacolor films, and Process P-122 for Ektacolor paper.

In the second group – Ektachrome films – there are two stages of develop ment, a first development which converts the latent images into negative silve images (this development is highly critical because it determines the amount an distribution of residual halides available for the formation of a second set of silve images) and a second stage, this time with positive tone gradation, produced b 'fogging' the film and re-developing it in a colour developer. This secon development is, in effect, equivalent to the single development of a negativ colour film, since the oxidation products released by the reaction of the develope with the couplers produce positive dye images. With a transparent base th result is a colour transparency, or with a white paper base, a colour print

Two Ektachrome processes are currently in use: E-2 and E-3 which are use as specified in the instruction leaflets packed with Ektachrome films marke Process E-2 or E-3 respectively.

Basic colour sensitometry

One of the principal methods by which the film manufacturer checks the qualit or characteristics of each new emulsion batch is by use of sensitometry. Thos already familiar with its application to black-and-white materials may note tha there is no basic difference in its application to colour materials except that th measurements must be interpreted in terms of colour variables.

Sensitometry requires five standardized conditions.

(1) A light-source of known intensity and of a specific spectral composition
(2) An instrument – known as a sensitometer – for exposing the materia under test to a series of graded exposures of known relative value.
(3) Standardized processing conditions.
(4) An instrument – known as a densitometer – for accurately measuring the density (quantity) of the silver or dye in the developed image.
(5) A method of interpreting these measurements – for example, as curves or numerical parameters such as speed numbers or gamma values.

But as well as affording an important means of quality control in manu facture and the investigation of experimental emulsions, sensitometry has prove an invaluable means of controlling the quality of large-scale processing unit such as those used by the manufacturer processing his own colour materials, by the film industry in processing millions of feet of movie film, and by commercia laboratories undertaking the developing and printing of amateurs' films. In thi latter respect sensitometry is usually limited to the use of control strips which ar processed at regular intervals and from which certain 'key' densities are read t determine, for example, the need for replenishment, the effect of replenishmen or merely the general behaviour of the plant. The use of such a control strip wit newly-prepared solutions is also a check on accurate composition.

Such a method of control is offered by Kodak to professionals and other undertaking the routine processing of colour films in the form of pre-expose control strips. When processed, specific densities are read by means of the Koda Colour Densitometer, and the measurements plotted on a special chart.

The densitometer, see fig. 20.1, is a kind of photometer applied specifically to the task of measuring the opacity or density (logarithm of opacity) of the silver or dye deposit in a film or paper. In the case of films the image is measured by transmitted light and an instrument specially designed for this purpose is known as a transmission densitometer. When the image is on a white opaque base, the measurement is made of the reflected light in relation to a standard white and the instrument is then known as a reflection densitometer. The Kodak Reflection-Transmission Colour Densitometer combines both these functions.

Fig. 20.1. Kodak Reflection-Transmission Colour Densitometer. It is designed to read densities from 0·0 to 3·0, but with an auxiliary density filter, the range can be increased to 4·0.

Opacity may be defined as the reciprocal of transmission, and transmission as the ratio between transmitted and incident light (multiplied by 100 it becomes percentage transmission). Density, as we have mentioned, is the logarithm of opacity and is the value normally used in densitometry. It is possible, however, to measure density in two ways: by confining the measurement to parallel rays of transmitted light, in which case it is known as 'specular' density, or by measuring all the transmitted light to obtain a diffuse density. In the case of a silver image the specular density is significantly higher, which accounts for the fact that negatives printed in a condenser-type enlarger are more 'contrasty' than when printed with one employing diffuse illumination. However, this difference is less significant in the case of dye images.

Densities may be measured visually by comparing an unknown density with a small spot whose intensity is controlled with a calibrated wedge of continuous gradually increasing density, both areas being illuminated with a constant light-source, or it may be done by measuring the transmitted light with a photocell coupled through an amplifier to a meter calibrated in density units. Visual density readings if made with reasonable care are quite suitable for quality control checks used in processing.

Kodak Reflection-Transmission Colour Densitometer

This is a visual instrument designed for measuring densities of both colour and black-and-white materials up to a value of 3·0, though with an auxiliary filter

the black-and-white range can be increased to 4·0, which can be considered th
maximum value for a visual reading. (A density of 4·0 means a transmission
only 0·01 per cent of the incident light). It incorporates a sliding filter holder t
take three filters (red, green and blue) needed for measuring cyan, magenta an
yellow dye densities in colour films. As well as for the use already indicated, it is
valuable aid for systematic control in colour photography, whether checking th
transmission densities of separation negatives and positives, transparencies
correction masks, or measuring the reflection densities of originals and colou
prints.

Processing control by visual comparison

Some photographers pride themselves on their ability to recognize correct colou
balance and most people would claim that they can recognize 'good' colou
rendering when they see it. But as we have shown in Chapter 1, our eyes ca
often be misled, and in any case unless we know the conditions of exposure it
not always possible to tell from the colour photograph whether the film or prin
has been correctly processed. In other words, errors in one may compensate fo
errors in the other. However, the Kodak control strips also provide a basis fo
visual control, as they are supplied with a reference strip which has been pro
cessed under controlled conditions. By direct comparison over an illuminato
the test strip may be compared with the reference strip to obtain an immediat
indication of whether processing is under adequate control.

Certain faults of a local nature due to contamination of one processin
solution with another, or with hand-controlled processing the omission of a ste
in processing, fogging during first development and so forth can only be diagnose
by visual inspection in conjunction with a fault-finding guide given on page 273

Kodak Colour Processing Chemicals

Complete kits of chemicals for making up all the solutions needed for an
particular process are available in various sizes or 'volumes'. In most cases
600 cc. (21 oz.) kit is available for amateur or professional photographers havin
only occasional films to develop. Accompanying each kit is a detailed instructio
leaflet on preparing and using the solutions. This should be studied with care b
the newcomer, and referred to on all occasions, even though it may have bee
committed to memory, in case some modification has been introduced. Normall
any such modification is well-advertised, but it is always possible to miss such a
announcement. The booklet contains a summary of the steps in bold print whic
can be pinned to the wall of the workroom for easy reference.

Small kits are used on the basis of capacity or, in the case of Process C-22 fo
Kodacolor films, with some time adjustment as well, see page 275. With large
volume kits, replenishers may be available as extras.

The purpose of replenishment is to extend the useful life of solutions whic
have reached a noticeable stage of exhaustion. In the case of developers it ma
also be limited by the relative instability of the solutions (keeping qualities).

Processing formulas

It is sometimes questioned why some colour film manufacturers publish the chemical formulas of various colour processes while others do not. However, there are good reasons for this latter attitude. By restricting the supply of chemicals to their own packed preparations, the manufacturers can assure the purity of the chemicals and their conditions of storage. They can assume responsibility for correct compounding and at the same time be free to make changes which lead to improved results or which may be required by modifications in the colour film itself. Bearing in mind the extraordinary progress which has been made by Kodak in the field of colour photography, it may be assumed that this last reason is a very important one. Finally it may be assumed that the manufacturer wishes to protect himself against the risk of unjustified complaints about colour materials actually arising out of the use of faulty chemicals.

However one may react to these arguments – for or against – there remains the undeniable convenience, and in most cases economy, of having the required chemicals provided in neatly packed kits.

Processing equipment

The most suitable types of tanks for processing depend on the kind of material, whether sheet, roll or 35 mm. film, and on the quantity to be handled at any one time or on the basis of continuous use. It is outside the scope of this book to deal with large-output, continuous-processing plants used in photo-finishing and full information on such equipment can be obtained from the Finisher Sales Division of Kodak Ltd.

Starting on a modest level, occasional films are most conveniently processed in one of the 600 cc. spiral-reel tanks designed primarily for amateur use, see Fig. 20.2. These usually have one adjustable flange so that the reel will accommo-

Fig. 20.2. Paterson Universal II and Triple 35 II developing tanks.

date any size of film. An additional flange may also be available to allow tw
36-exposure 35 mm. films to be loaded one above the other. Modern tanks ar
usually of the sealed type to enable the whole tank to be turned upside down fc
additional agitation. These tanks are also convenient in that with the lid fitte
the whole sequence of processing can be done in normal room lighting; only th
loading needs to be done in darkness, and in an emergency there is usually
cupboard or small room that can be temporarily blacked out. A minor objectio
to some amateur tanks is that it may take anything up to $\frac{1}{2}$ min. to pour the fir.
developer through the hole in the lid and a similar time to empty it. With suc
tanks it is usually better to carry out the beginning of the first step in a darkroor
with the lid of the tank open. The remaining steps can, of course, be carried or
in normal room lighting.

A wide variety of spiral-reel tanks exists. Some are made of stainless steel an
may be designed to take several spiral units at one time, though in this case th
capacity may be nearer 1 litre.

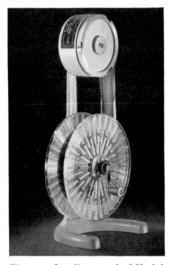

Fig. 20.3. Loading stand of Kodak Spiral Film Processing outfit. It is available for 35 mm. and 70 mm. wide films.

Fig. 20.4. Kodak 35/70 Spiral Film-Dryer Model 24.

The Kodak 35 mm. Spiral Processing Outfit offers a convenient method fc
processing bulk lengths of 35 mm. colour film. Two models are available, or
with a capacity of up to 24 ft. and the other up to 100 ft. The outfit includes
loading fixture for winding the film into the spiral grooves (see fig. 20.3), a spir.
reel, and four circular plastic processing dishes with a lid for the developing dis
and a key for dismantling the spools. Separate dishes may be obtained so that,

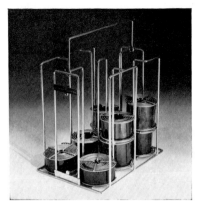

Fig. 20.5. No. 3 RM Processing Rack.

Fig. 20.6. No. 3C Sheet Film Processing Rack.

required, each sequence of the processing operation may have its own dish. An associated drying unit is also available, see fig. 20.4.

Roll film and 35 mm. film in small batches may be conveniently handled in the No. 3 RM Processing Rack (fig. 20.5), which will fit the Kodak No. 3 Processing Tank or one of similar dimensions. It will accommodate 30 reels loaded with 35 mm. or 828 film; 24 reels with size 127; and 18 reels of 120 or 620 film.

For sheet film or prints in small quantities, flat processing dishes may offer the simplest solution, especially if these have already been acquired for black-and-white processing. However, if a number of films or prints are to be processed at one time, a set of tanks with film racks or print baskets is required. These may be based on the No. 3 Processing Tank mentioned above, which will accept the

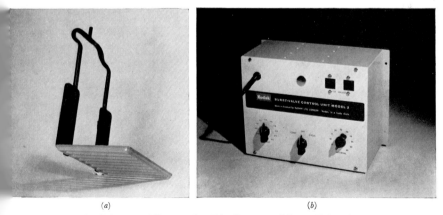

(a)   (b)

Fig. 20.7. Kodak No. 3 Nitrogen-Gas Distributor and Burst-Valve Control Unit.

261

No. 3C Sheet Film Processing Rack which embodies a P.V.C. gas distributor at the base for nitrogen gas agitation. The same tank will also take the No. 3 Colour Print Processing Basket which will take up to 30 prints 8 × 10 in. This can be used with the No. 3 Nitrogen-Gas Distributor for gas agitation, see fig. 20.7.

The No. 3 Processing Tanks are made of hard vulcanized rubber which is unaffected by any of the chemicals used in colour processing. Covers and floating lids are available as optional extras, but the latter are particularly important with colour developers in view of their rapid rate of oxidation.

The need for accurate processing control involves not only the maintenance of temperature and correct timing, but the application of regular amounts of agitation. This can be accomplished by lifting the rack or basket out of the solution at regular intervals, but it is highly desirable and more consistent to employ the use of nitrogen gas agitation. Being an inert gas as far as developing solutions are concerned, it has no harmful effect on either the film or solutions, and as nitrogen already makes up about 80 per cent of the air we breathe, it is equally harmless to the darkroom operator. The gas is supplied from the cylinder through a control unit such as the Kodak Burst-Valve Control Unit – shown in fig. 20.7 – by a No. 3 Nitrogen-Gas Distributor or the No. 3C Sheet Film Processing Rack which have already been mentioned.

Incidental equipment in the case of dish development would include storage bottles for the solutions, which should preferably be of glass and of the correct size for the mixed volume of solution. An accurate thermometer and a darkroom timer are also needed. When dealing with larger volumes of solutions an electric mixer having a long arm and paddle of stainless steel will be a worth-while time-saver.

Temperature control

One of the problems in colour processing involving the use of amateur processing tanks or dishes is the difficulty of maintaining the developer temperature to within the critical limits of $\pm \frac{1}{2}°$F. of 75°F. or 85°F. ($\pm \frac{1}{4}°$C. of 24°C. or 29·5°C.). Makeshift methods are discussed in the next chapter under the heading of Home Processing, but a more fundamental approach is required for routine professional work. Apart from some degree of temperature control of the workroom itself both for the comfort of the operator and to minimize the difference between room temperature and processing temperature, the normal procedure is to surround all the processing tanks with a water-jacket which is kept at constant temperature by an accurate thermostat.

Darkroom layout

Naturally in planning a new darkroom for professional or commercial activities involving the employment of assistants, due account must be taken of local by-laws and safety regulations, and it must also be observed that the water services comply with the Water Act of 1945. For this it is desirable to make use of

Plate 57. This portrait of a machine operator by Prudence Cuming was an 'assignment' during her three-month course as a Kodak scholarship holder in the U.S.A. She was required to take the portrait without interrupting the work of the machinist and for this reason chose to use flashbulbs as lighting. The lighting units enabled pilot lamps to be fitted – in this case important because of the man's spectacles – from which it was possible to make an exposure assessment. The Ektacolor negative was made with a 4 × 5 in. Calmut Monorail camera, and the print on Ektacolor paper.

Plate 58. Stained glass window in Cologne Station. The close viewpoint was necessary to obtain a clear area of sky behind the window. Kodachrome I Film, 1/125 sec. f/5·6

Plate 59. Ceramic name plate outside the Villa D'Este, near Rome. It was photographed with a 15 mm. lens at a distance to avoid having to tilt the camera. Kodachrome I Film, 1/125 sec. f/8.

Plate 60. Fresco painting at the entrance of Ravello Cathedral. Taken at noon when lit with sunlight reflected from paving stone. High Speed Ektachrome Film, 1/125 sec. at f

Photos: E. S. Bomback.

e services of a builder or architect. However, before consulting either of these, e photographer should use his experience to prepare a preliminary layout from hich the architect can draw detailed plans. Of considerable assistance in this spect is the booklet published by Kodak entitled *Professional Darkroom Design*.

The following notes are intended as a guide to the freelance and advanced mateur in setting up a darkroom in a spare room at home.

It is probable that the darkroom will also serve the purpose of a printing om and we have taken this into consideration in the layout shown in fig. 20.8. owever, there are a number of general considerations before considering details.

One of the principal enemies of the darkroom worker is dust and this requires at particular attention be given to the floor covering. Carpets, even of the aircord variety, though making for comfort, are collectors of dust, and to a sser extent we can include varnished wooden floor boards, tiled and concrete oors, which retain dust in cracks and uneven surfaces. At the same time it is ell to consider the possibility of spilt solutions, the bleach bath being particularly orrosive. The simplest floor covering is probably rubber sheeting, which is on le in a variety of attractive colours in most household and department stores. n existing linoleum floor is equally suitable if kept well-waxed as a protection gainst spilt fluids. A strip of rubber sheeting in the area where processing is arried out would give additional protection.

Next we may consider the exclusion of light, and, if work is to be carried on uring the hours of daylight, this means that any windows, ventilators and doors ust be made really light-proof. If the room is to be used permanently as a arkroom, a shutter over the window is relatively simple to provide, since any maining chinks of light can be covered with strips of black adhesive material. it is desired to admit daylight on occasions, some kind of framework must first e built into the window aperture with a recess into which the shutter is fixed. If e recess and the edges of the shutter are painted with blackboard paint, light akage should be negligible. Certain thin hardboard or masonite sheeting is not ght-proof to infra-red radiation and it may therefore be advisable to use $\frac{1}{2}$ in. lywood for the shutter. An existing ventilator should not be permanently closed; n the contrary it may form the ideal location for a light-trapped ventilation fan f the 'Ventaxia' type. Failing the existence of a wall ventilator, the ventilation n can be located in the window shutter, the window being left slightly open efore fitting the shutter. It is not always appreciated by the darkroom worker ow stuffy a smallish, light-proofed room can become after a few hours' work.

If the door leads out to a well-lighted passage it is as well to consider the dvisability of fitting a light-trap to the door. From the point of view of space it unfortunate that most doors are designed to open inwards and, depending on e position of the door, the light-trap may prove too wasteful of working space. n excellent compromise is to erect a curtain rail outside the door from which an be hung a pair of overlapping curtains of heavy but limp black material hich trail a little on the floor. The bottom edge of the door should be fitted with n additional strip of thick felt to make contact with the floor when the door is

265

swung on its hinges. A small red-signal lamp can be fitted above the curtains operated by one side of a double-pole switch of the type used for stairway illumination, so that when the white light is switched off in the darkroom the signal light comes on. This overcomes the necessity of locking the darkroom door as a precaution against chance visitors and allows a second person to enter the room if due precaution is taken to get inside the curtains before opening the door.

The walls and ceiling may need attention. An old plastered ceiling may suffer from flaking or old wall-distemper may have reached a powdery stage. Ideally, ceiling and walls should be given a coat or two of white glossy paint which can easily be washed down at intervals. A black line at a height of about 5 ft. from the floor on all four walls can be useful when working in almost total darkness as an aid to orientation. By having the walls and ceiling white it is possible to employ indirect safe-lighting when the room is used for black-and-white printing.

The question of a water supply and drainage is worth considering. For example, a room already fitted with a wash basin may provide the complete answer for a moderate amount of work merely by exchanging the wash basin unit for a large wooden trough made from 1 in. resin bonded plywood. If a hot-water supply is also available, a simple mixing tap may serve the purpose so long as due care is taken of variations of pressure caused by other users of the same hot and cold water system. It may be considered worth while to fit a separate water heater, though main washes can, of course, be carried out with cold water at temperatures as low as 50°F. (see page 276). Running water is by no means indispensible for the small darkroom, as intermediate rinses can be done on the basis of several changes of water, and lengthy washes done in a kitchen.

The need for safelighting will depend on whether the room is to be used for black-and-white work as well as colour. Colour-film processing requires the first three steps to be done in total darkness, but, after this, normal room lighting may be used. If the processing tank has a light-tight lid, total darkness is only needed for the loading operation and possibly in changing from developer to rinse and rinse to hardener if separate tanks are used. Brief inspection with the light from a Wratten 10H safelight screen may be used with both Ektacolor and Panalure papers and a safelamp of the Kodak Beehive type or similar which can be swung upwards when not required, is probably the best kind. Illumination for a darkroom timer can also be applied with such a safelamp, but fitted with a mask or hood to prevent light falling on the work bench. While on the question of safelights it is as well to test a newly constructed darkroom for light-tightness by exposing a piece of fast pan film face upwards on the work bench and partly covered with a coin for a few minutes. This is then developed and examined for signs of fogging.

The mixing of chemicals should be carried out in a separate room, care being taken, if done in a kitchen or bathroom, not to contaminate surrounding areas. Although none of the chemicals in use is a deadly poison, some are corrosive and others may cause skin rashes. The chemicals of the developing solution

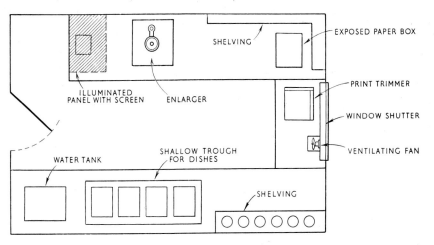

Fig. 20.8. Layout for a small general-purpose darkroom.

should be treated with particular respect, since continued contact with the skin over a period of time, far from building up an immunity, tends to make the skin more susceptible to rashes. Rubber gloves are therefore to be recommended, or, in the case of handling single prints, a pair of plastic print forceps.

Returning to the darkroom layout, it will be seen that the printing bench occupies the length of one wall and the processing bench the length of the opposite wall. At the extreme left of the printing bench is a 12 × 10 in. illuminated panel of flashed opal, screened by a kind of booth so that in the event of sensitive material being left accidentally exposed, fogging is reduced to smaller proportions. If, when working with a particular size negative, the panel is masked to this size and contains both a low-wattage guide lamp for positioning the negative and a second inspection lamp which can be switched on for inspection of a negative, the booth will afford more or less complete protection to a print processing operation which has just begun. Also the small amount of illumination will not destroy a state of dark-adaptation of the eyes. The enlarger with any associated exposure control occupies the central position and an exposed-paper box occupies the far end. Drawers or shelves under the bench provide paper storage and negative filing. The end bench, which can take the form of a hinged flap if access is required to the window, serves as a dry bench for cutting printing paper to smaller sizes or for test strips.

Turning to the processing bench, a set of shelves provide storage space for bottles of solution and the central area of the bench a shallow water-tight trough. The nature of the processing equipment and method of controlling the temperature of the solutions have been dealt with earlier in this chapter, and various improvised methods are suggested in the next chapter under home processing.

Processing Ektachrome Films

IT IS WORTH while for anyone intending to undertake the processing of an Ektachrome film for the first time to bear in mind that it is a complete process in the sense that the end product, the colour transparency, is a finished photograph. Assuming that the film has been correctly and carefully exposed with the object of obtaining both technically and pictorially excellent results, the successful outcome of these efforts will still depend on the accuracy with which the film is processed. Although the instructions packed with every kit of Ektachrome processing chemicals leave nothing unsaid by way of information, advice and precautions, the realization for the first time of the necessary conditions may produce unexpected departures from the ideal, for example, a rapid fall in temperature of the first developer when using a small processing tank or an unforeseen demand on the washing water supply. Also it is not impossible in the excitement of a first attempt to omit some vital step particularly when working at home where there is the likelihood of interruptions. Or bearing in mind human nature, the impatience to get started may lead to a rather cursory inspection of the detailed instruction booklet, or failure to dissolve completely all the chemicals in the manner described. For these and other reasons it is therefore preferable to start off with a film which contains photographs which, if need be, can easily be repeated. Such a film might well contain a few test exposures, one of which contains a grey scale and a coloured test object such as that provided by the Kodak Colour Separation Guides. This will provide a check on colour balance in processing provided that the correct colour quality of illumination has been used. On a professional basis the Kodak control strips provide a similar service.

However, the wise photographer will tackle his first Ektachrome film with the intention of achieving first class results and it is to this end that we present the following notes which give the essence, so to speak, of the instructions which accompany the processing kit. A summary of processing procedure is given below.

Capacity and storage

The smaller kits, 600 cc. and 2 litres, are packed in two separate units as a means of obtaining the maximum working life of the solutions. Unit No. 1 contains the

SUMMARY OF PROCESS E-2 AND E-3

Step		Temperature (°C)	Temperature (°F)	Time (minutes)
1	First developer	$24 \pm \frac{1}{4}$	$75 \pm \frac{1}{2}$	10
2	Rinse	23 – 25	73 – 77	1
3	Hardener	23 – 25	73 – 77	3

Remaining steps may be done in normal room lighting

4	Wash	23 – 25	73 – 77	3
5	Reversal exposure ..	Films must drain for at least one minute before colour development		
6	Colour developer ..	23 – 25	73 – 77	15
7	Wash	23 – 25	73 – 77	5
8	Clearing bath ..	23 – 25	73 – 77	5
9	Rinse	23 – 25	73 – 77	1
10	Bleach	23 – 25	73 – 77	8
11	Rinse	23 – 25	73 – 77	1
12	Fixing bath ..	23 – 25	73 – 77	6
13	Wash	23 – 25	73 – 77	8
14	Stabilizer ..	23 – 25	73 – 77	1
15	Dry	Not over 45 °C (113 °F)		

wo developers, and Unit No. 2 the hardener, bleach, clearing, fixing and tabilizing chemicals. The storage life of prepared solutions is given as 4 weeks for unused developers in tightly-stoppered bottles and 1 week for partly-used or for unused developers stored in a tank with floating lid. All the solutions made from Unit No. 2 may be safely used up to a period of 2 months whether unused or partly used as long as the capacity is not exceeded. In addition, the capacity of the latter solutions is roughly twice that of the two developers. While these limits are undoubtedly on the conservative side, they provide an essential basis for the quality control of processing in small quantities. There are two alternative approaches to the problem of a single film: one is to send it to a processing laboratory, though in fact if only Unit No. 1 chemicals have to be renewed there is little economy in this, and the other is to store the film in a refrigerator until additional films make another processing session worth-while. In general, exposed films should be processed as soon as possible and certainly within a month of exposure in moderately warm weather. In conditions of high temperature and humidity no time should be lost in processing, unless refrigerated storage is available.

The question of storage bottles for 600 cc. solutions may present something of a problem, since while bottles of 1 pint, and $\frac{1}{2}$ and 1 litres are commonly used for other purposes in all variety of shapes and coloured glass, few, if any exist which hold exactly 600 cc. (21 fl. oz.). In using 1 litre bottles the storage life is significantly affected by the large airspace that remains and which is renewed every time the solutions are returned to the bottle. To a greater extent this applies to storing 2-litre solutions in 80-oz. Winchester bottles, and although it doubles the number of bottles, it is preferable to store unused developer solutions in 1-litre bottles filled to the top. This, in any case, is an excellent method if the tank used for developing holds only 600 cc. since the capacity of half the developer can be used in the first bottle and the capacity of the second half (which keeps better in an unused condition) obtained from the second bottle.

Storage bottles should be carefully labelled, and since it is often convenient to stand them in a water bath as a means of maintaining the correct temperature the labels are best stuck with transparent adhesive tape round the neck of the bottle which stands clear of the water. The label should also bear the date of mixing. Certain types of plastic bottles are not suitable for storing developers.

Mixing

This should never be done where food is prepared, as splashes and chemical dust when emptying packets into the mixing water are extremely difficult to avoid. It is also advisable to wear rubber gloves, and after each stage of mixing to wipe thoroughly all surrounding surfaces and rinse out the mixing vessel. It is not necessary to use distilled water, though tap-water in some districts and that collected from the roof in districts remote from a mains supply should be filtered. At certain seasons of the year, rainwater from a roof may contain a high content of organic matter from adjacent foliage and it is then preferable to use distilled water which can usually be purchased from a garage. Metal vessels, except for stainless steel, should never be used for mixing. Some workers prefer mixing chemicals for small volumes in the storage bottle, and so long as none is spilled in pouring the ingredients into the bottle there is no objection to this method. A funnel will help in preventing the loss of chemicals, the water being poured in at intervals to free any blockage. One advantage of this method, if the bottle is tightly stoppered, is that it avoids splashes. However, if the chemicals are mixed in a separate vessel, the act of pouring them into the storage bottle can be accompanied with some filtration. A small wad of cotton wool laid over the neck of the funnel will serve the purpose. It is sometimes recommended that solutions be prepared 12 hours before being used, the object being for the developer to mature (perhaps like wine). The only good reason we can think of for doing this is that a lengthy job of mixing followed immediately by an hour's solid processing is apt to become somewhat tedious to anyone practising photography for pleasure.

Home processing

The chief problem is undoubtedly that of maintaining the temperature of the first development to within $\frac{1}{2}°$ of 75°F. during the colder months of the year. Prior to development, the bottles containing the processing solutions can be brought to the correct temperature by standing them in a deep bowl of water. If very cold, the water can be quite hot (though not so hot as to crack the glass until the temperature inside the bottle is 75°F. (24°C.). The water is then adjusted to this temperature. However, if the developing tank itself is very cold it may well reduce the temperature of the developer by 2° within a short while of starting the process. The simplest remedy, after the film has been loaded, is to place the tank in a warm airing cupboard for an hour, which is usually a convenient length of time to get everything ready for processing. As a precaution against variations of temperature during the first development, two bowls, one containing warm water and the other cold water, should be available for making rapid adjustments. If the temperature of the room itself can be temporarily raised to about 75°F. (with say an electric heater) such variations are unlikely to occur, and the latitude of 2° up or down in the remaining stages is no problem at all except in respect of the washing water. Failing a hot and cold mixing tap (plus an uninterrupted supply of water at constant pressure), the best method is to do the various washing stages by changes of water, taking the water from a large bowl, which is kept replenished and adjusted for temperature during the intervening steps of clearing, bleaching and fixing. Changes can be made at the rate of two every minute, the tank being well-drained after each soaking. Moderate agitation will help to promote adequate washing. If there is no hot water 'laid on', a large kettle should be kept going. With Process E-2 (but not Process E-3) the washing water temperature may be as low as 50°F. (10°C.) with washing times increased by 50 per cent.

It will be noted that the development time includes the time taken to drain the tank, and if an enclosed tank is being used for the convenience of working in normal room lighting, it may be found that both filling the tank and draining it takes anything up to 30 sec. It is logical to assume that proper development has not started until the tank is full or full enough to cover the film. However, the draining time should be considered part of normal development and should it be found to take 30 sec. then draining should start at $9\frac{1}{2}$ min. from the time the tank has been adequately filled. This draining time is also included in the times given for the remaining steps, but except for the first rinse which still requires that the lid be kept on the tank, draining need not exceed 10 sec. However, the first rinse which calls for not more than 1 minute in running water may seem a little difficult to achieve in terms of water changes if it takes 30 sec. to fill or drain the tank. Moreover it raises the question as to what extent the film is still reacting to the developer. Practice shows that a single rinse with continuous agitation for $\frac{1}{2}$ min. plus the $\frac{1}{2}$ min. draining time is adequate for this step.

It will be noticed that the final step is that of the stabilizer after which the film is dried. No further rinse in water should be given. Some photographers are in the habit of swabbing a film down with a sponge or leather, or with 35 mm. film, 'squeegeeing' it between two fingers. Providing there is no grit on the swab or fingers and it is done carefully no harm should result, though as the stabilizer contains a wetting agent surplus liquid rapidly drains from the surface. However this creates a danger of scum or sediment being left on the emulsion surface which, if allowed to dry may prove difficult to remove. One precaution is to

271

filter the stabilizing solution every time it has been used to ensure that it contains no sediment. Drying the film should also be carried out in a dust-free room.

Quality control for professional processing

We referred in the previous chapter to a system of processing control based on the use of sensitometric control strips pre-exposed by Kodak under standardized conditions. These strips are available for either the E-2 or E-3 processes (the two are not interchangeable) packed in boxes of 20, each strip bearing the latent images of a grey scale, two sets of filtered coloured patches, and a portrait photograph. The box includes a processed strip, processed under controlled conditions, as a reference guide for comparison.

Ektachrome Control Strips may be stored for periods of up to about one month in the freezer compartment of a refrigerator at a temperature not above 30°F.(−1°C.) to prevent changes in the latent image. The strips should be held at this temperature until required for processing and only sufficient withdrawn from the packet each day for estimated requirements. Only sufficient strips should be ordered for a month to six weeks ahead unless storage at below 0°F (−18°C.) is available.

Ideally, each batch of film developed should include a control strip, but when solutions have not been used or replenished for more than a week, a control strip should also be processed and inspected before another batch of film is undertaken. The control strip should be marked with the batch number of the films with which it has been processed.

The processed control strips provide the basis for visual assessment, and by means of density measurements plotted on a record chart over a period of time a valuable means of maintaining processing quality and also of diagnosing possible faults. The reader is referred to the Kodak booklet 'Quality Control Processes E-2 and E-3' for detailed information on the application of control strips.

However, there remain a number of errors which are more readily identified by visual inspection and some which are outside the scope of a control strip. A table of these is given at the end of this chapter.

Replenisher system of processing

When relatively large volumes of processing solutions are involved, the gradual exhaustion due to use and oxidation cannot be properly controlled by increasing the time of development, and the only satisfactory method is to add replenishers to adjust the chemical balance of the various solutions. As applied to Processes E-2 and E-3 special replenishers are needed only for the two developers, replenishers for the remaining solutions except the stabilizer being made up by the normal chemicals in two-thirds of the volume of water. Stabilizer replenisher is made up to the normal tank strength. Full details of the use of replenishers are packed with the chemicals.

VISUAL DIAGNOSIS OF FAULTS IN PROCESSING EKTACHROME FILMS

condition of film	*Probable cause: remedy*
contaminated with fungus or algae deposits	Processing tanks not cleaned properly or washing tanks not drained when not being used.
dirty with scum spots	Hardener or stabilizer solution contaminated with processing by-products. Filter or change solutions.
blue spots (iron spots, Prussian blue)	Bleach contaminated by iron, iron alloys or chemical dust.
reticulated or frilled	Excessively soft water used for rinse after first developer or wash after colour developer. Increase hardness of water: one gram of magnesium sulphate (Epsom Salts) per litre of wash water will increase hardness sufficiently. Or use cold water wash (50-70 °F).
light or greenish-light borders	Film borders covered by channel-type processing hangers during reversal exposure; faulty agitation.
completely opaque	Fixing bath or bleach omitted
extremely dense and green; slight trace of negative image.	First and colour developers reversed.
extremely yellow with overall density increase	Film exposed through base, or film immersed briefly in bleach bath after colour development. In the first case the reds are very degraded.
yellow with overall density increase: sometimes solarized	Film fogged during first development.
very light; higher densities are cyan	Colour developer contaminated or accidentally replenished with first developer replenisher.
dark and red (red stain in highlight areas)	Omission of clearing bath after colour developer.
green and light	Film fogged with green light. Hardener contaminated with stabilizer. Colour developer contaminated with hardener or bleach.
green (especially maximum-density areas)	Omission of reversal exposure.
greenish-blue, degraded colour	First or colour developer contaminated with fixing bath.
extremely blue	First developer contaminated with tin (possibly from re-soldering processing tank joint).
bluish-cyan and light	Colour developer contaminated with clearing bath.
red	Film fogged with red light.

Note: Some defects are visible in diffuse transmitted light such as that provided by the Kodak Transparency Illuminator. Other defects are easier to see in reflected light or in transmitted specular light.

22

Processing Kodacolor and Ektacolor Negative Films

MUCH OF WHAT has been written in the previous chapter regarding t conditions and equipment for processing Ektachrome film applies equally to t processing of Kodacolor and Ektacolor films. While there is certainly mc latitude in a negative-positive process, it should be remembered that Ektacol paper is only available in one 'grade' of contrast, whereas some black-and-whi printing papers are available in as many as five grades of contrast. Furthermo we are still dealing with a three-layer emulsion, the characteristics of which a designed to give their best results under certain standardized conditions exposure and processing. Even if it were permissible to vary the time of develo ment as a means of controlling contrast, such a procedure could only be appli to individual sheet films unless the whole of a roll film or 35 mm. film had be exposed under conditions of excessive lighting contrast. It is far better to adju the lighting contrast in lighting the subject so that all negatives may be given tl same treatment. It is also an advantage in printing colour negatives if bo density and contrast are kept as uniform as possible, and even more advantageo if the colour balance is reasonably constant.

Although the processing of colour negative materials does not diff essentially from processing panchromatic films, the need to remove the silv image formed during development requires the addition of a bleach ba between developing and fixing.

Kodak films for making colour negatives have coloured couplers incorpo ated in the emulsion layers at the time of manufacture. The unused couple remaining in the film after development provide automatic masking for colo correction. The effect of the coloured couplers is to give the negative an over orange colouring. While the coloured couplers effectively improve the absorptic characteristics of the dyes in the negative, they do not eliminate the need f supplementary masking procedures when a colour negative is used as an inte mediate in printing or duplicating a positive transparency, see page 243. Th is because the mask corrects only for the negative dyes and not for tl original.

274

rocessing kits (Process C.22)

hemicals ready for mixing are available in kit form to make up solutions of)0 cc., and 2 litres, and as separate components and replenishers in 3 gall., and ; litre sizes for large-scale processing units. Full instructions for processing are .cluded with each kit. The developer, used or partially used, may be stored r periods of up to 3 weeks in tanks fitted with floating lids, or for 6 weeks in ghtly-stoppered bottles. All the other solutions stored under the same conditions .ay be kept for a period of 8 weeks.

The 600 cc. kit is supplied in two units, Unit No. 1 containing the developer ad stop bath and Unit No. 2 containing the hardener, bleach and fixer. The tter solutions have twice the working capacity and a second developer and stop ath can be made up for further processing. The 2 litre kit already contains an *tra* set of developer and stop bath chemicals to enable full use to be made of the maining solutions.

In utilizing the full capacity of the developer, some increase in developing me is necessary. Since details of this are best taken from a current instruction aflet, the following example based on a 2 litre kit is given merely for interest.

The capacity of the developer may be conveniently expressed in units lated to the area of the film processed.

ktacolor film, types S and L

1 sheet film size 4 × 5 in.	0·75	unit
4¾ × 6½ in.	1·0	unit
8 × 10 in.	3·0	units

odacolor film

1 roll film size 828	1 unit
1 roll film size 127	1·5 units
1 35 mm. film, 12-exp.	
1 126 cartridge, 12-exp.	1·25 units
1 35 mm. film, 20-exp.	2·0 units
1 roll film 620 or 120	3·0 units

Each 2 litre (70 fl. oz.) volume of developer and stop bath will process 45 nits of film following the development time compensation shown below.

Type of film	Film processed before each developer time increase	Development times for processings of 9 units				
		1st	2nd	3rd	4th	5th
Ektacolor Print Film	9 units	12	12¾	13½	14¼	15
Kodacolor Film and Ektacolor Professional Films Types S and L	9 units	14	14¾	15½	16¼	17

Temperature control

As in the case of reversal film, this is critical during the time the film is in the developer, and every effort should be taken to maintain the solution at 75° (24°C.). Departures from this temperature are obviously not so serious as in the case of a reversal film since small variations may be corrected at the printing stage. Nevertheless it is sound practice to eliminate as many variable factors possible. The remaining solutions present little difficulty since there is a latitude of 2° either way.

If convenient, cold water not lower than 50°F. (10°C.) can be used for washing, but for temperatures between 73° and 50°F. (23°-10°C.) the washing time must be increased by 50 per cent. However, it should be appreciated that film which has been washed at a lower temperature will have the effect of reducing the temperature of the bleach and fixer solutions and these should therefore be kept at 77°F. (25°C.).

Quality control

A procedure similar to that already described for processing Ektachrome film can be applied to Kodacolor and Ektacolor film using Kodacolor control strips. A separate booklet *Quality Control Process C-22* is available from Kodak. In view the difficulty of judging whether the quality of a colour negative is within standard of speed, contrast and fog level, sensitometric checks may be considered even more important than for reversal films.

Visual comparison of processed control strips gives an immediate indication of the behaviour of the processing operation, but densitometric measurements are necessary to obtain the full benefit from this kind of quality control. The following conditions may be readily diagnosed by visual examination of the negatives.

Conditions of negative:	Cause and remedy:
Contaminated with fungus or algae deposits (occurs most often in the bleach and following wash)	Processing and/or replenisher tanks dirty. Drain water tanks whenever they are not being used. A water filter will help to prevent this trouble.
Scum and dirt adhering to emulsion or base	Final rinse contaminated with dirt and by-products processing: replace or filter
Blue spots (iron spots, Prussian blue)	Contamination of bleach by iron, iron alloys, or chemical dust. Change bleach bath
Reticulation or frilling	Washing water too soft or too warm. Hardness may increased by adding 1 gram of magnesium sulphate (Epsom Salts) per litre of wash water. Or use cold water wash
Completely opaque	Bleach or fixing bath omitted. Treat negative in bleach bath again and repeat the subsequent steps
Slow, uneven development (streaks, spots and mottle)	Insufficient agitation. Nitrogen-burst unit clogged or gas supply exhausted

Black-and-white processing by error

It is interesting to note that the mistake of processing a Kodacolor or Ektacolor film in a developer for black-and-white negative film is not necessarily a fatal one, though the practice is hardly to be recommended. The coloured couplers are not destroyed by normal black-and-white processing and by treating the negative in the C-22 bleach bath, the missing colour images can be brought to life (or very nearly so) by starting all over again, but this time with the correct solutions. However, before doing this, it is as well to make black-and-white prints from the negatives on 'Panalure' paper in case something should go wrong!

The following procedure should be adopted.

(1) Wash the negatives for 15 min. to ensure that all the chemicals from black-and-white processing have been removed.

(2) Place them in a C-22 bleach bath (at $73°$-$77°F$.) for 8 min. to convert the silver image to silver halide. The image will then appear a creamy colour.

(3) Wash for a further 15 min. in running water to remove all trace of bleach.

(4) Expose the film for a few seconds to the light of a Photoflood lamp to ensure that all the silver halide is developable. This is desirable even though washing may have been done in normal room lighting.

(5) Commence the normal C-22 process from the first step.

Although the results of this treatment depend on the type and condition of the black-and-white process, it usually works well enough for the reconstituted negatives to give acceptable colour prints.

23

Colour Printing

GIVEN A GOOD colour negative, individually-made colour prints using Ekt color paper can equal the quality of colour reproduction of those made with th Kodak Dye Transfer process, long considered by experts to provide as ne 'perfect' reproduction as is practicable. But as with all printing processes, mue depends on the quality of the negative, and though an expert may at great pai produce an acceptable print from a poor negative, economy of time ai materials in professional work requires, first of all, satisfactory exposure ai processing of the negative material. Naturally, in the large-scale production colour prints from negatives of varying quality, some departure from the be obtainable is inevitable, but this, of course, applies equally to black-and-whi printing.

The colour negative

If we examine the colour negative of a brightly coloured subject it can be see that not only are the tones reversed (as in an ordinary negative), but the colou are roughly complementary to those of the subject. For instance, a red popp would appear greenish-blue, its leaves a reddish-blue and, if photograph against a deep blue sky, the sky would appear brownish. This effect is mo noticeable in a negative made with a film which does not incorporate colour couplers. With negatives made on films containing coloured couplers the effe can still be seen but it is somewhat obscured by the orange mask formed by t unaltered couplers.

In order to understand why the colours are 'reversed' in this way, it necessary to realize that the colours of the colour positive are obtained by t subtraction from white light of their complementaries, and since the colo negative is an intermediate or half-way stage between the original subject a the colour photograph, it must subtract the original colours from the whi exposing light and transmit the complementaries. Just as a dark tone in t negative represents a light tone in the subject, a complementary represents t original colour.

Indeed people are under the impression that a negative colour film has entirely different colour-recording arrangement from that of a reversal film. B in fact the two films are basically the same in the way they record colour, t difference being that the colour development with reversal films does not occ

til after an initial negative development stage. In fact, unmasked colour
gatives may be obtained by developing an Ektachrome film in C-22 chemicals.

It may also be noticed by anyone used to colour transparencies that the
lours in the negative, even allowing for the orange mask, are by no means as
illiant or 'colourful' as in a transparency. This is partly due to its lower contrast
t even more so to the fact that the dyes are chosen for their absorption
aracteristics in colour printing and not for their visual effect. The appearance
a Kodacolor negative, in fact, gives very little clue to its pictorial value. It can
checked for sharpness, and if it includes a grey scale, densitometric measure-
ents can tell the photo-technician a great deal about the printability. With
rtain subjects, portraits for example, proof-prints in black-and-white may be a
ort cut to evaluating certain pictorial aspects or in preparing layouts. These
n be made on ordinary bromide paper or, if better tone rendering is required,
Panalure printing paper, which is fully panchromatic, see page 285.

ktacolor paper

his is printing paper intended specifically for making colour prints from
odacolor and Ektacolor negatives, though, with some adjustment to the filtering
th white-light exposures, it will produce excellent results from colour negatives
ade with other makes of colour film, masked or unmasked. It contains three
nulsion layers, sensitive to blue, green and red light respectively, coated on a
edium-weight paper base. The emulsion surface has a fairly high gloss, which
rmits the prints to retain a long tonal range. Prints may, if required, be glazed.

Ektacolor paper is supplied in moisture-proof bags of laminated foil, and
ly sufficient paper for immediate use should be withdrawn, the bag being
-sealed' by folding the foil over itself. Once a packet has been opened it is more
sceptible to changes in printing characteristics as a result of heat and humidity
d it is desirable to store the paper in a refrigerator. Failing this the coolest
ssible location should be chosen for storage. Paper which has been stored in a
frigerator should be removed about $\frac{1}{2}$ to 1 hour before use to prevent moisture
ndensation on its surface. If the contents of a package are used over an extended
riod, some adjustment in exposure conditions may be necessary to allow for
anges in its characteristics. For the prolonged storage of unopened packages a
ep freeze unit capable of maintaining temperatures at between 0° and − 10°F.
−18° and −23°C.) is ideal.

felight

ktacolor paper is necessarily very sensitive to light of all colours, though it may
handled for a limited time under a safelamp fitted with a Wratten Safelight
lter Series 10H (dark amber) using a 25-watt bulb. The darkroom itself, and the
larger must on no account admit leaks of white light. A small 'torch' safelamp
n be made for brief local inspection of a darkroom timer, or the paper itself, if
ing processed in an open dish, by fitting two layers of Wratten filter No. 72B
der the cover glass.

Colour balance in the print

Owing to the fact that the colour balance of a print – and this includes a te
strip – is influenced by the colour quality of the viewing illumination and by i
surroundings, it is desirable to use light of approximately the same quality a
that by which the print will normally be viewed. If this is not possible, for examp
when making prints in the evening for daylight viewing, a suitable compromi
can be effected by using colour matching fluorescent tubes or lamps. In a w
state a test print on Ektacolor paper appears slightly too dark and much to
cyan in colour balance. However, an approximate judgement can be made k
treating the print for 1 min. in Kodak AM-33 Rapid Liquid Fixer (undilute
and with no hardener added) directly after the formalin fixer (see page 293
If the test strip is to be preserved, the remaining steps should be completed wi
double the washing time at step 7.

Printing on Ektacolor paper

There are two basic methods: the first, and more usual, method employs a ligh
source which has been adjusted by filters to produce an image of the require
colour balance using a single exposure; the second method is to expose eac
emulsion layer of the paper separately using tri-colour filters over the enlarge
lens, the amount of each exposure being adjusted to give the required colou
balance. The first method is commonly referred to as 'white-light' printing an
the second as 'tri-colour' printing. Both can be made to yield prints of excellei
quality, but the former method, because it only involves one exposure (after th
filtration has been determined), is usually adopted by professional and comme
cial printers. However, it requires a fairly large range of filters and either
special 'colour' enlarger or one that has been adapted to take a filter drawer. Fo
this reason some amateurs prefer to use the tri-colour method, which can k
employed with almost any enlarger plus a set of tri-colour filters.

White-light method

This method is sometimes known as the 'subtractive' method because filters a
used in front of the light source to subtract light from certain regions of th
'white-light' spectrum so that the light transmitted by the colour negativ
balances the colour sensitivity of the printing paper. In a general sense it can k
compared with the use of light-balancing filters with a reversal colour film. I
practice there are more variables. Firstly, there is the light source – usually
tungsten filament lamp – which may vary in colour temperature according to i

---

Plate 61. Sardinian children. To avoid the problems attendant on strong overhead sunlight t
two children were invited to stand on the shadow side of the narrow street facing a light-colour
wall receiving direct sunlight. Being fairly neutral and receiving very little light from the bl
sky, the colour rendering is very nearly equal to that of sunlight. Exposure with High Spe
Ektachrome Film 1/125 sec. f/5·6 using a Retina Reflex camera fitted with an 85 mm. le
Photo: E. S. Bomback.

Plate 62. In the gardens.

Plate 63. At the opera.

Plate 64. Street scene.

Plate 65. At sunset.

attage and the voltage applied. Secondly, there is the colour balance of the egative: this could be 'normal' in the case of exposure made with clear flash or ungsten lamps and other artificial light-sources adjusted to the same colour mperature (3,800°K.) with suitable light balancing filters, or it could be a direct xposure taken by daylight. Thirdly, there is the small variation in the colour :nsitivity of the printing paper itself, resulting from batch-to-batch differences r storage conditions. Finally, the colour balance may have to be adjusted to articular viewing conditions.

Once an initial colour balance has been established for a first printing :ssion, provided the lamp voltage is kept constant, negatives from the same atch or of similar quality and made on the same batch of printing paper will ed little or no further adjustment in filtration. The filters used to achieve orrect balance are referred to as a 'filter pack', and may be either of the CP :olour printing) type for use between lamp and negative (e.g. in the enlarger mphouse) or of the CC (colour compensating) type for use near the enlarger :ns. The CP filters are available in cyan, (minus red), magenta (minus green) nd yellow (minus blue) in a range of seven densities (025, 05, 10, 20, 30, 40, and o) plus a CP2B (U.V.-absorbing filter) – making a range of 22 filters. The CC lters are available in cyan, magenta and yellow, *and* red, green and blue in a ange of six densities (05, 10, 20, 30, 40, 50) making a range of 36 filters.

Owing to its similarity to black-and-white printing, the white-light method ill obviously appeal to those printers used to applying local exposure control by ay of shading or dodging. Indeed local control may also be extended to colour alance by using CC filters in front of the lens during shading operations.

ri-colour method

his may also be referred to as the 'additive' method of colour printing, the three mulsion layers being exposed in succession. The colour balance is adjusted by arying the time of exposure through each filter according to the indications of :sts strips. Here again, once the basic ratio of exposures has been found, relatively nall adjustments only will be needed for negatives of similar colour balance

---

ates 62 to 65. These four table tops demonstrate the effect of background. Plate 62 was taken in e garden in weak sunlight using a sprig of box-tree to suggest a tree. Plate 63 made use of a ainting of the foyer of Covent Garden Opera House supplemented with a corner of a red rug, d was lit with two floods. Plate 64 involved the rather more elaborate construction of a small t, chiefly from insulating board. The lamp-post was based on the leg of a discarded what-not, e drain-pipe of wood dowelling, the shutters were made from cardboard and the door from wood ths. The set was lit with weak sunlight from an open window with a reflector as fill-in for the gure. Plate 65 made use of a piece of natural cork as a cliff-top and a back-projection sunset ffect'. The doll was lit with a single reflector spotlamp, the exposure being made in two stages; gure and foreground against black paper with spotlamp alight, then with the projector switched and the room otherwise in darkness, model left in position but black-paper removed. Exact ming was possible in all cases by use of a single-lens reflex camera. *Original Kodachrome ansparencies by E. S. Bomback.*

printed on the same batch of printing paper. An objection often put forward t
the tri-colour method is the danger of moving the enlarger head in changin,
filters and thereby destroying the exact registration of the three images. How
ever, if the head is tightly locked and the filter-changing device smooth and ligh
in operation, this danger can be minimized. Since the filters are normally place
below the lens their optical quality is critical. Wratten gelatine filters mounte
without glass in a sliding frame are ideal for the purpose. A skilful operato
should be able to employ limited shading with the tri-colour method, though i
is obviously a very tricky operation since it must be repeated for each exposur
in the correct ratio and the same manner.

Test prints and records

Nothing is more essential to good colour printing than an appreciation from th
very beginning of the need for standardization combined with the proper use c
test prints. In commercial printing on a large scale, electronic devices are used t
assess the printing requirements of a negative, but even these are by no mean
fool-proof, and it requires a visual appraisal of the finished prints to determin
which, if any, will need reprinting. Various methods of making test prints ar
discussed in the next two chapters, pages 288 and 298. Providing every stage i
the production of a colour print, from exposing the negative film to processin
the print, is standardized as much as possible, the first dozen or so test prin
should provide enough information, if records are kept, to reduce the number c
test prints required for each new printing session to little more than a routin
check. However, the more critical the work, the greater will be the need for tes
prints, and anyone admiring a superb colour print can be sure that its quality i
not the result of a lucky guess. It may be that a beginner will be satisfied with
much lower standard, feeling that his time has been much better spent in makin
half-a-dozen mediocre prints than a single print of high quality. Ultimately h
will be far more satisfied with the single print.

The Ektacolor print image

In common with all dye images, those of Ektacolor prints are subject to fading
exposed for prolonged periods to strong light. This applies particularly to direc
sunlight and fluorescent lighting. Retouching of the image can be carried ou
with artists' water colours, the dyes used in the Kodak Dye Transfer process, o
'Flexichrome' colours. Print mounting may be done with 'Ademco' Dry
mounting Tissue or with Kodak Photographic Rapid Mounting Cement. Whe
prints are mounted behind glass a slight separation between the print surfac
and the glass should be left.

Colour print services

Kodak and many independent colour finishing laboratories offer various colou
print services, chiefly for the amateur, but some laboratories offer 'specialis

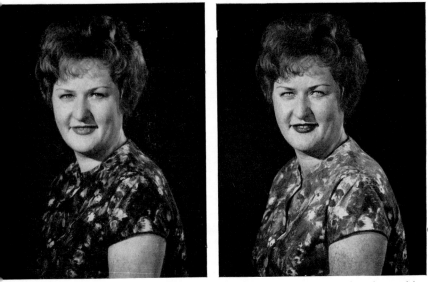

Fig. 23.1. Colour negatives can be printed on Bromesko or bromide paper, but the resulting prints have distorted tonal relationships. To obtain more pleasing results, particularly with portraits, Panalure paper, which has a panchromatic emulsion, is recommended. The print on the left shows the tone rendering of Panalure and on the right, ordinary bromide paper.

services for the professional. In some cases it may be more economic to use such services, particularly if only occasional prints are required.

Black-and-white prints from colour negatives

These may be made in exactly the same way as when making prints from black-and-white negatives using either Bromesko or bromide paper. Owing to the orange mask in Kodacolor and Ektacolor negatives the exposure time will be longer. However, since bromide paper is chiefly sensitive to blue light the resulting prints give a tone rendering similar to that obtained with a blue-sensitive film. To obtain a tone rendering equivalent to that obtained from a black-and-white panchromatic negative it is necessary to use a panchromatic printing paper such as Panalure, see fig. 23.1. Kodak Panalure paper is handled in the same way as Ektacolor paper in respect to safe-lighting, and may be developed in Kodak D-163 Developer or Kodak Soft Gradation Developer. No special filtering is required with exposures by tungsten lighting, but a CC20Y should be used to correct the rather high blue content of fluorescent lighting. Various tonal differences can be achieved with the use of coloured filters on the enlarger much as when using filters in black-and-white photography. For instance, a green filter will 'lighten' the greens of foliage and grass or darken its complementary colour, and so on. Thus anyone using a colour negative film has the best of both forms of photography – colour and black-and-white.

24

Exposing Colour Prints—Tri-Colour Method

ANY ENLARGER employing tungsten lighting and fitted with a high-grade lens can easily be adapted for tri-colour printing at no more expense than is necessary to make up a single filter holder and purchase a set of tri-colour filters. Some additional attention may be needed by way of avoiding leakage of light from the lamphouse and negative carrier, and by way of a luxury, an electronic timing device can be purchased or made up. Important points to bear in mind are as follows.

(1) The enlarger should be solidly supported and, if possible, the column made rigid by means of a wall bracket which is attached to the top of the column.

(2) The filter holder should be of the sliding type, as shown in fig. 24.1, and preferably fitted with a click stop so that the filters can be changed over

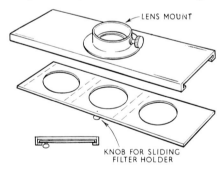

LENS MOUNT

KNOB FOR SLIDING FILTER HOLDER

Fig. 24.1. Sliding mount for tri-colour fittings.

in the dark without shaking the enlarger. The slide holder should provide top protection to the filters from dust. The filters can be mounted in a card which fits inside the framework of the slide. It is essential not to mount them between glass (unless cemented between glass of optical quality) as distortions in the glass will affect the print definition.

286

(3) Any method for preventing light leaks from the lamphouse should take into account the need for ventilation of the lamphouse. A tin or box painted black inside with ventilating holes situated so as not to align with those in the lamp house usually forms a satisfactory solution. Light leaks from the negative carrier slot can usually be screened by loosely tying a strip of black cloth around this section of the enlarger. Colour negatives must, of course, be masked in the negative carrier in the same way as for black-and-white negatives. Any white-light leaking around the edges of a colour negative is certain to produce an orange fog over the print.

(4) The exposure is best controlled by a switch in the lamp circuit which is mounted separately from the enlarger (e.g. a foot switch). It is also preferable to use a metronome or timer, no matter how skilful you are at counting seconds, since even small errors can produce deviations in colour balance. The illumination for the timer should be adequate but screened so that no light falls on the printing paper which is being exposed.

(5) It should be possible to control the voltage across the enlarger lamp since fluctuations in the mains supply may cause errors in print density and colour balance. The simplest method is to use a lamp rated for a lower voltage than the mains and have a rheostat in series with the lamp with a voltmeter across the lamp, see fig. 24.2. This will take care of general voltage reductions common at peak hours of consumption, and if the voltmeter needle and correct position on the scale are both painted with luminous paint, temporary fluctuations can be corrected should they occur during an exposure sequence. The working voltage should be that of the lowest value encountered. A more costly but efficient method is to employ an automatic constant-voltage transformer.

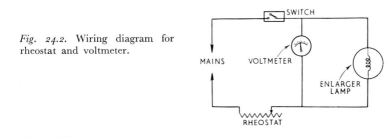

Fig. 24.2. Wiring diagram for rheostat and voltmeter.

Tri-colour filters

The recommended Wratten filters for printing from masked negatives are Nos. 70 (red), 99 (green) and 98 (blue). The normal colour-separation filters – Nos. 25, 58 and 47B – are not recommended, nor are the narrow-cut filters Nos. 29, 61 and 47B. No additional U.V.-absorbing filter is needed (as in the white-light method) since the Nos. 70, 99 and 98 filters already perform this function. I mounting the gelatine filters in a card mount, care should be taken to handl them only by the edges so as to avoid finger marks. Dust which may accumulat in the course of time can be removed with an anti-static lens brush, or cloth.

Test exposures

The nature of subtractive colour processes has been described in an earlie chapter, see page 23, but it is worth-while to remind the reader that each laye of a colour transparency, print and colour negative bears an image whose colou is complementary to that to which the layer is sensitized, the blue-sensitive laye forming yellow dye, the green-sensitive layer magenta and the red-sensitive laye cyan. In effect each layer is a filter which controls the amounts of red, green an blue light needed to reproduce the colours to which the colour film was originall exposed. In the case of a colour negative the filtration values are reversed an where, for example, the subject reflected only a small amount of blue light, th colour negative transmits a large amount of blue light, thereby producing heavy deposit of yellow dye in the print which reflects the original small amoun of blue light. If the deposit of dye in each layer is correct, then the overall prin density and colour balance are also correct.

The purpose of making a test print is to determine how much exposure eacl layer of the print material needs to produce a print of the required density an colour balance. Since we are dealing with a negative, an increase of exposur produces an increase in the density of the image (as in black-and-white photo graphy). However, an increase in the exposure of one layer without a proportiona increase in the exposure of the other two layers produces a change in the colou balance. These two forms of exposure variation used in conjunction form th basis of density and colour balance control in tri-colour printing. In making first trial exposure the objective is to establish both the overall level of exposur and the ratio of exposure between the three layers for the particular lamp bein used, a 'normal' negative and the printing paper.

In selecting a trial negative, one containing an area of neutral (grey) tone will provide a key to assessing the accuracy of the colour balance. It should hav been correctly exposed (neither under-exposed nor over-exposed) and is place in the negative carrier emulsion side facing the printing easel. If you are in an doubt as to which is the emulsion side, the arrow along the edge of a Kodacolo negative will be pointing in a clockwise direction when the emulsion side i facing you, while that of an Ektacolor negative is facing you when the cod notch is in the upper right-hand corner while holding the negative with the lon edge vertical. Needless to say it should be free of dust, and it is most importan that it be masked on all sides to the edges of the image. Failure to do this ma cause loss of contrast and degraded colours.

There are two methods of making a first trial exposure. If tungsten light i being used a number of test strips are exposed through each of the three filters i uccession based on an exposure ratio of 1 : 2 : 3 for the red, green and blue xposures respectively. A 'medium' exposure based on an enlargement of the negative by 4 could be 16, 32, and 48 sec. with the lens at f/8. Thus a second trip at 8, 16 and 24 sec., and a third at 32, 64 and 96 sec. would probably indicate he approximate level of exposure. The alternative is to make stepped exposures hrough each filter on a separate strip, the approximate level and exposure ratio being found by matching the three strips for a suitable density level. Whichever method is used, a further test will be needed to establish the accuracy of any djustments to colour balance. Let us suppose the test print in the first method is oo blue and also that it is estimated that the correct exposure level lies between he medium and lighter exposures at say, 12, 24 and 36 sec. As the blue requires educing, the actual exposures given could be 12, 24 and 30 sec. However, in educing the blue it may be found that the overall density is now a little too low, nd in addition a slight red bias is now visible. In this case a final test strip may stablish that 11, 26 and 32 sec. gives an acceptable result. To the experiment-lly-minded there may be considerable fascination in the effect of exposure ratio n colour balance, and a first session may easily produce nothing more than a collection of test strips! However, to evaluate fully the results of test exposures it s necessary to make a full-size colour print, since it is only from such a print that he actual colour balance under normal viewing conditions can be judged. Although colour print paper is on the costly side, test strips to be of any use must be at least 1 in. wide, and should also be exposed to a portion of the negative vhich is fairly representative and which also contains an area of grey tone. As it s important that the strips of paper are not moved between successive exposures, hey should be pinned in position.

Multiple test exposures

Once the exposure ratio has been determined for a typical negative, it can be used when tests are made on the same batch of paper from other negatives. A convenient method for dealing with a number of small negatives is to tape them o a sheet of plate glass, base side in contact with the glass, and lay the glass over a sheet of Ektacolor paper on the enlarger easel. The enlarger should be adjusted o give the same degree of magnification that is later to be used in printing the negatives, using a negative mask or carrier of the proper size in the enlarger head. For example, if 8 × 10 in. prints are to be made, the cone of light from the enlarger will be sufficient to cover a sheet of taped negatives of the same size. A sheet of 8 × 10 paper will take up to 30 negatives on 35 mm. film (five 6-negative strips), 12 exposures $2\frac{1}{4} \times 2\frac{1}{4}$ in. on 120 film and 8 exposures $2\frac{1}{4} \times 3\frac{1}{4}$ in. on 120 film. If prints of smaller size are to be made, the lens aperture should be reduced o compensate for the difference in light intensity. The exposure is made by aying the sheet of taped negatives over a sheet of printing paper in a printing frame and giving the same exposures as previously found by test. The contact print is then processed and dried. Assuming the exposure level for the contact prints turns out to be correct, the same exposure will apply when the negative are placed in the enlarger. However, in practice small differences in density and colour balance between different negatives will require some adjustment which, with experience, can probably be estimated without resort to a further test strip. If the negative previously enlarged is included among those from which contact prints are made, it will form a standard of comparison or 'master negative'. Each of the other contact prints can then be compared with the print from the master negative. In this way, only differences characterizing the individual negatives will enter into the comparison, since other variables, such as a departure of the test-print process from normal colour balance, will be eliminated. A more detailed application of a 'master negative' is discussed in the next chapter, page 301.

Sheets of contact prints form an ideal reference, and if records of the actual exposure conditions are kept, may serve as a guide to future printing. To begin with, at least, even test strips should be preserved accompanied with notes (written on the back) of the actual exposure given. In this way the photographer will rapidly gain skill in judging corrections for future printing sessions.

Print assessment

It is by no means easy for the untrained eye to make accurate and consistent judgments of density and colour balance, and as we have already stated, it requires first the establishment of standard viewing conditions. However, it is as well to remember that the incidence of colour blindness in men in one form or another is much higher than is usually realised, and anyone professionally engaged in making colour assessments should be tested for colour vision. It is also necessary to bear in mind the tendency of the eye to adapt itself to overall differences in colour rendering, particularly in viewing a print at a distance whereby it fills a wide angle of vision. Assessments should therefore be made rapidly, and with reference to a standard print. Side-by-side comparison between a standard print and a print under assessment might appear to be a logical procedure were it not that the eye will tend to 'split the difference' between the two prints, thus making the standard print appear off-balance, see page 70.

One method which will help in the early stages of printing done with the tri-colour method is to compare the test print with a 'ring-around' set of colour prints, obtained by printing the 'master negative' first on balance and then in steps of 'off-balance' in the directions of red, green, blue, magenta, cyan and yellow. The first three are obtained by decreasing the exposure through one filter (keeping the other two constant) in the equal steps equal to say a 10 per cent exposure decrease. For example, if the normal exposure were R = 10, G = 20 and B = 30, then the three red-bias prints are made with exposures 9, 20 and 30: 8, 20 and 30: 7, 20 and 30. The second three-colour biases represent either too little exposure through two of the filters or too much through one filter

Thus a magenta bias can be obtained by increasing the exposure through the green filter, giving three sets of exposures 10, 22 and 30: 10, 24 and 30: 10, 26 and 30: or by giving reduced exposures to red and blue, 9, 20 and 27: 8, 20 and 24: 7, 20 and 21.

In all, this will produce 19 test prints, 18 of which have varying degrees of colour bias. At the same time it may be worth making four additional prints of normal colour balance which vary in overall density. Two can be made at 1/3 and 2/3 of a stop below the correct and the other two at the same amounts above the correct level. With the aid of these test prints it should not be a difficult matter to determine in which direction, and by what amount, the exposure needs to be changed.

Exposure modifications

From what has been said in the foregoing paragraph the general principal of modifying tri-colour exposures may already have been grasped. However, the following table may simplify the matter:

If the print is too	increase exposure of	OR	decrease exposure of
red	red		green and blue
green	green		red and blue
blue	blue		red and green
magenta	red and blue		green
yellow	red and green		blue
cyan	green and blue		red

The choice as to whether the colour balance is to be corrected by increasing one or two of the three exposures or, alternatively, by decreasing one or two of the three exposures, will depend on whether the test print is too light or too dark. It may even be that a compromise is necessary and practical experience in using the tri-colour method is the best ultimate guide.

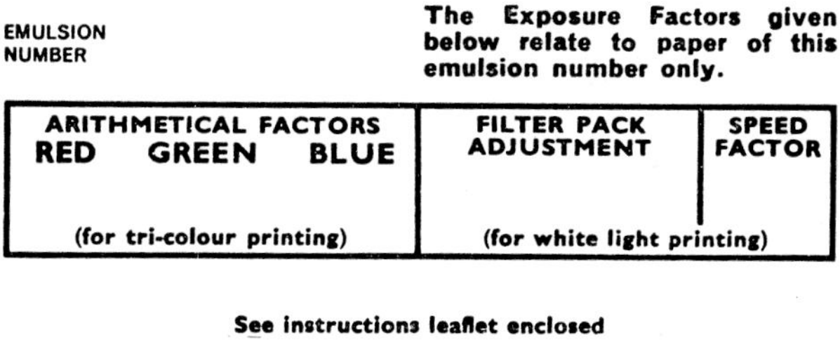

Fig. 24.3. Facsimile of label from packet of Ektacolor paper.

EMULSION NUMBER			The Exposure Factors given below relate to paper of this emulsion number only.		
ARITHMETICAL FACTORS			FILTER PACK		SPEED
RED	GREEN	BLUE	ADJUSTMENT		FACTOR
(for tri-colour printing)			(for white light printing)		

See instructions leaflet enclosed

Changing to a new batch of paper

Ektacolor paper varies slightly from one emulsion to another, and occasions may also arise when a gap of several weeks between printing sessions makes it advisable to establish the characteristics of an existing supply of paper. The problem of re-balancing the exposure ratios can best be solved by making a test with the master negative. Some guide to the use of a new batch of paper is given on th sealing label of the packet in forms suitable for both tri-colour and white-ligh printing, see fig. 24.3. In order to find the new ratios, the known printing tim for the old batch of paper is divided by the old exposure factor and the result i multiplied by the new exposure factor:

$$\text{New printing time} = \frac{\text{New exposure factor}}{\text{Old exposure factor}} \times \text{Old printing time}$$

Thus if the old factor for green were 80 and the new factor 90, then an established time of 16 sec. becomes:

$$\frac{90}{80} \times 16 = 18 \text{ sec.}$$

The same calculation is made for each of the three colours. Once the new exposure ratios have been established for the master negative all other exposures related to it can readily be worked out.

Densitometric evaluations

A densitometer provides another means for calculating the exposure require ments of a new negative from known exposures for a master negative. It i preferable that a reference area such as the Kodak Neutral Test Card be included at the edge of all negatives, otherwise it is necessary to take measurements o equivalent areas such as flesh tints, grey tones and so on depending on the natur of the subject. The density measurements may be made through narrow-cu filters or those used for tri-colour printing. The exposure times for the new negatives are then found by the following simple equation:

$$\frac{\text{New negative exposure time}}{\text{Master negative exposure time}} = \text{antilog} \left[\left\{ \begin{array}{c} \text{density} \\ \text{new} \\ \text{negative} \end{array} \right\} - \left\{ \begin{array}{c} \text{density} \\ \text{master} \\ \text{negative} \end{array} \right\} \right]$$

For example, let us suppose the red-exposure time for the master negative i 10 sec. and that the two density measurements are, master 1.12: new negative 1.26 giving a density difference of 0.14. The antilog of 0.14 is 1.380. The new red-exposure is therefore.

$$10 \times 1.380 = 13.8 \text{ sec.}$$

These density readings are best made with an electronic densitometer, but the Kodak Reflection-Transmission Colour Densitometer carefully used should give reliable density readings, see page 257.

Processing

The processing of Ektacolor paper in P-122 chemicals is dealt with in Chapter 26.

Ektacolor Print film

This film is designed for contact printing or enlarging direct from Kodacolor or Ektacolor negatives, and will yield brilliant positive colour transparencies for projection, displays or as originals or colour guides in photomechanical reproduction processes.

This material may be exposed by the tri-colour method in exactly the same way as described for Ektacolor paper. As a starting point the exposure time and filters (in the case of white-light printing) given in the supplementary instruction packed with the film should be used as the basis for a test exposure. If equipment different from that described in the leaflet is used, the difference found in making a satisfactory print may be taken as the factor of the equipment being used and the recommendations of future packets of print film can be modified accordingly.

Ektacolor Print film is exposed with the emulsion side towards the lamp and with a sheet of black paper placed behind the film to reduce halation effects and avoid light being reflected back through the film base. Accurate assessment of colour balance can only be made when the transparency is dry, but, as with Ektacolor paper, wet transparencies can be judged approximately if they are treated for one minute in Kodak AM-33 Rapid Liquid Fixer (undiluted and without the addition of hardener) after step 6 of the processing procedure. The remaining sequence of processing should then be completed in the normal way.

Print film is processed in C-22 chemicals (as used for Kodacolor and Ektacolor negative films), the time of development being 12 min. at 75°F. (24°C.). Full details of processing are packed with each C-22 Processing Kit, and Chapter 22 also deals with this process.

25

Exposing Colour Prints—
White-light Method

THE USE OF a single exposure in colour printing with multi-layer colour materials is more in keeping with their character than the tri-colour method described in the previous chapter. We could, for example, expose a colour reversal film in three stages using red, green and blue filters, and by using suitable exposure ratios, according to the colour quality of the illumination, produce well-balanced colour transparencies with a variety of different light sources – assuming, that is, that the subject is stationary. But this would be to defeat the whole object of a multi-layered film and the care which has been taken by the manufacturer to adjust its colour sensitivity for a single exposure with a certain quality of lighting. However, even when the illumination is not of the quality for which the film has been adjusted it is still possible to make a single exposure by using a light-balancing filter over the lens. This method is essentially equivalent to the use of filters in the white-light printing of colour negatives. And just as filters can be used over the light-source or the camera lens in colour photography, the filters in colour printing can be placed either between the enlarger lamp and the negative, or over the enlarger lens. The decision to use the filters in one position or the other depends somewhat on the kind of enlarger being used. If it is desired to use an enlarger designed for black-and-white printing with the minimum of modification, then the filter pack can be placed immediately in front of the lens. In this case it is necessary to use gelatine filters of the CC series which will not impair the image definition: as many as three gelatine filters can be used in this way, provided they are free from dust and scratches. With enlargers designed (or modified) for white-light colour printing a filter drawer is built into the enlarger lamphouse so that the filters are situated between the lamp and the negative. In this case the less-expensive and more robust CP filters may be used, though there is no objection to using CC filters if they have already been acquired for another purpose.

While almost any enlarger having a tungsten lamp is suitable, those with fluorescent light-sources are not recommended. Because the image of a colour negative is composed of dyes, a specular optical system, such as that given by condensers and a small light-source, is unnecessary and a more diffuse system is recommended, as it will not emphasize scratches on the negative. Any light-leaks from the enlarger head must be screened during exposure, see page 286, though the screening should allow access to a filter drawer if one is built into the lamp house. To prevent damage to the filters a heat-absorbing filter must be placed between them and the lamp (but not too close to the filters, as the heat filter itself becomes very hot.) A suitable arrangement for a filter drawer is shown in fig. 25.1.

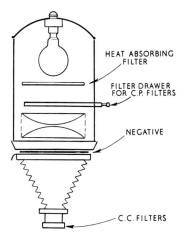

Fig. 25.1. Arrangement of filter drawer for CP filters and the position in front of the lens for CC filters.

HEAT ABSORBING FILTER

FILTER DRAWER FOR C.P. FILTERS

NEGATIVE

C.C. FILTERS

Some method of controlling the lamp voltage is necessary for work of a critical nature, and either of the two methods described on page 287 can be adopted.

Filters in white-light printing

The need for a flexible range of filters in colour printing with a single exposure is neither an indication of shortcomings in the colour materials, their exposure and processing, nor a device on the part of the film manufacturer to make the process more complicated than it need be. On the contrary, in this latter respect Kodak have done all they can to simplify, by way of calculators, nomograms and other devices, the various calculations which to a layman may seem to involve too much mathematics. Filters are needed to compensate for differences in paper batches, exposing equipment, differences in the colour balance of negatives, and to make fine adjustment to colour balance as dictated by viewing conditions and personal taste.

Filter characteristics are abbreviated for simplicity by the use of initial letters and the colour density of the filter. Thus a CP30M filter stands for Colour Printing, 0.30 density, and Magenta.

Colour-Printing filters

These filters are specially designed for use behind the negative, and are unsuitable for use in the image-forming light. The filters are supplied in cyan, magenta and yellow, and in the density range shown in the table below. Red, green and blue filters are not included because the number of filters behind the negative is not important, and these colours can be obtained, when needed, by using the proper combinations of cyan, magenta and yellow filters. The range of 22 filters, which includes the CP2B (U.V.-absorbing) filter, is available as gelatin film 7, 12, 16 and 23 cm. square ($2\frac{3}{4}$, $4\frac{3}{4}$, $6\frac{7}{8}$ and 9 in.).

KODAK COLOUR PRINTING FILTERS

CYAN	MAGENTA	YELLOW
CP025C	CP025M	CP025Y
CP 05C	CP 05M	CP 05Y
CP 10C	CP 10M	CP 10Y
CP 20C	CP 20M	CP 20Y
CP 30C	CP 30M	CP 30Y
CP 40C	CP 40M	CP 40Y
CP 50C	CP 50M	CP 50Y

Also CP2B (equivalent to Wratten No. 2B)

To ensure greater accuracy in colour printing, each of the nominal values CP40 and CP50 are subdivided into three groups of actual values: $37\frac{1}{2}$, 40 and $42\frac{1}{2}$ for the CP40, and $47\frac{1}{2}$, 50 and $52\frac{1}{2}$ for the CP50. Both 'nominal' values and 'actual' values are marked on the filter packets.

Colour-Compensating filters

Originally designed for colour printing, the colour-compensating filters have a wide range of uses in colour photography since they are suitable for use in front of the lens. However, in order to reduce flare and loss of definition, it is desirable to restrict the number of CC filters used in front of the lens to three. For this reason the range includes red, green and blue filters, thus making it possible to obtain practically any colour and density combination needed with not more than three filters. Although more expensive than CP filters, much smaller sizes can be used when used at the lens position.

KODAK COLOUR COMPENSATING FILTERS

CYAN	MAGENTA	YELLOW	RED	GREEN	BLUE
CC05C	CC05M	CC05Y	CC05R	CC05G	CC05B
CC10C	CC10M	CC10Y	CC10R	CC10G	CC10B
CC20C	CC20M	CC20Y	CC20R	CC20G	CC20B
CC30C	CC30M	CC30Y	CC30R	CC30G	CC30B
CC40C	CC40M	CC40Y	CC40R	CC40G	CC40B
CC50C	CC50M	CC50Y	CC50R	CC50G	CC50B

A U.V.-absorbing filter CP2B should, if possible, be placed between the negative and the lamp, and this position is desirable even when no special provision for accepting filters exists in the lamphouse, since the filter remains permanently in position. By including it with the filter pack below the lens it forms another component. However, if the lamphouse is inaccessible to a filter, a Wratten 2B can be placed with the other CC filters.

Naturally all filters used in the image-forming light must be free from dust, scratches and fingermarks. As the regular handling of gelatin filters, even when held only by the edges, inevitably involves some wear and tear, they should be regularly inspected and any which have suffered damage replaced. Damaged filters may still be useful for viewing test prints to help judge any colour correction needed.

Basically, the CP filters are similar to the CC filters but have improved colour transmission characteristics so that better neutrality is achieved when similar nominal values of cyan, magenta and yellow are combined. For this reason similar values of CP and CC filters may not produce identical results on a colour print, and it is therefore desirable that the two types of filters are not used together or interchanged.

Filter combinations

Obviously it is desirable that the combination of filters placed in the exposing light beam should consist of the least number of filters possible. The most important reason is the possible effect on definition when filters are used in the image-forming beam.

The simplest approach to using filters is to think of them in terms of the colours they absorb, not the colours they transmit. The following table shows what we mean.

ABSORPTION COLOURS OF CP AND CC FILTERS

Transmits	Absorbs	Equivalent to
red	blue and green	yellow + magenta
green	blue and red	yellow + cyan
blue	green and red	magenta + cyan
magenta (blue and red)	green	—
cyan (blue and green)	red	—
yellow (red and green)	blue	—

For really critical use it may sometimes be preferable to leave a particular filter pack containing the equivalent of a neutral density undisturbed, since a particular red, green or blue filter may not give exactly the same colour adjustment as the corresponding subtractive pair. However, disregarding this for the moment, the normal procedure is to convert any red, green or blue filters in the pack to their equivalents in subtractive colours. Thus a 30G = 30Y + 30C.

Then add up all the values for each colour. For example, suppose a filter pack consisted of 20G, 15Y and 10B then

$$
\begin{array}{lll}
20G = 20Y & + & 20C \\
15Y = 15Y & & \\
10B = & & 10C + 10M \\
\hline
35Y & 30C & 10M
\end{array}
$$

From this it can be seen that the pack contains a neutral density of 0.10. Thus:

$$
\begin{array}{lll}
& 35Y & 30C \quad 10M \\
\text{minus} & 10Y & 10C \quad 10M \\
\hline
& 25Y & 20C
\end{array}
= \text{neutral density } 0.10
$$

The final pack would therefore consist of three filters: 20Y + 05Y + 20C.

By observing this procedure carefully the use of excessive filtration will be avoided and any unnecessary filters which may have crept into the pack will at once be spotted.

Since the CP filters are only available in the subtractive primaries, the calculation is somewhat simpler. There may be occasions, particularly when using CP filters, when it is sometimes desirable to leave some neutral density in a filter combination, as, for example, when only a slight alteration is to be made to a filter pack containing several filters, when such an adjustment would mean changing several components of the pack. We may take the case of a filter pack containing CP30C + CP10M + CP37½M filters, a test print from which shows a very slight yellow bias, which needs for correction a CP025Y filter. It is preferable, and more convenient, to add the CP025Y to the existing pack (with due exposure allowance) than to remake the pack as CP025C + CP05C + CP20C + CP025M + CP05M + CP37½M.

Test exposures

A knowledge of the behaviour of filters in white-light colour printing will rapidly be gained in the practice of making test strips, but it is worth noting here that, since we are dealing with a negative-positive process, the effect of a filter is the reverse of using it with a reversal film. Thus if a test print appears too yellow, a yellow filter is *added* to the filter pack, whereas in making a camera exposure with illumination which contains too much yellow (thus making the colour rendering appear yellowish) a blue filter is used over the lens.

The need for test exposures in a first session is sufficiently obvious to need no further comment, but the need for test exposures on future occasions can be

---

Plate 66. Pincer's fish. The photograph has been made through the glass of an aquarium with electronic flash. When using flash under these conditions, care must be taken to avoid reflections off the surface of the glass. The original Kodachrome transparency was made with a Retina camera fitted with an NII close-up lens and using the Retina Close-up Rangefinder to focus and frame the subject. *Photo: Kroehnert.*

Plate 67.

Plate 68.

Plate 69.

Plates 67 to 69. Ceram
mask photographed agai
different backgroun
under identical conditic
of lighting, the exposu
being based on a grey-ca
meter reading. The to
appear lighter against
black background. T
piece of board with
remains of greyish pa
was chosen as a backgrou
in keeping with the subj
and the red netting as
in strong contrast. *Ko*
chrome II transparencies
E. S. Bomback.

greatly reduced by making or choosing from existing negatives a 'master negative' which is used as a standard and to which all future data on printing can be related.

The master negative

Essentially, a master negative is an average, normal negative which has been properly exposed under known conditions, has received standard processing, and yields an excellent print. This latter requirement will, of course, only become apparent after the first session, but it can be taken for granted that a negative produced under standardized conditions should yield an excellent print.

In choosing a master negative from an existing collection, it should be as typical as possible, both in subject matter and lighting, of the majority to be printed. It will be useful if the negative contains some areas which are relatively sensitive to minor colour-balance changes: skin textures, light, neutral tones, or near-neutral tones such as sunlit concrete or asphalt. If the subjects are chiefly of landscapes, flowers and the like, it will be useful to include a Kodak Neutral Test Card at the edge of a typical subject before it is photographed. The grey side of this card, which has a reflectance of 18 per cent, lends itself to exact and reproducible measurement. If two or more distinct classes of subject are dealt with – e.g. portraits and landscapes – it is useful to have two master negatives, each printed to give the most acceptable colour balance. Portraits in particular may need a colour balance which conflicts slightly with the best rendering of a neutral tone.

A first trial

Using an enlarger with tungsten illumination and with both a heat-absorbing glass and a CP2B or Wratten No. 2B U.V.-absorbing filter in position, the first test strip should be made without any CP or CC filters in the exposing light. With the enlarger lamp run at the rated voltage, the stepped exposures can be made at a lens aperture suitable for the normal printing of an average black-and-white negative at the same magnification. This assumes the colour negative to be of normal colour balance, namely, a Kodacolor or Ektacolor (Type S) negative exposed with light of 3,800°K. at an exposure time of about 1/50 sec. or one made with Ektacolor Film, Type L, with light of 3,200°K. at an exposure time of $\frac{1}{2}$ sec.

When this test strip has been processed and dried (see page 316), one of the steps should be approximately correct for density and this step can be taken as a guide to any colour correction required. A second test is then exposed using a range of densities of the CP or CC filter (or filter combination) chosen to correct the colour bias.

Two further points are worth noting for this first session. If a new lamp has been fitted to the enlarger (or the enlarger itself is a new one), the lamp should be run for at least an hour to stabilize its burning characteristics. Stepped test strips should be exposed on a time scale, e.g. a series such as 4, 8, 16, 32 sec., and

18

not with an intensity-scale device such as the Kodak Enlarging Exposure Scale which is intended for black-and-white printing. Owing to variations in sensitivity of the emulsion layers of Ektacolor paper with illumination level and exposure time, such a test range is not likely to lead to reliable exposure predictions.

On the basis of this second test strip, a further test may be needed to try out further colour adjustments or determine the exact exposure level, or it may be decided that such modifications can be estimated and a full size print be exposed. In any case, to arrive at a correct colour balance it will first be necessary to make a full-size print, which when dried, can be viewed under normal viewing conditions. The conscientious photographer will then press on with further prints until he arrives at one which he considers 'correct'. This, indeed, is important if the first negative is by way of being a master negative. Careful note should be made on the back of each print of the filter pack used and the exposure conditions.

Since the assessment of colour balance is not an easy task even for an expert, it is advisable to adopt some method of comparison, such as the 'ring-around' system described on page 290, or one based on viewing filters of known density such as those of the CP or CC series. In the first method the prints can show stages of off-balance in the directions of red, green, blue, cyan, magenta and yellow in steps equivalent to CP or CC densities of 10, 20, 30 and 40. The print showing correct colour balance can be made at density levels 1/3 and 2/3 stop less and the same amounts more than the correct level. The print to be assessed is then placed in the centre of such a ring of prints and a comparison made until a colour-balance match has been made. If the match turns out to be one of the off-balance prints, the necessary degree of correction can be effected by adding its colour density to the filter pack.

Use of viewing filters

If a test print is reasonably close to the required colour balance, viewing it through CP or CC filters provides a guide to the colour correction needed. Since a filter used in this way tends to over-correct the highlights and under-correct the shadows, the effect of the filter on the light middle tones should be observed. Naturally it is necessary to carry out this examination under proper lighting conditions, and due allowance must be made for the tendency of the eye to adapt itself to the colour of the filter. This can be done by holding the filter at such a distance that it is neither so close to the print that light falling on the print is affected by the filter nor so close to the eye that it occupies too large an angle of the field of view.

As the contrast of the print material is fairly high, a filter used in exposing a print tends to produce a greater change in colour balance than might be expected from its visual use. In general the filter added to the filter pack should be half the strength of, and *complementary* to, the filter that makes the lighter middle tones of the test print appear best. Thus if a CC10R gives the necessary visual correction then the filter to add to the pack is a CC05C.

Filter Pack modifications

While it is permissible to correct a colour bias by adding a filter of the same colour, it is preferable, whenever possible, to subtract a complementary filter. For example, if a print is too red it could be corrected by adding a red filter, but it would be preferable to subtract a cyan filter from the pack, if one is present. The following table may help to clarify the process.

Colour cast	Correct by subtracting these filters	OR	Correct by adding these filters
yellow	magenta and cyan OR blue		yellow
magenta	cyan and yellow OR green		magenta
cyan	yellow and magenta OR red		cyan
blue	yellow		magenta and cyan OR blue
green	magenta		cyan and yellow OR green
red	cyan		yellow and magenta OR red

The following rough guide may also be useful: when a slight shift in colour balance is needed, use a 05 or 10 filter change; when a moderate shift is needed, use a 15 (05 + 10) or 20 change. When the shift is too large to estimate, start by using a 30 change. The 025 CP filters are useful for making very subtle changes in colour balance.

The method for eliminating a neutral density from a modified filter pack follows the procedure already described on page 297.

Modifying exposure times

Whenever a filter is introduced into the exposing light some adjustment to the overall white-light exposure must be made to compensate for the density of the filter, and the change, if any, in the number of filter surfaces. In practice the values of the filter factors and densities have been modified to allow for both these effects simultaneously. A table of filter factors for CC filters is given on page 117, and this may, if preferred, be used in place of the nomogram method described below. The factors are given as increases in lens stops (since the table is primarily intended for the use of CC filters at the camera stage). These can be added arithmetically as 'densities' $1/3$ stop = 0.10, $2/3$ = 0.20, 1 stop = 0.30. However, these factors are rounded off and it is therefore preferable to use the densities given in the table associated with the nomogram.

		Densities of CP Filters			
Filter	Density	Filter	Density	Filter	Density
$CP_{025}Y$	0·07	$CP_{025}M$	0·08	$CP_{025}C$	0·08
$CP_{05}Y$	0·07	$CP_{05}M$	0·09	$CP_{05}C$	0·09
$CP_{10}Y$	0·07	$CP_{10}M$	0·11	$CP_{10}C$	0·11
$CP_{20}Y$	0·07	$CP_{20}M$	0·16	$CP_{20}C$	0·15
$CP_{30}Y$	0·08	$CP_{30}M$	0·21	$CP_{30}C$	0·18
$CP_{37\frac{1}{2}}Y$	0·08	$CP_{37\frac{1}{2}}M$	0·26	$CP_{37\frac{1}{2}}C$	0·21
$CP_{40}Y$	0·08	$CP_{40}M$	0·26	$CP_{40}C$	0·21
$CP_{42\frac{1}{2}}Y$	0·08	$CP_{42\frac{1}{2}}M$	0·26	$CP_{42\frac{1}{2}}C$	0·21
$CP_{47\frac{1}{2}}Y$	0·08	$CP_{47\frac{1}{2}}M$	0·30	$CP_{47\frac{1}{2}}C$	0·24
$CP_{50}Y$	0·08	$CP_{50}M$	0·30	$CP_{50}C$	0·24
$CP_{52\frac{1}{2}}Y$	0·08	$CP_{52\frac{1}{2}}M$	0·30	$CP_{52\frac{1}{2}}C$	0·24

		Densities of CC Filters			
Filter	Density	Filter	Density	Filter	Density
$CC_{05}Y$	0·04	$CC_{05}M$	0·07	$CC_{05}C$	0·06
$CC_{10}Y$	0·04	$CC_{10}M$	0·10	$CC_{10}C$	0·08
$CC_{20}Y$	0·04	$CC_{20}M$	0·16	$CC_{20}C$	0·12
$CC_{30}Y$	0·05	$CC_{30}M$	0·22	$CC_{30}C$	0·15
$CC_{40}Y$	0·05	$CC_{40}M$	0·27	$CC_{40}C$	0·18
$CC_{50}Y$	0·05	$CC_{50}M$	0·32	$CC_{50}C$	0·21
$CC_{05}R$	0·07	$CC_{05}G$	0·06	$CC_{05}B$	0·04
$CC_{10}R$	0·10	$CC_{10}G$	0·08	$CC_{10}B$	0·12
$CC_{20}R$	0·17	$CC_{20}G$	0·12	$CC_{20}B$	0·21
$CC_{30}R$	0·23	$CC_{30}G$	0·15	$CC_{30}B$	0·29
$CC_{40}R$	0·29	$CC_{40}G$	0·18	$CC_{40}B$	0·38
$CC_{50}R$	0·34	$CC_{50}G$	0·22	$CC_{50}B$	0·47

Use of the Nomogram

Exposure time changes can be calculated by using the table of densities given opposite the nomogram, fig. 25.2. The nomogram is used in the following manner:

(1) Find the densities of the filters used for the test print from the table.
(2) Add their densities and select their corresponding number on scale A.
(3) Locate the point on scale C which represents the exposure time in seconds used for the test print.
(4) Lay a straight-edge across the nomogram to join these points.
(5) Note the point where the straight-edge intersects scale B using the arbitrary reference figures.

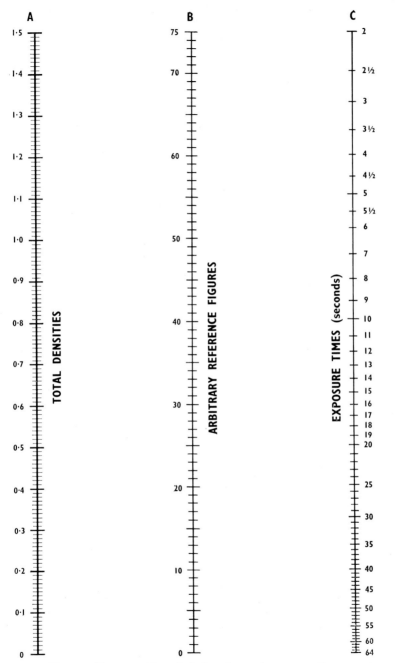

Fig. 25.2. Nomogram for calculating changes in exposure time.

(6) Add the densities of the new combination of filters and locate the number corresponding to this on scale A.

(7) Now lay the straight-edge across from this new point to the point previously noted on the reference scale B (as found in step 5).

(8) The intersection of the straight-edge with scale C now gives the exposure time required for the new filter combination.

If the exposure time exceeds 64 sec., the values of scale C can be taken as units of 10 so that the scale then reads from 20 to 640 seconds.

Example: Filter combination used for test print: CP10M + CP05C
Densities $= 0 \cdot 11 + 0 \cdot 09 =$ total of $0 \cdot 20$
Exposure was 13 seconds
This test print was too red
Assessed filter combination for final print: CP10Y + CP05Y + CP20M + CP05M
Densities $= 0 \cdot 07 + 0 \cdot 07 + 0 \cdot 16 + 0 \cdot 09 =$ total of $0 \cdot 39$
From nomogram exposure for new combination $= 20$ seconds

The Kodak Colour Print Exposure Calculator

This calculator is designed for use with colour printing filters only and consists of a rotating dial which contains the filter values, a base with a time scale and a cursor to enable the values of the old filters to be 'dialled out' and the new one to be 'dialled in'.

Comparing new paper with old

As already referred to in the previous chapter, page 291, the sealing label on each package of Ektacolor paper contains two sets of exposure factors as a guide in deciding the filter pack for the new batch of paper (or the exposure ratios for the tri-colour printing method). Owing to unpredictable storage conditions and use, time of exposure and other variables, these factors are only an approximate guide to the filter changes necessary when changing from one batch of paper to another. They cannot help in setting up an initial printing process.

The exposure factors given for white-light printing are the second set, which is divided into two sections. In the first part the speeds of the blue-sensitive and green-sensitive layers are rated relative to the red-sensitive layer in terms of CP or CC filter densities. Where the blue and green layers are faster than standard relative to the red layer, they are given plus values, and where they are slower, minus values. Thus the first two values labelled 'Filter Pack Adjustment' are used to modify the filter pack. The third value, labelled 'Speed Factor', is derived from the absolute speed of the red layer and is used to calculate an exposure time for a new batch of paper. The higher the value of this figure, the lower is the speed of the paper, and it can be thought of as representing units of exposure time. Thus a paper labelled 70 needs only half the exposure of one labelled 140.

The modification of the filter pack for a master negative (or one which was last printed on the old batch of paper) is relatively simple: the factors given for the old paper are subtracted from the filter pack and the new ones are then added. In practice it is simpler to work out the difference between the two batches of paper, and to add or subtract this (as the case may be) from the filter pack. The change in exposure time is found by taking the ratio of the new to the old speed factor.

The following example illustrates the use of exposure factors for filter pack adjustment. It is required to change from a batch of paper with 'white-light' exposure factors of:

$$+10Y \quad -20M \text{ Speed factor } 90$$

to a new batch with factors of:

$$-10Y \quad -15M \text{ Speed factor } 70$$

First subtract the 'old' from the 'new' factors

	Y	M	C	
	−10	−15	o	New factors
Subtract	+10	−20	o	Old factors
	−20	+05	o	*Difference*

Rule of thumb for subtraction: change the signs on the bottom line and add.
This *difference* figure is used to modify the working filter pack used for the standard negative on the old paper.

	Y	M	C	
	o	20	10	Old working filter pack (CP20M + CP10C)
Add	−20	+05	o	Difference (see above)
	−20	+25	+10	

To eliminate the minus sign add its value in CC or CP filter units (here 20) to each filter

	Y	M	C
	−20	+25	+10
	+20	+20	+20
	o	+45	+30

Thus the new working filter pack will be: CP40M + CP05M + CP30C.

More exposure is required because 20 density units were added to the pack to cancel out the minus filter. In this case the lens aperture is opened by two-thirds of a stop.

The new exposure time incorporating the speed factors of the old and new batches of paper is calculated from:

$$\frac{\text{New exposure time}}{\text{Old exposure time}} = \frac{\text{New speed factor}}{\text{Old speed factor}}$$

If the exposure time for the standard negative was 10 seconds then:

$$\text{New exposure time} = 10 \times \frac{70}{90} = 7 \cdot 78 = 8 \text{ sec.}$$

Note that the filter factors for the filters actually used in the working filter pack do not enter into the calculation of the new exposure time. Such factors have already been taken into account in determining the 'speed factor' from the filter pack adjustment values quoted on the packet of paper.

As an alternative to the use of exposure factors, make similar exposures on both the old and new paper batches using a standard or reference negative. Process the tests together and assess the changes needed.

Comparisons with a master negative

Most colour negatives of the same type of subject exposed under similar conditions will print similarly, but not identically. Differences may result from variations in lighting (colour temperature or colour quality), variations in film emulsion, film processing, and other factors. These differences are normal, and should be expected. However, the important thing is to think of these differences in terms of filter differences between each negative and the master negative.

Let us suppose that the filter pack for the master negative consists of 40M + 20Y and that the best print density is obtained at 10 sec. These filters remain in the optical system as an excellent starting point for similar negatives using the same batch of Ektacolor printing paper. For a particular negative it may be found necessary to add a 10M filter to the pack and adjust the printing time to 12 sec. to compensate for the additional filter and/or difference in the overall density of the new negative. This relative difference between the new negative and master can be taken as a constant, regardless of the characteristics of batches of paper which may be used in the future. Thus by recording these data on the negative bag (or whatever other reference system is kept), any future reprints from a production negative can be made without further test simply by modifying the current master negative filter pack with the same filter and by the same exposure ratio.

Negative evaluation by densitometric measurement

In the production printing of negatives of unknown characteristics, individual test printing is usually impossible for economic reasons, and a method based on densitometric measurements is commonly adopted. The usual practice is to select an area corresponding to a flesh tone or a neutral, and correlate density readings made through narrow-cut red, green and blue filters with printing exposures determined for a master negative of similar subject matter. An electronic densitometer rather than a visual one is usually preferable.

The principle applied to white-light printing is to take three-colour density readings of the reference area of the master negative and add these to the densities of the filters in the basic pack. The filters for any other negative are then chosen so that their densities plus those of the reference area of that negative come to the same totals.

As an example, consider a master negative requiring a basic filter pack of CP20Y + CP30M + CP05M and whose density measurements are R: 0·96, G: 1·08 and B: 1·24. The filter densities are added to their complementary colours, thus:

	R	G	B
Negative density	0·96	1·08	1·24
Filter density	0·00	0·35	0·20
	0·96	1·43	1·44

These figures represent the total amount of cyan, magenta and yellow in the master negative plus its filter pack.

The densities of the production negative are measured under the same conditions and subtracted from the above total. Suppose, for example, they turned out to be R: 1·08, G: 1·06 and B: 1·12, then we do the following sum:

R	G	B	
0·96	1·43	1·44	(Master negative + filter densities)
1·08	1·06	1·12	(Production negative densities)

$$-0·12 \quad +0·37 \quad +0·32$$

Now cancel out the neutral density by adding + 0·12 to each density and the final answer becomes R: 0·00, G: +0·49 and B: +0·44. These are then rounded off to the nearest filter value, which in complementary colours becomes a filter pack consisting of CP40Y + CP05Y + CP50M.

The neutral density of 0·12 represents the amount by which the production negative is denser than the master negative. If we suppose that the exposure time for the master negative is 17 sec., then the increase in exposure time for the production negative can be determined by using the nomogram on page 305. Alternatively the antilog. of the density difference can be taken as a multiplication factor.

To use the nomogram, place a straight-edge to join zero on scale A and the exposure time in seconds for the master negative – in this case 17 – on scale C, and note the reference point on scale B. Now place the straight-edge through the figure for the density difference – in this case 0·12 – on scale A and the reference point on scale B and read off the exposure time – 22 sec. – for the production negative on scale C.

Because some production negatives will be of lower density than the master, both negative and positive neutral-density differences need to be accommodated on scale A. To do this, either extend the lower end, or use 1·0 as a zero for scale A and add differences to or subtract them from this 1·0 value.

Multiple test exposures

A method which may appeal to the amateur is that of taping a number of sma
negatives on a sheet of plate glass, and making contact prints of them togeth
with a master negative of similar subject matter and colour balance. This meth
has already been described for tri-colour printing on page 289, and can be appli
equally well to white-light printing.

Shading and printing-in

Techniques normally applied to black-and-white printing can for the most pa
be adapted to white-light colour printing, but for the benefit of newcomers to tl
mysteries of the darkroom the terms shading and printing-in (along with othe
like dodging and holding-back) apply to local exposure control of the pri
image. For example, a heavy shadow can be lightened by shading it for part
the exposure time, or a sky area can be darkened by giving it more exposu
time than the rest of the print. The extent of shading or printing-in depends (
particular density differences and the effect required, and is an art that com
with practice and experience.

The basic tool for shading is an opaque card of size and shape simil.
to the area to be lightened, fastened to the end of a piece of wire, see fig. 25.
For printing-in, it consists of a large card containing an opening of the requir
shape. In either case the card is held in the image-forming beam between le
and paper, and is kept gently oscillating to prevent a sharp line of demarcatic
in the print. For best results it is advisable to practise the control measure
advance of making an actual exposure – better still to try it out using ordina
bromide paper. Experts often make use of their hands and fingers, varying tl
distance from the print to obtain larger or smaller areas of coverage or holes.

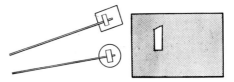

Fig. 25.3. 'Tools' for shading and printing-in which are used in the image-forming beam.

Local control should be used with discrimination, since too much may gi
rise to false tonal values. In reducing the density of shadow areas account shou
be taken of the extent of detail they contain. If, in fact, they represent areas
complete blankness it is better not to shade them at all. The effect of local contr
and the extent of shading or printing-in may often be judged from test strip
Thus, if it is required to darken the sky, a test strip across the sky area covering
range of exposures based on the normal will show by how much more the sl
area of the final print must be printed-in, and whether, in fact, this increase
exposure calls for any filter adjustment.

By using CC (not CP) filters of suitable shape, or moved about to cover a particular area, it is equally possible to make adjustments to local colour balance. Such a need frequently arises in bluish shadow areas where both the density and colour need adjustment. By using, say, a CC50B filter over the area for part of the exposure time, keeping the filter in motion, both density and colour can be improved. Similarly, a rather too ruddy complexion can be corrected by use of red filter. In general, a CC30 to 50 in density is suggested, as a weaker filter may not have enough effect. A filter on the strong side can always be used for a shorter time.

Filters are equally helpful in printing-in. For example, a white highlight might have a tendency to pick up too much colour when darkened by extra exposure. A filter of the same colour over the hole in the card will preserve the neutrality of the area.

The use of filters for local control may be roughly judged from an uncorrected print by viewing the area requiring to be changed through different CC filters. Having found a filter to give the desired visual change, the complementary of this filter and half its density value is used for correction.

There are numerous other situations in which local print control is desirable, not necessarily for any fault in the colour reproduction but to show the subject to better advantage or compensate for uneven lighting of the original scene. The colour of flesh tints – often a vital characteristic in good portraiture – dresses, buildings, and many other areas can be shifted, intensified, lightened or darkened so easily that local control should often be regarded as a routine part of high-grade printing.

Contrast control

Kodak Ektacolor paper is matched to the normal contrast characteristics of masked colour negatives. Occasionally, however, a subject is encountered that would reproduce better at a contrast level different from that afforded by the film-and-paper system. Since the paper is available in only one contrast grade, the best remedy is a supplementary mask to modify the printing characteristics of the negative. Masking is not often necessary, but in the comparatively rare instances that it is needed at all, it is usually able to produce a significant improvement.

Contrast reduction

Sometimes a negative contains too great a range of densities to print satisfactorily on Ektacolor paper. A typical subject is a back-lighted outdoor portrait in which no fill-in flash or reflector was used. In such cases, local control in printing may not solve the problem completely or even passably. However, a positive mask can be superimposed over the negative to compress its density range to a suitable level.

The positive mask is made by contact printing the colour negative on sheet of Kodak Pan Masking Film. It is convenient to use an enlarger with tungsten light source and to make the exposure in a printing frame on the base board of the enlarger. To facilitate registering the mask on the negative after has been developed, it is preferable to make the mask image slightly unsharp b placing a spacer between the negative and masking film.

To counteract the effect of the coloured couplers in the negative, filterin equivalent to CC200B is used in the light beam.

The exposure varies with negative density, but with the enlarger adjusted t give three foot-candles at the exposing plane (measured without the filters), negative of average density requires about 15 sec. The exposure should b adjusted, if necessary, to give a full-scale image having a slight density even i extreme highlight areas.

Suggested development is 3 min. at 68°F. (20°C.) in a dish of fres Kodak DK-50 developer, diluted one part developer to four parts water. Othe processing details are the same as given in the instruction sheet packed wit Kodak Pan Masking Film.

After it is dry, the mask is taped in register on the base side of the origina When the combination is placed in the negative carrier of the enlarger, th emulsion side of the negative should be down, as usual. Printing the combinatio requires about twice the exposure for the unmasked negative but no change i filtration.

SHADOW MASKING: When a contrast-reducing mask is used, it sometimes make the shadows come out smoky in the print. This effect can be eliminated by mask that removes the shadows from the principal mask, thus preventing the contrast from being lowered. The action is similar to that of a highlight mask c a transparency.

To make the shadow mask, use Kodalith Pan Film and develop it i undiluted D-11 developer for 2 min. at 68°F. (20°C.). Adjust the exposure t record only the deepest shadows – those devoid of any useful detail. In all othe respects, follow the recommendations given on the film instruction sheet.

Register the developed shadow mask on the emulsion side of the colou negative and, from the combination, make the contrast-reducing mask on Koda Pan Masking Film. Use only the contrast-reducing mask with the colou negative in exposing the colour print.

Contrast increase

On rare occasions, a negative may be encountered that is too low in contrast t make use of the full density range of the print material. The cause may be sligh under-exposure of the negative, camera flare, an unusually low lighting ratio i the illumination of the original scene, an unusually low reflectance ratio on th part of the subject material, or a combination of these factors. In such cases, negative silver mask can be added to the colour negative to increase its effectiv density range.

An interpositive is first made by contact printing the colour negative on Kodak Pan Masking Film, emulsion to emulsion. As in the case of a contrast-reducing mask, it is convenient to use an enlarger with a tungsten light-source and to make the exposure in a printing frame on the base-board. Filtering equivalent to CC200B should be used in the light beam. With three foot-candles at the exposing plane (measured without the filters), the exposure required to give a full-scale image is usually about 10 sec. The suggested development time $4\frac{1}{2}$ min. at 68°F. (20°C.) in a dish of fresh Kodak DK-50 developer, diluted one part developer to four parts water.

The interpositive is printed on Kodak Commercial Fine Grain Film with a spacer between the two films. The base side of the interpositive and emulsion side of the Commercial Fine Grain Film should face the light source. Again, the exposure should be sufficient to give a full-scale image. Suggested development for the negative mask is 4 min. at 68°F. (20°C.) in a dish of full-strength Kodak DK-50 developer. However, the development time can be varied, depending on subject requirements. After the contrast-increasing negative mask is dry, it is taped in register on the base side of the colour negative, and the combination is ready for printing.

HIGHLIGHT MASKING: This correction is useful with any subject which requires increased highlight contrast, and is of particular value in securing a clean white in reproductions of flat copy, such as charts or wash drawings. The mask can be made at the camera stage at the time the colour negative is made, or it can be made from an existing negative. In the latter case it should be borne in mind that highlight masking increases negative density range, which may then become too great to print properly without a contrast-reducing mask as well.

When made at the camera stage the same lens opening should be used for both colour negative, and mask. With a tungsten light-source a CC40B filter is needed over the lens to put equal densities into the three colour scales, and to make the exposure time for Kodak Pan Masking Film approximately the same as for the colour negative, neutral-density filters to make a total density of $1 \cdot 5$. If necessary the exposure should be adjusted (by changing neutral densities) to give a maximum density between $0 \cdot 20$ and $0 \cdot 25$ when the mask is developed for 2 min. at 68°F. (20°C.) in Kodak D-163 developer. When dry the mask is registered on the base side of the processed colour negative.

When made from an existing negative the first step is to make a full-scale interpositive by contact printing the negative on a sheet of Plus-X Pan Film, emulsion to emulsion, with the filtering equivalent of CC200B in the beam of light from a tungsten-source enlarger. The interpositive is developed for 3 min. at 68°F. (20°C.) in D-163 developer. When dry, the interpositive is contact-printed on Kodalith Pan Film, emulsion to emulsion, with the exposure adjusted to give a maximum density between $0 \cdot 15$ and $0 \cdot 25$ when the mask is developed for min. at 68°F. in undiluted D-11 developer. As the highlight mask has a short scale, no diffusion should be necessary. When dry, the highlight mask is taped in register on the base side of the colour negative.

26

Processing Ektacolor Paper

FULL INSTRUCTIONS for processing Ektacolor paper with Process P-1 chemicals are packed with each complete kit of chemicals, and these should be read with care before attempting to mix or use the solutions. As these instruction may be modified from time to time to incorporate improvements, constant reference should be made to the instruction leaflet with each new processing k to check that the procedure is unchanged. This present chapter is intended supplement these instructions and to give the reader a general idea of the natur of the process.

Colour-print processing differs fundamentally from the processing of prin on Bromesko or bromide paper. Firstly it must be carried out in total darkness or at best by the faint light from a safelamp fitted with a Wratten 10 safelight screen – until the first two steps have been completed. However, thi is no disadvantage from the point of view of print quality, since the imag appearing in the developer will give little guide to the quality of the fin print, and in any case it is unwise to try to correct even small errors exposure by altering the development conditions. While black-and-white prin ing offers considerable latitude at all stages of processing, the entire processir sequence of Ektacolor paper demands careful standardization. Indeed th validity of any tests carried out for print density and colour balance rests on exact repetition of processing conditions. And if we take into account the tin taken to expose a test print by the tri-colour method plus the fact that processir must continue for at least 20 min. before any assessment of the print can be mad it should be obvious to the most rebellious operator that the correct processir procedure really is the most sensible one.

Three basic types of equipment – dish, tank and continuous machine – ca be used to process Ektacolor paper, the choice depending on the size and quanti of the prints to be processed. We have chosen to describe dish processing in som detail because it offers the possibility of getting started with the minimum outla of equipment. For the black-and-white photographer already equipped f printing, it will involve only the purchase of an extra dish (three may be regarde as the minimum number for colour processing), an accurate thermometer, ar some kind of dish warmer. Tank processing lends itself to a wide variety production requirements, and if tanks such as the Kodak No. 3 have alrea

en acquired for processing sheet negative film, the addition of a print basket
d nitrogen-gas distributor may be all that is required. For processing large
antities of prints which have been exposed on rolls of paper, the Kodak Continu-
s Colour Paper Processor will tackle several hundred average-size prints an
ur, and is thus ideal for a photo-finishing establishment.

rocessing solutions

hese are made up according to the packed instructions to the volume specified.
o attempt should be made to 'split' the solid chemicals into equal parts with the
ea of extending the life of the solutions. However, the 1 litre (35 oz.) processing
t makes a useful unit for a first trial, though if several subsequent printing
ssions are visualized, it is an advantage to mix up a gallon-size kit, and when
ch component is properly mixed, store the solution either in two 80-oz. bottles
four quart-size bottles, since the storage life of unused developer in a tightly
oppered bottle extends to 6 weeks.

It may be desirable to filter the water used for mixing in some localities, and
so to boil the water to be used for mixing the developer (allowing it first to cool)
ith the object of expelling the air. Mixing should not be done in the printing
om, as the printing paper is particularly sensitive to contamination from
emical dust. If tanks are being used, it is preferable not to mix the solutions in
em, but to use a separate mixing vessel. Where an electric mixer is used to
ssolve chemicals, care should be taken that the stirrer does not suck air into the
lution, as this will promote oxidation.

apacity

he recommended capacity of the developer is 240 sq. in. of paper per litre of
eveloper, but when the ultimate in consistency is not required the solution may
e used to greater capacity by increasing the exposure time slightly after
ery 160 sq. in. of paper have been processed up to a maximum of 800 sq. in.
very small re-adjustment of filtering may also be necessary if an identical
lour balance is required from all prints throughout the life of the developer.
or tank development there are two ways of compensating for the normal
haustion of solutions: the first is by increasing the exposure time after every
asket of prints has been developed, and the second, with replenishment, keep-
g the time constant. With replenishment it is better to add the replenisher
ter each batch of prints on a pro-rata basis rather than to wait until a given
ea of paper has been used. Full details for the use of replenishers are packed
ith the chemicals.

andling chemicals

/hen processing is done in dishes particular care should be taken to avoid any
ntact of the developing solution with the skin: for this reason it is essential to
ear thin rubber gloves. A sprinkling of talcum powder inside the gloves will

make them more comfortable to wear. Be sure to read the section 'Precautions in Handling Chemicals' in the instruction leaflet for Process P-122.

Timing and temperature control

Both these aspects have been discussed in the general chapter on processing, see page 262. It should be noted, however, that the time required for each step includes draining time, and the print or prints should be lifted for draining 20 sec. before the end of the step so that the next step can be started on schedule. Anyone owning a tape recorder may use it to provide an audible time base, complete with reminder instructions and, perhaps, background music in the longer intervals!

The temperature control of solutions in dishes may present something of a problem if the room temperature is very different from the specified 75°F. or 85°F. (24°C. or 29·5°C.). While every effort to raise (or lower) the room temperature should be made, some kind of water-bath control for the developing dish is perhaps, the simplest method, though it must be large enough to maintain the temperature to within $\pm \frac{1}{2}$°F during development. A dish heater, using a low wattage household lamp with a simple thermostat control, offers another solution though care must be taken to see that it is electrically 'safe' and also light-proof. It should be well tested out for temperature control with a dish of water before being used for actual processing. The choice of temperature, either 75°F. or 85°F. depends on the photographer and if speed is essential, the higher temperature is the obvious choice.

Washing water

Although the wash times in the instructions apply to water at 75°F. or 85°F., temperatures as low as 50°F. (10°C.) are satisfactory providing the wash times are increased. It should be checked during the winter that tap water does not fall below 50°F., since at lower temperatures washing may not be effective even at prolonged times.

If a number of prints are being washed together in a dish, the agitation should be as efficient as when they are being developed.

Dish processing

Only two processing dishes plus a washing dish are required, since during the wash after the first two steps, the first two dishes can be emptied, thoroughly rinsed, and refilled for subsequent processing steps. Enamelled iron dishes which are chipped should not be used, as they may give iron contamination.

As the paper is slippery when wet and the emulsion soft, care must be taken to avoid scratching the emulsion of one sheet with the corner of another. With practice up to six prints may be processed at one time, but for best results no more than three should be processed at one time. The following procedure is recommended.

316

(1) Three dishes filled respectively with developer, stop-fixer bath, and water are placed in a sink or, if this is too small, on a suitable table or bench. To decrease the risk of contamination, they should be well separated. The developer dish in particular should have been previously filled with water at 75°F. or 85°F. or have stood in its water bath long enough to have reached the chosen temperature. If developing a number of prints at once, about 1 litre of solution will be needed for 8 × 10 in. prints in dishes for this size. If only one print (or two back-to-back) is to be handled, half this quantity will be sufficient. Less solution may be used for smaller dishes and correspondingly larger volumes when processing large prints in large dishes.

(2) Immediately before turning out the light, check that the developer is at the required temperature. If a water bath is used to maintain the temperature within the required tolerance of $\pm \frac{1}{2}$°F., check that it is at the required temperature and, if based on a flow of temperature controlled water, that there is no danger of the water level rising too high during processing.

(3) Turn out the white lights. Mark the first print (if more than one is to be processed) by notching or cutting off the corner just sufficiently to allow it to be identified during processing.

(4) Start the timer and immediately immerse the first print, emulsion side down, in the developer. Make sure that the whole of the print is pushed down to the bottom of the dish to ensure that it is thoroughly wet with solution and that no air is trapped beneath it. Start the next print in the same way after 20 sec., and any additional prints at the same interval. Take care to prevent the sheets from adhering to each other.

(5) During development, agitate the prints once every minute by pulling the bottom sheet out, placing it on top without draining it, and re-immersing it completely. Follow quickly with the other prints, taking care that they are pulled out in their proper order, and that two do not get stuck together. With practice, six prints can be handled in one complete rotation in about 15 sec. – the time a novice would take for three prints. Some workers find it worth while to count the prints as they change them round so that they know without feeling for the notch that the first print is always at the bottom at the end of the operation. The operation should be performed smoothly to avoid damaging the prints.

If only one print is being processed (or two back-to-back), agitation is best performed by tilting first the left side of the dish by about 2 in., then lowering it slowly; next raising and lowering the near side; then the right side and so on.

(6) 20 sec. before the first print has received the required development time withdraw it and allow to drain for 20 sec., and then place it in the stop-fixer bath. Follow immediately with the next sheet, and so on at 20 sec. intervals until all the sheets are in the stop-fixer bath.

(7) The possibility of agitation in the stop-fixer bath depends on the number of prints being handled, but with practice it should be possible to roc the dish during the draining periods to ensure efficient chemical actior

(8) 20 sec. before the first print has received the specified time it is with drawn, allowed to drain for 20 sec. and placed in the washing batl again contriving to maintain adequate agitation.

(9) As soon as the prints are all in the wash (step 3) the white light may b switched on, and the first two dishes emptied, thoroughly washed an refilled with the bleach and formalin fixer.

(10) During the final wash the buffer is poured into one of the availabl dishes after it has been emptied and well-rinsed.

Tank processing

When a number of prints are to be processed, the use of tanks is recommendec The usual size of tank capable of holding thirty 8 × 10 in. prints holds abou 3 gallons of solution. Stainless steel tanks fabricated with ordinary tin solder mus be avoided, as the contamination of the developer with tin will cause a cyan fog see table of processing faults, page 322.

There are several different ways in which the colour paper can be suspende in a tank. It is first necessary to take into account that the paper base expanc somewhat when wet. One possibility is to use clip-type hangers, each of whic holds one sheet of paper or two back-to-back. Fewer clip-type hangers can b hung in the tank at one time than when loaded with sheet film, as the expansio of the paper tends to make it bow outward, and, if over-crowded, parts of a shee may come into contact with the next. A moderate spring-loading of the clips wi help to restrain this tendency, but care must be taken that it is not so strong tha it tears the paper.

The lowered tensile strength of the paper must be considered when applyin agitation, and the safest method is a gentle 'jiggling' action for the first 30 sec. development, and thereafter for 5 sec. at 1 min. intervals.

Channel-type hangers, designed for sheet film, are not satisfactory fo holding paper, since even with gentle agitation the sheets tend to slip out of th channels. One way of overcoming this is to place two sheets, back-to-back an with a perforated sheet of cellulose acetate 0·010 or 0·015 in. thick between then Agitation should be applied in the same manner as for clip-type hangers.

The most convenient way of handling 8 × 10 in. prints in quantity is with device such as the Kodak No. 3 Colour Print Processing Basket – fig. 26.1 – whic has compartments formed of mesh supported by a stainless steel frame which fi in the No. 3 Processing Tank. Two sheets of paper can be loaded back-to-back i each of the 15 compartments. A stainless steel cover prevents the prints floatin out of the compartments when the basket is lowered into the solutions.

Basket processing of prints smaller than 5 × 7 in. is not recommended.] helps in removing prints of smaller size than 8 × 10 in. if the long dimension placed vertically in the basket.

Fig. 26.1. Kodak No. 3 Colour Print Processing Basket which is designed to hold up to 30 sheets of 8 × 10 in. paper.

Agitation is best provided by a No. 3 Nitrogen-Gas Distributor used with the Kodak Burst-valve Control Unit as described on page 261. This equipment gives bursts of nitrogen-gas bubbles which work their way up through the processing solutions. For processing Ektacolor paper a 1 sec. burst at 12 sec. intervals is recommended. For processing Ektacolor Print film 1 sec. bursts should be given every minute.

Drying

The simplest method is to hang the squeegeed prints, back-to-back, with film clips or spring plastic clothes-pegs. Prints can also be laid, picture side up, on frames covered with mesh material of plastic, muslin or on sheets of 'Fotonic' Photographic paper. On no account should a wet print be left to dry between blotters or face down on a glazing machine blanket, because the soft emulsion will adhere to any such surface.

For smaller batches of prints, gummed brown paper strip or decorator's masking tape can be used to fasten the wet prints to a sheet of hardboard which may then be placed inside a film drying cabinet, using an air temperature at 110° to 118°F. (43° to 47°C.) to dry the prints. The prints will then lie reasonably flat when they are dry.

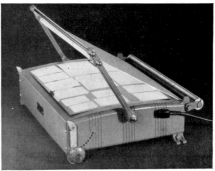

Fig. 26.2. Kodak Flat Bed Glazer Model 2. Glazing is performed with one 14 × 20 in. or two 10 × 14 in. glazing sheets.

Print glazing with heat

High-quality chromium-plated or stainless steel sheets or drums are recommend
ed for glazing colour prints. The surface must be free from scratches and pinholes
Black-japanned glazing plates are not suitable, as colour prints are liable to stic
to them. The glazing surface must be thoroughly cleaned just before use with
cleaning agent such as 'Silvo'. It can be applied with a cellulose sponge and
polished off with a clean, soft, lintless cloth.

The choice between chromium-plated or stainless steel drums or plates wil
depend on individual preference, operation and equipment. Prints can either be
air-dried after processing, then re-wetted for 1 to 2 min., and hot-glazed a
180°F. (82°C.), or directly after processing if the time of the formalin fixe
(step 6) is doubled. The other processing steps are normal, and the prints are
glazed directly after the buffer without washing.

Cold glazing

The recommended method is to squeegee prints on to polished metal glazing sheet
or plate glass. To prevent sticking, glass should be treated with a 3 per cen
solution in carbon tetrachloride of the silicone fluid M441 (marketed by I.C.I
Ltd.).* The solution should be applied with a pad of cotton wool to both sides o
each sheet of glass, followed by vigorous polishing with a soft cloth. Glass thu
treated may be used about a hundred times before a new silicone treatment i
needed.

To promote rapid drying, and at the same time prevent premature lifting o
the prints from the metal or glass, it is necessary to use absorbent pulp boards o
pads of felt at least $\frac{1}{4}$ in. thick, which have been impregnated in a 20 per cen
aqueous solution of calcium chloride and subsequently dried in a heated cabinet
The boards must be allowed to cool before placing them in contact with the back
of the prints, otherwise 'ferrotyping mottle' may result. Once treated, these board
need no further chemical treatment, but they must be dried and cooled each
time they are used.

Prints may be squeegeed on both sides of each sheet of glass and a 'stack
can be built up with a board or felt sandwiched between every two sheets o
glass. The stack is completed with a sheet containing prints on one side only
The time needed to complete glazing is from 1 to $1\frac{1}{2}$ hours.

An alternative method of cold glazing is to remove prints directly from the
wash (step 7) and place them in a dish containing the buffer plus 10 per cen
glycerine (9 parts of buffer to 1 part of glycerine). Rotate the prints from bottom
to top, as described earlier for dish development, for 3 min., then squeegee them

* Care should be taken when making up the silicone fluid to avoid contact with the skin or clothes
Goggles and rubber gloves are recommended for handling the silicone preparation but do no
allow carbon tetrachloride to come into contact with rubber. When using carbon tetrachloride
there must be plenty of ventilation and no-smoking rules must be observed, because a lighted
cigarette will decompose carbon tetrachloride into the toxic gas phosgene.

n to stainless steel or chromium-plated glazing sheets. The buffer-glycerine bath
s discarded after use.

Prints may also be completely processed and dried (to check their colour-
balance and density) and glazed later. However, the same modified buffer bath
treatment should be given for 3 min. just before glazing.

Mounting

Ademco Dry-Mounting Tissue can be used for mounting prints if the cover
sheet used over the face of the print has been pre-heated to remove residual
moisture and if the temperature of the mounting press is no higher than is
necessary to obtain a satisfactory bond. The actual temperature across the
heating plate should range between 200° and 220°F. (93° and 104°C.).

Kodak Photographic Rapid Mounting Cement is also satisfactory with
colour prints, providing that the instructions for its use are carefully followed.
Prints mounted behind glass should have a slight separation between the print
surface and the glass.

Fig. 26.3. Ademco Model J press
for heat mounting of prints up to
12 × 15 in. in one pressure.

Processing faults

There are a number of variables which can adversely affect the quality of colour
prints. Some of the more common causes underlying loss of quality are: lack of
cleanliness, incorrect mixing of chemicals or use of solutions, contamination of
solutions, and lack of adequate control in processing procedure.

For trouble shooting or simply as a routine check on processing, the use of a
master negative of the kind described on page 301 is invaluable. A small print
made carefully with controlled voltage from the master negative and processed
in the same batch with other prints will tell at a glance if there is any abnormality
in the processing solutions or procedure.

A supply of these control prints sufficient to last up to 6 months can be
pre-exposed. After exposure the prints are held at room temperature for 48
hours to stabilize them, and they are then wrapped individually in aluminium
foil (obtainable in rolls for kitchen use) to protect them against moisture, and
stored in a freezer operated at between 0° and −10°F. (−18° and −23°C.).

Before processing a batch of prints from other negatives, one of the contr prints is taken out of the freezer and allowed a few minutes to reach roo temperature. This warming-up time should be kept as consistent as possibl say, 10 min., to minimize changes in colour balance.

It should be noted that, if the stabilization period is omitted, the colou balance of the control prints will vary more readily with differences in th warming-up time. Also unless advance compensation for latent-image keeping made when exposing the control prints, their colour balance will usually diff from that of prints processed soon after exposure. This does not matter if a contr print used to check processing is compared only with other control strips expose at the same time on the same batch of paper.

A system of quality control based on the use of master negatives supplied b Kodak is available for photo-finishers using Kodak Colour Printers or Enlarger The information is available in the booklet *Quality Control—Process P-122*.

The following list will help to check specific errors associated with processing

WHITE-LIGHT FOG: A print made on paper which has been fogged by white ligl will show yellow, or in extreme cases, orange areas.

OVER-DEVELOPMENT: The result of over-development (excessive developmer time, temperature, agitation, or replenishment rate) is a print that is darker an slightly more contrasty than a normally developed print. There is also danger staining and of hue shifts over parts of the tone scale as a result of contra differences between the dye images.

UNDER-DEVELOPMENT: An under-developed print (insufficient development tim temperature, or agitation) is lighter and lower in contrast than a normal prir and usually tends towards a yellowish-green colour balance.

SAFELIGHT FOG: Prints fogged by the use of the safelamp too close, for too long time, or with a lamp of higher than recommended wattage, usually show a cya fog. The degree depends on the exposure.

DEVELOPER CONTAMINATION: If the developer becomes contaminated with one the fixing baths, a print will show cyan colour balance and in extreme cases cya fog as well.

Cyan fog, especially noticeable in highlight areas, may be caused by ti contamination of the developer as a result of the use of ordinary tin solder in th manufacture or repair of a stainless steel tank or rack. Such equipment should b welded.

Contamination with acid from the stop bath or buffer retards developmer and causes a pink stain, most noticeable in the highlights. Therefore prir baskets and dishes should be washed and dried after they have been used fc processing.

DEVELOPER EXHAUSTION: With exhaustion of the developer, the density level prints becomes lighter and the highlights go pink.

IRON CONTAMINATION: Iron or rust particles in the wash water or iron salts on the glazing surface will cause red spots. Iron particles in the bleach will cause blue spots.

OMISSION OF BUFFER: Failure to give this treatment may cause higher-than-normal stain in the white areas and will impair print stability. It may also cause blue stains to appear on the backs of prints.

HARDENING DIFFICULTIES: Inadequate hardening may lead to a lacy or blotchy blue-cyan pattern which becomes visible several days or weeks after processing. The effect of hardener exhaustion or insufficient agitation may be aggravated by excessive drying or mounting temperatures.

HIGH-TEMPERATURE DRYING: Prints dried at temperatures above 180°-200°F. (82°-93°C.) may show a yellow stain in unexposed areas.

INSUFFICIENT WASHING: Some time after processing, prints which have been poorly washed will exhibit blue stains which are most noticeable on the base side of the prints.

Large colour prints

The making of large colour prints in sizes up to 30 × 40 in. and in multi-section murals requires the same general processing procedure as that used for smaller prints. The difference is mainly that of handling large sheets. Dish development is usually sufficiently economical, but if large numbers are to be made a tank system is desirable. Details of such a system are available from Kodak Ltd.

Ektacolour paper is available in standard sheet sizes and also in rolls up to 40 in. wide. In the planning of large prints and murals that are to be wet-mounted, account should be taken of the fact that when wet the base of roll stock expands about 3 per cent in a crosswise direction and about 0·5 per cent in a length-wise direction. For exposing large prints, a horizontal enlarger, or one which allows the head to be set in a horizontal position, such as the Kodak Precision Enlarger, gives greater freedom of movement.

Dish processing of large prints

There are two alternative methods of dish processing. The choice will depend on the volume of work to be handled. Where there are a small number of large prints (up to about eight per day), it is possible to process, for example, 30 × 40 in. Ektacolor prints individually, each in 1 gallon of solution. In this method the developer is used for one print and then discarded, but the other solutions are used to capacity or replenished.

The second method utilizes deep dishes to process up to four 30 × 40 in. prints simultaneously. The developer and other solutions are replenished in the normal manner for use over an extended period. For processing 16 × 20 in. prints, dishes 20 × 24 × 6 in. are suitable. Proportionately larger deep dishes are necessary for larger prints. When not in use, the developer must be covered by a floating lid of suitable material to prevent developer oxidation. In addition a lid for the formalin-fixer, to minimize vapours of formaldehyde, is desirable.

Either method needs a minimum of two dishes and a washing tank although with large prints a separate dish for each solution makes for easier working.

It is possible to have the dishes in a sink with temperature control as described on page 316, but an alternative method of maintaining temperature is to have grid of copper tubing underneath each dish. A closed-circuit, thermostatically controlled system can be used to circulate hot water, at a suitable temperature through the grid to maintain each solution within the specified temperature limits.

Fig. 26.4. Kodak Drying Cabinet Model B, which is suitable for a small output. It is $3\frac{1}{2}$ ft. high and requires only 21 × 21 in. bench space.

For critical work, using the single print method, some slight difference between results from different mixes of developer may be found. Mixing two 3-gallon sizes of developer chemicals in a large crock and using six separate gallons to process one set of test prints and five 30 × 40 in. prints will give consistent results. The developer can conveniently be stored in 1-gallon stoppered bottles until required for use.

Uniform wetting and the agitation of prints must be tackled consistently particularly when working in large sizes. To immerse a large print in the developer, roll it up, hold the corners and draw the leading edge, emulsion down, through the solution pulling the body of the print behind it. When it is thoroughly wetted, turn the print emulsion side up. For the single print method, agitate each solution by lifting three adjacent sides of the dish in turn. This can be used to create an even, rolling motion of the liquid. In multiple-print dish processing immerse prints at 30-sec. intervals and interleave the prints, without draining at about 1-min. intervals. Be sure not to expose prints to the air unnecessarily during this agitation cycle. Remove the prints from the developer in the correct order – at 30-sec. intervals.

Try to adhere as closely as possible to the processing recommended in the instruction sheet packaged with P-122 chemicals. The development time may have to be increased in order to match the results of tank processing of 8 × 10 in. prints when the recommended time is used. Check processing as described on page 321. The washing times in the P-122 process should be increased by 2 min. if the efficiency of the water circulation in the dish is poor. When washing several prints, the washing efficiency is improved by interleaving all the prints, emptying out all the water from the dish and allowing it to refill.

When processing Ektacolor prints in dishes, clean rubber gloves must be worn to avoid skin irritation. The gloves must be kept clean and should be rinsed between processing steps to avoid solution contamination.

Drying

Prints may be dried by pinning them to racks and attaching weighted film clips to the bottom of each to minimize curl. Drying between muslin frames or by taping to hardboard can be accomplished as explained on page 319.

Mounting

Large prints up to about 30 × 40 in. can be dry mounted on hardboard using Ademco Dry-Mounting Tissue and a large press. (Fibrox hardboard obtainable from Rex Bousfields Ltd., 77 Carter Lane, London E.C.4, is suitable). It may be necessary to take several 'bites' to cover the complete area of the print.

Sectional mural prints should be wet mounted by using an adhesive such as Tub Paste (obtainable from A. Sanderson and Sons, Ltd., 52 Berners Street, London W.1, or wallpaper shops). Many adhesives are unsuitable for Ektacolor paper because they affect the dyes in the emulsion and cause a colour-balance shift. Other adhesives therefore, should be thoroughly tested before they are used on valuable large prints.

Prints may be mounted directly on to plaster walls, using wallpaper techniques, but such a wall must first be sealed with emulsion paint to prevent chemical and moisture staining. Hardboard or stout cardboard used as a support for wet-mounted prints must be similarly sealed. After the print has been mounted, cover its entire surface with muslin damped with buffer solution. This will retard the drying of the paper until the adhesive has partially set; the use of buffer solution will ensure maximum dye permanence.

27

Retouching Colour Negatives and Prints

SKILFUL photography and expert dark room technique should add up to a first class print in a wide range of subjects, but occasionally there remains the need for retouching, whether by way of repairing minor damage to the negative spotting pinholes caused by dust, or of effecting modifications to colour and density for display work, or of enhancing the appearance of a portrait. The final 'finish' of a colour print, even one that is not outstanding, can make a substantial impression on a client or exhibition judge, and one that is well-presented – properly mounted on a well-proportioned mount (with or without a flourishing signature) – and is free from small defects is far more likely to enhance the reputation than one that is poorly finished.

Darkroom cleanliness

A great many of the retouching chores originate from carelessness and lack of cleanliness both in the production of the negative and print. In portraiture, for example, retouching should not be the result of poorly applied or insufficient make-up. Fortunately the day when wrinkles and other signs of advancing age were systematically eliminated from a portrait has passed. The use of diffused lighting can lessen such features where desirable. Failure to notice undesirable coloured reflections from a dress or some other strongly coloured surface may create a major problem in the retouching department.

Dust of any description is a major enemy of darkroom work, but if it happens to be chemical dust the task of spotting out the effects in a colour negative or print are all the more tedious. Fingerprints have a way of intruding themselves. Neither negatives nor transparencies should ever be left out of their protective envelopes except for printing or copying. However, from whatever cause the need for retouching arises, it is comforting to know that anyone proficient in black-and-white retouching will not encounter any very great differences in colour work, and that in general colour negatives do not require so much attention from the retoucher as black-and-white ones.

Where a number of prints are to be made from one negative, correcting the

326

negative rather than the prints will save time and give more consistent results. Also, certain defects are easier to correct in the negative.

It is essential to realize that colour negatives and prints have three superimposed dye layers and that an etching knife cannot be used for lightening densities on any of these materials. Work that is normally done with a knife must be done by adding colour or neutral density, by means of dyes or pencil, to the colour negative or print. If the worker has little experience of retouching, experimenting with discarded or unimportant materials is advisable. If extensive retouching is to be done on a colour negative, it is also advisable to make a colour print before the work is started.

Retouching Kodacolor and Ektacolor negatives

In addition to the usual materials required for black-and-white negative retouching, some colour pencils and colour dyes are necessary. The following may be used, but other similar materials may also give satisfactory results.

PENCILS: Eberhard Faber 'Mongol' 860 Red and Blue combination, or Eberhard Faber 'Colarama' 8056 Crimson and 8025 Indigo, or Eagle Turquoise Prismacolor' 922 Scarlet and 901 Indigo. These are the most useful colours for portrait negatives, other colours may be necessary for other types of negatives.

DYES: Kodak Flexichrome Replacement Colours or Kodak Dye Transfer Dyes or 'Pelikan' Albumen Dyes (sold by G. H. Smith & Partners Ltd., 28 Berechurch Road, Colchester, Essex).

Some colour retouchers find it helpful to check their work by viewing it through colour filters such as the Kodak Wratten filters No. 29, 61 and 47B.

Preparation

Assessment of a colour proof (not a black-and-white print) will enable the retoucher to determine the areas to be corrected for a more satisfactory colour print.

In areas requiring heavy correction the retouching fluid should be applied to both sides of the film. Pencils can then be used to add a considerable amount of colour or density. Since Kodacolor negatives do not have as much surface tooth as Ektacolor negatives additional retouching fluid should be left on the negative. An alternative is to retouch Kodacolor negatives with dyes. It is also possible to bind a 'fixed-out' piece of black-and-white sheet film to a negative and to carry out the retouching on this supplementary surface.

Retouching techniques

There are three points which the retoucher must remember in viewing Ektacolor and Kodacolor negatives:

1. As in black-and-white negatives the densest portions of these negatives represent the highlights in the original subject.

2. The colours in these negatives are approximately complementary to the colours in the original subject. Thus a yellow object appears blue on the negative.

3. The orange colour of the coloured-coupler masks is superimposed on th subject colour in these negatives making precise colours difficult to identify.

PENCIL WORK. The major proportion of the retouching required by a colou negative is done with the same black lead as is used in black-and-white negativ retouching. In areas where colour must be neutralized, use coloured pencil in preference to black lead pencils.

Blemishes, lines and wrinkles. In a portrait negative, inspect the flesh areas for gree spots or lines (often faint) which represent red blemishes and wrinkles on th subject. Apply the red pencil until the green is no longer visible. If additiona density is needed after this colour correction, use the black lead to build up extr density. See Plate 38.

Veins. Blue veins in the original subject will appear yellowish red on the negative They may be removed or subdued by careful use of the blue pencil.

Highlights. It is possible to enlarge highlight areas or to work adjacent one smoothly together with a black lead. Where the eyes are in shadow, the catch lights will be small or may not appear at all. They can be restored or enlarge with black pencil lead or liquid opaque.

Pinholes and dust spots. Dark spots on the colour print result from dust or othe foreign matter on the film during exposure. Correct these spots in the negativ with neutral-grey dye or liquid opaque applied with a brush. The resulting ligh spot on the print can be retouched to match the surrounding area.

Dye retouching

Colour-negative retouching which has been accomplished with dyes shows les grain than pencil retouching and may therefore be desirable when large print are to be made from small negatives. Dye retouching is usually preferable t pencil retouching on Kodacolor negatives, since the lack of sufficient tootl prevents application of much pencil work.

Large areas of Kodacolor negatives can be dyed on the base side. Thi eliminates the possibility of wet dyes or water turning the emulsion surfac opalescent and the inconvenience of waiting for the surface to dry befor continuing the retouching. On the other hand, for fine or critical retouchin applying dye to the emulsion side will minimize dye bleeding.

The technique of applying dye is generally similar to black-and-white work Apply coloured dye first to remove unwanted colour in the negative; then appl neutral dye until the density is built up satisfactorily. As with pencil, mucl retouching can be accomplished using neutral dye only.

If too much dye is applied, some of it can be removed by sponging the are with slightly damp cotton wool. To remove the dye completely, wash th negative in water for several minutes.

Retouching Ektacolor prints

Also required, in addition to the materials usually used for black-and-whit print retouching, are a set of Kodak Flexichrome replacement colours and some water-free denatured ethyl alcohol, which can only be purchased when a icence from a local Customs and Excise officer has been obtained. It is also possible to use rectified spirit which may be purchased from a dispensing chemist. Kodak Dye Transfer dyes or artists' water colours may be used in place of, but not in the same manner as, the Flexichrome colours.

SPOTTING PRINTS: Much of the spotting of colour prints can be undertaken using black pencil in the same manner as for black-and-white work. Application of retouching medium may be necessary to give the print surface some tooth. After the retouching, apply some form of lacquer to preserve the pencil work. It is only in strongly coloured areas that this method is unsatisfactory.

The nature of various retouching dyes and water colours requires different techniques for their application and removal. An advantage of using Flexichrome colours is that if they are applied with pure alcohol in place of water, any excess can be wiped away with a cotton rag dipped in alcohol. When the desired effect has been obtained, steaming the print will render the Flexichrome colours permanent.

Flexichrome colours should be picked up from the dry cake with a brush moistened in alcohol. Two or more dyes can be mixed until the desired colour is obtained but it may be necessary to subdue this colour by adding Flexichrome neutral. Spotting is best carried out by the 'dry-brush' technique. The brush is lightly moistened by wiping lightly over a piece of clean cotton rag that has been 'wetted' in alcohol. After picking up some of the dye solution from the palette the brush is stroked over blotting paper to remove excess dye and liquid before it is applied to the print.

Dye Transfer dyes and water colours are diluted with water and mixed on a palette. They can be applied with the dry-brush technique described above. Because these colours dry rapidly and are absorbed by the emulsion, they are difficult to remove. Nevertheless where an excess of colour is deposited on a print, it can sometimes be removed with a tuft of cotton wool moistened with undiluted Kodak 'Photo-Flo' solution. Within one minute of applying the 'Photo-Flo' solution, blot the print area with clean newsprint.

Knifing. Not only is it difficult to remove dark spots on a colour print with an etching knife accurately, but the resulting hole is difficult to retouch satisfactorily. Adding dyes to the etched area will not fill the holes. Generally etching is not recommended.

Pinholes. Pinholes in the negative, caused by dust on the film during the camera exposure, show as black spots on the colour print. Apply white opaque to the spot on the print and when it dries, apply coloured pencils to match the surrounding area. Alternatively, apply dye to the opaque with the dry-brush technique or, before applying the opaque, tint it with the proper colour. It is, of course, preferable to spot the negative, as previously described.

If opaque colour is used to retouch a print from which colour separation negatives are required, the engraver should not apply petroleum jelly or other oily substances to the print. These would cause the opaque colour to photograph dark. An alternative is to spray the print with a lacquer: although this will also make the opaque darker; with experience, the retouching can be lighter to compensate for this density change.

Dust Spots. Prepare a weak solution of dye by mixing small amounts of colour in water or alcohol on a palette. Using the dry-brush technique, stipple the spot with the tip of the brush to build up the dye gradually.

Hairline Defects. It is difficult to brush the hairline several times with weak dye solution and keep the dye within the hairline borders. Rather, prepare a concentrated solution of dye of the desired colour and apply it with one smooth stroke of the brush.

Scratches. Surface scratches on a print may remove one or more of the three dye layers. If the scratch has removed the cyan and magenta dye layers, for example prepare a blue dye solution and apply carefully to cover up the defect. Print scuffs which do not penetrate through the gelatine supercoat layer can usually be removed by rubbing the area with cotton dampened with water.

Skin Blemishes. To subdue skin blemishes, build up a dye deposit around the blemish by light stippling with the tip of the brush to blend the spot into the surrounding skin areas. To subdue a dark blemish the dye colour should be slightly darker than the skin tone but lighter than the blemish.

Dye tinting

The colour in a specific area of a print can be changed by applying *dry* Flexi chrome colour with a tuft of cotton wool. This treatment is useful in warming bluish shadows; changing or enhancing the colours of skin or clothing and generally modifying the colour of specific areas. The technique has two major advantages; the retoucher can experiment until the desired effect is achieved before making the retouching permanent, and glazed colour prints can be retouched without spoiling the surface.

To apply the colours in dry tinting, breathe moisture on to the Flexichrome cake and rub a tuft of dry cotton wool over the cake surface to pick up dye Apply the colour with a light brushing motion. More colour may be deposited by a swabbing motion and even more by patting the cotton wool tuft on the print. Smooth out the dye with a clean tuft of dry cotton wool. Two or more dyes can be mixed directly on the surface which is being treated. To remove the dye completely, to clean up surrounding areas or to introduce highlights, wipe the area with cotton dampened with denatured alcohol.

To make the dye retouching permanent, apply steam to the retouched area for a few seconds. Avoid applying too much steam. When the surface mark caused by the dye application disappear, the surface has been steamed sufficiently.

It is important that the Flexichrome colours should not have been moistened at any time with water. The Ektacolor print and the cotton wool must be thoroughly dry. The source of steam should not be in the retouching room.

If Kodak Dye Transfer dyes or water colours are to be used for tinting, they are best diluted with a mixture of nine parts of alcohol and one part of water

The use of water alone causes the print emulsions to turn opalescent and bluish; the print must be allowed to dry before retouching can be continued in that area. The above alcohol and water mixture will still cause this opalescing effect but it dries out quicker.

Opaque retouching

Opaque colours can easily be applied to a colour print with sable spotting brushes to outline and accentuate objects, introduce specular highlights, retouch spots, etc. Also, opaque colours can be applied with an airbrush. In the hands of an expert, an airbrush is useful in dealing with larger areas of colour prints which need a change in density or colour.

A grey base which approximately matches the tone of the paper emulsion can be prepared by mixing white opaque water colour with small amounts of black and orange (yellow plus red) water colour in water.

This grey-white base material can be mixed with any of the chromatic water colours to obtain the desired retouching colour. The base material alone is often sprayed on the print area being retouched to cover dark colours before the final colour is applied. In areas where bright colours are desired, the pure chromatic water colours mixed only with water can be applied to an area opaqued with the base colours.

Colours should be mixed with enough water to let them flow easily through the airbrush. Colours which are too dry tend to produce rough textures, such as 'orange peel', on a print. Wet colours adhere better to the print and blend more satisfactorily with the print texture.

Airbrush colours should be applied in successive coats to build up the density gradually. Also, the colours should be feathered out to blend into the surrounding areas. A mask can be used to prevent opaque colours from being sprayed on any but the desired areas.

The water colours recommended for airbrush retouching are not absorbed by the print emulsion and, therefore, can be removed by wiping the retouched area with damp cotton.

Considerable judgement is necessary to select the proper density of opaque colours for a print that will be lacquered, since the lacquer will render opaque colours appreciably darker.

Lacquering

Various lacquers and other coating materials are available to give matt or glossy protective surfaces to colour prints and cover the changes in surface-reflective qualities caused by retouching. Since some matt lacquers reduce print contrast and brilliance considerably, they should be tried on a test to make sure the effect is satisfactory.

White shellac mixed with denatured alcohol provides a glossy, textured surface. The texture obtained depends on the amount of dilution of the shellac with alcohol; less alcohol gives greater texture.

28

Mounting Colour Transparencies

TO BE PROPERLY appreciated, small transparencies up to $2\frac{1}{4}$ in. square require to be viewed in some form of optical viewer or by projection as a screen image Except in the case of filmstrips, where a number of transparencies are printed on a single strip of film, individual transparencies must be mounted in some way In its simplest form, such a mount need consist only of two card frames glued together and supporting the edges of the transparency. 'Ready-mounts' of this type are fitted as a matter of course with Kodachrome transparencies of 24 × 36 mm. format, and those from 126 and 828 films, so that they are immediately ready for viewing on their arrival from the processing station. Ready-mounts or their equivalent in other makes are also available for sizes up to $2\frac{1}{4}$ in. square for mounting user-processed transparencies. These take the form of a card having two apertures which is creased for folding and coated on the inner edges with latex adhesive. Individual transparencies can be mounted in seconds merely by positioning the picture over one aperture, folding the card and pressing the edges together. Kodak Ready-Mounts with latex adhesive are available in boxes of 50 and Kodaslide Ready-Mounts for heat-sealing in boxes of 1,000. The latter are unprinted mounts intended for colour slide producers.

Card-mounted slides are satisfactory for viewing with an optical viewer, but when used in a projector, the heat of the lamp causes the transparencies to bow or buckle slightly after a few seconds. Thus if the focus is set for the 'bowed position, the slides are initially seen slightly out of focus. With certain slide projectors employing magazine loading, warm air is blown over the slides to

Plates 70 and 71. Two examples of the use of a small flash unit. As the principal interest of the altar carving lies in its colour and design it was decided to use the flash unit mounted on the camera. On the other hand, the shape and structure of the stalactite is of more interest than it colour and for this reason the flash was fitted to an extension lead and fired to one side.

Plate 72. To demonstrate the fall-off with a small flash unit it was fired at three distances with the aperture adjusted on the basis of the guide number. As can be seen, the guide number gave th correct exposure at a distance of 3 ft. but at half this distance, the wooden skier is about $\frac{1}{2}$ stop under-exposed while the background is very much darker. The behaviour of a flash unit at clos distances depends on the nature of the reflector and any diffuser employed, and the photographe intending to use flash for close-up work is advised to make tests with his own unit.

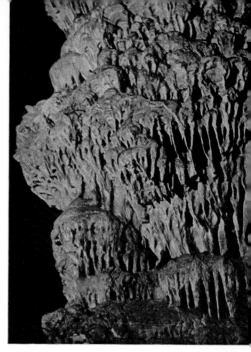

Plate 70. Wooden altar carving in Italian church – flash mounted on the camera.

Plate 71. Part of stalactite in the Grotta Verde, Sardinia – flash used from the side.

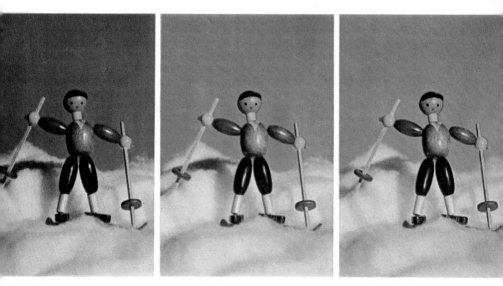

$1\frac{1}{2}$ ft. $f/22$ 3 ft. $f/11$ 6 ft. $f/5\cdot6$

Plate 72. A miniature set based on a model 2 in. high to illustrate the fall-off in using flash at close distances. The blue background was hung 12 in. behind the subject.   *Photos: E. S. Bomback*

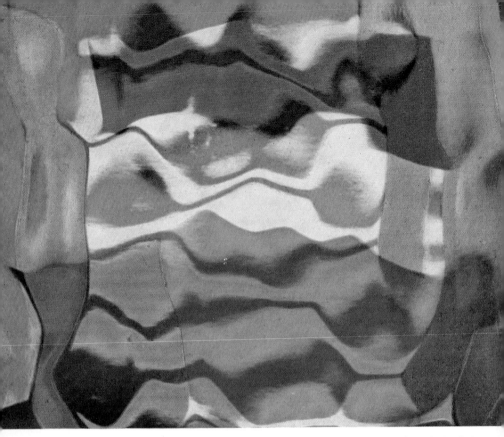

Plate 73. Abstract composition.   Devised by E. S. Bomback.

ause this expansion to take place before projection. A more satisfactory solution
to this problem is to mount the transparency between cover glasses.

While a card mount provides a satisfactory support for handling and storing
small transparencies, it offers no protection to the surfaces which are easily
scratched or finger-marked with careless handling. Here again, cover-glasses
seem to offer the best protection.

'Patent' slide mounts

The desirability of mounting transparencies between glass, plus the time-
consuming operation of effecting this with binding tape, have led to the appearance of a wide variety of easy-to-fit slide mounts which embody cover glasses.
These usually consist of plastic or metal frames with hinges, clips, lugs or other
devices for holding the various components together. Some are more robust and
practical than others. Common faults are lack of a proper seal against dust, fran-
gibility of plastic lugs and hinges, the tendency of the transparency to slip, and in
most cases difficulty in applying additional masking to the image. Some advantage
may be gained in choosing differently coloured plastic mounts as a means of
classifying different subjects.

Binding with cover glasses

The traditional method of binding a transparency between two cover glasses
using black lantern-slide binding tape is undoubtedly still the best method when
slides are to be presented for public viewing. If the job is tackled systematically,
the results in terms of projection quality are well worth the effort. Experienced
slide-binders each have their own pet methods of reducing the time factor per
slide, and in suggesting the following procedure we are simply giving what to us
seems a logical way of making a batch of slides.

Firstly, it is an advantage to use cover glasses of constant thickness so that
once the focus of a projector lens has been set for one slide, all subsequent slides
will also be in focus. Kodak Slide Cover Glasses are recommended, as they have
smooth rounded edges and corners: they are available in squares 2, $2\frac{3}{4}$ and $3\frac{1}{4}$ in.
The possibility of Newton's rings (light-interference rings between two smooth
surfaces) may suggest the use of etched cover glasses, but the effect is only troublesome with subjects having large areas of light, uniform density, and where these
occur, they may be treated separately, see page 338.

---

see page 338

Plate 73. The use of a camera to create abstract pictures may be considered by the serious-minded
well outside the useful range of colour photography. Nevertheless to judge from modern art
forms, a camera loaded with a roll of colour film offers a medium limited only by the imagination
of the operator. The example given shows one method of building up a design from a simple
geometric pattern made by laying strips of coloured paper on a sheet of blue paper. Two exposures
were made through a sheet of Large Flemish glass to give transparencies on the 'thin' side.
These were $3\frac{1}{4} \times 2\frac{1}{4}$ in. in size and were laid one over the other, one being reversed laterally to
the other, and viewed over a standard 35 mm. slide mask until a suitable combination was
obtained. The original transparencies were made with Ektachrome Film.

335

It is also convenient to make up a small mounting desk consisting of a bo containing a low-wattage lamp which illuminates a square of flashed opal glass see fig. 28.1. This enables the transparency to be located in its mask. A simpl stand to hold cleaned cover glasses may also be useful, but by stacking clea glasses on edge there is less chance of dust settling on them. Depending on th size of the transparency image, a supply of masks should be obtained: those mad of aluminium foil have the merit of being thin, and since they reflect heat, c keeping the slide cooler. Some workers use two masks, one each side of th

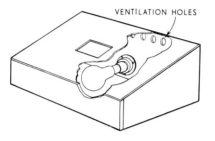

VENTILATION HOLES

Fig. 28.1. Slide binding desk with small illuminated panel.

transparency, with the object of creating a small air space on both sides. How ever, the natural curve of the transparency requires a thicker airspace if it i intended to prevent Newton's rings, and even under moderate heat furthe expansion increases the curvature. A secondary reason for using two masks is t give the slide a better appearance.

Slide-binding material of black gummed paper is to be preferred to adhesiv plastic tape, since the latter tends to extrude adhesive under heat, causing slide to stick together or, worse still, fouling the cover glasses. Slide-binding paper i available in reels or cut to lengths suitable for specific glass sizes. In the forme case it is an advantage to cut the tape to the required lengths using a simpl template, and store it flat so that it is easy to handle. It is also useful to clean packet of, say, 50 cover glasses in advance of requirements.

Undoubtedly the most important requirement for the slide-binding operation is a dust-free workroom. Dust suspended in the air or stirred up a every movement has a way of creeping *between* the cover glasses in the mos insidious manner. And there are few more frustrating experiences than t discover that five or six slides out of twenty contain specks of dust or lint. A smal room that has been well cleaned with an efficient vacuum cleaner, is fre from carpets, curtains and other soft furnishings and is fitted with a filtere ventilation fan that draws air *into* the room from the outside is as near perfect a one could wish for production slide-binding. In addition the operator shoul wear a well-boiled lintless overall.

Provision must be made for the projection guide spot and, if needed, separate label. There is much to be said for having the spot and any label insid

336

ae cover glasses, as there is then no danger of their coming adrift or becoming
oiled with handling. Many workers content themselves with a rather larger
aan normal spot which also bears the sequence number of the slide. Gummed
pots numbered from 1 to 999 are available from most photographic stores.

A number of spring clothes pegs will be useful to hold the prepared
andwiches' until ready for binding, so will a shallow dish of tepid water for
vetting the binding tape, a clean polishing cloth or Selvyt duster, and an anti-
tatic brush for removing dust from the surfaces of the transparency and cover
lasses. If the transparencies have been previously handled for any length of
ame in card mounts, film-cleaning fluid such as that supplied by Kodak for
leaning cine film will be needed. All Kodak colour films are 'super-coated' as a
rotection, and light fingermarks may be removed by gently breathing on the
urface and rubbing it with a soft lens cloth. If this does not remove the offending
lirt, apply a trace of cleaning fluid to the cloth and repeat the rubbing opera-
ion. Adhering specks of dirt which were picked up during the film drying
eriod may prove difficult to remove, hence the need for a dust-free atmosphere
vhen drying processed films.

Transparencies already in card-mounts are most easily removed by cutting
$\frac{1}{4}$ in. strip off one side of the mount with a pair of scissors. With Kodachrome
ransparencies 24 × 36 mm. the cut can be made through the word 'Transpar-
ncy'. The two layers of cardboard can then easily be separated without
lamaging the transparency. Transparencies and masks should be dried thorough-
y in a drying cabinet or airing cupboard before mounting.

When all the materials have been set in convenient positions on the working
able, the procedure follows the lines of small-scale industrial production. A mask
s placed over the illuminated panel and a transparency, emulsion side down,
laced over the mask. When the picture has been correctly positioned a small
trip of thin adhesive tape is stuck along one edge so as to overlap both film
ebate and mask. Small pieces of inch-wide Sellotape can be previously cut on a
heet of glass, and lifted as required with the tip of a pocket knife. The projection
pot is then stuck on the bottom left-hand corner of the mask when the picture
mage is upright and with the base side upwards, fig. 28.2. If additional masking

Fig. 28.2. Position of projection spot. It is useful
to mount this on the mask so that it is bound up
behind the cover glass.

o sides, top or bottom of the picture is required, this can be done by cutting
trips of foil almost as long as the full width of the glass and smearing the ends
vith rubber solution, such as Cow gum. The additional masking should be
uch that the final picture area is centrally placed in the mask. Some workers

prefer to cut such masks from foil or black paper, but this is something of refinement and makes no difference to the projected image.

When all the slides have been masked, spotted and labelled – a neat stack being built – a cover glass, carefully dusted, is placed so that it extends a little over the edge of the table (or mounting desk), and a masked transparency, also carefully dusted on both sides, is placed on top, a second glass then completing the sandwich. It is now lifted by the edge, adjusted so that the various edges coincide, and inspected through a magnifier for signs of dust. At this stage it is relatively simple to start again. When satisfied that the slide is free of dirt, a clothes-peg is applied to keep the sandwich in position. When all the sandwiches are complete, the tape-binding operation is started. A strip of tape is passed through the water and placed glue-side up on a thick layer of blotting paper. As it must be left a minute or so to dry off to the 'tacky stage', several strips may be wetted and laid at convenient intervals on the blotting paper. As soon as the first has reached a tacky stage, one of the sandwiches is applied edgewise to one end of the tape, the next edge can then be turned over and so on until all four edges have, so to speak, rolled up the binding tape. At this stage, the perfectionist cuts out mitred corners so that when the tape is pressed down on either side there is no overlap In fact a single cut with a sharp knife is all that is needed, two opposite sides then being folded round the edges, followed by the remaining pair. With a little practice this operation takes less than a minute. The finished slides are then stacked neatly so that their weight helps to keep the binding tape in position until dry.

A skilled worker can do as many as twenty slides an hour, but a good average is a dozen, and even if only six are properly mounted, the satisfaction of first-class projection may be considered ample repayment for the time spent.

Newton's rings

Unfortunately these may not manifest themselves until the slide is heated in the projector, when the audience may then become fascinated with the mysterious growth of faintly coloured shapes materializing in a thin sky area like visitors from another planet. The beauty and interest of the picture suffers in consequence. Etched glass has been put forward as the only sure cure, but as the irregularities of the glass may show on the screen, the cure may not suit everyone. There are various part-remedies: newly-processed transparencies should be allowed at least 48 hours to dry out properly; storing the slide with a dessicator composed of active silica gel may help; the use of lycopodium powder or fine starch grains is another remedy used by microscopists; or the use of thicker masks.

Cementing transparencies to glass

Perhaps the complete answer to Newton's rings is to cement the transparency image side down, on to a cover glass free from defects, backing it with a mask and a second cover-glass for protection. Properly done, the image remains perfectly flat and even with only a thin mask between the base and the second cover glass, there is no danger from Newton's rings. The method described below works well with recently processed Kodachrome transparencies. Old transparencies which have become thoroughly dried out, and particularly those which have been frequently projected, may not adhere so firmly to glass.

The cement consists of a gelatin solution containing a suitable wetting agent. Good adhesion is also more likely by using gelatin-coated glass, and this stage of the operation should be done on the previous day. As an alternative to coating glass, thoroughly fixed-out, washed and dried lantern plates can be used.

The operation demands the utmost cleanliness at all stages, and first attempts should be carried out on valueless transparencies. These experimental slides should also be tried out in the projector to determine a safe drying time. Normally-cemented transparencies should be left overnight, but the drying time can be reduced by placing the slides in an airtight vessel containing active silica gel. If the slides are projected before they are properly dry, the heat may cause vapour bubbles to form.

The gelatin adhesive is made up as follows:

1,000 cc.	Distilled water	(80 oz.)
100 cc.	Photo-Flo 1 per cent solution	(8 oz.)
22 grams	Gelatin	(1 oz. 325 grains)

The 1 per cent Photo-Flo solution can be made by adding 1 part of concentrated solution from a $\frac{1}{2}$ gallon size pack to 99 parts of distilled water: with 20 oz. and 4 oz. packs, 3 parts should be added to 97 parts of distilled water.

The cement is made up by heating the solution to 100°F. (38°C.), stirring constantly until the mixture is homogeneous and clear. It should then be allowed to cool to room temperature, but if it becomes too viscous should be slightly reheated.

The following steps should be carefully observed:

(1) The emulsion side of the transparency must be thoroughly clean and free from oil and grease. The use of Kodak Movie Film Cleaner is recommended.

(2) The transparency should next be placed on a piece of clean, dry cloth or Fotonic Photographic paper, with its base side uppermost, and a length of cellulose tape attached to one of the long edges of the transparency, allowing the tape to overhang the edge by about half its width. A glass plate with its gelatin surface face up is then placed alongside the transparency, which is then held over the plate until it is seen to be in the correct position. The tape is then pressed down to form a hinge.

(3) With the glass plate held between thumb and forefinger by the edge opposite the hinge, the transparency is folded away from the plate and both surfaces dusted with an anti-static brush. The transparency only should then be dipped into the cement, though it will not matter if a

small portion of the glass becomes immersed in order to coat the film thoroughly.

After complete immersion, and with the film still held away from the glass, the edge nearest the hinge is inserted between the roller of rubber wringer, and with a slow, even motion the transparency is rolled into contact with the glass. The film must be rolled down into contact with the glass, and not allowed to fall down against the glass as this may trap air-bubbles. Any hand-operated wringer having smooth, soft rollers may be used, and the pressure should be adjusted so that the sandwich can be rolled without difficulty. After each slide, the roller should be cleaned with warm water, and at the end of the session all traces of gelatin removed from the wringer, as remaining traces will cause the surface to become hard and rough.

(4) Immediately after being rolled through the wringer the slide should be dipped in a dish of cold water containing 1 per cent Photo-Flo. As this step is to harden the gelatin the water should be as cold as possible. After immersion for about 10 sec. the adhesive tape should be carefully removed by drawing it back at an acute angle, the slide then being immersed again and gently rubbed with the fingers to remove any traces of gelatin. After allowing the slide to drain it is examined with both reflected and transmitted light for signs of air bubbles and other defects. If the cementing is imperfect, the transparency is removed as described in the next step, otherwise it is placed in a rack to dry.

(5) If the transparency is to be removed immediately after cementing, the slide should be held under a stream of warm water, but not warmer than can be borne by the hand. After 30 sec., a corner of the transparency is lifted up and the warm water allowed to run into the opening. With gentle pulling the film is now lifted away from the glass, but only as rapidly as the softening of the gelatin will permit. When free the transparency is held under warm water and gently freed of gelatin with the fingers. It is possible to tell if any gelatin remains since the new layer will be softer and more slippery than that containing the image.

If the cement has already dried, the glass and transparency should be left to soak in warm water for about 24 hours.

The transparency is then dried for at least 8 hours in a dust-free atmosphere and re-cemented as described in the previous steps.

Finished slides should be bound up with a mask and cover glass in the normal way to obtain maximum protection.

Surface scratches

Superficial surface scratches may be greatly reduced by dipping the transparency in a solution of gelatin and allowing it to dry in a dust-free atmosphere. Alternatively the surface may be lacquered with a clear photographic lacquer.

lide storage

wide range of storage boxes and cabinets is available, and the choice is largely
personal one. Many modern slide projectors employ magazine loading, in
hich case it may be preferable to use steel filing drawers of a suitable depth for
toring the magazines. In warm, humid climates a slide storage box or cabinet
hould be airtight and contain a compartment for a tray of silica gel. It is essential
o re-activate the desiccant at regular intervals, and also to inspect the slides for
igns of mould.

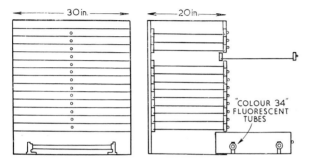

Fig. 28.3. Slide cabinet for easy reference. It consists of trays
with glass bottoms. The bottom drawer is fitted with a sheet
of opal glass with two strip-lights, against which any tray of
slides may be viewed.

ndexing

The simplest method, if started in time, is to number each slide in sequence
eeping a written index of the subject matter and any other detail required. Any
rrangement of slides for lecture or entertainment, which is keyed to a written or
aped commentary, can then be recorded as a list of numbers, and the slides
eturned to their normal numerical sequence in the storage cabinet. The
nterprising and critical slide collector (namely, one who knows when to use the
vaste-paper basket) may like to consider making a cabinet of the type shown in
ig. 28.3. The dimensions can be made to suit individual requirements, but a 20
× 30 in. drawer will take 150 slides of 2 × 2 in. dimensions. A cabinet with 12
uch drawers will hold nearly 2,000 slides. Fluorescent strip lighting in the
ottom illumination drawer is preferable as it is cool and can be chosen to give
ood colour balance.

29

Projection of Colour Slides

THE PRESENTATION of colour photographs as screen pictures is regarded by many photographers as the ideal mode. Technically it offers a brilliant image of high colour saturation, which is normally viewed at a distance to give natural perspective. Psychologically it commands almost the exclusive attention of the viewer, enabling maximum accommodation to the brightness and colour balance of the image, which frequently combine to give an effect little short of reality. Projection therefore provides an excellent method for displaying instructional and educational matter, display photographs of manufactured goods – particularly those of high artistic quality, such as china, glass and metal ware – and also subjects of general interest and travel pictures.

The projector

This may be compared with a photographic enlarger, and consists basically of a light-source with a mirror reflector, a condenser system, a slide carrier and a projection lens. The light-source is enclosed within a lamphouse, which acts as a screen to unwanted illumination. The heat of the lamp is dispersed by a convector system for lamps of up to 250 watts, and with an electric fan for higher-wattage lamps. The lens is of fixed aperture and is provided with a focusing movement to accommodate a normal range of projection distances. However, there are many variations and refinements in modern slide projectors, some of which are worth considering in some detail.

The wattage of a projector is a nominal guide to the maximum size of image it will throw having a satisfactory screen brilliance. A well-designed projector of 150 watts will provide satisfactory screen brightness with a slide of average density projected to fill a 40 × 40 in. white screen. This size could be increased (though at some sacrifice in the viewing angle) by using a metallic or glass beaded surface. Projectors of twice this wattage may be expected to give satisfactory brightness for a screen of about 5 ft. square, while those of 500 watts or more will cover screens of 7 ft. square or larger. However, the screen brightness depends on the efficiency of the condenser system, the aperture of the projection lens, the age of the projector lamp (which tends to blacken), and to some extent on the cleanliness of the entire optical system, which may have a

Fig. 29.1. Kodaslide 50 Projector fitted with Kodamat Rapid Slide Changer and Automatic Motor.

dozen or more air-to-glass surfaces. In choosing a projector some account should therefore be taken of the maximum screen size it may be desired to fill. If projection is to be restricted to a medium size room, a projector such as the Kodaslide 50 Projector is ideal, see fig. 29.1. The use of a high-wattage projector for small screen sizes may result in loss of picture quality owing to excessive screen brightness. However, it should be borne in mind that a low-wattage projector cannot be fitted with a lamp of higher wattage, as the cooling system will be inadequate.

Correctly designed and adjusted, the mirror and condenser system should give a uniform brightness over the whole picture area. This is best tested and, if need be, adjusted, without a slide in position.

Screen brightness

While the adaptation of the eye to different levels of brightness allows considerable latitude in screen brightness, some attempts have been made to lay down

Fig. 29.2. Kodak 500 Projector.

desirable standards of brightness for the projection of colour slides. That of the Photographic Alliance may be taken as a suitable guide. It is based on the use of a white screen, the measurement being made at the centre of the screen and without a slide in the gate, the meter being pointed towards the projector: a value of 12-18 foot-candles is recommended for average colour slides. An alternative method of measuring screen brightness also without a slide in the gate is to take a reflected-light reading with an exposure meter held near the screen, taking care that the reading is not influenced by any shadows cast by the hands or meter. A reading between 6·5 and 13 on the scale of a Weston meter (pre-model V) is very satisfactory. With a meter giving exposure values this is equivalent to an E.V. of 6 to 6½ with the speed scale of the meter set to 40 ASA.

The reflected brightness depends on the reflectance of the screen surface, and an 'off-white' screen may reflect up to 30 per cent less light than one which is perfectly white. A silvered-surface screen reflects the highest percentage of light, but the reflection is considerably more specular and falls off rapidly as the viewing angle exceeds about 20° from the lens axis. The specular nature of the light tends to give rather a contrasty image and the metallic surface detracts somewhat from the 'reality' of the image. A glass-beaded screen is very nearly as efficient as a metallic one, but is also somewhat specular in nature and tends to give a grainy appearance to the image. A good white screen is undoubtedly the best choice for colour projection.

However, the apparent screen brightness is strongly influenced by the ambient illumination, and a satisfactory level, as measured with an exposure meter, may prove inadequate in a room not properly darkened or if the projector itself is not properly screened. Some ambient illumination is desirable, but the light from the screen itself reflected from walls and ceiling in an average room is sufficient.

Projection distance and picture size

For a given size of slide, the relation between projector-to-screen distance and picture size is governed by the focal length of the projector lens. The following simple formulas may be useful to the projectionist:

$$\text{Width of screen picture} = \frac{\text{Projection distance}}{\text{Focal length}} \times \text{width of slide image}$$

$$\text{Projection distance} = \frac{\text{Width of screen picture}}{\text{Width of slide image}} \times \text{focal length}$$

$$\text{Focal length} = \frac{\text{Projection distance}}{\text{Width of screen picture}} \times \text{width of slide}$$

The choice of projection distance will depend a great deal on the nature of the room or hall (whether long and narrow or short and wide) and on the size of

PROJECTION DISTANCE AND SCREEN WIDTH

For 2 × 2 in. slides masked to 34 mm. in width

Projection Distance in ft.	Focal length of lens and screen width in ft. and in.					
	85 mm.	100 mm.	120 mm.	135 mm.	150 mm.	200 mm.
6	2 4	2 0	—	—	—	—
7	2 9	2 4	—	—	—	—
8	3 4	2 8	2 3	2 0	—	—
9	3 7	3 2	2 6	2 3	2 0	—
10	4 0	3 5	2 10	2 6	2 3	—
12	4 9	4 1	3 5	3 0	2 9	2 0
16	6 5	5 6	4 7	4 1	3 8	2 9
20	8 1	6 10	5 9	5 1	4 8	3 5
32	12 10	11 0	9 2	8 2	7 4	5 6

For 2 × 2 in. slides masked to 40 mm. in width

Projection Distance in ft.	Focal length of lens and screen width in ft. and in.					
	85 mm.	100 mm.	120 mm.	135 mm.	150 mm.	200 mm.
6	2 8	2 3	—	—	—	—
7	3 2	2 7	2 3	2 0	—	—
8	3 7	3 0	2 7	2 3	2 0	—
9	4 1	3 6	2 11	2 7	2 3	—
10	4 6	3 11	3 3	2 11	2 7	—
12	5 5	4 8	3 11	3 6	3 1	2 4
16	7 2	6 3	5 3	4 8	4 2	3 2
20	9 3	7 10	6 7	5 10	5 3	3 9
32	—	12 6	10 6	9 4	8 6	6 3

Note: The inclusion of screen sizes in the above table does not imply acceptable screen brightness.

the audience. The best viewing distance for slides which have been made with a lens equal in focal length to the picture diagonal can be taken to equal the diagonal of the screen picture if the whole of the picture area is projected. Thus a 4 ft. square picture should be viewed at about 6 ft. This distance is independent of the focal length of the projector lens and remains the same whether the screen picture is the result of a long projection distance with a long-focus lens or not. Home projectors are usually fitted with a lens which gives the best viewing distance at about midway between screen and projector. This distance relates to the so-called standard lens, and if shorter or longer focal lengths are used for the same camera, different viewing distances should be chosen to obtain the effect of natural perspective. In practice this is scarcely possible, and with a large audience seated in a long hall, those at the back could be as much as six times the 'ideal' distance. Movie cameras employ a 'standard' lens of focal length about twice the picture diagonal, and the correct viewing distance thus becomes twice the screen picture diagonal. Anyone taking pictures solely for projection to public audiences would do well to adopt a similar standard.

Fig. 29.3. Kodak Transparency Viewer. The 14 × 17 flashed opal screen can be adjusted in brightness with a six-position switch.

Cooling and slide temperature

In addition to a cooling system adequate to keep the body of the projector reasonably cool, or at least not so hot as to cause discomfort in touching it, it is necessary to restrict the heat radiation reaching the slide. This is accomplished by means of a glass heat-absorbing filter, which must on no account be left out if the various components of the optical system are dismantled for cleaning. Naturally, excessive heating up of a colour slide is extremely undesirable, and even if it does not cause actual damage it may cause premature fading of the image. Thermometer 'slides' are available for testing the temperature at the gate of a projector, but if a glass-mounted slide that has been in the projector for about 60 sec. is unbearably hot to the back of the hand, the heat filter is not adequate. Normally, after an average projection time of 15 sec., the slide should only just be appreciably warm, but one must, of course, allow for much longer projection times for instructional material.

Automatic projectors

The usual system for a hand-operated projector is a slide carrier with two apertures which is moved from one side to the other as a new slide is put in in place of that already screened. At the same time the projectionist is also responsible for seeing that the picture is sharply focused on the screen. Both of these movements are accomplished electrically on an automatic projector, some of which have as many as four electric motors incorporated. Slides are pre-loaded into a special magazine, and from this are selected in sequence by operating a push-button switch. In some projectors this can also be coupled to a variable time-switch which automatically changes the slide at regular intervals. Some projectors with a circular-type magazine enable this feature to be used for continuous window-display projection, a sequence of, say, 50 slides being repeated until a master switch turns the projector off.

The second movement, that of lens focusing, usually enables a limited degree of focusing (sufficient for average variations in slide thickness, etc.) to be accomplished. The three switches with a sufficient length of cable enable the projectionist to sit near the screen both to enjoy the pictures and to maintain sharp focus. It offers the advantage that a lecturer himself, standing to one side of the screen, can also be his own projectionist.

Back-projection

The method described in Chapter 16, page 230, for back-projection may offer a solution to projection in a long hall in the absence of a long-focus lens, or when a small room opening off a larger room offers space for the projector behind the screen. The screen brightness tends to fall off at wider viewing angles, and it is desirable to use a material giving good diffusion.

Dual projection system with dissolve unit

A system of still projection pioneered by Kodak at public shows makes use of two slide projectors fitted with variable diaphragms which may be operated by a single control so that as one opens the other closes. Skilfully applied, the effect is almost that of a movie picture, the suggestion of movement coming from the dissolve from one scene to the next.

Display of large transparencies

Transparencies which are too large for projection can be presented, properly masked, on an illuminator having an opal diffusing screen. Such an illuminator can be made up with one or more fluorescent strip lights such as Philips Colour 34 or Mazda Kolorite enclosed in a shallow case, the front of which is fitted with an opal screen. The same unit fitted with legs can be used as a slide-editing desk, see page 349. A range of Kodak Transparency Illuminators and Viewers is available.

30

Presenting Slide Shows and Lectures

IT IS TO BE regretted that colour slide shows, along with magic lantern lectures, have become something of a music hall joke, and even Richard Dimbleby, that most courteous of television commentators, when presenting a review of slide projectors could not refrain from referring to the boredom of being subjected to a prolonged session of someone's colour slides. The original novelty of colour has now largely worn off, and mere exhibitions of the colour capacities of modern colour films, unless skilfully staged as in the case of Kodak Colour Shows, are apt to leave the unspoken phrase 'So what!' in the spectator's mind. We are indeed tempted to speculate whether or not colour slide shows have passed their peak of popularity in spite of the impressive range of projection equipment now available. Whether this is so or not, anyone with respect for his reputation as a photographer and showman should think very carefully before putting on a slide show or accepting an invitation to lecture before a critical audience.

Yet in spite of this pessimistic appraisal of colour slide shows in general, we remain essentially enthusiastic in the power of a well-selected and well-presented colour show to entertain, or in the case of educational matter, to inform and instruct in an entertaining manner. The aim of this chapter is to offer advice and suggestions in this most difficult and exacting mode of presentation.

Quality of slides

The question of subject matter does not really matter; almost any subject can be made interesting. What does matter is that each and every slide should be as near technically perfect as possible. By this we mean well-exposed, sharp, properly framed and free from obvious blemishes. Needless to say there are occasions when, for the sake of continuity, a slide of poorish quality may have to be included: if it adds substantially to the interest of the subject matter as a whole, its defects are less likely to be noticed, but it should not be so poor in quality as to require excuses. While it is usually preferable to keep the picture size constant so as to fill the screen on each occasion, the judicious masking of unwanted edge material will greatly improve the presentation. Some people consider that all the slides should be of the same format, in keeping with the cinema or TV screen. But it can be equally well-argued that still pictures are a mode on their own and have no need to conform to the conventions (compulsory ones at that) of motion picture photography. In our opinion the use of horizontal, vertical and square formats in a slide sequence can add variety and interest. On occasions, even circular or oval shapes may suggest themselves – a photomicrograph, for example used in an otherwise normal series, could be given a circular mask.

Editing a series of slides

While it is possible to examine the quality of individual slides by the simple process of projecting them, the task of editing a series of slides from the point of view of subject matter, continuity, colour balance and so forth requires a large illuminated editing desk. This can either be adapted from an existing piece of furniture, or constructed to individual requirements. The following suggestions are worth considering,

(1) The top of an ordinary card or bridge table can be replaced by a sheet of plate glass under which a sheet of thin white diffusing material is attached. The sides of the table can be screened with black cloth and a reflector-type display lamp is placed at floor level mounted on a flat base, see fig. 30.1. A table 30 × 30 in. will accommodate a series of 100 slides with sufficient room for additional slides to be set out in the lower half.

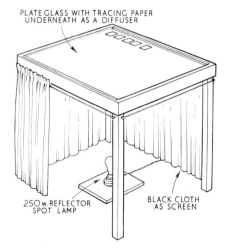

PLATE GLASS WITH TRACING PAPER
UNDERNEATH AS A DIFFUSER

Fig. 30.1. Simple card table with recessed top adapted as an editing desk with a sheet of plate glass.

250 w. REFLECTOR SPOT LAMP

BLACK CLOTH AS SCREEN

(2) A large drawer can be fitted with a sheet of opal glass (supported on a recess just below the upper edges) and the interior of the drawer fitted with two fluorescent striplights of suitable length and colour quality. If a top drawer is used, it can be fitted with stops to prevent its coming fully out and a front leg support, which can be attached when required with a wingnut, see fig. 30.2.

349

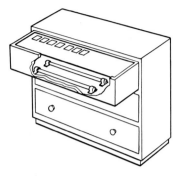

Fig. 30.2. The top drawer of an old tallboy adapted as slide viewer with strip-lighting.

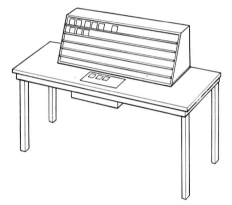

Fig. 30.3. A tilted slide-editing panel with ledges to support slides. A small, horizontal panel allows close examination and matching of slides.

(3) A vertical illuminator having a small back-tilt and slots for carrying slides can be constructed as shown in fig. 30.3, and placed at the back of a long table or work-bench. It can be an advantage to have a small illuminator of, say, 8×10 in. in the work-bench as well for close scrutiny with a magnifier. Opal glass with fluorescent lighting is recommended.

Whatever form the editing desk takes, it permits a series to be seen at the same time, thus enabling subject matter to be built up on the basis of a previously worked out script, or, depending on how you prefer to work, to arrange slides into some kind of order and then work out a script, making such additional adjustments in slide order as might be necessary in preparing the script. At the

Plate 74. One of several compositions representing different countries which was used as a double-page spread in the Penrose Annual 1962 as an advertisement for Kodak colour materials. With such a complex subject arrangement careful lighting is needed to separate the various planes and avoid distracting shadows. *Ektachrome transparency by E. W. Johnson.*

Newspaper text:
Schach dem Beraten...
Wochenau...
Wie bleibe ich
● **jung**
● **gesund**
● **schön!**
Jede Frau ist zur Venus geboren

Stein text: ...erhalte...

Photo: E. W. Johnson.

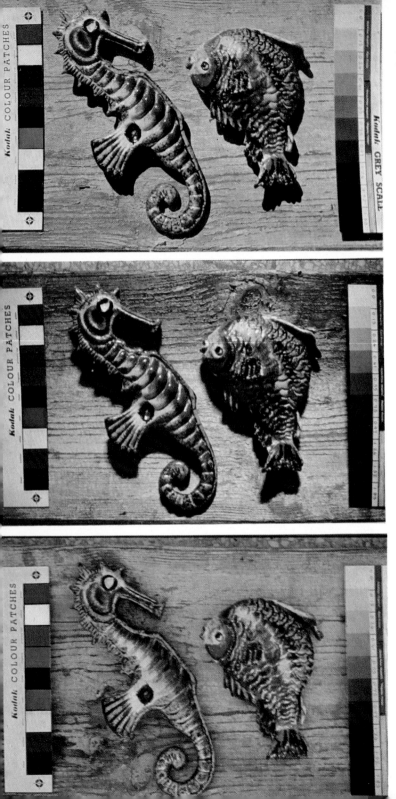

Plate 75. Strong overh[ead]
sunlight, Kodachrome[II]
Film, 1/125 sec. *f*11.

Plate 76. Full moon
night, Kodachrome II F[ilm]
1 hour at *f*/2.

Plate 77. Light from [blue]
sky, Kodachrome II F[ilm]
1/125 sec. at *f*5·6.

,ame time the illuminated area permits slides to be compared for colour balance, and either rejected as unsuitable or arranged in such a way that differences in colour balance appear natural or unnoticed. Fortunately the adaptation of the eye is a great ally in slide projection provided that substantial differences are not allowed to occur between successive slides. For example, foliage and grass in sunlight would make a following slide of similar subject matter photographed on an overcast day appear rather too blue and lacking in contrast. By interposing a slide of different subject matter and colouring, the eye will lose its adaptation to the sunlit greens and will more readily accept the rather more sombre and bluish greens which result from different lighting conditions. Account should be taken of the fact that a strong predominating colour in one slide will tend to emphasize its complementary colour in the next slide. Thus a strongly green landscape could make a portrait appear rather too pink.

Commentaries

Whether you prefer a 'spontaneous' commentary, or one that is read or recorded, an editing desk provides the ideal initial stage for deciding what you are going to say. Just as the best 'snapshots' are often the result of the most careful planning on the part of some professional photographer, so the spontaneous commentary is usually the result of writing a script that suits the slides. Even the best lecturers are liable to suffer lapses of memory, perhaps even moments of stage fright. But if a commentary has been written, a mere glance at it from time to time may be sufficient to keep to the point and at the same time maintain the desired effect of being spontaneous. Many lecturers make their notes on small index cards and as each slide is changed automatically move the card relating to it to the back of the pack. In this way, whether the notes are used or not, a reminder involves no more than glancing at the top card.

The danger of an unscripted slide show is that the enthusiasm of the lecturer may greatly prolong the showing of each slide – particularly if he has been well-dined and wined beforehand by the club president. In the normal way, one should allow 15 sec. average showing time per slide with the object of limiting a slide show to about 30 min. Naturally the subject matter may call for somewhat longer or shorter screening times, and material of an instructional nature may average 30 sec. per slide, while pictorial material or travel subjects may be better presented in fairly rapid succession with an average of 7 sec. per slide. But unless

---

Plates 75 to 77. This test was made to illustrate the statement made on page 73 that moonlight, being of similar composition to sunlight, will give roughly the same colour rendering in a colour photograph if given sufficient exposure. The slight green bias can be attributed to reciprocity, but if it were not for the background this would hardly be noticeable. On the other hand the visual appearance of the test object in moonlight showed very little of the red and yellow colours of the ceramics. It is of interest to note that blue skylight, to which the eye readily adapts itself, has produced a much greater shift in colour balance.

353

21

the material is exceptional the number of slides should not take longer than 30 to 40 min. to screen. Unfortunately many photographic societies expect their lecturers to 'fill-in' a 2 hour session, and, perhaps, longer.

Projection conditions

Anyone accepting the invitation to lecture should, if possible, verify personally and beforehand that the room or hall is suitable, can be adequately darkened at the scheduled time, is sufficiently provided with seats, is properly ventilated (we have known occasions of fainting due to lack of ventilation), and allows for emergency exits by members of the audience who have buses to catch, etc., without creating a disturbance for those who want to see the show to its end. Unless the club or society is known to have good projection conditions, it is never wise to rely on the (often well-meaning) assurances of the programme secretary that everything will be ready. Experience shows that it rarely is, and the lecturer is advised to arrive at least half an hour before the scheduled time and to do his best to make good any deficiencies before the audience arrives. If he is bringing his own projection equipment, it should include a multi-plug arrangement (or a 'universal' plug), several lengths of rubber cable with extension plugs and two spare projector lamps. Unless he is to project his own slides, he should be sure that the slides are properly arranged and 'spotted' for the official projectionist. Any special effects he may want should be clearly described to the projectionist, together with some agreed system for signalling slide changes. A dry battery

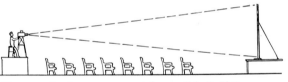

Fig. 30.4. Seating arrangement for small hall. If the screen does not possess tilting adjustment it can be held with string.

and torch bulb with a length of wire and push switch is the most usual system, and is preferable to audible signals which can be disturbing to the audience.

If an automatic slide projector is being used, check that the magazines are correctly loaded (nothing is more demoralizing than to create a hiatus with a magazine loaded with a slide upside down!). Even when the lecturer has taken the precaution of bringing everything, including a tape-recorded commentary, he must be prepared for the unexpected. A tape-recorder may be the wrong model or may break down, and unless the lecturer has a good memory or is skilled at improvising, a typed copy of the script should be carried.

It is preferable to have the projector located behind the audience, and if the seats are level, to have both projector and screen raised clear of the audience. One arrangement is to have the screen tilted slightly downwards as shown in fig. 30·4, and to avoid having the front row so near that they are likely to suffer from stiff necks. Seats should also be in 'staggered' rows for the benefit of junior members.

Recorded commentaries and music

The skilful presentation of slides with attractive titles, nicely delivered commentary and unobtrusive background music can raise the quality of a slide show to the level of the best professional entertainment. A good main title-slide should be considered indispensible, as also an 'END' slide. Methods of producing these may be found in Chapter 16 of this book, and the imaginative photographer will have no difficulty of recognizing natural titling material in the course of his wanderings.

A musical accompaniment may be provided from long-playing records, using two turn-tables if changes are required from one record to another. A tape-recorder offers considerable freedom in making such changes, but due attention must be given to the fact that all musical performances on the radio or TV, whether recorded or otherwise, and all gramophone records are protected by copyright. Various recording-rights societies exist for those wishing to use music for public slide shows.

There is, of course, no restriction in recording commentaries, sound effects (such as bells, song birds and so on), or amateur recitals of music out of copyright or of original compositions. The traveller collecting photographs abroad now frequently carries a small portable tape-recorder with the object of incorporating realistic background sounds to particular slides. Such sound effects are, perhaps, more in keeping with movies and may even tend to draw the attention of the audience to the shortcomings of still pictures. Unless you have a good 'microphone' voice, it may be preferable to obtain the services of a member of the local drama circle or even to hire a professional commentator. Before doing either, the commentary should be tried out while the slides are being projected for its general effect, due allowance being made for audience reaction if humour is introduced in picture form or evoked by the commentary. This latter point is one of the principal objections to recorded commentaries, since no two audiences react in the same way, and a pause left for laughter may appear nothing more than an ill-timed gap in the commentary.

The technicalities of recording are beyond the scope of the present book and the reader is referred to the bibliography for titles of books dealing with this subject.

31

Colour-Separation Negatives for Colour-Print Processes

IN SOME systems of making colour prints on paper, it is first necessary to make separation negatives through red, green and blue filters. In the subsequent processes of printing, suitably coloured positive images made from the three separation negatives are superimposed in register on a paper support to give the final colour print.

Separation negatives may be made directly from a still-life subject by using a conventional camera and exposing three panchromatic plates or films separately through Wratten red, green, and blue tri-colour filters, or in other circumstances by using a 'one-shot' camera to expose the three plates or films simultaneously. Separation negatives may also be made indirectly by copying a colour transparency.

The steps in making direct-separation and indirect-separation negatives are outlined in the following pages. There are, however, certain fundamental considerations which apply to the making of all separation negatives, and the worker making colour prints should study and understand these before commencing to make separation negatives.

The exposure and development times quoted in this chapter should be taken only as a guide; they must be confirmed by practical trial.

Lenses

It is essential for a lens which is used in making colour-separation negatives, directly or indirectly, or when exposing colour transparencies, to be fully colour-corrected, in order that the three images may register perfectly. Kodak Ektar lenses are corrected for lateral colour aberration and the 2 in., 3 in. and 4 in. lenses supplied with the Kodak Precision Enlarger are highly suitable for colour-separation work. To test a camera lens for colour correction, make separation negatives of some register marks or white threads stretched across a black background. The register marks or cross threads should be arranged so that they are recorded in the corners and centre of the plate. Use gelatin tri-colour filters over the lens and expose each plate in the same dark-slide. The lens is adequately corrected if a contact positive made from the red-filter negative registers exactly with the green-filter and blue-filter negatives.

To test enlarging lenses, use a scribed plate in the negative carrier and make the separation negatives by projection.

Lighting and exposure

When lighting the subject from which the colour print is to be made, several points should be observed carefully, whether direct separation negatives or colour transparencies are to be exposed. The lamps should be of the same colour quality, i.e., have the same colour temperature, and this can best be assured by using lamps which burn at a specified colour temperature when run at their rated voltage. Care should be taken to see that all the reflectors are of matt metal finish or, if painted white, that they are not in any way discoloured. The most satisfactory method of checking the colour temperature of the light-sources is to use a colour temperature meter. A less accurate method, but one that will give a good guide, is to hinge together two large pieces of identical white card and stand them on edge so that the hinge is towards the observer with the cards at right angles. Place the two lamps to be compared so that each illuminates one piece of card only, and adjust their position until the same reading is obtained on an exposure meter from each side. Then, by viewing from the front, differences above 100°K. can be detected after a little experience. As long as no difference is perceptible under this test the lamps may be used together, see fig. 31.1.

Fig. 31.1. A rough method of comparing the colour quality of two different light sources.

The lighting used for colour photography should be kept very soft: except for occasional special effects, the lighting contrast should not exceed 3 : 1, i.e., there should not be more than three times as much light on the highlight side of the subject as there is on the shadow side. Remember that *colour* contrast is as effective in colour photography as *lighting* contrast in black-and-white photography.

Generally the lighting should be even over the whole of the subject area, and care should be taken to see that the intensity of the light on the background is of the same order as that on the main part of the subject. See page 131.

357

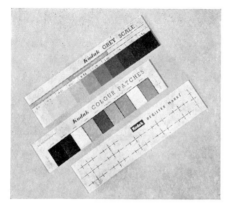

Fig. 31.2. Kodak Grey
Scale, Colour Patches and
Register Marks.

As regards exposure, transparencies which are to be used for reproduction are best under-exposed by about half a stop, whereas separation negatives should be exposed so as to avoid any loss of quality in the highlights or shadows.

Grey-scale record and negative identification

If good colour prints are to be obtained, it is most important that the separation negatives match each other exactly for density and contrast. The balance of the separation negatives, i.e., their density and contrast, is controlled by exposure and development, and can be checked accurately only by including a grey-scale (or step-wedge) image on each negative. When the three separation negatives are properly balanced, corresponding steps on the grey-scale image will show equal densities in all three negatives.

Two types of grey-scale are available. One, printed on paper, is included in the Kodak Colour-Separation Guide (supplied in 9 in. size) and should be placed at the margin of the subject so that it will be recorded alongside one edge of the negatives. The grey-scale should receive the same amount of light as the most important part of the subject. The second type of grey-scale is a transparent step-wedge made on film. Its special use is in making indirect separation negatives from Ektachrome and Kodachrome transparencies. It is mounted alongside the transparency and both are copied together. Suitable transparent step-wedges can be supplied as Kodak Photographic Step Tablets in the following overall sizes:

Tablet No. 1 – 2·2 × 7·5 cm. ($\frac{7}{8}$ × 3 in.)
Tablet No. 2 – 2·2 × 14 cm. ($\frac{7}{8}$ × 5$\frac{1}{2}$ in.)
Tablet No. 3 – 2·2 × 25 cm. ($\frac{7}{8}$ × 9$\frac{7}{8}$ in.)

Included on the Colour-Separation Guide and Nos. 2 and 3 of the above Step Tables are colour patches which make the identification of the separation negatives a very simple matter. With sheet-film material identification may be

358

simplified by cutting one corner off the film for the red-filter negative, two corners for the green and three for the blue. If developing hangers are used, the top bar can be notched for easy identification in the dark.

The densities of the grey-scale images recorded on the negatives should be measured accurately with a densitometer such as the Kodak Reflection-Transmission Colour Densitometer, which gives a direct reading from a calibrated scale.

If a grey-scale image is not included in the negative, the highlight density can be measured from the image of a neutral white or light grey object and the shadow density from a black object or deep shadow. The specular highlights obtained on metals, china and glass should be avoided when determining highlight densities.

Materials for colour-separation negatives

Kodak Colour Separation Negative Films Type 1 and Type 2 (this latter gives higher contrast) are ideal for making colour separation negatives because the straight-line portions of their characteristic curves are exceptionally long. Kodak P.900 plates are also suitable, but plates are less convenient to use than film. The high order of the dimensional stability of glass plates has now been offset by the introduction of the Type 1 and Type 2 films which are coated on 0·007-inch thick polyester plastic base which provides the best dimensional stability obtainable with flexible film base.

Another reason for choosing the Type 1 or Type 2 film is that it can be punched with the Kodak Register Punch and exposed in the Kodak Register Printing Frame; when making separation negatives from masked colour transparencies this solves tedious registration problems.

Processing

When processing separation negatives, the utmost care must be taken to see that conditions are rigidly controlled to ensure uniformly satisfactory results. Negatives may be developed in a dish or a tank, but in either case the developer should be accurately prepared and used at the specified standard temperature. After being used once, developer in a dish should be discarded, and developer in a tank replenished according to the instructions given on page 361.

With dish development, the most satisfactory results will be obtained if the negatives are developed in separate dishes one size larger than the material to be processed; but, since the degree of agitation seriously affects the rate of development and the density of the negatives, every effort must be made to see that the agitation is identical. This is best accomplished by making a simple hand-operated rocker to take three dishes. The rocker should consist of a flat board surface or arrangement of slats to take the three dishes: to the base are fixed two curved blocks or bowed slats set at right angles to each other, as shown in fig. 31.3. The dishes should be placed on the rocker and filled with water at such a temperature as to adjust their temperatures to 68°F. (20°C.). A sufficient quantity of developer should be diluted and brought to the same temperature. The three dishes are then emptied, an equal quantity of developer quickly poured into each, and the temperature of each checked to ensure that it is 68°F. The amount of developer used for each plate or film should be constant for every set of negatives; 200 cc. (7 oz.) is sufficient for a half-plate developed in a whole-plate dish, and 400 cc. (14 oz.) for a whole-plate in an 8 × 10 in. dish. Throughout the

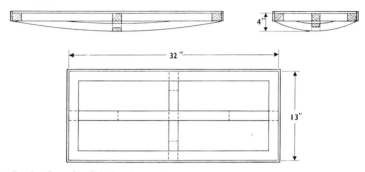

Fig. 31.3. Rocker base for dish development.

development, the rocker with its three dishes must be kept agitated with an out-of-phase motion, to prevent setting up any uniform currents. The rate of agitation must be the same during the whole of the development, and every effort must be made to ensure that the same agitation is given for each set of negatives. When the negatives are made on the smaller sizes of films or plates, they may be processed together in a large dish. The dish should be placed in a larger dish of water to maintain the temperature of the developer at 68°F. (20°C.). The dish should be agitated in all directions to prevent the setting up of uniform currents. Care must, of course, be taken to see that the water does not get into the developing dish.

With tank development, considerable care must be taken to ensure uniform development, and it may sometimes be necessary to experiment with the actual tanks available, in order to find the most suitable routine of agitation. Very successful results will be obtained by using Kodak No. 3 Processing Tank Assembly and the Kodak No. 3 Sheet Film Processing Rack or No. 3 Plate Processing Rack, when the instructions for agitation given below are followed. It is most important that the films or plates are set a half-inch or more apart in the racks, with the emulsion facing the same direction and with the corresponding edge of the picture uppermost. The rack is lowered into the developer, given two complete up-and-down movements and thereafter slowly raised two or three inches and slowly lowered, the whole operation taking 5 sec.; after a pause for 5 sec., the agitation and pauses are continued throughout the development cycle.

Kodak DK-50 Negative Developer is suitable for either dish or tank development. When used in the tank specified it should be replenished with

Kodak DK-50R Replenisher; 1 fl. oz. of replenisher should be added after processing every 4 half-plates or 2 whole-plates.

Development is followed by a stop bath (formula SB-1), fixing (formula F-54a) and washing, after which the plates may be rinsed with dilute Kodak Photo-Flo to aid even drying.

The three negatives may be dried naturally or in a drying cabinet, but it is important that they be oriented in the same direction during drying.

Separation negatives direct from the subject

Direct separation negatives may be made from appropriate subjects by three different means:

1. An ordinary camera may be used on a rigid tripod and the three negatives made one after another through the appropriate filters. It is important that the movements of the camera be firmly locked to prevent any displacement during or between exposures, and that the various dark-slides hold sensitive material in exactly the same plane. Dark-slides can be tested for register, adapting the method described for testing lenses; if matching dark-slides cannot be found, one slide must be used for all three negatives, the sensitive material being changed for each exposure.

2. A repeating-back may be fitted to a suitable stand camera. With this apparatus three panchromatic plates or films are held in a single slide behind filters of the same size as the negative material. A repeating-back, which may be operated either manually or automatically, allows the three negatives to be taken in rapid succession.

3. A 'one-shot' camera may be used. Cameras of this type have an optical system which splits the beam of light coming through the lens and divides it between three plates or films, in front of which are the appropriate separation filters.

Direct separation negatives are made through Kodak Wratten tri-colour filters – red No. 25, green No. 58, and deep-blue No. 47B. Typical development times are given in the following table; this information is based on average conditions. It should be checked by trial, and modified as necessary to produce matching grey-scale images in the separation negatives. Filter ratios are given for Separation Negative Film Types 1 and 2 and for P.900 plates.

The exposure and development times should be adjusted to give negatives with a minimum density in the shadow areas (or the lightest step of the grey-scale) of between $0 \cdot 3$ and $0 \cdot 4$, and a density range suitable for the particular print process used. With the Kodak Dye Transfer process, the density range should not be less than $1 \cdot 0$ nor greater than $1 \cdot 8$; but a minimum density range of $1 \cdot 2$ is recommended when cold-cathode illumination is to be used.

The density range of a negative is the difference between the densities of the darkest and the lightest areas: these densities should be determined with a densitometer. The difference in density range between the individual negatives of a set should not be greater than 0·1, as measured either on the grey-scale image or on parts of the subject which are neutral in colour.

Filter Ratios relative to Wratten Filter No. 25

Exposure times with the other filters should be determined by multiplying the red filter exposure by the appropriate filter ratio.

Material—with Photoflood Illumination	No. 25	No. 58	No. 47B
Separation Negative Type 1	1·0	1·5	4·0
Separation Negative Type 2	1·0	1·5	6·0
P.900 Plates	1·0	1·2	2·0

Development times in Minutes at 68°F. (20°C.).

Material	Developer	Dilution	Agitation*	Times for each negative		
				No. 25 (red) filter	No. 58 (green) filter	No. 47B (blue) filter
Separation Neg. Type 1	DK-50	1 + 1 undiluted	dish tank	4½ 7	4½ 9	5½ 10
Separation Neg. Type 2	DK-50	1 + 2	dish tank	3½ 4	3½ 4	4 4½
P.900 Plates	DK-50	undiluted	dish tank	4¾ 5½	5¼ 6	5½ 6½

* Dish agitation should be continuous. Tank agitation once a minute, brief but thorough.

Separation negatives from colour transparencies

Separation negatives are best made by contact printing from sheet-film and roll-film transparencies, and by projection from 35 mm., sizes 126 and 828 transparencies. The equipment for exposing the separation negatives from sheet-film transparencies consists of a light-source over which the separation filters may be placed, and a good printing frame with a strong spring back; if it is proposed to make negatives from 35 mm., sizes 126 and 828 transparencies, a suitable miniature enlarger such as the Kodak Precision Enlarger will be required.

A Kodak Beehive Safelamp mounted on its stand makes a suitable lamphouse for contact-printing. A 60-watt bulb should be used in it and the normal safelight screen should be replaced with an opaque mask with a cut-out aperture suitable for carrying a sheet of flashed opal and the various filters used in the separation of transparencies. If this lamphouse is used 3 ft. from the printing frame, exposures will be of reasonable length. Exposures should not be much shorter than 20 sec. or they become difficult to control with any accuracy.

The transparencies from which the best colour prints can be made are those which are slightly under-exposed (i.e., a little heavy for projection) and critically sharp. Transparencies which when placed on a sheet of white paper make a recognizable colour print are not suitable for reproduction.

To copy transparency originals successfully, retaining all the gradation of tone whilst compressing the overall brightness, it is first necessary to reduce the overall contrast by means of either one or two 'contrast masks' – unsharp, black-and-white negative masks of low contrast. Such masks are made by contact from the original on to a P.900 plate exposed to a light-source covered by, for example, the red filter. The red filter ensures that density is recorded behind the whites, reds and yellows, thus brightening relatively the blue and green areas, which are usually reproduced too dark. The unsharpness is obtained by interposing a clear celluloid spacer of 0·005 in. clear film base between the support side of the transparency and the emulsion of the plate during the exposure. The diffuseness of the mask facilitates registration between mask and transparency, because the need for precise registration is obviated; and at the same time it increases the effective definition.

Contrast masks may also be prepared using Kodak Pan Masking Film. An advantage when using this material is that it can be punched with the Kodak Register Punch (see page 373) and exposed in the Kodak Register Printing Frame. When the original transparency is taped to a strip of film (preferably 'Estar') together with a step tablet, it can also be punched and all the exposing, both masks and separation negatives, can be done in the printing frame without the need for visual registration and taping.

Procedure from sheet or roll Ektachrome originals

Contrast masks: With Ektachrome originals, it is recommended that two masks be made – one through a Wratten No. 29 deep-red filter and one through a Wratten No. 61 deep-green filter. The steps for making these masks are as follows:

1.   Clean the transparency, if necessary, by gently polishing with a soft chamois leather. Slightly moistening the leather with Kodak Movie Film Cleaner will assist in the removal of the more obstinate marks.

2.   With a densitometer measure the brightest highlight and the deepest shadow in which it is desired to record detail in the finished print, and note the nearest corresponding densities on a transparent step-wedge such as the Photographic Step Tablet No. 2. (In this operation specular highlights should be ignored.) Mount the transparency and step-wedge, emulsion-side down, on a sheet of glass from the printing frame or, if pan masking film and the register printing frame are used, tape both the step wedge and the transparency together to a register-punched strip of film. The transparency and wedge should be masked with black adhesive paper stuck to the front of the glass to prevent extraneous light spreading into the picture area. The steps on the Step Tablet which extend beyond the highlight and shadow densities of the transparency may conveniently be masked off at this stage. Mount over the transparency and the wedge

(between transparency and sensitized material) a sheet of 0·005 in. clear film base to act as a spacer when making the unsharp contrast mask (Kodak Matrix Film with the emulsion washed off is quite suitable for this purpose).

3.   Two contrast masks should be made. The exposures are made to a light source screened in one case with a Wratten No. 29 deep-red filter and in the other, with a Wratten No. 61 deep-green filter. In each case the exposure should be adjusted to give a minimum density of between 0·15 and 0·20 in the image of the darkest step of the grey-scale which corresponds to the deepest shadow of the transparency. Dish-develop the film or plate for 2½ min. at 68°F. (20°C.) in Kodak Soft-Gradation or D-165 developer, diluted 1 + 5. This development time gives a gamma of about 0·3 and the resulting density range will therefore be about 30 per cent of the density range of the transparency.

Separation negatives by contact: For making the red-filter and green-filter separations, the Ektachrome original is combined with the mask made through the red filter; and for making the blue-filter separation, the transparency is removed from the first mask and registered with the mask made through the green filter.

After processing and drying the masks, register the transparency and wedge with each one in turn, omitting the celluloid spacer. Again mask the transparency and the wedge with black adhesive paper stuck to the glass side of the contrast mask.

Separation negatives from colour transparencies are made through the Wratten red, green and blue filters given in the table below. The exposure and development should be adjusted to give negatives with a density range suitable for the particular printing process. The exposure should be such that the density of the shadow areas is not less than 0·3 and not greater than 0·4. The Kodak Dye Transfer process for making colour prints on paper can accommodate negatives with density ranges of between 1·0 and 1·8: hence when copying transparencies it is not necessary to adjust the development time for each set of negatives, and only the exposure requires altering to produce the correct minimum density. It is therefore possible to determine the exposure required,

Development times in Minutes at 68°F. (20°C.).

Material	Developer	Dilution	Agitation*	Times for each negative		
				No. 29 (red) filter	No. 61 (green) filter	No. 47B (blue) filter
Separation Neg. Type 1	DK-50	undiluted	dish	5	4	6
			tank	10	10	11
Separation Neg. Type 2	DK-50	1 + 1	dish	4½	4	4½
			tank	5½	5	5½
P.900 plates	DK-50	undiluted	dish	4	4	4
			tank	5	5	5

* Continuous agitation in a dish, or brief but thorough agitation once each minute in a tank.

with fair accuracy, from the shadow density of the transparency. Instructions for preparing a simple chart for this purpose are given in the last section of this chapter.

Work extremely carefully to ensure that the differences in density range between the negatives of a set are not greater than 0·1.

The red-filter mask is registered with the transparency while making the red-filter and green-filter negatives, and the green-filter mask is registered with the transparency while the blue-filter negative is made.

Procedure from 35 mm., sizes 126 and 828 Kodachrome or Ektachrome originals

Contrast mask: The steps in making the contrast mask from 35 mm., sizes 126 or 828 Kodachrome or Ektachrome transparencies are:

1. Clean the transparency by gently polishing with a soft chamois leather. Slightly moistening the leather with Kodak Movie Film Cleaner will assist in the removal of the more obstinate marks.

2. Mount the transparency, together with the step wedge, in a cut-out mask or onto a piece of estar film that can be punched to fit the register printing frame.

3. With a densitometer, measure the brightest highlight and the deepest shadow in which it is desired to record detail in the finished print, and note the nearest corresponding densities on the transparent step-wedge. (In this operation specular highlights should be ignored.) Steps at either end of the wedge should then be masked off, if necessary, so that the densities left on the wedge correspond as nearly as possible with the highlight and shadow densities of the transparency. Mount over the transparency and the wedge a sheet of 0·005 in. clear film base to act as a spacer when making the unsharp contrast mask (Matrix film with the emulsion washed off is quite suitable for this purpose). This assembly is now ready for the making of the contrast mask.

4. The contrast mask is made on a P.900 plate or Pan Masking Film, making the exposure through a Wratten No. 33 medium magenta filter. The exposure should be adjusted to give a minimum density of between 0·15 and 0·20 for the darkest step of the grey-scale, which corresponds to the deepest shadow of the transparency. Dish-develop for $2\frac{1}{2}$ min. at 68°F. (20°C.) in Soft-Gradation or D-165 developer, diluted 1 + 5. This development time gives a gamma of about 0·3 and the resulting density range will therefore be about 30 per cent of the density range of the transparency.

Separation negatives by projection: The contrast mask is registered with the transparency, the register checked with a magnifying glass and they are then bound together. When binding is completed, check that the register has been maintained. The contrast mask is left in position for all three separations.

Place the mask and transparency in the negative carrier, and make the negatives by projection through clean, flat Kodak Wratten gelatin filters which have been mounted close to the lens of the enlarger.

365

With a filter in position, focus the transparency on to a plate which is the same thickness as that on which the negatives are to be made if P.900 plates are to be used for the separation negatives. If the transparency is dense use a clear gelatin or light-coloured filter in place of the Wratten tri-colour filter. On no account vary the aperture to control the exposure time for the different negatives of the set, because this generally results in a slight change of image size and the negatives will not fit.

The filters used are Kodak Wratten tri-colour filters – deep-red No. 29, deep-green No. 61, and deep-blue No. 47B. Since the exposure conditions for suitable miniature enlargers vary considerably, it is not possible to specify average exposure conditions. It is recommended therefore that a simple exposure chart be prepared according to the instructions given below. The development times for an average transparency are given in the table on page 364.

Exposure charts for making separation negatives

Where greater accuracy than is usually employed in black-and-white photography is required, the application of a little elementary sensitometry will enable an operator to produce work of a consistently high standard with a minimum waste of material, time and effort. The making of well-balanced separation negatives from colour transparencies requires considerable skill and practice and, since the densities of the highlight and shadow areas may vary considerably from transparency to transparency, the operator with no knowledge of sensitometry can achieve the high standard required only by trial-and-error: this generally means making several trial strips to ascertain the correct exposure and development times for each new set of negatives.

The Dye Transfer process allows considerable latitude in the density range of the separation negatives; and it is therefore possible to determine once for all the development times for the separation negatives and to adhere to these times so long as the particular batch of photographic material for which they were calculated remains in use. The exposure charts and instructions set out below will enable an operator without any previous knowledge of sensitometry to produce sets of separation negatives from transparencies with confidence that they will be properly matched. Operators who are making several sets of negatives a week, as well as those who make only an occasional set, will find these charts are both simple and worth-while to prepare. The only conditions that must be fulfilled are to work carefully using a densitometer which will read densities from $0—3 \cdot 0$ and to control accurately the conditions affecting development and exposure. Development of the separation negatives is best controlled by tank processing, where a standard agitation procedure is adopted and the developer is properly replenished. The temperature of the solutions can be controlled with a water-jacket. Where the voltage supply is reasonably stable, the exposures are best controlled by seeing that they are of not less than 30 sec. duration. An error of $\frac{1}{2}$ sec. in this exposure time is only $1 \cdot 6$ per cent, whereas a

366

½ sec. error in 5 sec. is 10 per cent. If the voltage fluctuates, some type of voltage control should be installed – see page 287.

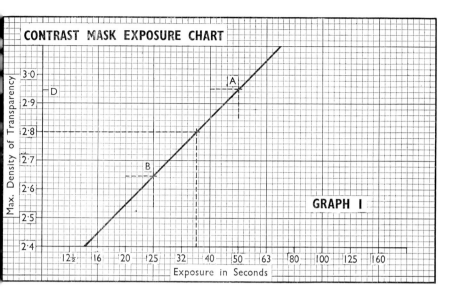

To prepare exposure chart for contrast mask

1.   Mount a Photographic Step Tablet No. 2, emulsion-side down, on the glass sheet of a printing frame and mask it with black tape to prevent extraneous light spreading over the wedge area during exposure. Cover with a clear celluloid spacer of 0·005 in. thickness.

2.   Place the film or plate over the wedge and give an exposure of, say, 50 sec. under the conditions recommended on page 364. Process as described on page 364. If the conditions of working are not the same as those described on pages 363 and 364, then 50 sec. exposure may not be correct and the exposure time and/or lamp, or lamp-to-printing frame distance, must be adjusted until a low-contrast negative, as described in the next step, is obtained.

3.   Mark out on a sheet of graph paper vertical and horizontal scales exactly as shown in Graph 1. When the test strip is dry, find on it the step which has a density of about 0·17 (intermediate between the 0·15 and 0·20 specified on pages 364 and 365) and note the density of the corresponding step on the No. 2 Density Strip: this density will be referred to as D. In the example, density D is 2·95.

4.   Opposite the density D on the vertical scale of the graph and directly above 50 sec. (or the exposure given) on the horizontal scale indicating exposure time, plot a point A.

5.   Now from the density D subtract 0·3, and opposite this total density plot a second point B, immediately above the exposure time in seconds arrived at by halving the exposure given to the test wedge. For the example given in Graph 1 this is 25 sec.

Alternatively, if more convenient, add 0·3 to the density D, and opposite this figure plot the point B immediately above the time arrived at by doubling the original test exposure.

6.   The two points A and B are joined by a straight line (of 45°) which is extended in both directions, and the chart is complete.

To use the chart, read the density of the deepest shadow area of the transparency in which detail is required in the finished colour print. The exposure required is found by reading from the maximum shadow density on the vertical scale to the time in seconds on the horizontal scale. For example, following the dotted line in Graph 1 :

Maximum density of transparency (shadow area) = 2·8
therefore exposure for contrast mask = 36 sec.

When a new batch of films or plates is used for making the contrast masks or when the light-source is changed, the exposure chart must be checked and, if necessary, modified by the operator.

The test described here must be carried out for each different contrast-mask filter, but for convenience the exposures through the different filters can be made in different positions on the same plate as long as precautions are taken to note the filter through which each negative was made. Similarly the lines for the two contrast masks may be plotted on the same graph as long as they are appropriately identified.

To prepare exposure chart for separation negatives made by contact

1.   When preparing the exposure chart for making separation negatives from Ektachrome transparencies, select on a Photographic Step Tablet No. 2 two steps, one with a density of about 3·0 and the other with a density of about 0·5. This will represent the greatest density difference likely to be encountered in an Ektachrome transparency.

2.   Mount the wedge on a glass sheet from a printing frame, mask it with black tape and make a contrast mask giving the exposure indicated by the exposure chart already prepared. Process and dry the contrast mask and register it with the wedge.

3.   Expose the film or plate, behind the combination of wedge and contrast mask, to light filtered by the Wratten No. 29 filter. Find by experiment the exposure and development time necessary to make a negative copy of the wedge which has a minimum density of 0·4 and an overall density range of 1·5—1·6.

If the wedge is properly masked off, a number of test exposures may be made on one plate.

4. By trial and error find the exposure and development times necessary to reproduce identical wedges exposed to light filtered by Wratten No. 61 and No. 47B filters.

5. When the matched wedges have been obtained, prepare on a sheet of graph paper vertical (density) and horizontal (exposure) scales exactly as in Graph 2. Above the exposure times given for each filter, and opposite the sum of the maximum density selected on the wedge (i.e., 3·0) and the density of the corresponding step on the mask (i.e., a density of between 0·15 and 0·20), plot three points R, G, and B for the red, green and blue filter strips respectively.

6. Follow the procedure described in steps 5 and 6 (page 368), under the heading of 'To prepare exposure chart for contrast mask', for each of the points plotted.

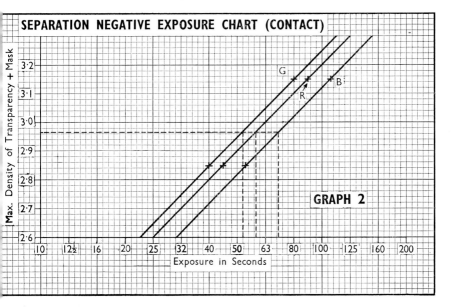

To use the graph, mark off on the vertical scale the density representing the sum of the maximum density of the transparency and the corresponding minimum density of the contrast mask and read off, on the horizontal scale, the appropriate exposure for each filter.

The example shown in Graph 2 is for an Ektachrome transparency with a maximum density of 2·8 plus a contrast mask density of 0·17, giving a total density of 2·97. The exposures indicated are red filter, 58½ sec.; green filter, 52¼ sec.; and blue filter, 70 sec.

The development times remain constant for the same batch of films or plates although, when the developer is in constant use, it may be found that all

369

the negatives are a little too flat or too contrasty; in that event the development times will require to be adjusted accordingly.

To prepare exposure chart for separation negatives
made by projection

The procedure for preparing this chart is similar to that used for the previous one.
The chart will normally be used for miniature Kodachrome or Ektachrome
transparencies mounted with a step wedge (see page 365). When separation
negatives are made by projection, allowance has to be made for the filter factors
by adjusting the length of the exposure, and not the size of the light-source
aperture. This necessitates the use of a more compressed scale for the exposure
time. Therefore instead of the exposure time intervals of 10, $12\frac{1}{2}$, 16, 20, 25, 32,
40, 50, 63, 80, 100, 125, 160 and 200 sec. given in Graph 2 mark the following
exposure times at the same intervals 10, 16, 25, 40, 63, 100, 160, 250, 400, 630,
1,000 and 1,600 sec.

32

Kodak Dye Transfer Process

ALTHOUGH in some measure superseded in speed and simplicity by the making of direct colour prints with Ektacolor paper from Kodacolor and Ektacolor negatives, the Kodak Dye Transfer Process offers a most elegant method of making superb colour prints on paper using dyed relief images, known as matrices. The matrices are made from a set of colour-separation negatives which can be made either directly from the subject or from a Kodachrome or Ektachrome Transparency. When Kodak Pan Matrix film is used, the relief matrices can be made direct from a Kodacolor or Ektacolor negative, since a colour negative is, in effect, a set of colour-separation negatives on one sheet of film.

Methods of making colour-separation negatives suitable for the Dye Transfer Process have been dealt with in the previous chapter, and we shall deal here solely with making the matrices and the colour print.

The process in brief

The process depends on the imbibition of dyes from gelatin relief images by premordanted Dye Transfer paper. Regardless of the starting point – whether separation negatives or a colour negative – the printing procedure is substantially the same. The matrix film is exposed through the base, either by contact or projection, to one of the separation negatives. The three exposed matrices are developed in a tanning developer which renders the gelatin insoluble in proportion to the density of the silver image formed. Development is followed by fixing in a non-hardening fixing bath and the films are then washed in hot water to remove all the gelatin which has retained its solubility. Shadows are thus represented by a thick layer of gelatin, middle tones by intermediate proportions, and highlights by little or no gelatin; in each case the corresponding silver deposit of the image is allowed to remain. The matrices are then dried and they are ready for printing. Printing is accomplished by soaking each of the matrices in a solution of dye of the complementary colour: thus the matrix made from the green-filter separation negative is soaked with magenta dye, the red-filter matrix with cyan dye, and the blue-filter matrix with yellow dye. Each matrix takes up dye in proportion to the thickness of the gelatin, and at this stage the three matrices may be regarded as colour-separation positives. The dye

371

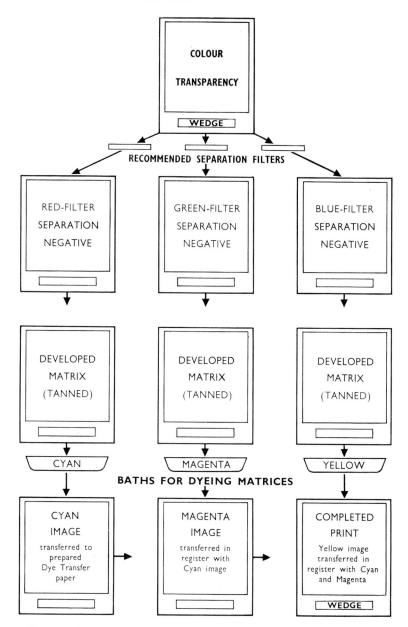

Fig. 32.1. Steps in preparation of Dye-Transfer prints from a transparency.

images are now transferred to a premordanted gelatin-coated paper in exact register in the sequence cyan, magenta and yellow; the result is a full colour print. The time taken to produce the first finished print from the dyeing of the first matrix is about 30 min., and subsequent prints take about 20 min. each.

The process provides a high degree of control over both contrast and colour balance, and the matrices are suitable for the production of a considerable number of duplicate prints.

Basic equipment

This consists of developing dishes, storage bottles, measuring cylinders for 250 cc. and 50 cc., and 10 cc. pipette, thermometer, print roller; Kodak Register Punch, Register Pin Bars and Register Board (or Dye Transfer Blanket). These last items and the dishes, together with chemicals for making up the various processing and dyeing solutions, may be obtained from Kodak Ltd. Full working instructions are also available from Kodak Ltd., and these should be studied carefully by anyone undertaking the Dye Transfer process for the first time. The description of the process given in the following pages should therefore be considered as a résumé and not as a working guide.

Fig. 32.2. Kodak Register Punch.

Kodak Matrix film

This film, the emulsion of which is soluble in hot water, consists of a transparent base on one side of which is coated a yellow-dyed emulsion, primarily blue-sensitive, since exposures are made through black-and-white negatives. The exposure is made through the base. The yellow dye is incorporated to limit the penetration of the exposing light, thus keeping the image near to the base. Kodak Matrix film can be handled by the light of a safelamp fitted with a Wratten Series I (red) filter and a 25-watt bulb at a distance of not less than 4 ft. from the film.

The film should be stored with as much care as for colour film; once a packet has been opened, dimensional changes affecting register may occur under adverse temperature and humidity conditions. For best register, changes in temperature and humidity during the handling of Matrix film should be kept as few and as small as possible. Even more important, the films should be handled in such a way that matrices forming a set receive as nearly identical treatment as possible during exposure, processing and printing.

Kodak Pan Matrix film

This film is designed specifically for preparing Dye Transfer matrices from colour negatives and it has a clear base the same as that of Matrix film. Since exposures are made on to this film through tricolor filters, the emulsion is fully panchromatic and must be handled and developed in total darkness. The emulsion of Pan Matrix film contains a black pigment to limit the penetration of the exposing light; the gelatin relief image obtained with it is otherwise the same as that obtained with ordinary matrix film, and is dyed and transferred in the same manner.

Registration of Matrix film

When printing from a set of separation negatives, the matrix exposures are made from three separate originals and locating the image identically on each matrix so that all three can be transferred in register is difficult. The usual practice is to register the matrices visually after processing.

When the processed and dried matrices have been superimposed in exact register and taped together, one of two procedures can be adopted. The matrices can be punched with the Kodak Register Punch so that they will fit the register pins of the Kodak Register Pin Bar or the Kodak Register Board for transferring in register. Alternatively, they can be trimmed so that the trimmed edges will fit against the locating discs on the Kodak Dye Transfer Blanket.

This latter method of registration has been the most widely used in the past, but is being replaced by the pin register system which is faster, more flexible and gives greater accuracy. Furthermore, it makes the transfer procedures identical for printing from both colour separation negatives and colour negatives.

Registration of Pan Matrix film

When printing from a colour negative, three matrices are exposed from a single original, the position of which need not be changed between exposures. Since Pan Matrix film is used this way, it is punched during manufacture so that the three matrices can be exposed in register and subsequently transferred in register, using the Kodak Register Board or register pin bars set into suitable printing and transferring surfaces.

Exposure of Matrix film

Printing can be done by contact in a printing frame or by projection with an enlarger. For contact printing it is desirable to use a small light-source and a safelamp can be adapted for the purpose in the manner described on page 362. However, if an enlarger is available, this will offer a suitable printing light with the advantage of greater control. The exposure is made through the base of the matrix film. In printing, each negative should be oriented in the same way.

The Matrix film should be masked so as to leave a ⅜ in. border for handling during processing.

When a correctly exposed and processed matrix is dyed, and the dye image is transferred to paper, any diffuse highlight area shows a just perceptible transfer of colour. The exposure given to the cyan printer (the matrix exposed from the red-filter separation negative) determines the over-all print density. With a properly balanced set of dyes, whites, greys and blacks will be produced as neutrals when all three matrices have equal densities in the white, grey and black areas. While slight adjustment may be required at the transfer stage, the first objective is equal densities in the neutral areas. Any adjustment for density differences among the colour-separation negatives at the density corresponding to a diffuse white highlight must therefore be made in exposing the individual matrices.

For contact printing it is preferable to cut a sheet of Matrix film into strips 1½ in. wide and to expose them successively to a series of timed exposures based on steps of ×2. For projection printing trial exposures can be made of a selected part of the subject, such as a face or an area of neutral grey. Alternatively, exposures can be determined with a densitometer by reading the highlight densities in the separation negatives.

Exposure of Pan Matrix film

Pan matrix film can also be exposed by either contact or projection. A suitable enlarger must be equipped with a lamphouse which does not allow stray light to reach the film during exposure, and it must be perfectly rigid; any movement of the enlarger between exposures will result in registration difficulties. Additionally, the enlarger should be equipped to take the tricolor filters through which the exposures are made: Wratten filters numbers 70 (red), 99 (green) and 98 (blue).

A correctly exposed pan matrix will show, after processing, a just perceptible density in the diffuse white highlights of the subject. The exposure necessary to produce this density can be found by making trial exposures through the red filter first to determine overall print density. The colour balance of the final print will then depend upon the relative exposures received by the other two matrices. A balanced set of matrices will show equal densities in those areas which were neutral in the original subject. Alternatively, exposures can be determined with a colour densitometer.

Processing

The exposed films may be developed separately, using fresh developer for each film, or together using interleaving agitation. The developer is a two-part

375

solution which is mixed just before use. It is relatively unstable and turns brown very quickly and must be discarded after being used once. The time of development is 2 min. for matrix film and 3 min. for pan matrix film and should be accompanied with a gentle irregular rocking motion. With interleaving development the procedure recommended for Ektacolor Prints on page 317 should be adopted to ensure that all films receive identical treatment. Development is followed by a 30 sec. water rinse, and fixation for 2 min. in a non-hardening fixing bath.

Wash-off

Two dishes are required if three films are being handled together, both being filled with water at 120°F. (48°C.). The first film is placed in the hot water and given fairly vigorous agitation for 1 min. This removes the bulk of the untanned gelatin. The film is then transferred to the second dish for 30 sec. with normal agitation. When the matrix is removed from the water, any gelatin adhering to the edges of the film should be removed by running the fingers along the edges, taking care not to damage the image. The film should be given two further warm-water rinses, each in fresh water of 120°F. This is followed with a 30 sec. rinse in water at 68°F. (20°C.) to chill the gelatin, after which the matrix is drained and hung up to dry.

Contrast control

One valuable feature of the Dye Transfer Process is the degree of control of both contrast and colour balance that it provides. This control can be effected at the matrix exposure stage by controlling the densities of the matrices (and their contrast in the case of ordinary Matrix film); at the matrix development stage by adjusting the developer, and at the dyeing stage by adjusting the dyes.

Conditioning the paper

The number of sheets of Dye Transfer paper to be used are submerged for at least 10 min. (longer does no harm) in a Conditioner solution. Any paper unused may be squeegeed and dried for future use.

Dyeing the matrices

After preparing the dye solutions, each matrix is placed in its respective dye bath – the red-filter matrix in cyan, the green-filter matrix in magenta and the blue-filter matrix in yellow; this will apply whether the filter specified was used to produce a separation negative or a matrix direct from a colour negative. The dishes should be agitated continuously for about 5 min., when the dyeing will be complete. A longer period in the dye bath does no harm. For example, the magenta and yellow matrices can be left in their dye baths while the cyan matrix is being transferred.

376

First acid rinse

Starting with the cyan matrix, it is first allowed to drain until the solution runs off in droplets, and is then placed in a 1 per cent solution of acetic acid at room temperature with agitation for 1 min. The time should be exact (except when contrast must be increased or reduced) to produce a proper balance in the colour print. It is also important to use the same amount of solution each time, which is discarded after treating one matrix. For example, an 8 × 10 in. print requires about 150 cc. of solution.

Second acid rinse

This second acid rinse is also known as the 'holding bath', because matrices may be left in it for the time ranging from ½ to 3 min. during the period that the paper is being positioned, or in the case of the magenta and yellow matrices, while the preceding matrix is being transferred. The bath is filled to about three-quarters of its depth with 1 per cent acetic acid, and can be used for rinsing until it becomes discoloured.

Positioning Transfer paper

The paper should be positioned and squeegeed on to the transfer surface so that the image will fall on it when the matrix is registered over the register pins. The transfer surface can be a sheet of plate glass equipped with a register pin bar or the Kodak Register Board can be used. If a Dye Transfer Blanket is used, this should be placed so that matrices transfer squarely onto the paper positioned on the transfer surface.

Transfer of cyan image

The matrix is removed from the second rinse and drained for 2 or 3 sec. only and, with the emulsion down, the punch holes are located in the register pins, care being taken to keep the matrix raised so that it does not touch the paper. If a transfer blanket is used, the matrix should be positioned against the locating discs with the blanket held taut and swung away from the transfer paper. The roller is then applied firmly, starting at the register, or blanket end, until the far edge of the print has been reached. Transferring takes about 5 min., and this time should not be exceeded unless the room temperature is below 65°F. (18°C.), or the matrix may be difficult to separate from the paper. During this period the magenta matrix is treated in the two acid rinse baths and held ready in the second while the cyan matrix is being removed. This is accomplished by placing the roller at the far edge of the matrix and rolling it back just far enough to be able to grasp the edge of the matrix. Then the matrix is pulled back slowly, allowing it to push the roller back at the same time. The cyan matrix is now placed in a bath of running water, and the magenta matrix applied in the manner already described for the cyan matrix. When the cyan matrix has been

377

washed for 3 min. it can be returned to the dye bath if further prints are to be made. Otherwise it is given a 5 min. wash at 100°F. followed by a 3 min. wash in water at 68°F. and then hung up to dry. The yellow matrix is applied after the removal of the magenta matrix.

Drying the prints

The finished print can be briefly blotted between photographic blotting paper to remove excess moisture. Drying should be as rapid as possible and the print can be kept flat and the shrinkage minimized by fastening it to a stout board, such as hardboard, with adhesive tape.

Kodak Dye Transfer prints may be mounted and retouched using the same procedure as for Ektacolor prints, see page 321 and page 328.

33

Data on Kodak Colour Films

Acknowledgement is made to Kodak Limited for permission to use their Data Sheets as a basis for this section.

IMPROVEMENTS in products are constantly being made with the result that published recommendations must be changed from time to time. The information contained in this section should therefore be checked with the instructions packed with the film.

Page

KODACOLOR-X FILM

A negative colour film designed for exposures in daylight or with clear flashbulbs. The negatives can be used to obtain Kodacolor prints and enlargements, or they can be printed on Kodak Ektacolor paper. Kodacolor transparencies can be ordered from negatives made with miniature cameras, and enlarged transparencies can be made on Ektacolor Print film.

	Speed and meter settings				
	ASA	B.S.	Weston I and II	DIN	Filter (if any)
Daylight	64/4°	29°	50	19	—
Photoflood ..	40/3·5°	27°	32	17	Wratten No. 82A

The first ASA number is for use with meters and cameras marked for ASA Speeds or Exposure Indices: the second number in the pair (given in degrees) is the ASA Speed Value for the additive exposure system. These meter settings apply to reflected-light and incident-light readings of average subjects.

Light sources. Kodacolor film does not require the use of filters when it is exposed either in daylight or with clear flashbulbs.

When prints are to be made by the user with Ektacolor Paper it is recommended to bring all negatives to approximately the same balance by using filters over the camera lens. One way of working is to expose without a filter when using clear flashbulbs, using a Wratten No. 85C filter for daylight exposures, and a No. 85 filter for electronic flash. With the No. 85C filter, use an ASA setting of 50 or the same lens settings given in the daylight exposure table.

Daylight exposure table. Lens apertures for a shutter speed 1/100-1/125 sec. For the hours from 2 hours after sunrise to 2 hours before sunset.

Bright or Hazy Sun (Distinct Shadows)	Weak Hazy Sun (Soft Shadows)	Cloudy Bright (No Shadows)	Cloudy Dull	Open Shade
$f/11$	$f/8$	$f/5·6$	$f/4$	$f/4$
Exposure Values				
14	13	12	11	11

Light subjects (beaches, distant views, high-altitude snow): ½ stop less exposure. Nearby side or back-lit subjects under bright sun: 1-2 stops more exposure. In winter increase all exposures by 1 stop, but expose for snow scenes as in table.

ill-in flash. In bright sunlight the lighting contrast is frequently excessive with close-up subjects lit from the side or back. Harsh shadows can be lightened by the use of fill-in flash in the form of blue flashbulbs or electronic flash. The following table gives distance ranges at which to use blue flashbulbs.

Daylight exposure	No. 1BS or PF 1B	PF 24/97
$f/22$ at $1/25$–$1/30$ sec.*	7–12 ft.	—
$f/11$ at $1/100$–$1/125$ sec. (M)	11–20 ft.	7–12 ft.

* For all cameras without full XM synchronization.

Clear flashbulbs – guide numbers. To determine the recommended f/number for average subjects, the guide number should be divided by the selected flashbulb-subject distance in feet. For capless bulbs the guide numbers apply to use in average domestic rooms, those for large bulbs to use in large areas (i.e. commercial and industrial interiors). Increase exposure by at least 1 stop in large dark interiors, outdoors at night, or for dark subjects. Decrease exposure by 1 stop in small light rooms or for light subjects. For flashbulb-subject distances less than 5 ft. $\frac{1}{2}$ stop additional exposure is advised. For open-flash with focal-plane shutters, use the bulbs and guide numbers for diaphragm shutters.

Shutter speed and synchronization for diaphragm shutters	Diaphragm shutters					Focal-plane shutters	
	AG 1	PF 1 No. 1	PF 5 No. 5	PF 60 No. 22	PF 100 Open-flash or M synch. only	PF 24	PF 45
Open flash — ⎫ Up to 1/30 X ⎬	125	100	160	280	360	—	—
1/50–1/60 M	110	90	140	250	—	100	140
1/100–1/125 M	100	80	125	220	—	72	100
1/200–1/250 M	80	64	100	180	—	50	72

The figures for PF 1 and No. 1 bulbs apply to 4-inch reflectors. When 2-inch reflectors are used, open the lens by $\frac{1}{2}$-stop.

Electronic flash. When exposing negatives intended for ordering Kodacolor Prints, a Wratten No. 85 filter should be used over the lens for indoor exposures. Guide numbers recommended by the manufacturer of the unit may be taken as the basis for trial exposures.

Processing. The film should be processed as soon as possible after exposure. It may be returned to a dealer for processing (the price of the film does not include processing), or it may be processed by the user in chemicals available as Kodak Colour Film Processing Chemicals, Process C-22.

Sizes available. CX 135, 12 and 20-exposure cassettes, and 828, 127 and 120/620 roll film, also 12-exposure Kodapak cartridges.

381

KODAK EKTACOLOR PROFESSIONAL FILM, TYPE S (PROCESS C-22)

A film designed for making colour negatives at exposure times of 1/10 sec. or shorter. It is balanced for exposures without a filter by electronic flash, daylight, or blue flashbulbs, and with clear flashbulbs with a Wratten No. 80C filter. The negatives can be printed on Ektacolor paper, and can also be used to obtain positive transparencies on Ektacolor Print film, or black-and-white prints on Kodak Panalure paper.

	Speed and meter settings			
	ASA*	B.S.	Weston I and II	DIN
Daylight	80/4·5°	30°	64	20

* The figure given in degrees is the ASA Speed Value for the additive exposure system. The meter settings appy to properly-made reflected-light and incident-light readings of average subjects.

Caution: Do not expose Type S film for times longer than 1/10 sec., because the resulting negatives may contain colour-reproduction errors that cannot be corrected satisfactorily in the printing operation. For long exposures use Type L film.

Light-sources and filters. The use of Photoflood lamps is recommended only if sufficient light can be obtained to permit an exposure time of 1/10 sec. or shorter. The ASA speed of the film with Photoflood lamps and a Wratten 80B filter should then be taken as 32/3·5°.

Daylight Exposure Table. Lens apertures based on a shutter speed of 1/100-1/125 sec. For the hours from 2 hours after sunrise to 2 hours before sunset.

Bright or Hazy Sun (Distinct Shadows)	Weak Hazy Sun (Soft Shadows)	Cloudy Bright (No Shadows)	Cloudy Dull	Open Shade
f/16	f/11	f/8	f/5·6	f/5·6
Exposure Values				
15	14	13	12	12

Light subjects (beaches, distant views, high-altitude snow): ½ stop less exposure. Nearby side or back-lit subjects under bright sun: 1-2 stops more exposure. In winter increase all exposures by 1 stop, but expose for snow scenes as in table.

Fill-in flash. In bright sunlight the lighting contrast is frequently excessive with close-up subjects lit from the side or back. Harsh shadows can be avoided by the use of fill-in flash in the form of electronic flash or blue flashbulbs. The following table gives distance ranges at which to use blue flashbulbs.

Daylight exposure	No. 1BS or PF 1B	PF 24/97
f/22 at 1/25–1/30 sec.*	7–12 ft.	—
f/11 at 1/100–1/125 sec. (M)	11–20 ft.	7–12 ft.

* For all cameras without full XM synchronization.

Blue flashbulbs – guide numbers. To determine the recommended f/number for average subjects, the guide number should be divided by the selected flashbulb-subject distance in feet. For capless bulbs the guide numbers apply to use in average domestic rooms, those for large bulbs to use in large areas (i.e. commercial and industrial interiors). Increase exposure by at least 1 stop in large dark interiors, outdoors at night, or for dark subjects. Decrease exposure by 1 stop in small light rooms or for light subjects. For flashbulb-subject distances less than 5 ft. ½ stop additional exposure should be given. For open-flash with focal-plane shutters, use the bulbs and guide numbers for diaphragm shutters.

Blue Flashbulbs						
Shutter speed and synchronization for diaphragm shutters	Diaphragm shutters				Focal-plane shutters	
	AG 1B PF 1B No. 1BS	Atlas Double-lite	PF 60/97 No. 22B	PF 100/97 Open-flash or M synch. only	PF 24/97	PF 45/97
Open flash — ⎫ Up to 1/30 X ⎬	110	160	250	320	—	—
1/50–1/60 M	100	140	220	—	80	110
1/100–1/125 M	90	125	200	—	56	80
1/200–1/250 M	72	100	160	—	40	56

The figures for PF 1B and No. 1BS bulbs apply to 4-inch reflectors. When 2-inch reflectors are used, open the lens by ½ stop.

continued over page

Kodak Ektacolor Professional Film, Type S, *continued*

	Clear Flashbulbs (with Wratten 80B filter)						
Shutter speeds and synchronization for diaphragm shutters	Diaphragm shutters					Focal-plane shutters	
	AG 1	PF 1 No. 1	PF 5 No. 5	PF 60 No. 22	PF 100 Open-flash or M synch. only	PF 24	PF 45
Open flash — ⎫ Up to 1/30 X ⎬	90	72	110	200	250	—	—
1/50–1/60 M	80	64	100	180	—	72	100
1/100–1/125 M	72	56	90	160	—	50	72
1/200–1/250 M	56	45	72	125	—	36	50

The figures for PF 1 and No. 1 bulbs apply to 4-inch reflectors. When 2-inch reflectors are used open the lens by ½ stop.

Electronic flash. This can be used as the sole light or for fill-in flash. No filter is needed when used as the sole light. Guide numbers recommended by the manufacturer of the unit can be taken as the basis for trial exposures.

Processing. Ektacolor Professional Film, Type S is not processed by Kodak Ltd. Packed chemicals for preparing a complete set of solutions are available as Kodak Colour Film Processing Chemicals, Process C-22.

Sizes available. Sheet film $2\frac{1}{2} \times 3\frac{1}{2}$, $3\frac{1}{4} \times 4\frac{1}{4}$, 4×5, $4\frac{3}{4} \times 6\frac{1}{2}$, 5×7 and 8×10 inches. The film is also available in 35 mm. long lengths and as 120-size roll film.

KODAK EKTACOLOR PROFESSIONAL FILM, TYPE L (LONG EXPOSURE)

A sheet film designed for making negatives at exposure times of 1/10 sec. to 60 sec. with 3,200°K lamps or, with appropriate filters, by Photoflood lamps or daylight. The negatives can be printed on Ektacolor paper, and can also be used to obtain positive transparencies on Ektacolor Print film or black-and-white prints on Kodak Panalure paper.

			Speed and meter settings				
Light-source	Wratten Filter No.	Exposure Time	ASA*	B.S.	Weston I and II	DIN
3,200°K	None	1/10 sec.	80/4·5°	80	64	20
3,200°K	None	1 sec.	64/4°	64	50	19
3,200°K	None	5 sec.	50/4°	50	40	18
3,200°K	None	60 sec.	25/3°	25	20	15
Photoflood	81A	1 sec.	50/4°	50	40	18
Daylight	85	1/10 sec.	50/4°	50	40	18

* The figure given in degrees is the ASA Speed Value for use with the additive exposure system.

If the length of the exposure time is not known, the meter can be set tentatively to the settings given for the 5 sec. exposure time. The exposure setting should then be changed, in accordance with the table above, if the exposure time calculated for a particular lens aperture is substantially greater or less than that for 5 sec., and the exposure time re-calculated.

Caution: Do not expose Type L film for times shorter than 1/10 sec. or longer than 60 sec., because the resulting negatives may contain colour-reproduction errors that cannot be satisfactorily corrected in the printing operation. For short exposures, use Ektacolor Professional Film, Type S.

3,200°K lamp exposure table. Based on the use of two 500-watt (photopearl) lamps in studio lighting units, both being at the same distance and within 45° of the camera-subject axis. One lamp (as fill-in) should be as near the camera as possible. Exposures will vary to some extent according to the shape and surface of the reflectors used, and also the amount of reflected light from walls, ceiling, etc.

The lens apertures given are for an exposure time of 1 sec. (64/4° ASA).

Lamp-subject distance	20 ft. 6·5 m.	14 ft. 4·5 m.	10 ft. 3 m.	7 ft. 2·3 m.	5 ft. 1·7 m.
f/number	f/4	f/5·6	f/8	f/11	f/16

Processing. Ektacolor Film is not processed by Kodak Ltd. Packed chemicals for preparing a complete set of solutions are available as Kodak Colour Film Processing Chemicals, Process C-22.
Sizes available. Sheet film of $2\frac{1}{4} \times 3\frac{1}{4}$, $3\frac{1}{4} \times 4\frac{1}{4}$, 4×5, $4\frac{3}{4} \times 6\frac{1}{2}$, 5×7, and 8×10 inches.

23A

KODAK EKTACHROME-X FILM (PROCESS E-2)

A reversal colour film designed for user-processing and balanced for exposure in daylight. After reversal processing it yields positive transparencies for projection. The transparencies can be used to obtain Kodachrome prints and enlargements, direct duplicate transparencies, and, via an internegative, black-and-white prints, colour prints and enlarged transparencies.

	Speed and meter settings				
	ASA	B.S.	Weston I and II	DIN	Filter (if any)
Daylight	64/4°	29°	50	19	—
Photoflood ..	25/3°	25°	20	15	Wratten No. 80B

The first ASA number is for use with meters and cameras marked for ASA Speeds or Exposure Indices: the second number in the pair (given in degrees) is the ASA Speed Value for the additive exposure system. These meter settings apply to reflected-light and incident-light readings of average subjects.

Daylight exposure table. Lens apertures for shutter speeds 1/100-1/125 sec. For the hours from 2 hours after sunrise to 2 hours before sunset.

Bright or Hazy Sun (Distinct Shadows)	Weak Hazy Sun (Soft Shadows)	Cloudy Bright (No Shadows)	Cloudy Dull	Open Shade
f/11	f/8	f/5·6	f/4	f/4
Exposure Values				
14	13	12	11	11

Light subjects (beaches, distant views, high-altitude snow): ½ stop less exposure. Nearby side or back-lit subjects under bright sun: 1-2 stops more exposure. In winter increase all exposures by 1 stop, but expose for snow scenes as in table.

Fill-in flash. In bright sunlight the lighting contrast is frequently excessive with close-up subjects lit from the side or back. Harsh shadows can be lightened by the use of fill-in flash in the form of blue flashbulbs or electronic flash. The following table gives distance ranges at which to use blue flashbulbs.

Daylight exposure	No. 1BS or PF 1B	PF 24/97
f/22 at 1/25–1/30 sec.*	7–12 ft.	—
f/11 at 1/100–1/125 sec. (M)	11–20 ft.	7–12 ft.

* For all cameras without full XM synchronization.

Light sources. In general, the best colour rendering is obtained in clear or hazy sun. The bluish cast which is evident in pictures taken in the shade under a clear blue sky can be minimized by the use of the Kodak Skylight Filter (Wratten 1A), which requires no increase in exposure. This filter is also useful for reducing bluishness in pictures taken on an overcast day and in distant scenes, mountain views, sunlit snow scenes, and aerial photographs.

Blue flashbulbs – guide numbers. Although intended for supplementing daylight, blue flashbulbs can be used as the sole light-source.

To determine the recommended f/number for average subjects, the guide number should be divided by the selected flashbulb-subject distance in feet. For capless bulbs the guide numbers apply to use in average domestic rooms, those for large bulbs to use in large areas (i.e. commercial and industrial interiors). Increase exposure by at least 1 stop in large dark interiors, outdoors at night, or for dark subjects. Decrease exposure by 1 stop in small light rooms or for light subjects. For flashbulb-subject distances less than 5 ft. $\frac{1}{2}$ stop additional exposure is recommended. For open-flash with focal-plane shutters, use the bulbs and guide numbers for diaphragm shutters.

Shutter speed and synchronization for diaphragm shutters	Diaphragm shutters				Focal-plane shutters	
	AG 1B PF 1B No. 1BS	Atlas Double-lite	PF 60/97 No. 22B	PF 100/97 Open-flash or M synch. only	PF 24/97	PF 45/97
Open flash — ⎫ Up to 1/30 X ⎬	100	140	220	280	—	—
1/50–1/60 M ⎭	90	125	200	—	72	100
1/100–1/125 M	80	110	180	—	50	72
1/200–1/250 M	64	90	140	—	36	50

The figures for PF 1B and No. 1BS bulbs apply to 4-inch reflectors. When 2-inch reflectors are used, open up the lens aperture by $\frac{1}{2}$ stop.

Electronic flash. These units can be used as the sole light-source or for fill-in flash. Normally no filter is needed when used as the sole light-source, but pictures showing a bluish cast will suggest the use of a Wratten No. 81A filter. The guide numbers provided by the manufacturer of the unit can be taken as the basis for trial exposures.

Processing. The film should be processed as soon as possible after exposure. It may be returned to a dealer for processing (the price of the film does not include processing), or it may be processed by the user in chemicals available as Ektachrome Film Processing Chemicals, Process E-2.

Sizes available. EX 135, 20- and 36-exposure cassettes, and 127 and 120/620 roll film, also 20-exposure Kodapak cartridges.

23B

KODAK EKTACHROME FILM, DAYLIGHT TYPE (PROCESS E-3)

A colour sheet film balanced for exposure in daylight and designed for reversal processing to produce positive colour transparencies. These are suitable for viewing by transmitted light or by projection, and can be printed in colour by photo-mechanical methods, the Kodak Dye Transfer process, or via an inter-negative on Ektacolor paper and Ektacolor Print film. This film is also available in No. 120 roll film as Kodak Ektachrome Professional Film, Daylight Type (Process E-3).

Important. These instructions are based on average emulsions used under average conditions. Information applying to a film of specific emulsion number is given as supplementary data in the instruction sheet packed with the film.

Speed and meter settings				
	ASA	B.S.	Weston I and II	DIN
Daylight	50/4°	28°	40	18

The first ASA number is for use with meters and cameras marked with ASA Speeds or Exposure Indices: the second number of the pair (given in degrees) is the ASA Speed Value for the additive exposure system. These meter settings apply to properly-made reflected-light and incident-light readings for average subjects.

Daylight exposure table. Lens apertures at a shutter speed of from 1/50–1/60 sec. for average emulsions, from 2 hours after sunrise to 2 hours before sunset.

Bright or Hazy Sun (Distinct Shadows)	Weak Hazy Sun (Soft Shadows)	Cloudy Bright (No Shadows)	Cloudy Dull	Open Shade
f/16	f/11	f/8	f/5·6	f/5·6
Exposure Values				
14	13	12	11	11

Light subjects (beaches, distant views, high-altitude snow): ½ stop less exposure. Nearby side or back-lit subjects under bright sun: 1-2 stops more exposure. In winter increase all exposures by 1 stop, but expose for snow scenes as in table.

Fill-in flash. In bright sunlight the lighting contrast is frequently excessive with close-up subjects lit from the side or back. Harsh shadows can be lightened by the use of fill-in flash in the form of blue flashbulbs or electronic flash. The following table gives distance ranges at which to use blue flashbulbs.

Daylight exposure	No. 1BS or PF 1B	PF 24/97
f/22 at 1/25–1/30 sec.*	7–12 ft.	—
f/16 at 1/50–1/60 sec.	9–15 ft.	7–12 ft.

* For all cameras without full XM synchronization.

Light sources. In general the best colour rendering is obtained in clear or hazy sunlight. Other light-sources may not give equally good results even with the most appropriate filters. The bluish cast which is evident in pictures taken in shade under a clear blue sky can be minimized by the use of the Kodak Skylight Filter (Wratten No. 1A), which requires no increase in exposure. This filter is also useful in reducing bluishness in pictures taken on an overcast day and in distant scenes, mountain views, sunlit snow scenes, and aerial photographs.

Blue flashbulbs – guide numbers. Although intended for supplementing daylight, blue flashbulbs can be used in an emergency as the sole light-source. To determine the recommended f/number for average subjects, the guide number should be divided by the selected flashbulb-subject distance in feet. For capless bulbs the guide numbers apply to exposures in average domestic rooms, those for large bulbs to exposures in large areas (i.e. commercial and industrial interiors). Increase exposure by at least 1 stop in large dark interiors, outdoors at night, or for dark subjects. For flashbulb-subject distances less than 5 ft. ½ stop additional exposure is recommended. For open-flash with focal-plane shutters, use the bulbs and guide numbers for diaphragm shutters.

Shutter speed and synchronization for diaphragm shutters	Diaphragm shutters				Focal-plane shutters	
	AG 1B PF 1B No. 1BS	Atlas Double-lite	PF 60/97 No. 22B	PF 100/97 Open-flash or M synch. only	PF 24/97	PF 45/97
Open-flash — ⎱ Up to 1/30 X ⎰	90	125	200	250	—	—
1/50–1/60 M	80	110	180	—	64	90
1/100–1/150 M	72	100	160	—	45	64
1/200–1/250 M	56	80	125	—	32	45

The figures for PF 1B and No. 1BS bulbs apply to 4-inch reflectors. When 2-inch reflectors are used, open up the lens aperture by ½ stop.

continued over page

Kodak Ektachrome Film, Daylight Type (Process E-3) *continued*

Electronic flash. These units can be used as the sole light-source, though some filtration may be necessary as indicated in the supplementary data in the instruction sheet packed with the film. The guide numbers provided by the manufacturer of the unit can be taken as the basis for trial exposures.

Processing. The film should be processed as soon as possible after exposure, and is designed to be processed in chemicals available as Ektachrome Film Processing Chemicals, Process E-3.

Sizes available. Sheet film sizes $2\frac{1}{2} \times 3\frac{1}{2}$, $3\frac{1}{4} \times 4\frac{1}{4}$, 4×5, $4\frac{3}{4} \times 6\frac{1}{2}$, $6\frac{1}{2} \times 8\frac{1}{2}$, 8×10 inches, and 9×12 centimetres. Also available in No. 120 roll film under the name, Kodak Ektachrome Professional Film, Daylight Type (Process E-3).

KODAK EKTACHROME FILM TYPE B (PROCESS E-3)

A colour sheet film balanced for exposure with 3,200°K lamps and designed for reversal processing to produce positive transparencies. These are suitable for viewing by transmitted light or by projection, and can be printed by photo-mechanical methods, the Kodak Dye Transfer process, or, via an internegative, on Ektacolor paper and Ektacolor Print film.

Important: These instructions are based on average emulsions used under average conditions. Information applying to film of a specific emulsion number is given as supplementary data in the instruction sheet packed with the film.

ASA speed and meter settings					
	ASA	B.S.	Weston I and II	DIN	Filter (if any)
3,200°K lamps ..	32/3·5°	26°	24	16	—
Photoflood lamps ..	25/3°	25°	20	15	Wratten No. 81A
Daylight	25/3°	25°	20	15	Wratten No. 85B

The first ASA number is for use with meters and cameras marked for ASA Speeds or Exposure Indices: the second number in the pair (given in degrees) is the ASA Speed Value for the additive exposure system. These meter settings apply to properly-made reflected-light and incident-light readings of average subjects.

3,200°K lamp exposure table. Based on the use of two Photopearl lamps (500-watt) in studio lighting units, both being at the same distance and within 45° of the camera-subject axis. One lamp (as fill-in) should be as near the camera as possible. Exposures will vary to some extent according to the shape and surface of the reflectors used, and also the amount of light reflected from walls, etc.

Lamp-Subject Distances	20 ft. 6·5 m.	14 ft. 4·5 m.	10 ft. 3 m.	7 ft. 2·3 m.	5 ft. 1·7 m.
f/number at ¼ sec.	f/4	f/5·6	f/8	f/11	f/16

Daylight exposures. Used with a Wratten No. 85B filter the film has the same speed as Kodachrome II Film Daylight Type. The exposure table given in the data sheet for this film may therefore be used as a guide to exposing Ektachrome Film Type B.

Clear flashbulbs – guide numbers. The recommended guide numbers are based on the use of a Wratten No. 81C filter. To determine the f/number for average subjects, the guide number should be divided by the selected flashbulb-subject distance in feet. For capless bulbs the guide numbers apply to exposures in average domestic rooms, those for large bulbs to use in large areas (i.e. commercial and industrial interiors). Increase exposure by at least 1 stop in large dark interiors, outdoors at night, or for dark subjects. Decrease exposure by 1 stop in small light rooms or for light subjects. For flashbulb-subject distances of less than 5 ft. an additional ½ stop in exposure is recommended. For open-flash with focal-plane shutters, use bulbs and guide numbers for diaphragm shutters.

Shutter speed and synchronization for diaphragm shutters	Diaphragm shutters					Focal-plane shutters	
	AG 1	PF 1 No. 1	PF 5 No. 5	PF 60 No. 22	PF 100 Open-flash or M synch. only	PF 24	PF 45
Open flash — ⎫ Up to 1/30 X ⎭	72	56	90	160	200	—	—
1/50–1/60 M	64	50	80	140	—	56	80
1/100–1/125 M	56	45	72	125	—	40	56
1/200–1/250 M	45	36	56	100	—	28	40

The figures for PF 1 and No. 1 bulbs apply to 4-inch reflectors. When 2-inch reflectors are used, open the lens by ½ stop.

Processing. The film should be processed as soon as possible after exposure. It is designed to be processed in chemicals available as Ektachrome Film Processing Chemicals, Process E-3.

Sizes available. Sheet film sizes 2½ × 3½, 3¼ × 4¼, 4 × 5, 4¾ × 6½, 6½ × 8½, 8 × 10 inches, and 9 × 12 centimetres.

391

KODAK HIGH SPEED EKTACHROME FILM, DAYLIGHT TYPE (PROCESS E-2)

A reversal colour film for miniature cameras and recommended for photography of fast action, interiors lit by daylight, close-ups which require the utmost depth of field, etc. It is balanced for exposure by daylight, and is also suitable for exposure by blue flashbulbs and electronic flash. When processed, it yields transparencies for projection which can also be used to obtain colour prints and enlargements.

	Speed and meter settings				
	ASA	B.S.	Weston I and II	DIN	Filter (if any)
Daylight	160/5·5°	33°	125	23	—
Photoflood ..	80/4·5°	30°	64	20	Wratten No. 80B

The first ASA number is for use with meters and cameras marked for ASA Speeds or Exposure Indices: the second number in the pair (given in degrees) is the ASA Speed Value for the additive exposure system. These meter settings apply to properly-made reflected-light and incident-light readings of average subjects.

Most shutters, except focal plane shutters, have the high speed settings calibrated for the maximum lens openings. They are relatively more efficient at small lens openings, and so pass more light than calculated. Therefore under lighting conditions which call for small lens apertures at high shutter speeds, use an aperture ½ stop smaller than that indicated by the exposure meter. The following table makes allowance for this shutter speed efficiency.

Daylight exposure table. For average front-lit subjects from 2 hours after sunrise to 2 hours before sunset.

Bright or Hazy Sun (Distinct Shadows)	Weak Hazy Sun (Soft Shadows)	Cloudy Bright (No Shadows)	Cloudy Dull	Open Shade
f/16	f/11	f/8	f/5·6	f/5·6
Exposure Values				
16	15	14	13	13

Light subjects (beaches, distant views, high-altitude snow): ½ stop less exposure. Nearby side or back-lit subjects under bright sun: 1-2 stops more exposure. In winter increase all exposures by 1 stop, but expose for snow scenes as in table.

Fill-in flash. In bright sunlight the lighting contrast is frequently excessive with close-up subjects lit from the side or back. Harsh shadows can be lightened by the use of fill-in flash in the form of blue flashbulbs or electronic flash. The following table gives distance ranges at which to use blue flashbulbs.

Daylight exposure	No. 1BS or PF 1B	PF 24/97
1/100–1/125, f/22	9–18 ft.	6–10 ft.

Light sources. In general, good colour rendering is obtained under most forms of daylight. With subjects in open shade and lit by a clear blue sky, it is desirable to use a Kodak Skylight Filter (Wratten No. 1A). The film can be used without a filter for subjects lit with white fluorescent lighting, but is not recommended for use with tungsten light sources since the necessary filtration results in a substantial loss of speed. For Photoflood, photopearl and other tungsten light-sources, the Type B version of this film is recommended.

Blue flashbulbs – guide numbers. The following table applies to the use of blue flashbulbs as the sole light-source. To determine the recommended *f*/number for average subjects, the guide number should be divided by the selected flashbulb-subject distance in feet. For capless bulbs the guide numbers apply to use in average domestic rooms, those for larger bulbs to use in large areas (i.e. commercial and industrial interiors). Increase exposure by at least 1 stop in large dark interiors, outdoors at night, or for dark subjects. Decrease exposure by 1 stop in small light rooms or for light subjects. For flash-subject distances less than 5 ft. ½ stop additional exposure is recommended. For open-flash with focal-plane shutters, use the bulbs and guide numbers for diaphragm shutters.

Shutter speed and synchronization for diaphragm shutters	Diaphragm shutters				Focal-plane shutters	
	AG 1B PF 1B No. 1BS	Atlas Double-lite	PF 60/97 No. 22B	PF 100/97 Open-flash or M synch. only	PF 24/97	PF 45/97
Open-flash — ⎫	160	220	360	450	—	—
Up to 1/30 X ⎬						
1/50–1/60 M ⎭	140	200	320	—	110	160
1/100–1/125 M	125	180	280	—	80	110
1/200–1/250 M	100	140	220	—	56	80

The figures for PF 1B and No. 1BS bulbs apply to 4-inch reflectors. When 2-inch reflectors are used, open up the lens aperture by ½ stop.

continued over page

Kodak High Speed Ektachrome Film, Daylight Type (Process E-2) *continued*

Electronic flash. These units can be used as the sole light-source and for fill-in flash. No filter is normally needed when used as the sole light-source, but pictures showing a bluish cast will suggest that a Wratten 81A filter should be used. The guide numbers provided by the manufacturer of the unit can be taken as the basis for trial exposures.

Processing. The film should be processed as soon as possible after exposure. The film may be returned to a dealer for processing (the price of the film does not include processing), or may be processed by the user. It is designed to be processed in chemicals available as Ektachrome Film Processing Chemicals, Process E-2.

Sizes available. EH 135 20-exposure cassettes; No. 120 roll film.

KODAK HIGH SPEED EKTACHROME FILM, TYPE B (PROCESS E-2)

A colour reversal film balanced for exposure with 3,200°K. lamps. It is a special-purpose, high-speed film intended primarily for use under existing tungsten light conditions. When processed, it yields transparencies for projection or direct viewing.

Speed and meter settings					
	ASA	B.S.	Weston I and II	DIN	Filter (if any)
Photopearl (and 3200°K lamps)	125/5°	32°	100	22	—
Photoflood lamps ..	100/5°	31°	80	21	Wratten No. 81A
Daylight	80/4·5°	30°	64	20	Wratten No. 85B

The first ASA number is for use with meters and cameras marked for ASA Speeds or Exposure Indices: the second number in the pair (given in degrees) is the ASA Speed Value for the additive exposure system. These meter settings apply to properly made reflected-light and incident-light readings of average subjects.

Photopearl lamp exposure table. Based on the use of two lamps in studio lighting units, both being at the same distance and within 45° of the camera-subject axis. One lamp (as fill-in) should be as near the camera as possible. Exposures will vary to some extent according to the shape and surface of the reflectors used, and also the amount of reflected light from walls, ceiling, etc.

Lamp-Subject Distances	20 ft. 6·5 m.	14 ft. 4·5 m.	10 ft. 3 m.	7 ft. 2·3 m.	5 ft. 1·7 m.
f/number at 1/15 sec.	f/4	f/5·6	f/8	f/11	f/16

Trial exposure settings for existing-light conditions. Sports Arenas: about 30 to 40 foot-candles of incident illumination: 1/50 sec. at f/2. Work Areas – Store Interiors: about 60 to 80 foot-candles of incident illumination: 1/50 sec. at f/2·8. *Daylight exposures.* Used with the Wratten No. 85B filter, the film has half the speed of High Speed Ektachrome Film, Daylight Type. The recommendations given in the daylight exposure table for Daylight Type film should therefore be increased by 1 stop.

Clear flashbulbs – guide numbers. The recommended guide numbers are based on the use of a Wratten No. 81C filter. To determine the f/number for average subjects, the guide number should be divided by the selected flashbulb-subject distance in feet. For capless bulbs the guide numbers apply to use in average domestic rooms; those for large bulbs apply to use in large areas (i.e. commercial and industrial interiors). Increase exposure by at least 1 stop in large dark interiors, outdoors at night, or for dark subjects. Decrease exposure by 1 stop in small light rooms or for light subjects. For flashbulb-subject distances of less than 5 ft. an additional ½ stop exposure is recommended. For open-flash with focal-plane shutters, use bulbs and guide numbers for diaphragm shutters.

Shutter speed and synchronization for diaphragm shutters	Diaphragm shutters					Focal-plane shutters	
	AG 1	PF 1 No. 1	PF 5 No. 5	PF 60 No. 22	PF 100 Open-flash or M synch. only	PF 24	PF 45
Open flash — ⎫ Up to 1/30 X ⎰	140	110	180	320	400	—	—
1/50–1/60 M	125	100	160	280	—	110	160
1/100–1/125 M	110	90	140	250	—	80	110
1/200–1/250 M	90	72	110	200	—	56	80

The figures for PF 1 and No. 1 bulbs apply to 4-inch reflectors. When 2-inch reflectors are used, open the lens by ½ stop.

Processing. The film should be processed as soon as possible after exposure. It may be returned to a dealer for processing (the price of the film does not include processing), or it may be processed by the user. It is designed to be processed in chemicals available as Ektachrome Film Processing Chemicals, Process E-2. *Sizes available.* EHB 135 20-exposure cassettes; No. 120 film.

KODACHROME II FILM, FOR DAYLIGHT

A colour film designed for use in miniature cameras and balanced for exposure in daylight. After reversal processing, it yields positive transparencies for projection. The transparencies can be used to obtain Kodachrome prints and enlargements, direct duplicate transparencies, and, via an internegative, black-and-white prints, colour prints, and enlarged transparencies.

	Speed and meter settings			
	ASA	B.S.	Weston I and II	DIN
Daylight	25/3°	25°	20	15
Photoflood*	12/2°	22°	10	12

* Not recommended: in emergency use Wratten No. 80B filter

The first ASA number is for use with meters and cameras marked for ASA Speeds or Exposures Indices: the second number in the pair (given in degrees) is the ASA Speed Value for the additive exposure system. These meter settings apply to properly-made reflected-light and incident-light readings of average subjects.

Daylight exposure table. Lens openings at shutter speeds stated from 2 hours after sunrise to 2 hours before sunset.

Bright or Hazy Sun (Distinct Shadows)	Weak Hazy Sun (Soft Shadows)	Cloudy Bright (No Shadows)	Cloudy Dull	Open Shade
Shutter at 1/100 or 1/125 sec.		Shutter at 1/50 or 1/60 sec.		
f/8	f/5·6	f/5·6	f/4	f/4
Exposure Values				
13	12	11	10	10

Light subjects (beaches, distant views, high-altitude snow): ½ stop less exposure. Nearby side or back-lit subjects under bright sun: 1-2 stops more exposure. In winter increase all exposures by 1 stop, but expose for snow scenes as in table.

Fill-in flash. In bright sunlight the lighting contrast is frequently excessive with close-up subjects lit from the side or back. Harsh shadows can be lightened by the use of fill-in flash in the form of blue flashbulbs or electronic flash. The following table gives distance ranges at which to use blue flashbulbs.

Daylight exposure	No. 1BS or PF 1B	PF 24/97
f/16 at 1/25–1/30 sec.*	7–12 ft.	—
f/11 at 1/50–1/60 sec.	9–15 ft.	7–12 ft.

* For all cameras without full XM synchronization.

Light sources. In general, the best colour rendering is obtained in clear or hazy sunlight. The bluish cast which is evident in pictures taken in shade under a clear blue sky can be minimized by the use of the Kodak Skylight Filter (Wratten No. 1A), which requires no increase in exposure. This filter is also useful for reducing bluishness in pictures taken on an overcast day and in distant scenes, mountain views, sunlit snow scenes, and aerial photographs.

Blue flashbulbs – guide numbers. Although intended for supplementing daylight, blue flashbulbs can be used as the sole light-source. To determine the recommended f/number for average subjects, the guide number should be divided by the selected flashbulb-subject distance in feet. For capless bulbs the guide numbers apply to use in average domestic rooms, those for large bulbs to use in large areas (i.e. commercial and industrial interiors). Increase exposure by at least 1 stop in large dark interiors, outdoors at night, or for dark subjects. Decrease exposure by 1 stop in small light rooms or for light subjects. For flash-to-subject distances less than 5 ft. ½ stop additional exposure is advised. For open-flash with focal-plane shutters, use the bulbs and guide numbers for diaphragm shutters.

Shutter speed and synchronization for diaphragm shutters	Diaphragm shutters				Focal-plane shutters	
	AG 1B PF 1B No. 1BS	Atlas Double-lite	PF 60/97 No. 22B	PF 100/97 Open-flash or M synch. only	PF 24/97	PF 45/97
Open flash —⎫ Up to 1/30 X⎬	64	90	140	180	—	—
1/50–1/60 M	56	80	125	—	45	64
1/100–1/125 M	50	72	110	—	32	45
1/200–1/250 M	40	56	90	—	22	32

The figures for PF 1B and No. 1BS bulbs apply to 4-inch reflectors. When 2-inch reflectors are used, open up the lens aperture by ½ stop.

continued over page

397

24

Kodachrome II Film, for Daylight *continued*

Electronic flash. These units can be used as the sole light-source and for fill-in flash. Normally no filter is needed when used as the sole light-source, but pictures showing a bluish cast will suggest that a Wratten No. 81A filter should be used. The guide numbers provided by the manufacturer of the unit can be taken as the basis for trial exposures.

Processing. Kodachrome II Film should be sent to a Kodachrome Processing Laboratory as soon as possible after exposure. Instructions as to where to send it are contained in the leaflet packed with the film.

Sizes available for still cameras. KR135 20- and 36-exposure cassettes and KR 828 12-exposure roll film.

KODACHROME II FILM, TYPE A

A colour film designed for use in miniature cameras and balanced for exposures with photoflood lamps (3,300°-3,400°K). After reversal processing, it yields positive transparencies for projection. The transparencies can be used to obtain Kodachrome prints and enlargements, duplicate transparencies, and, via an internegative, black-and-white prints, colour prints, and enlarged transparencies.

Speed and meter settings					
	ASA	B.S.	Weston I and II	DIN	Filter (if any)
Photoflood ..	40/3·5°	27°	32	17	—
Photopearl ..	32/3·5°	26°	24	16	Wratten No. 82A
Daylight	25/3°	25°	20	15	Wratten No. 85

The first ASA number is for use with meters and cameras marked for ASA Speeds or Exposure Indices: the second number in the pair (given in degrees) is the ASA Speed Value for the additive exposure system. These meter settings apply to properly-made reflected-light and incident-light readings of average subjects.

Photoflood exposure table. The lens openings apply to shutter speeds of 1/25 to 1/30 sec. for two lamps arranged so that the beams from each lamp are superimposed on the subject. Separate back-lighting does not affect the exposure of the subject. One lamp should be placed near to the camera (as fill-in) to avoid deep shadows, and the other, as mainlight, at about 45° to the camera-subject axis and 2 to 4 feet higher than the fill-in light.

Lamp-Subject Distances	20 ft. 6·5 m.	14 ft. 4·5 m.	10 ft. 3 m.	7 ft. 2·3 m.	5 ft. 1·7 m.	3½ ft. 1·2 m.	2½ ft. 0·8 m.
No. 1	—	$f/1\cdot4$	$f/2$	$f/2\cdot8$	$f/4$	$f/5\cdot6$	$f/8$
No. 2 or SM	$f/1\cdot4$	$f/2$	$f/2\cdot8$	$f/4$	$f/5\cdot6$	$f/8$	$f/11$
NM	$f/2$	$f/2\cdot8$	$f/4$	$f/5\cdot6$	$f/8$	$f/11$	$f/16$

Clear flashbulbs – guide numbers. The recommended guide numbers are based on the use of the Wratten No. 81C filter. To determine the recommended f/number for average subjects, the guide number should be divided by the selected flashbulb-subject distance in feet. For capless bulbs the guide numbers apply to use in average domestic rooms, those for large bulbs to use in large areas (i.e. commercial and industrial interiors). Increase exposure by at least 1 stop in large dark interiors, outdoors at night, or for dark subjects. Decrease exposure by 1 stop in small light rooms or for light subjects. For flash-to-subject distances of less than 5 ft. an additional ½ stop exposure is advised. For open-flash with focal-plane shutters, use the bulbs and guide numbers for diaphragm shutters.

Shutter speed and synchronization for diaphragm shutters	Diaphragm shutters					Focal-plane shutters	
	AG 1	PF 1 No. 1	PF 5 No. 5	PF 60 No. 22	PF 100 Open-flash or M synch. only	PF 24	PF 45
Open flash — ⎫ Up to 1/30 X ⎬	80	64	100	180	220	—	—
1/50–1/60 M	72	56	90	160	—	64	90
1/100–1/125 M	64	50	80	140	—	45	64
1/200–1/250 M	50	40	64	110	—	32	45

The figures for PF 1 and No. 1 bulbs apply to 4-inch reflectors. When 2-inch reflectors are used, open up the lens aperture by ½ stop.

Daylight exposures. Kodachrome II Film, Type A with a Wratten No. 85 filter gives excellent results with daylight. As the No. 85 absorbs ultra-violet it provides the effect of a Kodak Skylight filter under conditions when Daylight Type film tends to give bluish results. With the No. 85 filter it is the same speed as Daylight Type Kodachrome II Film, and the table for daylight exposures given for this film may be used with equally good results.
Processing. Kodachrome II Film should be sent to a Kodachrome Processing Laboratory as soon as possible after exposure. Instructions as to where to send the film are contained in the leaflet packed with the film.
Sizes available for still cameras. KRA 135 20-exposure cassettes.

KODACHROME-X FILM

A colour film designed for use in miniature cameras and balanced for exposure in daylight. As well as being faster than Kodachrome II Film, it gives somewhat higher contrast and is therefore ideal for subjects having flat lighting and for exposures in overcast weather. After reversal processing it yields positive transparencies for projection. They can be used to obtain Kodachrome prints and enlargements, duplicate transparencies, and, via an internegative, black-and-white prints, colour prints and enlarged transparencies.

	Speed and meter settings				
	ASA	B.S.	Weston I and II	DIN	Filter (if any)
Daylight	64/4°	29°	50	19	—
Photoflood ..	25/3°	25°	20	15	Wratten No. 80B

The first ASA number is for use with meters and cameras marked for ASA Speeds or Exposure Indices: the second number in the pair (given in degrees) is the ASA Speed Value for the additive exposure system. These meter settings apply to reflected-light and incident-light readings of average subjects.

Daylight exposure table. Lens apertures for shutter speeds 1/100-1/125 sec. For the hours from 2 hours after sunrise to 2 hours before sunset.

Bright or Hazy Sun (Distinct Shadows)	Weak Hazy Sun (Soft Shadows)	Cloudy Bright (No Shadows)	Cloudy Dull	Open Shade
$f/11$	$f/8$	$f/5\cdot6$	$f/4$	$f/4$
Exposure Values				
14	13	12	11	11

Light subjects (beaches, distant views, high altitude snow): ½ stop less exposure. Nearby side or back-lit subjects under bright sun: 1-2 stops more exposure. In winter increase all exposures by 1 stop, but expose for snow scenes as in table.

Fill-in flash. In bright sunlight the lighting contrast is frequently excessive with close-up subjects lit from the side or back. Harsh shadows can be lightened by the use of fill-in flash in the form of blue flashbulbs or electronic flash. The following table gives distance ranges at which to use blue flashbulbs.

Daylight exposure	No. 1BS or PF 1B	PF 24/97
$f/22$ at 1/25-1/30 sec.*	7-12 ft.	—
$f/11$ at 1/100-1/125 sec. (M)	11-20 ft.	7-12 ft.

* For all cameras without full XM synchronization.

Light sources. In general, the best colour rendering is obtained in clear or hazy sun. The bluish cast which is evident in pictures taken in the shade under a clear blue sky can be minimized by the use of the Kodak Skylight Filter (Wratten 1A), which requires no increase in exposure. This filter is also useful for reducing bluishness in pictures taken on an overcast day and in distant scenes, mountain views, sunlit snow scenes, and aerial photographs.

Blue flashbulbs – guide numbers. Although intended for supplementing daylight, blue flashbulbs can be used as the sole light-source.

To determine the recommended *f*/number for average subjects, the guide number should be divided by the selected flashbulb-subject distance in feet. For capless bulbs the guide numbers apply to use in average domestic rooms, those for large bulbs to use in large areas (i.e. commercial and industrial interiors). Increase exposure by at least 1 stop in large dark interiors, outdoors at night, or for dark subjects. Decrease exposure by 1 stop in small light rooms or for light subjects. For flashbulb-subject distances less than 5 ft. ½ stop additional exposure is recommended. For open-flash with focal-plane shutters, use the bulbs and guide numbers for diaphragm shutters.

Shutter speed and synchronization for diaphragm shutters	Diaphragm shutters				Focal-plane shutters	
	AG 1B PF 1B No. 1BS	Atlas Double-lite	PF 90/67 No. 22B	PF 100/97 Open-flash or M synch. only	PF 24/97	PF 45/97
Open flash — ⎫ Up to 1/30 X ⎬	100	140	220	280	—	—
1/50–1/60 M	90	125	200	—	72	100
1/100–1/125 M	80	110	180	—	50	72
1/200–1/250 M	64	90	140	—	36	50

The figures for PF 1B and No. 1BS bulbs apply to 4-inch reflectors. When 2-inch reflectors are used, open up the lens aperture by ½ stop.

Electronic flash. These units can be used as the sole light-source and for fill-in flash. Normally no filter is needed when used as the sole light-source, but pictures showing a bluish cast will suggest that a Wratten No. 81A filter should be used. The guide numbers provided by the manufacturer of the unit can be taken as the basis for trial exposures.

Processing. Kodachrome-X Film should be sent to a Kodachrome Processing Laboratory as soon as possible after exposure. Instructions as to where to send it are contained in the leaflet packed with the film.

Sizes available. KX 135, 20- and 36-exposure cassettes, also 20-exposure Kodapak cartridges.

FILTER RECOMMENDATIONS
(All filters are Wratten

Illumination	Daylight Type			
	Ektachrome Sheet and Roll Film (Process E-3)	Ektachrome-X Film (Process E-2)	High Speed Ektachrome Film (Process E-2)	Kodachrome II Kodachrome-X Films
Daylight—bright and hazy sun ..	*No filter	*No filter	*No filter	*No filter
Open shade—blue sky	No. 1A	No. 1A	No. 1A	No. 1A
Electronic flash	No filter normally, but some units give better results with one of the following: No. 1A, 81, 81A, 81B.			
†Colour matching fluorescent tubes	CC 10M	CC 10M	No filter	CC 10M
†Daylight fluorescent tubes ..	CC 30M	CC 30M	CC 30M	CC 30M
†Warm-white De Luxe fluorescent tubes	N.R.	N.R.	N.R.	N.R.
Clear flashbulb	Not Recommended—use Blue flashbulbs			
Photoflood lamp (3,400°K) ..	‡No. 80B	‡No. 80B	‡No. 80B	‡No. 80B
Photopearl lamp (3,200°K) ..	‡No. 80B with No. 82A	‡No. 80B with No. 82A	‡No. 80B	‡No. 80B with No. 82A
Tungsten lamp 150-200-watt (2,850°K)	N.R.	N.R.	N.R.	N.R.

N.R. Not Recommended.
* Distant scenes, mountain scenery, etc. use No. 1A.
† Different makes of tube have slightly different characteristics. These filters provide a starting point for tests. It is better to avoid fluorescent tubes if possible.

FOR KODAK COLOUR FILMS
unless with prefix CC)

Type A	Type B		Type L	Type S	Daylight and flash
Kodachrome II Film	Ektachrome Sheet Film (Process E-3)	High Speed Ektachrome Film (Process E-2)	Ektacolor Professional Film (Process C-22)	Ektacolor Professional Film (Process C-22)	Kodacolor-X Film (Process C-22)
No. 85	No. 85B	No. 85B	No. 85B	No filter	¶No. 85C
No. 85	No. 85B	No. 85B	No. 85B	No filter	¶No. 85C
No. 85	N.R.	No. 85B	N.R.	No filter	¶No. 85
No. 85 +CC10M	No. 85B +CC10M	No. 85B	N.R.	No filter	¶No. 85
CC 30M with CC 10Y	N.R.	N.R.	N.R.	No filter	¶No. 85
No. 82A	No filter	No filter	No filter	N.R.	N.R.
No. 81C	No. 81C	No. 81C	N.R.	N.R.	No filter
No filter	No. 81A	No. 81A	No. 81A	No. 80B	No. 82A
No. 82A	No filter	No filter	No filter	No. 80B with No. 82A	No. 82C
No. 82 with No. 82C	No. 82B	No. 82B	N.R.	N.R.	N.R.

‡ These filters represent a compromise and it is preferable to use the appropriate type of film where available.

¶ Kodacolor-X Film does not normally need a filter for daylight and similar light-sources, but the No. 85C is recommended when the resultant negatives are to be printed manually.

Index

Note: page numbers in italics indicate colour plates.